The Sequential Dynamics
of Narrative

The Sequential Dynamics of Narrative

Energies at the Margins of Fiction

Ken Ireland

Madison • Teaneck
Fairleigh Dickinson University Press
London: Associated University Presses

Associated University Presses
440 Forsgate Drive
Cranbury, NJ 08512

Associated University Presses
16 Barter Street
London WC1A 2AH, England

Associated University Presses
P.O. Box 338, Port Credit
Mississauga, Ontario
Canada L5G 4L8

The paper used in this publication meets the requirements of the American National Standard for Permanence of Paper for Printed Library Materials Z39.48-1984.

Library of Congress Cataloging-in-Publication Data

Ireland, Ken, 1941–
    The sequential dynamics of narrative : energies at the margins of fiction / Ken Ireland.
        p.   cm.
    Includes bibliographical references and index.
    ISBN 0-8386-3863-5 (alk. paper)
    1. Narration (Rhetoric)   2. Fiction—Technique.   3. Fiction—History and criticism.   I. Title.

PN3383.N35 I74   2001
808.3—dc21   00-035441

PRINTED IN THE UNITED STATES OF AMERICA

For my parents

Contents

List of Figures

Acknowledgments

IN ITS DISTANT ORIGINS, THE IDEA FOR THIS PROJECT GOES BACK TO A
volume by Gérard Genette, borrowed from a French colleague on a
campus in West Africa during the 1970s. Since then, the implications of what I later came to term sequential dynamics, have increased in scope and depth. The various features examined here
have been applied and tested in a wide range of teaching contexts,
in conference presentations and in academic papers. I should like
to record my appreciation and thanks to my students and colleagues, and to those who at different times have found time to
read draft sections, to discuss in person or to respond in writing.
Among those who have raised critical points and offered stimulat-
ing suggestions about the material, I should like to mention, especially, Seymour Chatman, Hillis Miller, Franz Stanzel, Gerald
Prince, Mieke Bal, Wolfgang Zach, Meir Sternberg, Jakob Lothe,
Mick Short, Paul Simpson, Monika Fludernik.

To the organizers of PALA conferences at the Universities of
Brighton, Amsterdam, Sheffield Hallam and Belfast, I am particularly grateful for the opportunity to have explored related issues. I
am similarly indebted to the organizers of an AUMLA conference
at Macquarie University, Sydney, of an American Literature Association of Japan meeting at Sugiyama University, Nagoya, of the First
International Conrad Conference in Africa at Potchefstroom and
Cape Town Universities, and of the Joseph Conrad Society (U.K.)
at the University of Kent at Canterbury, for invitations to try out a
variety of approaches.

I would also like to acknowledge my gratitude to Aichi Shukutoku
University, Japan, for granting me a sabbatical leave of absence,
and to the administration of the Japanese Private Universities
Research Bursary, for financial support during 1993–94. The resources of Cambridge University Library, and the ready coopera-
tion of its staff, have been invaluable throughout my research.

In earlier and somewhat different versions, parts of this work
have previously appeared in print, and are published here with the
kind permission of the editors of the respective journals: "Towards

a Grammar of Narrative Sequence: The Model of *The French Lieutenant's Woman*," in *Poetics Today* 7:3 (1986), 397–420; "Future Recollections of Immortality," in *Novel: A Forum on Fiction* 13.2 (Winter 1980), 204–20. Copyright NOVEL Corp. © 1980. Reprinted with permission; "Dark Pit of the Past: Gide's 'mise en abyme' and Natsume Sōseki's *Mon*," in *Comparative Literature Studies* 20.1 (Spring 1983), 66–76. Copyright 1983 by The Pennsylvania State University. Reproduced by permission of The Pennsylvania State University Press; "End of the Line: Time in Kourouma's *Les soleils des Indépendances*," in *Présence Francophone* 23 (Automne 1981), 79–89; "Amphibian of the Fens; postmodernist dis/continuities in Graham Swift's *Waterland*," in *Parlance* 3.2 (Winter 1991), 73–89; "Chronotope in Hawthorne: Bakhtin and *The Scarlet Letter*," in *POETICA: An International Journal of Linguistic-Literary Studies* 33 (1991), 63–74.

For permission to reproduce diagrams, tables or formulae, I should also like to thank the following authors and publishers: Boydell & Brewer Ltd, for lower diagram, from Helmut Bonheim, *The Narrative Modes: Techniques of the Short Story* (Cambridge: D. S. Brewer, 1982), 44; Edward Arnold, for time scheme, from Jonathan Raban, *The Technique of Modern Fiction: Essays in Practical Criticism* (London: Edward Arnold, 1976), 66; International Thomson Publishing Services Limited, for Figure 2.1: 'story time', from Edward Branigan, *Narrative Comprehension and Film* (London: Routledge, 1992), 41; Dr. Ann Shukman, for Figure 2.2: 'Time structure of "The Shot," from "Ten Russian Short Stories: Theory, Analysis, Interpretation," *Essays in Poetics* 2.2 (Sept. 1977), 51; Editions L'Harmattan, for the 'Diagramme du récit', from Marc Gontard, *"Nedjma" de Kateb Yacine: Essai de la structure formelle du roman* (Paris: Editions L'Harmattan, 1985), 38; Yale University Press, for table of time blocks, from Robert Scholes, *Semiotics and Interpretation* (New Haven: Yale University Press, 1982), 93–94; Blackwell Publishers, for formula, from Gérard Genette, *Narrative Discourse*, trans. Jane E. Lewin (Oxford: Blackwell, 1980), 41; Mouton de Gruyter, for diagram of plot structure of Kundera's *The Joke,* from Lubomir Dolezel, "A Scheme of Narrative Time," in *Slavic Poetics: Essays in Honor of Kiril Taranovsky,* ed. Roman Jakobson, C. H. Van Schooneveld, and Dean S. Worth (The Hague: Mouton, 1973), 97; Dr. Renate Jungel, for Figure 2.3, from *Die Zeitstruktur in den Romanen E. M. Forsters* (Ph. D. diss., University of Graz, 1953), 54.

Finally, at crucial moments in the writing, England's cricket team has managed a rare victory, and the shock has triggered off a creative mood of unexpected euphoria, which I am happy to acknowledge here. For more continuous inspiration, however, over a more extended innings, my thanks go out, for their unfailing support, to my wife and family.

Introduction

The question is, shall it or shall it not be linear history? I've always thought a kaleidoscopic view might be an interesting heresy. Shake the tube and see what comes out. Chronology irritates me. There is no chronology inside my head. I am composed of a myriad Claudias who spin and mix and part like sparks of sunlight on water. The pack of cards I carry around is forever shuffled and re-shuffled; there is no sequence, everything happens at once.

—Penelope Lively, *Moon Tiger*

There I go again! Can't keep a story going in a straight line, can I? Drunk in charge of a narrative.
Where was I?

—Angela Carter, *Wise Children*

AT LEAST, SOME MIGHT ARGUE, THIS WAS *ONLY* A NARRATIVE: NO PENALties, legal or otherwise, for deviation. As for the concern of Angela Carter's Dora about going in a straight line: what readers, narratively charged, could possibly be upset? And if one event follows *this* rather than *that* event in the act of narration, what difference should it make? The musings of Penelope Lively's Claudia, by contrast, are grounded in her pragmatic conviction that experience, far from being linear and chronological, tends rather to be kaleidoscopic and simultaneous. Such issues are multiplied and enriched, when literary works from diverse eras and traditions are taken into account, and their narrative lines closely, even soberly, scrutinized.

What then does the notion of *sequential dynamics* imply? Initially, it relates to the textual arrangement and interplay of elements between demarcated units in narrative.[1] The term conveys, too, a proactive stance on the part of readers, and suggests the involvement of forces that instigate changes of state and direction. Early on, therefore, issues of ordering and continuity, isotopic and causal relations, accompany the core sense of one thing following another. That "thing" is itself protean. In fiction, it may mean a paragraph, a chapter, a series of chapters on the level of the text, or a narrative event represented by that text. Both orders of repre-

15

sentation and represented world are implied. Thus, sequential dynamics may be regarded provisionally as an operation for organizing narrative material, and communicating its impact on readers with maximum efficiency.[2]

Why do sequential dynamics merit discussion? For a start, they are less commonly examined than taken for granted, by readers and critics alike. Eclipsed by more superficially attractive elements of plot, they often seem invisible until hinge-points of tension are exposed, or the spatial blanks of new chapters or parts appear. Different types of narrative (oral and written; autobiography and historiography; film and visual art; reports and case studies; advertising and comic strips) elicit different types of sequence. Their operation is, however, often neglected, even when their relevance is admitted.

Assuming that material has been freely chosen and freely deployed by an author, readers are entitled to speculate *why* certain deployments have in fact been made. Some texts are self-conscious; they may parade their workings, allude to earlier and foreshadow later events, record meticulously where these occur. Other texts hide their traces, inviting or compelling readers to seek orientation for themselves, to construct meaning by resort to intuition or logic, fictional or real-life experience.

Why categorize sequential dynamics? One reason is the imprecision of terminology on hand, as well as the need to relate a given instance to a general theoretical framework. Alluding to a pair of chapters in *Bleak House*, for example, one critic comments that together they form, "the most powerful succession of set-scenes in the novel. Several things contribute to this. Most unusually, the two chapters run on, with no break in the narrative; they also give us a brilliant example of Dickens's use of suspense" (Storey 1987, 76–77).

It is of value here to establish and appreciate: how sequentially unusual these chapters actually are in the contexts of novel, writer, and period; how they should be classified; why their lack of break aptly projects the topic of Nemo's death; why their momentum straddles serial divisions; the fact that they are not viewed from Esther's perspective; that their suspense, typifying the apparently unconnected, paradoxically contributes to the novel's sense of ultimate connectedness.

What then are the larger implications of noting, for instance, that two crucial scenes in *The Scarlet Letter* open at chapter end rather than chapter start? that short chapters characterize *War and Peace* and *Wilhelm Meister*? that three successive chapters in *Ivanhoe* commence with an identical event? Why does simultaneous phase govern the longest chapter of *Madame Bovary* and join three plot lines in *The Return of the Native*, or nocturnal phase punctuate *The Mysteries of Udolpho* and *Northanger Abbey*? How are key scenes in *The Ambassadors* and *Daniel Deronda*, or interwoven plot lines in *Don Quixote* and *Tom Jones*, *Anna Karenina* and *Vanity Fair* sequentially signaled? Do switches of focalization at the start of *Our Mutual Friend*, or a stress on linear ordering in *Effi Briest* and *Buddenbrooks* project underlying concerns?

It is equally valuable to speculate, for example, whether contrasts of time-ratios in different books of *Adam Bede* and *The Brothers Karamazov* can be thematically justified, or melodramatic elements in *Notre-Dame de Paris* and *Oliver Twist* can be recognized by use of similar technical devices. Are the continuity spans in *Moby-Dick*, *The Egoist*, and *Lord Jim*, or the split perspectives in *The Woman in White* and *Kater Murr* operating identically? In what way do generic and formal choices, such as epistolary format in Behn, Richardson, and Laclos, the absence of segmentation in Bunyan and Defoe, episodic diversions in Fielding and lyrical interweavings in Mörike, framework narrative in *Frankenstein* and *Wuthering Heights*, affect issues of continuity? When, for instance, are chapter ellipses in *Tess* and *The Secret Agent* registered by characters and readers, and do they typify overall attitudes to temporality?

Questions of this nature must certainly have arisen in negotiating such texts, but it is by creating taxonomies of temporal and continuity relations, that suitable analytic tools become available to describe with precision the dynamics across, as well as within narrative units, and the gaps and transitions they involve. These relations can illustrate semantic interests, such that the sequential status of a given chapter or group of chapters may be seen to carry more than formal significance. A fresh focus is directed on energies in operation at margins, which may then in retrospect be identified as key junctures of the total narrative. Invoking analogies from music, it is apposite to speak of subtleties of harmonic and polyphonic effects, which are sponsored by the activity of sequential dynamics.

Analyses that employ sequential categories can help to display the actual pacing and proportions of works, by identifying broad rhythms and shifts of direction. Inferences from the frequency or rarity of particular types may reinforce or disappoint reader expectations, while the prevalence of patterns can be correlated with developments in a writer's oeuvre, or may project tendencies of a specific historical period. An attention to sequential dynamics can enhance an appreciation of authorial skills, or reveal flaws in organization often apparent only at the end of a text, when the reader's charitable suspension of doubts must be lifted. Within an individual work, moreover, sequential concerns also further a view of narrative as evolving and changing, as process rather than product, constructed rather than consumed by readers.

In the present study, basing itself on factual evidence from given texts, the role of sequential dynamics is examined within the larger rubric of *temporal and continuity relations*. By proposing specific taxonomies of *narrative transitions* and *order transforms*, especially, and demonstrating their roles in a wide gamut of examples, it is hoped to suggest the value of sequential dynamics as a separate approach to the general enterprise of narrative.

Such analytic categories—which involve changes of state, location, and event; passages from one unit to the next; and intratextual arrangements on the *microsequential* level of sentence and paragraph, or the *macrosequential* level of the whole work—are necessarily bound up with other features. These include the scale and grouping of narrative units; type, proportion, and positioning of dialogue; choice of generic format and text layout; framework devices and narrative focalization; ranges of time-cover and relationships with calendar time; principles of symmetry and contrast.

Most recent commentators on narrative temporality are still in debt to Gérard Genette (1972), and are either developing, modifying, or contesting his work. This study also acknowledges his "Discours du récit" as starting point and framework. Use, too, has been made of forerunners, in Günther Müller (1947) and Eberhard Lämmert (1955), untranslated from German; of works, insufficiently known, on chapter (Stevick 1970), tempo (Grabo 1928), sequence versus structure (Wetherill 1974).

In addition to monographs on narrative temporality in individual authors, which serve to substantiate general theories, specific critical approaches have been profitable. Stylistics has aided analysis of the presentational level; film theory and aesthetics have offered analogical insights and narratological strategies; comparative literary techniques have encouraged a focus on texts across national and disciplinary bounds; reader theory has seemed central to studying the effects of sequential dynamics.

Texts for analysis and illustration have been chiefly drawn from the European canon of the past four centuries, and this, together with contemporary international examples, helps to furnish exempla and detailed case studies. Of particular interest are non-Anglophone texts, which remain influential in their own linguistic territories, but are often unfamiliar outside. Contributions from the period of German Romanticism, and from the genre of the *novelle*, might be especially cited. Other texts epitomize specific types, such as the historical and autobiographical novel, the picaresque and bildungsroman, or project sociocultural phenomena, such as serial publication in the Victorian era.

Organizationally, the study falls into three parts. In Chapter 1, "Theory," the broad issues raised by sequential dynamics are considered in critical and conceptual frameworks that survey temporal and spatial relationships. The discussion then deals with types of segmentation, involving the creation of narrative units, gaps and cohesive relations; and topics of ordering, focusing on chronology and anachrony, linear and nonlinear distinctions. Tempo, affected by variable unit scales, perspective shifts and discourse types, is examined, and in the final section of the chapter, the theoretical issues already broached culminate in a detailed analysis of continuity relations and categories of transition. These are seen to embrace a multiplicity of types, from varieties of forward phase to parallel and simultaneous, alternate and analeptic phases.

In Chapter 2, "Practice," theoretical findings are applied in case studies from British, African, and Japanese texts, to observe how specific narrative features appear in action, and to underscore the universal role of sequential dynamics. In Chapter 3, "History," a broad diachronic survey highlights key contributions to sequential dynamics in European and American fiction, over the period from Cervantes to Conrad. It attends, in particular, to the functions and effects of the taxonomies introduced in Chapter 1, pointing up the relevance of developments prior to our own century of ostensible "time-novels." A brief conclusion reviews the value of sequential dynamics within fiction, and its implications outside.[3]

The Sequential Dynamics
of Narrative

1

Theory

CRITICAL AND CONCEPTUAL ISSUES

An hour, once it lodges in the queer element of the human spirit, may be stretched to fifty or a hundred times its clock length; on the other hand, an hour may be accurately represented on the timepiece of the mind by one second. This extraordinary discrepancy between time on the clock and time in the mind is less well known than it should be and deserves fuller investigation.

—Virginia Woolf, *Orlando*

Die Zeitgestaltung und ihre Technik sind ein zwar schwieriges, aber lohnendes Feld für die Untersuchung von Kunstwerken.

[The techniques of temporal arrangement represent an admittedly difficult, but rewarding field for the investigation of works of art.].

—Wolfgang Kayser, *Das sprachliche Kunstwerk*

IN HISTORICAL TERMS, *SEQUENTIAL DYNAMICS* BELONG TO THE GENERAL category of temporality, which since 1900, in particular, has claimed the attention of science and philosophy, from Einstein and Bergson onwards, and radically affected developments in the arts.[1] In its dual aspect as constitutive and referential, articulating narrative and supplying its subject matter, time in twentieth-century literature has increasingly accented thematics. This move is most widely apparent in fiction. Novels of the 1920s by Proust, Joyce and Woolf, Faulkner and Thomas Mann thematize time, thereby displacing traditional plot, as well as emphasizing inwardness and the activity of individual consciousness. If these "time-novelists" register a new perceptual awareness and worldview, they trigger, in turn, critical studies which analyze time in literature as a whole.

At the height of Modernism, both Anglo-American and Russian critics make valuable contributions to the topic. In the wake of Henry James, issues of formal presentation inspire Percy Lubbock

23

(1921) and Carl Grabo (1928); plot and structure engage E. M. Forster (1927) and Edwin Muir (1928). Lesser known, but ultimately of greater influence theoretically, are the technical analyses of Russian Formalists: Viktor Shklovsky and Boris Tomashevsky, Boris Eichenbaum, Vladimir Propp, and Yuri Tynyanov.

During the 1920s and 1930s, they introduce, among other seminal concepts, those of *fabula* and *syuzhet*. Roman Jakobson and Mikhail Bakhtin, moreover, as Formalist "outriders" fuse literary with linguistic and ideological concerns. Other approaches to time during the 1930s and 1940s range from ontological (Ingarden 1931), poetical (Staiger 1939), and morphological (Müller 1944), to existential (Pouillon 1946) and phenomenological (Poulet 1949).

Internationally, the 1950s open with some of the most insightful studies of time in literature (Mendilow 1952, Van Ghent 1953, Jauss 1955, Lämmert 1955, Meyerhoff 1955), before the next decade sees the reemergence, via translation and commentary, of Russian Formalism (Erlich 1955, Todorov 1965, Lemon and Reis 1965). The advance of French Structuralism proceeds, meanwhile, via anthropology, film and linguistics (Lévi-Strauss 1958, Barthes 1966, Metz 1968, Todorov 1969). Structuralist literary successes lie, significantly, in fiction, even as the accent shifts toward semiotics: Roland Barthes (1970) stimulated by Balzac, Gérard Genette (1972) by Proust, A. J. Greimas (1976) by Maupassant.

In North America, conceptual studies of time in terms of Modernism (Church 1963) and Victorianism (Buckley 1966), are followed by a history of narrative forms (Scholes and Kellogg 1966), analyses of division (Stevick 1970), structural patterns (Kroeber 1971), and text/film affinities (Chatman 1978). In Austria, Franz Stanzel (1955, 1979) offers typologies of novelistic perspectives; in Russia, Boris Uspensky (1970) abstracts perceptual and temporal categories; in England, David Higdon (1977) crystallizes novelistic time patterns; in Israel, Meir Sternberg (1978) and Menachem Perry (1979) apply textual dynamics.

During the same decade, valuable collections of essays treat interdisciplinary topics of time (Patrides 1976), and temporal aspects of fiction (Ritter 1978). By the 1980s, Tzvetan Todorov's *narratologie* has encouraged wider links, and refinements of Genette's theories continue in Mieke Bal (1977), Gerald Prince (1982), Shlomith Rimmon-Kenan (1983). The decade is also marked by key synoptical works from Paul Ricoeur (1983–85), David Bordwell (1985), and Wallace Martin (1987). These are supplemented by studies of move-grammar and text linguistics (Pavel 1985, Segre 1988), of

chronology and teleology (Sternberg 1990, 1992). In historiographic studies, especially in the work of Hayden White, the role of
narrativity has become central (Rigney 1991).

In transmission theory, the importance of the contact channel
has been reinforced by an analysis of generic types, and documentary techniques (Duyfhuizen 1992). Cross-disciplinary models of
narrative now apply extensively in the social sciences (Riessman
1993) and educational studies (Cortazzi 1993), while recent narratological developments promote "energetics" over "geometrics,"
conceiving text as polymorphous, and space as heterogenous and
pluralized (Gibson 1996). In a nanosecond culture of computer
and information technology, fiction itself offers a labyrinthine vision of multiple temporalities (Heise 1997).

Few titles, however, devote much space to sequencing and sequential dynamics per se. One of the most balanced accounts surveys critical methodology (Wetherill 1974); another places
sequence and plot in an intercultural context (Miner 1990); a third
exploits Formalist time-play of original and textual sequences
(O'Toole 1982). Practitioners of the *nouveau roman*, such as Alain
Robbe-Grillet (1963) and Michel Butor (1964), have commented
acutely on chronological order and spatial discontinuity, and the
notion of spatial form (Frank 1945) has been further developed as
an overall approach to twentieth-century literature (Smitten and
Daghistany 1981). Useful distinctions have been drawn between
spatial, logical, and temporal order (Todorov 1968), memory relations and causal order (Meyerhoff 1955), the role and function of
narrative phase (Lämmert 1955).

Film semiotics, after Christian Metz's *Grande Syntagmatique*
(1968), with its types of narrative syntagmas or autonomous units,
has utilized general narrative theories, including schemata and ordering (Branigan 1992). At the same time, film criticism has applied Genette's pioneering categories to its own corpus (Henderson
1983). In literary criticism, specific moments of discourse—
beginnings (Said 1975) and endings (Kermode 1967, Smith
1968)—have taken on philosophical status. The most incisive work
on types of exposition (Sternberg 1978) combines cognitive psychology with pragmatic text analysis. In literary history, Jakobson's
notion of the shifting dominant has been fruitfully applied, by contrasting Modernist epistemology and Postmodernist ontology, together with their paradigmatic genres of detective and science
fiction (McHale 1987).

In conceptual terms, sequential dynamics are clearly involved in
the operation of narrative temporality. Drawing upon the Stoics' di-

vision of time into *chronos* and *aion*, a closed and measurable, as opposed to an open and measureless conception, critics like Gilles Deleuze assert the relevance of *aion* in contemporary culture (Gibson 1996, 179–81). In culture as a whole, at least five broad philosophical views of time can be identified. These range from a Christian concept of human history, to time as cyclical repetition, as linear progress, in both pessimistic and optimistic senses, and as chaos and flux (Harvey 1965, 102–3). In practice, these views have rarely been held independently of each other. The notion of time as linear progress, is perhaps most influential on the novel in its classical stage.

To pair mechanical and organic conceptions of time (Mumford 1963, 9–18) is to invoke a familiar combination. This may occur in a historical framework of Enlightenment versus Romantic models (Abrams 1958), of vernacular cultures where market days and lunar eclipses prevail over clocks, or of literary phenomena such as "stream-of-consciousness" fiction, where Bergsonian *durée* and mental time counter public, linear measurement (Graham 1949).

In Mann's *Der Zauberberg [The Magic Mountain]*, a time-novel of the 1920s, the narrator stresses the common factor of time, fundamental both to narrative and life: "die Zeit ist das *Element* der Erzählung, wie sie das Element des Lebens ist" ([1924] 1974b, 748).[2] Though they share the same phenomenon, the experience of time in everyday life patently differs from that in a literary context. The "objective" time of the real world has been defined as continuous or sustained ["ein kontinuierliches Medium" (Ingarden 1960, 251)], with no gaps. The represented time ["dargestellte Zeit"] of fiction, by reason of the differing lengths and interests of the genre, is necessarily asymmetrical with real time, and may run parallel with it only at irregular intervals and for varying stretches. By comparison with the continuum of real time, the represented time of narrative, punctuated by gaps, remains in essence discontinuous, and thus offers only an analogue or modification of the structure of real time and events.[3]

At its simplest, narrative displays a group of characters who live in a given place as time passes in succession (Miner 1990, 149). In order of increasing importance, the three essential elements are time, place, and characters—the hierarchy being motivated by the fact that places and time may be changed without changing the people, but that "to change the people, on the other hand, is to change the plot" (155). However we accentuate the elements, a majority of narratologists give priority to time, less in terms of what results from the effects of change on the other elements, than of its fundamental role.[4]

There is also near-consensus that narratives involve human beings, and that the events they feature, display that continuity of subject matter that A. J. Greimas calls the *isotopic* principle (Jonnes 1990, 65–67).[5] Gerald Prince's account of narrative remains the most comprehensive: "the recounting . . . of at least two real or fictive events . . . neither of which logically presupposes or entails the other . . . communicated by . . . narrators to . . . narratees" (1989, 58). He signals an etymological root in the Latin *gnarus*, its connotation of a mode of knowledge, exploring and devising what can happen. In sum, narrative "illuminates temporality and humans as temporal beings" (60).

Two novelists, especially, reflect on the operation of narrative temporality. Henry James, as a practicing nineteenth-century writer, famously singled out the "eternal time question" for particular mention: "always there and always formidable; always insisting on the *effect* of the great lapse and passage . . . of compression, of composition and form" (James [1875] 1986b, 44). He tellingly acknowledges in his 1907 New York Edition preface to *Roderick Hudson* the inadequacy of his own time scheme, whereby what should be the "gradual process" of its hero's disintegration, "swallows two years in a mouthful" (43).

A twentieth-century novelist-critic, E. M. Forster, insists that, whereas in daily life an allegiance to time may not be necessary, no novel could be written without it. Intelligibility itself is at stake: "The author may dislike his clock. Emily Brontë in *Wuthering Heights* tried to hide hers. Sterne, in *Tristram Shandy*, turned his upside down. Marcel Proust . . . kept altering the hands" (Forster [1927] 1993, 20), verdicts all inviting correction. Tracing how the time sense is consciously celebrated in Arnold Bennett's *The Old Wives' Tale* (1908), Forster then posits its negative pole in the contemporaneous writings of Gertrude Stein. Her syntactical experiments in *Three Lives* (1909),[6] represent an instructive failure. In her attempts to abolish time, pulverizing her clock and scattering its fragments, Stein has only demonstrated its vital role: "as soon as fiction is completely delivered from time it cannot express anything at all" (Forster 1993, 28).

Within fiction, a basic duality exists between time as a *constitutive* element, part of the armature of a work, discussible in technical terms, and time as a *referential* or thematic factor, supplying its plot material. James's problems with *Roderick Hudson* illustrate the *internal* aspects of constitutive time: its distribution and proportioning. Such aspects may go unnoticed by readers, until difficulties of interpretation occur, or issues are deliberately and blatantly foregrounded. Critical studies may examine temporal discrepancies or inconsistencies, reconstruct a chronological order, linearize events.[7] The *external* aspects of constitutive time, on the other hand, are represented by wider studies of chronometry. These may relate datings and seasonal references within the text to calendars, almanacs, and time charts from the outside world,[8] establishing different degrees of accuracy and verisimilitude between text and context.

With time in its *referential* or thematic aspect, the roles of memory and history, of anticipation and projection, are foremost. The repression and suppression of past events, apprehension and pessimism about events ahead, can be thematized, for example, as trauma, violence, sterility, physical and material legacies, mental guilt, stigma, and anxiety. Detective fiction, reliant on data concealed in a narrative past, or science-fiction, in its future or fantasy trajectories, typify genres that exploit temporality for thematic ends. To try to narrate time, in a pure state, would anyway be self-defeating. A narrative written in the vein of "die Zeit verfloss, sie verrann, es strömte die Zeit"[9] (Mann [1924] 1974b, 748), would not merit the name of narrative. The thematization of time must, therefore, be partial and relative at best.

Assuming a different value in different genres, time approaches near-evanescence in lyric poetry, where brevity of expression lends a point-present impact. With longer, narrative poems, however, density yields to an extended series of events as in fiction. In dramatic performance, on the other hand, a direct mode means that dialogue and events on stage occur in a dimension akin to the spectator's "real" time. In the dramatic text, directions about the duration of movements and speech delivery are necessarily approximate, suggesting the genre's sense of *near-isochrony*.

While the principal forms of narrative tradition have been epic, romance, and novel, it is in the third that time plays the most crucial role. By contrast with drama, moreover, where what is recounted is distinct from what is presented, in the novel, "all is narrative" (Leech 1968, 327), and where drama at its simplest has a ritual, hieratic function, narrative "puts us into the flux" (328). The major changes wrought by time inevitably occur offstage in a play. A youthful character and new house in act 1 may reappear, in act 3, as, respectively, gray-haired and dilapidated. What happens between the acts, is "the body of the novel, and it cannot happen before our eyes in the 45 minutes of Act Two" (Hutchens 1972,

221). While drama and fiction alike are discontinuous forms, the extensive flux of narrative involves varied types of discourse and, as a consequence, of varied temporal relations.[10]

Since literary works use the symbolic medium of language, they are also subject to its syntactic, grammatical, and semantic constraints. Unlike the plastic arts, which the observer confronts without mediation, natural language necessarily interposes itself between the poetic object and its reader or audience. Thus, the linear movement of a text and its linguistic base convey the linear unfolding of narrative events, with the dynamics of the text emerging from the "sequential nature of the verbal medium as a continuum of signs" (Sternberg 1978, 34).

Historically, the simple linear plot of epic,[11] unified by its protagonist's movement in time from one event to another, by its chronological record of heroic deeds, provides the model for the picaresque novel. The "multifoliate plot" (Scholes and Kellogg 1975, 209) of the romance,[12] and its shift during the Middle Ages from bipartite to interlaced narrative (Ryding 1971, 139), represents an alternative not taken up by the early prose form. Though the progress of the *picaro* may be unheroic, his encounters unepical, and the textual scale modest, the episodic, linear picaresque offers an uncomplicated model for later and more extensive fiction.

While consecutiveness, transience, and irreversibility, Mendilow's three principles of time (1952, 236), apply forcefully to picaresque, the third principle implies that the reader can only move in one direction, cannot reverse reading without loss, and memory must constantly relate what has gone to what is going on (124). Irreversibility may also be formulated as directionality, and adduced as a principle that separates drama from film, to the extent that dramatic time, like real time, must move forward. For traditionalists, only present time should be directly accessible on stage; the past has to be recalled through memory and dialogue, and not by resort to cinematic flashback (Ross 1987, 29). Plays by J. B. Priestley and Arthur Miller, Jean Anouilh and Caryl Churchill,[13] among others, testify, nonetheless, to violations of stage norms of chronological order and directionality.

If the reader's experience of fiction is "inescapably sequential" (Harvey 1965, 112), the response to particular works may be more qualified. The concept of spatial form, for example, tries to account for developments from 1900 on. Behind the poetry of Eliot and Pound lies the intention, "to undermine the inherent consecutiveness of language," by frustrating normal expectations of sequence, and forcing the reader to perceive elements "juxtaposed in space rather than unrolling in time" (Frank 1945, 227).[14] This strategy is applied to the prose of Proust and Joyce, Faulkner and Dos Passos, the French *nouveau roman* and Latin-American *nueva novela*.

In the great Modernists, the reader is meant "to apprehend their work spatially, in a moment of time, rather than as a sequence" (1945, 225). Proust's discontinuous presentation of character means that the reader must juxtapose, in an instant, images widely separated in narrative time; Joyce's *Ulysses* enforces simultaneity of perception, through the need to link allusions together by reflexive reference; the dense patterning in Djuna Barnes's *Nightwood* (1937), results from a spatial interweaving of images and phrases independent of temporal sequence.

Joseph Frank notes sporadic anticipations of spatial form in Sterne and Diderot, in Flaubert's handling of simultaneous actions in *Madame Bovary*, in Mallarmé's radical linguistic dislocations, and experiments with perspective and time shifts in James, Conrad, and Ford Madox Ford. More general technical features, such as the role of description, or Benveniste's notion of "discours,"[15] also affect the relative importance of the spatial factor (Frank 1981, 239–40). Later spatial formalists have ranged back to antiquity, focussing on thematic variation in Apuleius's *Golden Ass* (Mickelsen 1981, 74–76) or chapter alternation in Longus's *Daphnis and Chloe* (Rabkin 1981, 82–83). Elsewhere, claims that George Eliot's approach to character is predominantly temporal, Dickens's basically spatial (Garrett 1969, 55–57), have guaranteed lively debate.

In proposing that the history of the novel charts a tension between the linear-temporal nature of its linguistic medium, and the spatial elements "required by its nature as a work of art," Frank (1981, 235) assumes that no example is purely temporal or spatial. By 1900, however, the principle of juxtaposition begins to triumph over transition (Shattuck 1959, 256–66), paratactic over hypotactic expression (Hayman 1987, 209) in the verbal arts. A stylistic shift in the visual arts moves painting away from naturalism and three-dimensional depth toward abstraction, and encourages spatiality of perception. The new century becomes attracted to myth, whose timeless realm now replaces the nineteenth-century's sense of progress in time.

Spatial form is thus presented as an essentially twentieth-century mode, dependent on whether a given work strikes the reader more, "as an image of a complex *situation* or as that of an *enfolding* process" (Vidan 1981, 140). Less cautious spatial formalists seem to ignore the temporal dimension completely, so that it is salutary to speak of particular tendencies and priorities, of relative, not absolute weightings. Fictional texts, in the final analysis, despite effects of spatialization and simultaneity, remain, to greater or lesser degree, sequential. Devices of repetition, circularity, and fragmentation at best neutralize, disrupt and detract, but the use of natural language and the process of reading ensure that temporality is never annulled, but minimized.

Rather than view spatial form as diametrically opposed to temporal sequence, it would ultimately be more fruitful to consider it as a different accentuation within a temporal-verbal medium, and to treat both aspects in terms of a constructive interaction, not as a disparity of poles. Spatial form as a concept is at first attractive in its application to literary works. In treating texts as physical objects, however, the spatial dimension is clearly already involved as a measure of the number of words and paragraphs on a page, and of the length of chapters and volumes.

Spatiality serves to distinguish narrative units, while in poetry it contributes an important visual dimension to layout, by interstanzaic and marginal presence. Lyric poetry tends toward the spatial rather than temporal, in being less concerned with the movement of outside events than with the personal record of inner thoughts and emotions. To this end, Roman Jakobson's paradigmatic axis associated with metaphor is patently more relevant than the syntagmatic axis associated with metonym; the former, in turn, typical of nonnaturalistic discourse, the latter of naturalistic discourse incarnated in the classic realist novel.

In more recent narrative theory, new connections between elements have been hypothesized, and different spatial models have been conceptualized by a preference for uncommon metaphors. For the geometric image of the text as pyramid or box, Jacques Derrida substitutes the opening and closing fan, Gilles Deleuze the rhizome, Michel Serres the intersystemic parasite, while computer-generated "interactive fiction" (IF) offers "decision trees" and labyrinths. As static and hierarchical models of all kinds are deconstructed, new configurations obtain: "Fluent form, nomadic distributions, the hymen, heteroplasty, transversals, multiplicities, the excluded third, the *chora,* vectors, lines of force and flight" (Gibson 1996, 212).

Spatial form itself, adopted in a literary context, remains in the final analysis a metaphor, a rhetorical figure designed to make its case as powerfully as possible, by persuading the reader that in a given instance an ontological shift has occurred. At most, the concept points to a sharp bias within a verbal medium, rather than any metamorphosis into a plastic medium. It affords a graphic image of certain emphases within a text, but its shorthand character should not mislead the reader into an interpretive error of *pars pro toto*.

In addition, the concept may lead to an oversimplified view of complex narratives, whereby material not obviously linear and unfolding can be too readily labeled as spatial, and careful discriminations and refinements of treatment on the part of the writer glossed over. In the sections below, some of these subtleties of narrative technique will be recovered, by allowing the notion of sequential dynamics to embrace the spatial as well as temporal aspects of fiction. The implications of the ways that sequencing is affected by the art of segmentation now need to be examined.

SEGMENTATION

> It becomes an author generally to divide a book, as it does a butcher to joint his meat, for such assistance is of great help to both the reader and the carver.
> —Henry Fielding, *Joseph Andrews*

In her celebrated monologue at the end of Joyce's *Ulysses*, Molly Bloom delivers herself of forty-five pages, virtually unpunctuated, and indented only seven times (Joyce [1922] 1961, 738–83). The feat of continuity is not surpassed even in the linguistically more radical *Finnegans Wake*, but in fiction overall such uninterrupted stretches of print are exceptional. Generally, texts are divided into units that the reader can encompass with relative ease, and that thereby sponsor a grasp of content. A cursory glance usually indicates how both page and book have been apportioned, even prior to relating those divisions to the material they communicate.

Earl Miner identifies four possible kinds of narrative units: the work as a whole, division into chapters or other parts, larger groupings of such chapters or parts, and subchapter units (Miner 1990, 179). He distinguishes between the first two kinds, given by the author, and the second pair, matters of interpretation and debate, to be resolved by the reader. In actuality, of course, if the author chances to be Trollope, and chapters in *Barchester Towers* are headed "Ullathorne Sports—Act I" (ch. 36), "Act II" (ch. 40), "Act III" (ch. 42), a larger grouping already suggests itself. Subchapter units, in novels as various as Turgenev's *Fathers and Sons* and Woolf's *Jacob's Room*, are distinct by an increase in typographical spacing, or, in the case of H. G. Wells's *Mr. Britling*, by numbered sections. Isolated sentences, or sentence-paragraphs, particularly where they fulfil a summarizing function, form the briefest narrative units, as *Tristram Shandy* illustrates.

It is the chapter, however, that remains the standard unit of narrative fiction, even if works on the scale of Hugo's *Les Misérables* or Tolstoy's *War and Peace* adopt, respectively, the larger units of book and part. The notion of division itself goes back to Homer, the Bible and conventions of rhetoric (Stevick 1970, 163–8). The *Odyssey* and *Iliad* share twenty-four books apiece, while the twelve books of Virgil's *Aeneid* likely influence Fielding's identical arrangement in his *Amelia*. On the title page of *Joseph Andrews* (Fielding [1742] 1983, 47), the author acknowledges his debt to Cervantes, whose *Don Quixote,* adopting the episodic divisions of romance, is one of the first novels to use chapters.

By introducing his own novel as a comic epic in prose, Fielding lays down a serious, poetic model from Greek and Roman culture, which he then proceeds to modify or invert. His Classicist outlook means that earlier practice serves to legitimize his own, so that the art of dividing narrative carries the "sanction of great antiquity" (124). The *locus neoclassicus* of his views is placed, like the other three critical prefaces in *Joseph Andrews*, and the eighteen in *Tom Jones*, at the opening of a new book (2.1), typifying, as such, the balance and symmetry of Classicism.

Denying that division inflates material unnecessarily, Fielding draws analogies with travel, to illustrate the practical advantages of segmentation: "those little spaces between our chapters may be looked upon as an inn or resting-place where [the reader] may stop and take a glass or any other refreshment as it please him" (123). In the blank pages between the larger units of books, the reader enjoys longer pauses for reflection, for recovery of eyesight and restoration of spirit. The contents prefixed to new chapters, like inscriptions over inns, telegraph the entertainment in store. Mischievously deeming the art of dividing "too mysterious" for the uninitiated, Fielding concedes that at least it prevents a book's being spoiled by having its leaves turned down (124). Like a butcher's jointing meat, he concludes, the author's division of his text benefits himself and reader alike.

Fielding's sister, Sarah, likens segmentation to "the acts and scenes in a play; the main design of which must be to give time for shifting the scenes and conveying the audience without hurry or apparent absurdity to and from the several places and apartments where the poet had laid his action" (Fielding [1749] 1979, 67). Credibility and smoothness of transition, therefore, are the qualities she highlights, while a later female writer, Charlotte Brontë, draws a similar stage analogy in *Jane Eyre*, as she appeals directly to the imagination of the reader-as-spectator: "A new chapter in a novel is something like a new scene in a play; and when I draw up the curtain this time, reader, you must fancy you see a room in the George Inn at Millcote" (Brontë [1847] 1978, 125).

In James Fenimore Cooper's *The Prairie*, which adopts Shakespearean epigraphs for nearly all its chapters, it is scarcely surprising that a new chapter should be colored by this metaphorical framework: "The curtain of our imperfect drama must fall to rise upon another scene. The time is advanced several days, during which very material changes had occurred in the situation of the actors" (Cooper [1827] 1980, 281). To the extent that any analogy with drama, however, involves the stage norm of successivity, the notion is frequently disregarded in fiction, with its greater flexibility, as the *categories of transition* (§1.5) demonstrate.

The length of narrative units depends as much upon the total economy of a work, as upon the weight and importance of constituents. To the reader of Smollett's *Peregrine Pickle*, for instance, it is clear, even without computing an average length for the other chapters, that the "Memoirs" of Lady Vane (ch. 88), by virtue of their vast scale, almost assume the status of an independent novella within the novel (Smollett [1751] 1983, 432–539). A distortion in overall balance results, despite a quantitative indicator that correlates the amount of narrative space with the degree of aesthetic relevance or centrality (Sternberg 1974, 45).

With luck, helpful authorial narrators, such as those in Scott, themselves rationalize chapter breaks. Thus, in successive chapters of *The Fair Maid of Perth*, a new narrative unit is justified by a shift from the "lower parties" in an armourer's hut to those of a "higher rank and greater importance" in a royal council room (13i; [1828] 1969, 154), by a thematic parallel between the Maid's outdoor confessional (14i) and Robert III's similar action in a Gothic monastery, at the beginning of an earlier chapter (9i).

In gestalt theory, the size of a narrative unit needs to be limited by the pattern-making ability of the reader. It is for similar reasons of facilitating access, that scenes change, and irrelevant periods of time are disposed of between rather than within chapters, that adjustments of tone and contrasts of ideas find easiest entry there (Stevick 1970, 26–28). Chapter breaks also serve, the same critic points out (63, 79–81), as comic devices (*Alice in Wonderland*), as means to delay synthesis (*The Great Gatsby*) or to create startling discontinuities (*Ulysses*).[16] Despite changes during the twentieth century, conventions of segmentation, Stevick argues, remain important perceptual means by which we understand fiction. By "extending, refining, or modifying our initial sense of what is related and what can be grouped together, [the art of division] becomes a technical means by which the novelist compels the reader to see as he sees" (144).

In terms of spatial form, the chapter has been regarded as the "most important architectural unit" for the novel (Kestner 1978, 113–14). It articulates such functions as antithesis, gradation, and parallelism. Its ability to control sequence is patent in its use of digression to affect overall rhythm, of prefiguration to adjust scale. For cognitive psychology, the absence of segmentation in Bunyan and Defoe means, nonetheless, that scenes combine more closely in retrospect. An effect of foreshortening causes details and connective material to fade out in the reader's mind, as a continuous narrative makes it easier, to "consolidate episodes in memory where they may operate together more powerfully than when encountered separately during reading" (Alkon 1979, 115).

Authorial decisions about breaks in narrative obviously affect the whole shape of a work. In the hypothetical case of a meeting between two people, for example, the scene can be represented in a single unit, extended over two, further expanded by embedded material, descriptive or reflective passages, analeptic or proleptic episodes, according to whim or design. When, moreover, a text left unfinished by one hand is completed by another, subtle changes in articulation inevitably occur. The continuation by "Another Lady" of Jane Austen's *Sanditon* (Austen 1976), for instance, differs from the 1817 fragment not only by its trebling in scale of the original, but also by its handling of division and transition, and its doubling in length of an average chapter.[17]

If the physical arrangement of narrative units includes spatial separation between chapters, and more extensive blanks between larger units, other "paratextual" (Genette 1987) material (titles, dedications, prefaces, tables, notes) may intervene to blur clear transitions from one unit to the next. Fielding's resort to precise notation of time spans at the head of each book of *Tom Jones*, and his often elaborate and ironic summaries for individual chapters (as in 4.6), contrast, for example, with the practice of simple numbered chapters in Austen.

Scott's rationale, stated in *Rob Roy*, for his popularization of initial epigraphs, is at least candid: "to seduce your continued attention by powers of composition of stronger attraction than my own" (Scott [1818] 1991, 24). His disciples of superscription include Elizabeth Gaskell and George Eliot, though most Victorian novelists restrict themselves to chapter-start numbers and brief summaries, before even these disappear by the 1900s. When Postmodernists such as John Barth, in *The Sot-Weed Factor* (1960), and John Fowles, in *The French Lieutenant's Woman* ([1969], henceforth, *FLW*), resurrect verbose chapter summaries and epigraphs, their purposes are essentially parodic and playful, subverting earlier conventions.

The absence of print between the end of one chapter and the opening of the next is obviously, in the first instance, a visual phenomenon, a punctuation sign employed by author or printer, and factually registered by the reader. Whereas gaps between stanzas of a poem tend to be identical, even if constituent lines vary in number, their counterparts in fiction may be more elastic, reserving a new chapter for a fresh page, out of aesthetic or dramatic grounds. Both literary kinds, however, share the possibility of exploiting gaps between units for text-dividing or text-unifying functions, so that these visual gaps take on a status of fruitful indeterminacy.

Such gaps qualify as "minus devices" (Lotman 1977, 51), since they act as unused but meaningful elements, becoming organic parts of graphically fixed texts. Thus, their silence is efficacious by the very manner in which they break off or discontinue texts, violating expectations and disrupting routines established in the previous narrative. They may reinforce kindred elements on either side of the segmentation, drawing attention to what Frank Kermode terms "connexity" (1980, 87), or A. J. Greimas (1966) "isotopy" or "isotopic discourse."

While inter-chapter or inter-unit gaps have a visual impact, they patently fulfill a conceptual purpose too. Iconically, the empty space can signify a narrative stretch void of interest from the narrator's view, void of information from the reader's, though diegetic events may simply be omitted here on tactical grounds, to reappear more effectively at a later stage. These gaps serve also to suggest an accelerated passage of time, contributing to an overall sense of rhythm and tempo, but may, conversely, run counter to accepted norms, by drastic reduction of time-lapse between units, as the range of *categories of transition* (§1.5) indicates.

Although the blanks with which the reception theory of Wolfgang Iser deals may be those which precede new chapters, and so may affect the reader's changing views of the text, they are more generally represented by "gaps of indeterminacy" *[Unbestimmtheitsstellen]* within the narrative units themselves. Iser's phenomenological approach, influenced by Roman Ingarden, traces back the dynamism of a story to its "inevitable omissions" (Iser 1971, 285), which include unexpected twists and turns, and blockages in the stream of thought, since no tale can ever be told in its entirety. It is the reader's role to fill in the gaps left by the text.[18]

As Karl Kroeber argues, what Iser does is to focus on a paradox central to narrative: "the *lacunae*, what is *not* told, constitute the dynamic effectiveness of narrative art. The supreme skill of a storyteller is knowing what to leave out" (Kroeber 1992, 62). At any reading moment, only segments of textual perspectives are available to what Iser terms the "wandering viewpoint" of the reader, who, throughout, is engaged in a complex operation of prediction and recollection, and must constantly modify expectations and transform memories. Thus, the text cannot at any one moment be grasped as a whole, its unfinished and provisional character being caught in a dialectic between a future horizon to be occupied and a past horizon already filled.

Since Iser posits no definite frame of reference to regulate this process, any successful communication "must ultimately depend on the reader's creative activity" (Iser 1978, 112), concretizing the potentialities of the text's *schemata*. If that reader has been criticized as insufficiently ideological in terms of social and historical positioning (Eagleton 1983, 83), the very mobility of the role, nonetheless, crucially affects the way a text is viewed. It ceases to be treated as a static object and becomes a changing gestalt. A text, "no longer a timeless aesthetic object, is experienced as an unfolding temporal sequence" (Selden 1989, 125).

The image of volumes on bookshelves, silent until taken down and opened by human hands, crystallizes the literally vitalizing power of the reader. Thus, printed material resolves itself into a series of discrete units, presenting themselves one after another to the gaze. Without the creative collaboration of the reader, therefore, the text can hardly be actualized as a temporal sequence, but must remain dormant and static in its graphic fixity. Sequential dynamics relate, then, both to the manner in which sequences are arranged, in terms of overt authorial division of a text, and to the manner in which the reader, proceeding through that text, registers temporal and continuity relationships, and creates sequential ties.

In certain cases, even where major narrative units are marked, subchapter boundaries remain aporetic. The lack of any punctuation in the early Japanese classic, Lady Murasaki's *The Tale of Genji*, makes every reader an exegete (Miner 1990, 180). When Roland Barthes, on the other hand, dissects a short story by Balzac, his "commentary" is nearly seven times the length of the original, and he fragments *Sarrasine* [*sic*] into well over five-hundred *lexias* or reading units. Their length, he concedes, is purely arbitrary, a matter of critical convenience and connotative density (Barthes 1970, 20).

Of the five codes into which Barthes reassembles Balzac, the hermeneutic and proairetic bear especially on temporal sequence. The first often retains its enigmas until the closing stages of a text. It tends, moreover, to work against "the chronological flow of the story and operates through the distribution of *retards*, which hinder recuperation by the reader" (Duffy 1992, 67). The second, the code of actions, countering the occlusive and stalling tactics of the hermeneutic, relates to chronology and sequence.

Where a text is already divided into chapters and supplied with titles, that task may not be problematic, but the brief *lexias* of S/Z represent Barthes's own microdivisions of another's text, and the data composing proairetic sequences needs to be pieced together by the reader. In his own appended list (Barthes 1970, 259–63), only the most basic actions, such as arrival and departure, occupy successive *lexias*. The remainder, including those which Barthes cites under generic headings ("Promenade," "Assassinat," "Rendez-vous"), appear in *lexias* dispersed throughout the text.

In an earlier essay, Barthes (1966) classifies narrative events into the more crucial "noyau," the less vital "catalyse" (Chatman's "kernel" and "satellite" [1978, 53–54]). Satellites are merely consecutive or chronological; kernels are both consecutive and consequential, or chronological and logical. The mainspring lies precisely in the confusion of consecution and consequence, what comes *after* being read in narrative as what is *caused by*. As such, narrative systematically applies post hoc, ergo propter hoc, and the notion has complex resonances. Barthes's advocacy of re-reading, of multiple forward processing, as a textual strategy (1970, 22), is borne out by Culler's stress on the reader's need to perceive teleologically organized structures, and to place actions in sequences retrospectively (1975, 136). Chatman, too, recognizes that the first kernel can only be properly identified and its sequence named, after finishing the entire narrative (1978, 56).

As a "whole within which nothing is repeated" (Barthes 1977, 124), a narrative sequence comprises a logical succession of kernels, each of which may be relatively unimportant in isolation. So trifling an event as the offer of a cigarette may comprise *microsequences* of offering, accepting, lighting, smoking, at every juncture of which an alternative is possible. James Bond's express refusal, at the third juncture, of Du Pont's lighter (Fleming [1959]

1964, 14), indeed, projects his instinctive wariness. 007's world of contingency thus endows the commonplace with uncommon relevance.

Another narrative fragment from *Goldfinger* ("the telephone rang") illustrates a kernel, allowing the choice of response or non-response, before a variety of possible satellites gives way to the next kernel ("Bond answered"), completing another brief sequence (Barthes 1977, 94). The examples happen to be drawn from initial chapter segments of Fleming's novel, but they could be gathered from any other segment, or, as in S/Z, disseminated throughout. Such is the case with one of Chatman's own examples of a kernel: Strether's dilemma in James's *The Ambassadors*, whether to advise Chad to remain in Paris or to return. A different example, Achilles's choice in *The Iliad* between surrendering Briseis to Agamemnon or refusing, derives from a medial segment of the epic's opening book (Chatman 1978, 53).

The kernels that constitute Barthes's narrative or actional sequences ("suites d'actions") vary considerably in their positioning. Though *Sarrasine* is too short for major textual divisions, the approach clearly implies that in larger-scale works, the formation of sequences would rely on kernels assembled from separate units or chapters. The creative role of a reader, even Superreader, in interpreting and naming the material of sequences, remains paramount, but, just as clearly, their number and selection are not the result of overt authorial decisions, and are thus open to debate.

Other critical approaches to sequence refer to a series of situations and events, of which the last in time constitutes a partial repetition or transform of the first (Prince 1989, 86): "Susan was unhappy; then Susan met Flora, and she became happy." An elementary, minimal sequence, or triad, basic to a taxonomy of narrative roles (Bremond 1973, 131), may be more abstractly described as a combination of three terms. These correspond to the three stages in the unfolding of any process: 1) virtuality, 2) actualization or nonactualization of the possibility, 3) achievement or non-achievement. Examples are provided by two strings, such as "villainy, intervention of the hero, success," and "villainy, intervention of the hero, failure" (Prince 1989, 100).

From the above, there appears a fundamental discrepancy between the narrative sequence of Barthes, and textual sequence, as manifest in the narrative flow within and between units. Texts which embody Prince's transform or Bremond's triad, moreover, could equally well occupy a short story or a long novel. In the latter, the separate stages of the process would normally unfold in different narrative units. The issue then becomes one of charting the distribution of material across chapter boundaries. In another approach, Greimas outdoes even Barthes, expanding a six-page story into a "commentary" over forty times as long.

Maupassant's *Deux amis* is broken into twelve *séquences* of varying lengths, to which Greimas gives a name or *lexeme*, and only one of the series is not immediately successive. In this exceptional case (SQ III: "La promenade"), a paragraph from the first page joins a passage from the second, representing a rare instance of non-agreement between textual sequence and narrative syntagm (Greimas 1976, 69). Thus, a brief, unsegmented text generates a succession of virtually self-contained *lexeme-sequences*, which Greimas exploits to play syntagmatic against paradigmatic axis, the surface Realist against the potential Symbolist in Maupassant.

Whereas Greimas segments a text into a linear succession of *lexemes*, and Barthes into dispersed proairetic sequences, a different emphasis appears in German analysts. For Günther Müller, the basic unit of all narrative is the *Phase:* "das im Erzählen gebildete Gefüge eines Vorgangs, der in einem Einsatz zu einem Ende geführt wird"[19] (Müller 1950, 29). The formulation, which implies the self-contained and completed character of an event, often introduced by the "one day" marker, composed of part-phases and in turn composing a larger entity, remains, nevertheless, insufficiently precise and detailed.

Müller's chief concern is to establish morphologies according to large-scale patterns of page/time ratios, of amounts of textual space *[Erzählzeit]* used to cover story-time *[erzählte Zeit]*. Thus, lengthy texts, thematically disparate, may share a sequential kinship in the way they shift from expansive representation *[breite Darstellung]* at their opening, to subsequent telescoping *[Raffung]* of events. They may alternate between both patterns, or show little initial action (Müller 1950, 28).

Application of Müller's approach to a specific writer, produces a division of texts in terms of the number of chapters occupied by individual phases (Jungel 1953). In novels by E. M. Forster, an increment in the length and number of phases can be demonstrated in successive works. The notion of phase here connotes a self-contained portion of action, but not necessarily coinciding with the single chapter-unit. For Jungel, the fifth phase of *A Passage to India* (Forster [1924] 1981), for example, spans the nine chapters of the Marabar Caves episode (chs. 13–21; 139–98), and its phasal limits are uncontentious (see page 276). Other phases marked by Jungel, however, are much more debatable. The exact nature of the phase-linkages, whether by telescoping, ellipsis, or direct succession, is left relatively vague, their typology unexplored.

If Müller and Jungel too easily equate phase and chapter boundaries, without allowing for preemptive material and *delayed presentation*[20] within chapters, Eberhard Lämmert at least relates his narrative phases *[Erzählphasen]* to concrete situations occurring on specified days or series of days (Lämmert 1955, 76). The similarity with and foreshadowing of Genette's category of singulative frequency is clear (Genette 1972, 145–46). Lämmert himself defines phases in terms of the way they represent individual events through a combination of relatively restricted time-cover with relatively detailed narration, and of their equal ability to accentuate large-scale movements over many years as well as day-long events (1955, 73–76). His coinage of a proleptic *Hakenstil* category (171), suggests a more elastic view of narrative and textual division than Müller's.

Both Lämmert's championship of succession as the determining criterion of narrative, and Müller's spatiotemporal ratios, however, have been attacked as irrelevant to contemporary literature. In discussing Arno Schmidt's fragmentary novel *Das steinerne Herz* [1956], Reimer Bull concludes that such linear and organicist approaches, which imply a sense of narrative continuity and coherence, can scarcely apply to a novelist committed to quite opposite values (Bull 1970, 64–65). They apply no more easily, either, to *Finnegans Wake*, close to " 'incoherence' in the sense of 'unintelligibility' " (Wales 1989, 75). For Schmidt and his generation, spatial models of narrative seem more appropriate.

To consider a text from the reader's perspective, as an unfolding temporal sequence, involves, therefore, a discrepancy between narrative sequences and phases, as perceived by critics, and textual sequences, as marked by authors. While critics are free to override textual divisions, it is authors, in the main, who have freely created them in the first place, so that when chapter boundaries do not correspond to those of subject matter, a sense of deliberately planned asymmetry may result. This lack of fit between physical unit and discourse unit, may be illustrated by resort to episodes that *commence* at chapter end rather than chapter start, to overflow thereafter into the following chapter.

In the more radical, but actual case of a work such as *Tristram Shandy*, the mismatch has a creative, comic, contrapuntal effect. Sterne's novel demonstrates how a physical paragraph can function, as "a pattern maker (as distinct from being merely a pattern marker) in its own right" (Halliday and Hasan 1976, 297). Crucially, in Tristram's unconventional world, transformations of scale appear; paragraphs operate like sentences, and chapters like paragraphs. Thus, his bizarre chapter lengths and divisions stem partly from the treatment of a new chapter as if it were a new paragraph in ordinary writing, and from dividing a single discourse unit into absurdly brief physical units (Sultana 1987, 193–95).

Where the text-unifying, rather than text-dividing functions of the gaps between narrative units are at issue, the concepts of cohesion and coherence come into play. Text itself has been variously defined as a "coherent sequence of linguistic signs" (Bertinetto 1979, 1.154), a "stretch of language which seems appropriately coherent in actual use" (Quirk et al. 1985, 1423), and narrative as "coherent textual order" (Jonnes 1990, 9). Common to each approach, then, is the factor of coherence. The pair of cohesion and coherence is differentiated succinctly by Tanya Reinhart, who sees the former as a "label for overt linguistic devices for putting sentences together," while the latter is a "matter of semantic and pragmatic relations in the text" (Reinhart 1980, 163).

Since they share a verb and are related etymologically, the two concepts have often been confused. A more expansive account identifies cohesion with the various phonological, grammatical, lexical, and semantic means of linking sentences into larger units, such as paragraphs or chapters, of making them "stick together." Equivalent terms might be *intersentence linkage/concord, suprasentential relations,* or *connectivity* (Wales 1989, 75). In the same account, "coherence" refers to the underlying development of propositions in terms of speech acts, and it is particularly significant for literary forms. "Narrative coherence" implies a logical consistency and clarity in the working out of plot, "discourse coherence" a clear and plausible narration.

The value of cohesive relations to a consideration of sequential dynamics is apparent in terms of intersentence linkage. Where the relevant sentences are separated by a textual divide, discussion at the level of *microsequence* then shifts to that of *macrosequence,* since the sentences may derive, respectively, from the closing and opening stages of quite different narrative units. Halliday and Hasan (1976, 4) view the principal cohesive ties as lexicogrammatical: reference, substitution, ellipsis, conjunction, and lexical repetition.

Defining the text as a "semantic unit . . . realized by . . . sentences" (2), the same critics take cohesive relations to be relations of meaning, and the continuity they bring about is semantic too. Cohesion, moreover, serves as a criterion for recognizing the boundaries of a text. A new text begins, "where a sentence shows no cohesion with those that have preceded" (295). To this linguistic dimension of linkage needs to be added that of a discourse or narrative context.

If "new episode" is substituted for "new text," in the sense of a topically coherent part of discourse, or a sequence of sentences dominated by a macroproposition, at least seven possible types of transition can be identified (van Dijk and Kintsch 1983, 204). Neither a new text, nor a new episode, however, presupposes the presence of a new chapter or narrative unit. An episode may be broached, for example, by the surface structure mark of a paragraph indentation, by a pause in spoken discourse, or the new macroproposition may be signaled by various markers of topic change.

These comprise a change of possible world; of time or period; of place; the introduction of new participants; a full noun phrase reintroduction of old participants; a change of perspective or viewpoint; a different predicate range in terms of a change of frame or script (204). Depending on how inclusively these topic markers are understood, they may be supplemented by other types of transition, such as pronounced shifts of mood and feeling. Our chief concern here lies with the second category, a new episode broached by change of time or period. More extensive analysis, however, "deserves a chapter to itself" (Sterne [1767] 1967, 346), and it is the topic of ordering that we next address.

ORDERING

> If I were to relate it in the order in which it reached me, I should commence in the middle, and when I had arrived at the conclusion, go back for a beginning. It is enough for me to say that some of its circumstances passed before my own eyes. For the remainder I know them to have happened. . . .
> —Charles Dickens, *The Pickwick Papers*

> Gern hätte [ein Historiograph oder Biograph] angefangen: In dem kleinen Städtchen N. oder B. oder K., und zwar am Pfingstmontage oder zu Ostern des und des Jahres, erblickte Johannes Kreisler das Licht der Welt!—Aber solche schöne chronologische Ordnung kann gar nicht aufkommen, da dem unglücklichen Erzähler nur mündlich, brockenweis mitgeteilte Nachrichten zu Gebote stehen, die er, um nicht das Ganze aus dem Gedächtnisse zu verlieren, sogleich verarbeiten muss.

> [(A historiographer or biographer) would like to have started thus: In the small town of N. or B. or K., on Whit Monday or at

Easter of a particular year, Johannes Kreisler first saw the light of day!—Such a fine chronological arrangement, however, cannot occur, since the information made available to the unfortunate narrator has been only piecemeal and by word of mouth, so that he has to transcribe it immediately in order not to forget it completely.]

—E. T. A. Hoffmann, *Lebensansichten des Katers Murr*

In Dickens's case, old Jack Bamber admits rearranging his "Tale about the Queer Client" to make it more accessible for an audience that includes Mr. Pickwick. The account, for whose veracity the Old Man personally vouches, differs, therefore, in its ordering, from that by which he allegedly gleaned the material. In Hoffmann's case, Kreisler's unnamed biographer would prefer to have introduced his subject chronologically, but the secondhand, oral, and partial nature of his sources, as well as a weak memory, opt against rearrangement.

This serves the larger strategy of an ironic *Doppelroman*, which alternates between tomcat Murr's progressive autobiography, and the discontinuous fragments of the *Kapellmeister*'s life. With Dickens, the difference between the Formalist *fabula* and *syuzhet* seems minimal, since the Old Man has linearized events[21] before communicating them; with Hoffmann, it is the reader who is left to create linear out of nonlinear sequences.

As imaginary construct, a *fabula* is created progressively and retroactively by a reader, adopting narrative cues and applying various schemata. The latter may be prototype, template, or procedural (Bordwell 1985, 49). Reconstituted along a chronological line of cause and effect, the *fabula* necessarily omits elements from the *syuzhet*. These include atemporal interpolations such as the prefatory chapters in *Tom Jones*, as well as perspectival refractions, analogical patterns, and the whole verbal play of the text (Sternberg 1978, 10). The *syuzhet*, as actual presentation of the *fabula*, does not depend on being embodied in any specific medium. Since it is not a speech act, the same *fabula* could be inferred from a novel, film, painting or play. It can thus avoid forced analogies between linguistic categories and nonverbal phenomena (Bordwell 51).

In addition to the *fabula/syuzhet* pair, Sternberg draws attention to E. M. Forster's celebrated distinction between *story* and *plot* (Forster [1927] 1993, 60). The first emphasizes chronological sequence ["and then?"], the second, causality ["why?"]. Since Forster's pair is governed by mode of linkage rather than by degree of anachrony or deformation, Sternberg proposes a set of four terms, by conflating Forsterian and Formalist concepts.[22] Deeming the terms not interchangeable but complementary, Sternberg faces problems in promoting their use. *Story* and *plot*, as he himself notes, are English renditions of Boris Tomashevsky's Formalist pair (Lemon and Reis 1965), while Chatman, in the title of his influential *Story and Discourse* (1978), already repeats the same Englished term for *fabula*. Despite their greater precision, then, Sternberg's concepts need renaming to avoid appearing tautological.

Some sense of the diverse terminology employed in critical discussion of ordering, is conveyed by Monika Fludernik's tabulation of the narrative levels assumed by six leading narratologists (1993, 62).[23] Whichever labels and couplings we prefer, the justification for applying the concepts of *fabula/syuzhet*, even after more than seventy years, remains strong.[24] For Peter Brooks, the distinction is central: it allows us "to juxtapose two modes of order and in the juxtaposing to see how ordering takes place" (Brooks 1984, 13).

For David Lodge, this tool of comparison enables us to uncover formal choices in handling time and perspective (Lodge 1990, 123). Identification of discrepancies between *fabula* and *syuzhet* can direct attention to turning points of plot, narratorial priorities, and assumptions (Duffy 1992, 44). It may contribute to intenser reading, bring about aesthetic or psychological effects, and point to subtle differences between expectation and realization (Bal 1985, 52–53). An author is enabled to vary focusing patterns, and create powerful stylistic effects (Pavel 1985, 35).

In specific cases, reconstitution of a *fabula* genuinely illuminates a work. How nearly the paths of Adam and Hetty cross, how nearly tragedy could have been averted, becomes graphically clear by linear rearrangement of events in *Adam Bede* (1859) (Harvey 1957, 436–37). The study of a nineteenth-century Russian story, Vladimir Korolenko's *Makar's Dream* (1885), shows that time reversal is essential to its theme. In itself a *fabula* holds little interest, since a writer "is unlikely to have thought up the facts of his story in strict chronology and then rearranged them" (O'Toole 1982, 162). Lest conceptual gains mask other shortcomings, Wallace Martin warns against overconcern with a *fabula*. This might imply that, "what the narrator is *really* telling is a chronological story . . . and that the elements of narration are deviations from a simple tale that existed beforehand" (Martin 1987, 109).

Though Lewis Carroll's *Alice* is broadly chronological, its topsy-turvy world is typified by the White Queen. She recommends living backwards and remembering forwards. Verbally, she cites the King's Messenger: punished in prison, prior to his trial and well before his crime; physically, she applies a plaster, before screaming, and only then pricking her finger with a pin (Carroll [1865] 1947, 204–6). Exempting, on surrealistic grounds, this regal subversion of the "normal" order of events in the empirical world, the problematics of determining a "true" order are still acute.

A causal sequence in the "real" world may first be signified by pain, then, if not Queen's pin, at least mosquito. It is the *effect* that drives us to produce a cause, and a tropological operation then reorders the sequence pain→mosquito as mosquito→pain (Culler 1981, 183). Menakhem Perry suggests that more than a single *fabula* may be possible, where elements of the text participate in several temporal frames at once, with a sequence in the external world and in a character's consciousness being as equally "natural" (1979, 39–40).

The choice of material is crucial. Thus Kant, in his *Critique of Pure Reason*, identifies a necessary order in perceiving an event. With a static object like a house, perception can begin and proceed in any direction, and the sequence may be termed "subjective"; the dynamic motion of a boat on a river, however, ensures that it must be seen first at one point, then another, in an "objective" sequence (Docherty 1983, 147). Freud's analysis of the Wolf Man produces four separate elements: the history of the neurosis; the order of past events that provide its aetiology; the order in which events emerge during treatment; the order of reporting in the case history (Brooks 1984, 272).

This fourth option functions as *syuzhet*, alternately selecting its *fabula* from among the other three elements, and meaning ultimately resides in the effective interrelationship of all four. In his novel *The White Hotel* (1981), D. M. Thomas supplies, on the level of imaginative fiction, a virtuoso set of generic variations on another Freudian subject. Here, phenomena of transference, displacement, sublimation, and condensation are projected into a typical asymmetry between orders of representation and represented world.

While the concepts of *fabula* and *syuzhet* have relevance within narrative, they are more restricted in their application to the world outside. For this reason, the terms *linear* and *nonlinear* may serve as more inclusive categories to describe the operation of ordering, and to span both narrative and extranarrative experience. As movement along a straight line, in a single direction, *linear* implies an arrangement of elements in a chronological sequence, and from cause to effect. It need not mean tightly connected elements in unbroken succession, or absence of temporal and informational gaps.

Since a text often mingles linear and nonlinear stretches, we may allude to predominant rather than exclusive bias.

The linear/nonlinear pairing usefully designates broad arrangements or macrosequences in a text, though different commentators apply the categories in different ways. For Shklovsky ([1925] 1990, 101), it is the role of the reader that separates "temporal sequence" (as in *War and Peace*, where events unfold one after another, without significant omissions), from "temporal transposition" (as in Dickens and detective fiction). Here, the omission of an incident and its appearance after the consequences have already been revealed, make what is happening incomprehensible to the reader.

For other critics, "fugal" replaces nonlinear. Its musical connotations are exploited, together with its contrast of axis; a temporal succession of states and events is set off against a spatial network of relationships. In a fugal novel, "the horizontal melodic line with its succession of notes is transformed into the vertical chord of simultaneous notes" (Boa and Reid 1972, 16). The difference between linear and fugal here remains one of emphasis, with the categories overlapping, since the linear novel also invites us to see beginning and end, past and present as a unity.

While identifying linear and fugal as basic time structures in fiction, it is salutary to recall that in life and literature, *all* time is in one sense linear. Even though the fictional ordering may be C-B-A-D, the reader starting at page one reads forwards: a-b-c-d, and ends with a compound time of aC-bB-cA-dD (Rodway 1979, 284). However jumbled by memory and imagination the ordering may be, the individual memories or imaginings still occur successively, and are experienced linearly. For a critic of Conrad, strict chronological method is contrasted with "broken method," the novelist's equivalent of a musical fugue (Crankshaw [1936] 1976, 175). Here, fugal-as-nonlinear actively imitates the effect of counterpoint, in treating characters and motifs simultaneously, making each thread self-supporting, but never allowing individual subjects to overshadow the importance of the whole.

Linear order may be set against the dynamic order of memory relations (Meyerhoff 1955, 21). A neutral arrangement by clocks and dates in the physical world yields to another causality. Links between events within memory, therefore, no longer constitute an objective, uniform, consecutive order of "earlier" and "later" as they do for events in nature. Seen from outside, the flow of free association and the fusion of past, present and future in this internal world, take on a quality of timeless copresence, recalling earlier paradigms of fugue and vertical chord.

The novelist William Golding seems to corroborate the notion that dynamic order results in a sequence determined by *significant* associations, rather than objective causal connections. Through the mouth of his artist Samuel Mountjoy in *Free Fall*, a linear view of time (compared to an endless row of bricks) is opposed by a second mode, that of memory, a sense of "shuffle fold and coil." This accentuates what is valuable to the individual, highlighting personal values, patterns of analogy and difference. It thus renders "that day nearer than that because more important . . . that event mirroring this, or those three set apart, exceptional and out of the straight line altogether" (Golding [1959] 1988, 6).

Distinguishing a chronological sequence of action from a sequence of presentation, Mendilow (1952, 124) subsumes in the latter such genres as detective story and stream-of-consciousness novel. Leech and Short, on the other hand, divide the nonlinear into psychological and presentational sequencing, grounded in the relationship between fictional point of view and the order in which information is conveyed (1981, 176–80). Psychological sequencing is typified by detective fiction: the reader adopts the investigator's perspective and order of pursuing the case; in stream-of-consciousness writing, too, textual order reflects the way impressions occur in the mind. With presentational sequencing, the narrator's role is more evident, by omission and playfulness, by commencing *in medias res* and ending with solutions still pending. While such motivation is largely artistic, other grounds may be philosophical, political or social (Prince 1982, 67), tonal or emotional (Ishiguro 1989, 342).

Media-specific, cultural and historical factors, too, affect attitudes toward the linear/nonlinear distinction. In film theory, Bordwell (1985, 77) proposes four possible orders of events and presentation, depending on their successive or simultaneous status.[25] Fiction, since it lacks the equivalents of separate sound and image channels, can effectively realize only two of the options. These harness successive presentation to either simultaneous or successive events. Another critic notes that interartistic linkages favour one of the linear/nonlinear pair. Between "readable" Pre-Raphaelite pictures, and the mid-Victorian novel's fusion of elaborate yet resolved plots, solid detail and emphasis on the *moral aspect of cause and effect*, the connection seems scarcely accidental (Flint 1990, 51), and linearity entirely appropriate.

In historical terms, the linearity of heroic epic and unheroic picaresque on the one hand, has been contrasted with nonlinear types on the other. These include the "multifoliate plot" of romance, and cyclical narratives based on lunar and solar movements (Scholes and Kellogg 1966, 208–22). Different views of history and time also produce different types of plot. From Kermode's "tick-tock" plot, typical of Realism, in which history appears progressive and evolutionary, and time as a plenum, two nonlinear types emerge (Docherty 1983, 135). The circular "tick-tock-tick" plot of Modernism reflects a static view of history; the discontinuous "tock-tick" plot of Postmodernism acknowledges gaps in time, a revolutionary approach to history which fractures not only the "instant" but also the "subject."

The sense of forward motion may also be reinforced by material modes of production. Nineteenth-century serial publication, for instance, in limiting the reader's ability to ascertain subsequent developments, still less to turn forward to an ending, stresses the dual line of empirical and literary experience. A month of real time separates an unfinished narrative from the next tranche of a whole, as yet likely incomplete in its creator's mind. The reader, therefore, is repeatedly "in the middle of a story whose past was earlier installments and whose future [is] 'to be continued' " (Hughes and Lund 1991, 60–61).

In practical terms, chronological deviations are less likely to appear with serialization than with whole texts, since the latter permit linearization by the reader. A typical view of fiction: "presumably written to be read from front to back, once" (Sammons 1965, 35), would also support a claim that linear ordering of events, which matches the reader's linear processing of texts, appears more "natural" than nonlinear arrangement.

It is Meir Sternberg who urges the prochronologist cause most vigorously. Challenging truisms that "going straight is going wrong" and that "breaking time is making art," he argues that theory has been geared to disorder, that critics from Shklovsky to Barthes and Genette have been biased against chronological narration. Although the line from early to late follows nature and causality, promotes plot coherence, intelligibility and memorability, these very features seem defects to antilinearists: "too akin to the way of the world, too mimetic and transparent for art" (Sternberg 1990, 903). The chronological tendencies of omniscient narration, which allows telling without gaps, and of direct quotation, have been devalued, while history-telling in its largest sense has been ignored.

For Sternberg, this genre has produced some of the masterworks of narrative, from the Bible and Thucydides to Gibbon, not so much despite as owing to their mimesis of sequence, their "alignment of events into grand chronological-causal design" (922). Denying that chronologizing comes easily, Sternberg argues rather that capturing the visible world comes hard, that linear narrative is as flexible and wide-ranging in means as it is variable in ends and scales. It may be "potentially subtler, *more* artistic, than the open ruptures of anachrony" (924). His alternatives to anachrony are simultaneity and types of nontemporal logic: hierarchical, perspectival, and suprasequential patterning or spatial form.

After Sir Walter Scott, George Watson suggests, the European novel has stepped outside chronology less often than its predecessors, and cites the popularity of seventeenth- and eighteenth-century exemplary tale and epistolary novel. His conclusion reiterates the force of chronology: "most readers still demand development, preferring a novel to move steadily forward than to recoil or zigzag. To this day, then, most novels are a matter of one thing after another, like life itself" (Watson 1979, 94). If the concepts of "most readers" and "most novels" are contentious enough in their generalities, Watson's view of life as linear succession is no less problematic.

Even Scott's French contemporary, Balzac, in an age of classic realism, is led to debate the difficulties of introducing a new character into a novel. When an author, in real life, encounters someone long since forgotten, details may emerge from a third party, either the following day or month, perhaps in fragments, about those missing years. Balzac contrasts history-telling with biography, and resignedly abandons the effort at strict chronological ordering in fiction: "Il n'y a rien qui soit d'un seul bloc dans ce monde, tout y est mosaïque. Vous ne pouvez raconter chronologiquement que l'histoire du temps passé, système inapplicable à un présent qui marche"[26] ([1841] 1965, 1.602).

Nearly a century later, Ford Madox Ford refutes any linear parallels between life and fiction. In justifying time shift, he maintains that the traditional novel goes straight forward, whereas the reality of establishing human contact is quite different. To produce an effect of life upon the reader, authors must first grasp their subject "with a strong impression, and then work backwards and forwards over his past" (Ford 1924, 137). Writing of *Lord Jim*, Hillis Miller echoes the same phrase. Conrad's very material, he implies, forces the narrator, "to move back and forth across the facts, putting them in one or another achronological order in the hope that this deeper meaning will reveal itself" (Miller 1982, 35). Unsurprisingly, Ford's own work attracts similar comments. Thus, *The Good Sol-*

dier (1915), with its "piecemeal chronology" (Schow 1975, 207), and "rich arabesque of forward-looking and backward-amplifying hints" (Vidan 1981, 143), tends toward the omnitemporal quality of spatial form.

In ideological terms, the case against chronology seems to go by default, grounded in the assumed superiority of skewed over straight telling. Even unpartisan critics hint at the somewhat color-less identity of chronological sequencing, its "neutral" order, by contrast with psychological or presentational modes (Leech and Short 1981, 177). The Formalist notion of defamiliarization *[ostra-nanie]*, which works to prevent perception becoming automatic, enlists nonchronological narration to achieve its ends. A critique of chronology might object to a lack of overtones, or to sentences that contribute no more than their own face value to the total effect. The result is a "waste of space" and "thinness of texture" (Crank-shaw [1936] 1976, 170).

Conrad's "broken method," by contrast, yields an extreme close-ness of texture "very satisfying to the adult mind" [*sic*], in novels dealing in atmosphere and the effects of facts, rather than in the "purely superficial matter of physical suspense" (172). To these points, sobering both for prochronologists and nonadult minds, Crankshaw adds that to write *Nostromo* according to strict chronol-ogy would have been "easy," but the outcome unreadable. William Golding, as practicing novelist, only reinforces the antilinearist po-sition, declaring that the straight line is a "dead thing." Formalist echoes linger in his definition of linearity, as "effortless perception native to us as water to the mackerel" (Golding [1959] 1988, 6).

Disputing any literary-historical progression from a period of naïve synchrony to one of sophisticated anachrony, Barbara Herr-nstein Smith contends that absolute chronological order is as rare in folkloric narratives (*pace* Genette) as in any literary tradition. Such order is "virtually *impossible*" for any narrator to sustain out-side the most minimal utterance (Smith 1980, 227). Nonlinearity represents "the rule rather than the exception in narrative ac-counts," and if *perfect* chronological order occurs at all, it is likely only in "acutely self-conscious, 'artful', or 'literary' texts." In the lack of evidence, however, it may be asked how many critics of liter-ature ever in fact assume such total linearity, or reject entirely a narrative's "social and circumstantial context" (234).[27]

Even Sternberg does not posit perfect chronology, and cites cross-cutting in Thucydides and digressions in Herodotus (Stern-berg 1990, 924). One model of everyday discourse, the oral-sponta-neous studies of William Labov, seems to support a monochronic system of events and presentation (Labov 1972, 378). Within literary narration, however, even proponents of spatial form, such as Joseph Frank, make no case for the existence of works completely purified of either spatial or temporal elements.

At the opposite end of a spectrum from Claude Simon's mosaic-like *La Route des Flandres* (1960), Jeffrey Smitten offers Trollope's *Can You Forgive Her?* (1864) as chronological model with "few violations" (Smitten 1981, 20).[28] In Fontane's *Effi Briest* (1894), however, even the preliminary exposition is couched in dialogue form, and so does not shift outside present events. This novel, with the single but vital exception of paraliptic love letters between Crampas and Effi, comes closer than Trollope to a model of linear ordering.

Beyond ideological contests for the souls of prochronologists or achronophiles, is a need to accept the fact that specific texts already exist in linear or nonlinear arrangements, and usually involve both. Further analysis of narrative ordering, therefore, has to proceed from that basic and pragmatic recognition.[29] Within the linear category itself, chronological and causal elements may combine to greater or lesser degree, and exist in a more or less pure state. Literature has traditionally shunned that unadulterated extreme. As Tzvetan Todorov has pointed out, pure chronological order, stripped of all causality, is dominant in chronicles, annals and diaries; pure causality dominates the discourses of logician, lawyer, and political orator (1981, 42). Certain literary works, nonetheless, gesture toward these pure forms: Mann's *Buddenbrooks* (1902) or Galsworthy's *Forsyte Saga* (1922) as chronicle, Gogol's *Diary of a Madman* (1835) or Tanizaki's *The Key [Kagi]* (1960) as diary.

The portrait and descriptive tale illustrate causality, while logic rather than narrative prevails in the literary essay and sermon. With different genres, different tendencies appear. The bildungsroman, concerned with growth and development, is markedly chronological; framework narrative *[Rahmenerzählung]*, especially prevalent in the German *novelle*, fractures progression. Picaresque fiction, discarding causality, accentuates change of place rather than time (Mickelsen 1981, 67). Despite its linear basis, multiplot narrative, with its repeated breaks and transitions, reduces the importance of forward succession, in favor of a more static unity based on analogical relationships, with no necessary order (Garrett 1969, 5).

Within the nonlinear category, in which possibilities for "dis-orderly" arrangement can reach Shandean extremes, some of the most notable types may be termed *order transforms*. In a sequence such as *A-C-B*, the second and third elements are presented in the text in the reverse order of their supposed occurrence. According to generative-transformational grammar, the operation constitutes an order transformation of a deep-structure string (Prince 1989, 98–99). Such relations are *intratextual*, as opposed to the kind of *intertextual* transformations observed in folktale and myth, whereby functions (Propp) or versions (Lévi-Strauss) change from one tale/set of tales or one myth to another. Order transforms in a single text may vary in their proportions. They can operate at a *part-text* or *microsequential* level, between successive sentences, paragraphs or chapters, as well as at a *whole-text* or *macrosequential* level, accounting for broad movements of a work.

An element *B*, omitted from its expected place in a microsequence *A-B-C* and reordered as a *medial reverse transform*, *A-C-B*, might be only briefly postponed, depending on role and status. Since absolute ellipsis cannot be perceived, any forward leap between *A* and the succeeding element in the text must be registered retrospectively. The existence of *B* may be explicitly signalled, implicitly assumed by the reader, or remain unsuspected until a later stage, when narratorial paralipsis acknowledges its omission. In extent, element *B* may range from a mere hint or forward reference, even begging its own designation as a separate element, to a fully developed scene, and its importance may likewise vary greatly.

Its relocation may be linked to the type of material treated, *heterodiegetic* (new or different characters or events), rather than *homodiegetic* (same characters or events), relative to adjacent elements. Instead of an *A-C-B* sequence, the *B* element could be situated in a more complex arrangement such as *A-C-D-E-F-B*. Here, the effect of delayed presentation is to increase curiosity and tension, while there may be no clue given at element *C* as to when the missing stage is to be supplied, nor any reason offered for its delay. Element *C*, meanwhile, could serve as the equivalent of a filmic flash forward, to reassure readers of future developments, to play down the loss of the intervening stage, or to fuel speculation as to the identity of *B*.

In Turgenev's *Virgin Soil* (1877), a dinner (*B*) at Sipiagin's house is assigned to the gap between the end of chapter 11 (*A*) and the start of chapter 12 (*C*). The temporary withholding of details serves here to reduce emphasis on direct observation of the meal per se. It directs attention, instead, to Nejdanov's retrospective thoughts and sensations, ultimately of greater relevance. By choice of verb form, too, a chapter opening might immediately announce material omitted or deferred. In Bennett's *The Old Wives' Tale* (1908), new-

Medial Reverse	A-C-B-D	(Conrad, *The Secret Agent*)
	or	
	J-L-K-M	(Turgenev, *Virgin Spring*) [Part-text]
Initial Reverse	B-A-C	(Gray, *Lanark*)
/Extended	B-A-C-D	(Hugo, *Notre-Dame de Paris*) [Part-text]
Extended Reverse	C-A-B-D	(Faulkner, *The Sound and the Fury*)
Alternating	A-B-A-B	(Ackroyd, *Hawksmoor*)
/Initial Reverse	B-A-B-A	(Clarke, *The Chymical Wedding*)
Final Reverse	B-C-A	(Walpole, *The Castle of Otranto*)
/Delayed	B-E-C-D-A	(Churchill, *Top Girls*)
Progressive Reverse	E-D-C-B-A	(Howard, *The Long View*)
/Loop	C-B-A-D	(Desai, *Clear Light of Day*)
/Semi-Return	C-B^1-A-B^2	(Storm, *Der Schimmelreiter*)
/Delayed	C-B-E-A-D	(Eliot, *Daniel Deronda*) [Part-text]
Random Sequence	*Date-Explicit*	(Huxley, *Eyeless in Gaza*)
	or	
	Date-Implicit	(Sterne, *Tristram Shandy*)

Figure 1.1   Types of Order Transforms

lyweds Gerald and Sophia leave London at chapter end (*[A]* 3.2.1f),
but their arrival in Paris (*[B]* 3.2.2i2) is only confirmed after reference to their excursion to Versailles (*[C]* 3.2.2i1).

Reordering the sequence into *A-C-B*, therefore, helps to stress
the role of the Versailles trip, at new chapter start, as the highpoint
of the honeymoon, before disillusion and humiliation intrude. In
another medial reverse transform, from Moore's *Esther Waters*
(1894), a new chapter (ch. 15) begins with a set of conversational
"turns" unassisted by speech-tags (*[C]*, 15i1). Forward ellipsis here
serves to eliminate an unwanted and unspecified lapse of time (*B*),
and to delay confirmation of the fuddled state of Esther's father,
revealed only at the end of the exchange (15i2).

In all these microsequences, the designation *A-C-B* is relational
rather than absolute, since *A* does not mark the starting point, but
a later stage of the narrative; *J-L-K* or *P-R-Q* may in fact offer more
accurate coding. At a macrosequential level, however, *A-C-B* or another permutation can register the large-scale course of a work.
Where a novel is textually segmented into parts or books not sequentially linear, it is statistically unlikely that the first of them will
follow an *A-C-B* format. Far more probable is a permutation such

as B-A-C or C-A-B, with the earliest event *(A)* delayed in its presentation.

Since narrative beginnings and endings are both "arbitrary disjunctions in a sequence of events that is presumed continuous" (Welsh 1978, 10), extending before and after the events actually narrated, issues of ordering necessarily deal with the textual position of this earliest event. It may not be obvious at once that the opening part or book is in fact not the first in order of occurrence; or how and when its status is to be clarified; or how its length and significance compares to that of other divisions.

Order transforms can reveal themselves as such by *explicit dating* or *implicit relationship* of events to one another. The latter is illustrated by Raphael's account to Emile of a disastrous life *(A)*, in the central chapter of Balzac's *La Peau de Chagrin* (1831). His history grounds developments in the final chapter of a novel using *initial reverse transform*, B-A-C, thus avoiding the block exposition prevalent elsewhere with Balzac. At the core of Thornton Wilder's *The Bridge of San Luis Rey* (1927), are the three chapters that chronicle the victims *(A)* of the disaster sketched in a prologue *(B)*, with consequences in the last chapter *(C)*. By positioning the crisis not toward the close but at the very outset of the narrative, Wilder removes suspense, and encourages concentration on the biographies, bound by a common framework and fate.

In the original 1934 version of F. Scott Fitzgerald's *Tender Is the Night*, a sequence of chapters that evokes Dick Diver's meeting at the Swiss clinic with Nicole Warren, is placed at the beginning of book 2, rather than of book 1 where, chronologically, it belongs. In the revised 1951 version, the novel is linearized.[30] The advantages of tracing a relationship from first encounter to final parting, and of focusing on Diver's psychological development, are exchanged for the reader's sense of underlying enigmas, together with the symmetry of the original B-A-C ordering. This allowed contrast and comparison between two quite different scenes at Gausse's Beach, in the very first (1.1) and very last (3.12) chapters.

Another novel in two versions, Gottfried Keller's *Der grüne Heinrich*, suggests different effects from different ordering. In the 1855 original, Keller follows the nonlinear B-A-C macrosequence of Wieland's *Agathon* (1766), the first German bildungsroman, but Heinrich's retrospective threatens aesthetically to overbalance the whole work, and lend undue weight to his early Zürich years. Thus, the revised 1880 version linearizes and unifies its hero's career, focalizing entirely by first person, its forward progression now reflecting organic growth and development, one of the strengths of the bildungsroman. For a group of modern novels, the same initial reverse transform, B-A-C, serves other purposes.

In V. S. Naipaul's *The Mimic Men* (1967), Ralph Singh's memories of the disorder of a Caribbean youth (A) as viewed from exile in postwar London (B), force him to reappraise his career, to recognize that the process of biographical re-creation itself can restore clarity and order (C). A similar principle of "reculer pour mieux sauter," of strategic withdrawal to prepare for later advance, operates in Susan Hill's *In the Springtime of the Year* (1974). Here, temporal reversion from a bleak present (B), yields to revelations about a husband's sudden death in part 2 (A), and the gradual strengthening of a widow's resolve to survive (C). Formal echoes of pastoral elegy inspire a movement from present grief to reassessment of the past, to projected hope in the future.

In Alasdair Gray's Postmodernist *Lanark*, by contrast, initial reverse transform reflects the influence of Sterne, with book 3 opening the work (B), followed by the prologue, books 1 and 2 (A). An ironic, highly self-conscious narrator himself highlights this large-scale book renumbering. He playfully situates an epilogue three chapters before the end, where it will offer comic distraction, fine sentiments and critical notes. The latter, he adds thoughtfully, "will save research scholars years of toil" (Gray [1981] 1985a, 483).

If these initial transforms display their nonlinearity by implicit relationship of events, other types may use *explicit dating*. In examples of another macrosequence, *extended reverse transform*, C-A-B-D, each of four books proclaims the year of its events. While Isherwood's *The Memorial* (1932) loops back from 1928 to 1920, then forward to 1925 and 1929, for its account of family affairs in the wake of the Great War, Faulkner's *The Sound and the Fury* (1929) likewise begins in 1928, but focuses on Quentin's suicide at Harvard in 1910, before returning to two contiguous days of Easter 1928. Crucial to Faulkner's arrangement are a sense of past events still alive in the present, presaging family decline, and four shifts of perspective, contributing to a sense of partial access to "truth" and of prismatic instability.

With another type of macrosequence, *alternating transform*, different principles apply. To the musical problem of setting twin poems of 1631 by Milton, Handel's solution of 1740 in his oratorio, *L'Allegro, il Penseroso ed il Moderato,* was to move between each in turn, highlighting their contrasting qualities, and avoiding the dangers of evoking separately the spirits of mirth and melancholy. Fiction with plots unrolling at different historical periods may choose to imitate Handel, or shift in regular alternation from chapter to chapter. Peter Ackroyd's *Hawksmoor* (1985) changes consistently from eighteenth to twentieth century on an *A-B-A-B* basis throughout its twelve chapters.

Lindsay Clarke's *The Chymical Wedding* (1989), by contrast, uses an *initial reverse transform* in its *alternating B-A-B-A* macrosequence, moving over fourteen chapters between the 1980s and 1848. As if simultaneously to accentuate and eschew absolute symmetry, its penultimate chapter 13 comprises fourteen alternating segments: a sequential and numerological *mise en abyme* of the whole novel. Its final chapter 14 then departs from the expected shift to 1848, and remains in 1980s Norfolk. Intriguingly, it is made up of seven segments, an appropriately "magic" figure, together with its multiples: such as 1848.

Two examples of *final reverse transform*, *B-C-A*, demonstrate the crucial issue of defining the scale and importance of the dislocated element, and of characterizing its formal mode. In Horace Walpole's pioneering *The Castle of Otranto* (1765), the *(A)* element is represented by Manfred's verbal disclosure of past secrets in the last two pages of the novel, making up a tiny proportion of the whole. By contrast, in a *delayed* version of the type, *B-E-C-D-A*, Caryl Churchill's *Top Girls* (1982) allows the *(A)* element to occupy the whole final act of a play. Here, the element's generic mode is patently scenic, but a fictional equivalent of such events placed a year earlier than the first two acts, could select either *recounting* or *enactment*,[31] either Walpole's oral-memorial form, or a full spatiotemporal shift back to the original episode as it occurred.

A further type of nonlinear macrosequence, *progressive reverse transform*, offers a mirror-image of the linear novel. In Elizabeth Jane Howard's *The Long View* (1956), each of the five dated Parts shifts consistently but in exact retrograde motion, *E-D-C-B-A*, from 1950 *(E)* back to 1926 *(A)*. By a steady process of peeling away layers of earlier events, the unpromising liaisons of offspring are traced back to the failures of grandparents. The reader is activated to reread the novel in the light of the characters' past, which furthers an understanding of their descendants' present.

In a *loop* variant of this type, a final part takes events forward from their initial articulation, in a *C-B-A-D* arrangement. Thus, in Anita Desai's *Clear Light of Day* (1980), the fourth part of the novel moves toward family reconciliation and reintegration in the present, after inner parts mark the bondage of the past during Indian Partition *(B)* and childhood *(A)*. A *semi-return* version, in Theodor Storm's framework *novelle, Der Schimmelreiter* (1888), brings the reader, after a recessive movement from 1880 to 1756, back to the middle-frame narrator of the 1830s, tracing out a pattern of C-B^1-A-B^2. A similar transform can operate at a part-text or micro-sequential level. Almost one-third (twenty-one of seventy chapters) of Eliot's *Daniel Deronda* (1876) is devoted to a leisurely exposition of its main figures, in a *delayed* version, C-B-E-A-D.

Another part-text example juxtaposes dated linearity with its mirror-image. Part 4 of John Banville's *Kepler* (1981), entirely comprises a group of ten letters penned by the astronomer between Ash Wednesday 1605 and April 1612, succeeded by a further group of ten. These are deliberately arranged in a precisely reverse order, from December 1611 to Easter Day 1605. So studied a presentation not only dramatizes Kepler's relations with a variety of correspondents, but creates a subtle sense of disorientation for the reader, who learns of calamities before their contributory causes.

At a macrosequential level again, Martin Amis's *Time's Arrow* (1991) is a tour de force of progressive reverse transform. The whole of the text appears in reverse order, establishing an unusual and uneasy tension between sentences and paragraphs that the reader processes forward, and narrated events that unroll backward, between the horrifying central topic of the Holocaust, and the essentially comic device of narrative reversal.

Sterne's *Tristram Shandy* (1767) remains very much *sui generis*, a macrosequence best described as *total random transform*. This is to forget, however, that a verifiable chronology for the novel has long been established. A calendar-time of events between 1689 and 1750 has been related to characters' experience, so that, far from being wild and whimsical, the text actually turns out to be an "exactly executed historical novel" (Baird 1936, 819).

The detection of a rationale for narrative ordering becomes easier where units are explicitly dated, as in Aldous Huxley's *Eyeless in Gaza* (1936). None of its fifty-four chapters resumes chronologically from its predecessor, but each time-marked unit can be related to all the others. A measure of forward continuity is assured by the occasional entries from Anthony Beavis's diary. Even in this apparently total random transform, the novel's longest chapter (ch. 6) is set at the earliest point of the period, from 1902 to 1935, covered by the text. The same tendency applies in virtually every case of macrosequence cited, from initial and extended, to alternating and progressive transform.

This chronologically prior element (A), though it nowhere appears in initial position, occupies most pages, underlining the force of the earliest in relation to later events. The very fact that this prior element is presented out of linear sequence, may contribute to its being more acutely focused than otherwise. Where the tension between past and present has thematic importance, moreover, the adoption of one or other type of macrosequential transform can only foreground this contrast, by allotting an entire narrative division to events at a different temporal level, and by a clear rupture of continuity and linearity. If *Time's Arrow*, which even presents lines of dialogue in reverse order, radicalizes the concept of effect before cause, all nonlinear texts do likewise, though to less startling degrees.

In Hardy's last novel, *Jude the Obscure* (1896), Sue Bridehead offers to make her cousin a *new* New Testament like her own:

> "I altered my old one by cutting up all the Epistles and Gospels into separate *brochures*, and re-arranging them in chronological order as written, beginning the book with Thessalonians, following on with the Epistles, and putting the Gospels much further on. . . . My University friend . . . said it was an excellent idea. I know that reading it afterwards made it twice as interesting as before, and twice as understandable."
> "H'm!" said Jude, with a sense of sacrilege. (3.4m; 1975b, 171)

The daring of a subversive New Woman at the end of an era of crumbling religious belief, may bring wry smiles to secular sophisticates at the start of a new millennium. To appreciate Jude's reaction to the flouting of Scriptural order, here ironically involving *relinearization* rather than its converse, it may be necessary, a century later, to seek some equivalent. *Time's Arrow* exemplifies how much more radical a means the writer must employ, to renew the reader's interest and understanding, not of the New Testament, but of narrative ordering itself.

TEMPO

> He was enchanted by the red-haired beauty with her sexy prominent teeth, who stood beside him, so ready to edge away. She thought him all right to look at provided he didn't put on more weight.
> They were married within four months.
> —Muriel Spark, *Symposium*

> Are we for ever to be twisting, and untwisting the same rope? for ever in the same track—for ever at the same pace?
> —Lawrence Sterne, *Tristram Shandy*

Common practice encourages natural links between tempo and speech: we allude to slow, deliberate speakers, measured delivery, rapid-fire utterance, and can quantify such judgments by counting syllables or words per minute. Variations in sentence length have been described as "compositional tempo" (Nash 1980, 99), and changes of pace associated with emphasis and aesthetic satisfaction. Contrasts of meaning can be marked by an increase or decrease in speed (Crystal 1992, 334), but tempo, as in verbal transcriptions of a sports commentary or state funeral, has been typically regarded as an element of spoken discourse (Crystal 1969). Such definitions as "relative speed or rate of movement" (*OED* 1993), still beg questions about written texts. What kind of movement is involved, and speed relative to what?

In musical practice, the situation is more clearcut: tempo alludes to the speed of the beats, to the "uniform rate of rhythmic units" (Tovey 1981, 438). The metronome, moreover, sponsors objective measurement, so that a score can be interpreted at a pace marked by its composer. Meter in poetry, together with devices of punctuation and enjambement, particular choice of vowels and lexical items, can influence overall shifts of speed. The inevitable tendency in prose towards diffusion rather than distillation, means that such effects, even where present, are not as readily apparent.

Shifts of tempo, occasioned, for example, by a series of short vowels, of short or run-on lines, are difficult to reproduce in prose. Even the ground of debate seems to move from technical features to content. The kind of analysis performed on a Baudelaire sonnet (Jakobson and Lévi-Strauss 1962), in an essay where abstract formulae and patterns predominate, is hard to apply to prose, with its multiple systems of speed. At least four different tempi are apparent: "the author gives us a summary, which we read in two minutes (he might have spent two hours writing it), of a narrative which a certain character might have told in two days, of events extending over two years" (Butor 1970, 21).

As an important constituent of sequential dynamics, tempo particularly affects the reader's perception of how narrative events are represented, how quickly or slowly they seem to proceed, how variable treatment of plot elements produces contrast and variety in texts as a whole. Historically, three key influences may be noted. Since Russian Formalism in the 1920s, the partnership of *fabula* and *syuzhet* has proved its value. By the late 1940s and 1950s, Günther Müller had undertaken statistical, intertextual studies in morphological poetics, tracing out types of temporal gestalt. His basis is the ratio between the number of lines and pages which narrative events take up in the text *[Erzählzeit],* and the period of time, in minutes or months, which those events allegedly cover [erzählte Zeit].

The third important contribution dates from the 1970s: Gérard Genette's seminal taxonomy of temporal relations in *Figures III* (1972). Drawing upon Proust, Genette distinguishes order, duration, frequency, voice, and mood. He proposes, as closest to an ideal pace constant, the tempo of dialogue, in which words transcribed on the page most nearly correspond to their putative delivery in real life. Against this measure of near-isochrony, Genette introduces four variations of speed or *anisochronies*; in ascending order from deceleration to acceleration: descriptive pause, scene, summary, and ellipsis. Chatman adds a fifth, stretch, exemplified by inserted material in texts, or slow motion in film (Chatman 1978, 72–73). In all cases, the duration of *fabula* is compared with *syuzhet*, and the balance determines the tempo type. It is the scene, embodying dialogue, which represents the quasiconstant, the sole type remotely able to be gauged by the clock time of real life.

Lacking the equivalent of a metronome, fiction registers no absolute tempo, so that the debate has to deal with varying degrees of objective measurement. Even within narrative studies, tempo has not been allotted a significant role, either in works of general theory or on specific authors. Paul Alkon's book on Defoe, therefore, is exceptional. In a chapter devoted to tempo, he quotes from a passage where Robinson Crusoe reacts to a shipwreck, with "earnest Wishings, That but one Man had been sav'd! *O that it had been but One!* I believe I repeated the Words, *O that it had been but One!* A thousand Times" (Defoe [1719] 1972, 188).

Alkon then distinguishes "objective" from "subjective" tempo, the former being affected here by triple repetition of a single phrase, which makes this passage seem to go more slowly, because for a time it does not progress to a new statement. Subjective tempo is decelerated by invoking the aural powers of readers, to imagine what Crusoe silently thinks (Alkon 1979, 191). Alkon points out how objective pace is affected by text divisions, by increasing or shedding clauses, sentences and paragraphs, to occupy more or less of the reader's clock time. Subjective pace is slowed down by the reader's need to imagine events or complete details not supplied, by repetitions that turn attention backward: it is speeded up, by making readers anticipate future developments.

At this point, the concept of iconicity, whereby a code "imitates, in its signals or textual forms, the meanings that they represent" (Leech and Short 1981, 233) might be usefully introduced. Thus, major examples of syntactic iconicity are chronological sequencing and juxtaposition. In the former, textual time imitates real time, so that sequencing bears a mimetic force; in the latter, words close in the text may evoke an impression of closeness or relatedness (temporal, psychological or locational) in the fiction. On the level of microsequence, the sentence, as smallest graphic unit, already offers indications of pace: "He caught [the portrait] up, rushed into the next room, tore, cut, and hacked it in every direction, and eagerly watched the fragments that burned like tinder in the turf-fire" (Maturin [1820] 1968, 60). Here, the textual representation closely matches the speed of putative events, so that discourse- and story-time are virtually identical (DT = ST), and the passage can be designated iconic. Each comma is co-occurrent with the end of a separate bit of action, while dynamic, onomatopoeic verbs, asyndeton, and monosyllables suggest rapidity, and proximity in text echoes succession in events.

To be more significant, however, a sample needs to be suprasentential, since its tempo can be better appreciated in relation to other portions of text. Its typographical status may, from the outset, be relevant. As a set of visual signals to the reader, a print format can exercise reactions before the level of content is broached. Thus, punctuation of Shandean dashes or Richardsonian exclamation marks prepares the ground for disconnected or irregular tempi. An obvious preference for hypotactic, paratactic, or verbless sentence formations, together with observation of their overall distribution, can again signal trends.

The paragraph, with its unifying character, and capacity to promote regular eye rhythms by its appearance at roughly similar intervals, is a prime graphological feature. On a purely perceptual level, any wide fluctuations or flurries of single sentence-paragraphs attract the reader's immediate attention. Laconic paragraph and sentence sequences, in D. H. Lawrence's *Studies in Classic American Literature* (1924), for example, provide a remarkably unconventional tour de force.

A dozen lines, comprising five brief paragraphs, two of only two words each, envelop sixteen whole years of Frédéric's life in Flaubert's *L'Education sentimentale* (3.6i; [1869] 1989, 455). Contrasts of pace, influenced by paragraph length, animate the shortest chapter (ch. 27) of Meredith's *The Ordeal of Richard Feverel* ([1859] 1984, 252–56). This opens with half-page paragraphs of abstract speculation, before focusing on a score of single-line exchanges between the lovers, so that achrony counters isochrony.

Typical of the thriller genre is the resort to brief paragraphs, and abrupt shifts of pace:

> Springer wound down his window, Sam leant in and shot him dead.
> Springer's car had been parked in the corner of the car-park, it was four whole days before anyone even noticed something was wrong. (Elton 1992, 290)

Although both sentence-paragraphs are externally focalized, and feature monosyllabic items, the first equates discourse- and story-time (DT = ST). In the second, a rapid shift via a past perfect form (recording a state prior to the event of the first sentence) toward another state four days later, marks a sharp contrast of pace between two graphologically similar units. Ongoing action is opposed to summary, and story-time greatly exceeds discourse-time (ST>DT) in the second unit.

Another text-division below chapter level, is the segment, authorially marked by superior line spacing. The graphological gap may serve to project an informational gap, requiring readers to supply their own continuity. As in Woolf's *Jacob's Room* (1922), regular segment gaps advance fictional events in the manner of vignettes or snapshots, so that overall pace depends as much on elimination of unwanted material as on presentation of that selected. In a more recent novel, chapter-segments are separated by quadruple spacing, which creates an elliptical rhythm, recording consistent shifts of subject, place, and time.

To match these regular permutations, new chapters in Susan Hill's *Air and Angels* (1991) are also discontinuous with previous chapters; events in Calcutta are marshalled into separate chapters from those in Cambridge. Gradually, the rigidity of thematic boundaries represented by different segments weakens, and by 1.5 the regular tempo is interrupted. Segments now resume the same rather than different topics, or flash briefly to Norfolk or India, underscoring breaks in the harmony of Cavendish's life. Thereafter, the initial segment norms are set in question by decreasing time gaps, associational linkages, direct thematic continuity between segments and chapters. By part two, the fragmentation of textual and emotional stability is complete.

The location of specific passages in relation to narrative units, and the nature of those units, must also be considered. An initial paragraph or section of a chapter, for example, invites comparison with the final paragraph or section of a preceding chapter. In the final section of a chapter, reader expectations of a narrative climax can be deliberately frustrated if the event is delayed until the next chapter, or blandly recorded without elaboration or comment. Thus, the penultimate line in chapter 24 of Hardy's *The Woodlanders*, brings us to the wedding-morn of Grace Melbury; a single sentence-paragraph abruptly terminates the scene: "Five hours later she was the wife of Fitzpiers" ([1887] 1975f, 195), and the new chapter, accelerating still more rapidly, moves on another two months.

The standard narrative unit of chapter may change, in longer works, to part (*War and Peace*) or book (*Les Misérables*), affecting overall and individual tempi. A diary or journal format may shift pace swiftly, reflecting the momentary whims of its writer, while the pulse and extent of epistolary fiction depends, in addition, on the nature of its recipients. Where a single correspondent can unify the diary or journal format, the novel-in-letters usually involves multiple correspondents and sequential discontinuity, with new perspectives bringing new tempi. With genuine letters, such as those printed in Boswell's *Life of Johnson*, furthermore, real duration enters into the debate. We as readers take as long to peruse them as the original recipients, and this pace differs from the recorded time of invented correspondence (Alkon 1973, 250).

Since reading-speeds can vary so markedly among different readers, less subjective criteria for establishing tempo must be sought. In terms of discourse elements, such recurring features in fixed positions as the initial essays in *Tom Jones*, imply a whole-unit pace and clear deceleration, by comparison with the rest of the novel. More typical of fiction in general is the interplay of description, comment, report and speech, and such a taxonomic approach can be fruitful (Bonheim 1982, 41–46).[32]

A scene from Voltaire's *Candide*, the auto da fé after the Lisbon earthquake, may illustrate the linkage of discourse elements and tempo markings:

(1) Pangloss and Candide were led off separately and closeted in exceedingly cool rooms, where they suffered no inconvenience from the sun, (2) and were brought out a week later to be dressed in sacrificial cassocks and paper mitres. (3) The decorations on Candide's mitre and cassock were penitential in character, inverted flames and devils without tails or claws; but Pangloss's devils had tails and claws, and his flames were upright. (4) They were then marched in procession, clothed in these robes, (5) to hear a moving sermon (6) followed by beautiful music in counterpoint. Candide was flogged in time with the anthem; (7) the Basque and the two men who refused to eat bacon were burnt; and Pangloss was hanged, though that was not the usual

practice on these occasions. (8) The same day another earthquake occurred and caused tremendous havoc. (Voltaire [1759] 1964, 36–37)

Apart from description in (3), the entire passage uses noniconic
report, so that story-time exceeds discourse–time (ST>DT). In the
absence of direct speech as a quasi-constant, the pace ranges from
medium (1), very fast (2), stopped (3), medium (4), slow (5–6), to
fast (7–8). Wide oscillations between (2), covering a whole week,
and (3–8), a single day, between calamities personal (6–7) and
general (8), convey sharp contrasts of content and speed. In addition to the ironically protracted account of apparel (3), the function
of tempo itself is given musical point in (6). An air of satirical improbability, and a strong narratorial perspective, furthermore, reduce reader expectations of any balanced treatment of events.

With dialogue, as near-isochronous discourse, the proportion of
a narrative unit that it occupies, and its distribution in the work
overall needs to be analyzed. The presence in *Emma* (1816) of the
voluble Miss Bates, helps to make it the most dialogue-rich of any
novel by Austen, with even its opening chapter dominated by direct
speech. No single chapter of Cooper's *The Prairie* (1827), for example, lacks dialogue, which, as in *Emma*, accounts for half its total
pages, reinforced by the garrulous Obed Batt. In writers as various
as Ivy Compton-Burnett and Roddy Doyle, a high proportion of dialogue, by comparison with other modes, sponsors certain effects. It
allows characters to reveal themselves through their own mouths,
take charge of narrative, accentuate the dramatic impact of the
present, and enables readers to approximate the tempo of text and
clock time.

The positioning of dialogue within the chapter, and its capacity
to emphasize continuity or discontinuity, is also significant. At the
start of Mann's *Buddenbrooks* (1.1i; [1902]), for instance, dialogue
plunges the reader immediately in medias res. At chapter end, by
contrast, an abrupt truncation of final words may not coincide with
the termination of events, but be succeeded at new chapter start by
complete change of tempo, place and subject. Akin to the sudden
emergence and disappearance of radio signals, or a direct cut from
one film sequence to the next, speech and its varied tempi can exploit a range of effects. Thoughts, letters and diaries can, of course,
be severed at chapter end, or minimal speech-tags used to create
brief distancing, but direct speech carries greater force.

In Hardy's *The Return of the Native,* three of the six books end
with direct speech. 1.11f thrusts the reader forward to Clym's arrival in Egdon from France, in the next book:

"Where has he been living all these years?"
"In that rookery of pomp and vanity, Paris, I believe."

([1878] 1975d, 124)

Jem Wilson's reiterated question "Where is she?" at chapter end, after the trial in *Mary Barton*, sustains the reader's interest in the fate of the heroine (Gaskell [1848] 1983, 400). Little Time's words: "I should like the flowers very much if I didn't keep on thinking they'd all be withered in a few days" (Hardy [1896] 1975b, 309), end *Jude the Obscure* 5.5 on a note of gloomy foreboding. In Gaskell's *North and South*, four successive chapters (chs. 41–44) close with direct speech from four different characters delivered at varied pace, but none of these new chapter starts features dialogue.

The case is common. Both in James's *Portrait of a Lady* (1881) and Fontane's *Effi Briest* (1894), nearly half the chapters end, but no single one begins with dialogue. In *The Ambassadors* (1903), there are merely three (out of thirty-six), though two are foregrounded at the opening of new books (4.1, 9.1). In *War and Peace* (1869), the ratio of dialogue-end to dialogue-start exceeds 4:1, typifying the relationship in most fiction. *Anna Karenina* (1877) shows unusual flexibility of tempo, by introducing several cases in which dialogue unifies chapter end and new chapter start, emphasizing that fictional characters are in control on both sides of the textual divide. Such chapters may be joined by *immediate ties* (§1.5), with minimal temporal separation, or combine with other chapters to form *immediate continuity spans* (§1.5), as in the scene between Dolly and Anna in the country (6.17→20). Readers then experience tautness, a fluency and momentum seemingly achieved without narratorial intervention.

Supratextual comparisons in analysing pace are recommended by Michael Toolan, who cites certain kinds of duration linked with certain kinds of "culturally-salient narrative incident": scenes from early childhood, love and death (1988, 61). We might add the representation of weddings: leisurely detailed in *Madame Bovary*, consigned to chapter gap or extranovelistic future in *North and South*, famously disrupted, then briefly noted in *Jane Eyre*. Not only topoi or schemata, but also similar periods of time may be compared, intra- and intertextually, to suggest elasticity in the handling of duration. Three chapters, for instance, are devoted to Sir Kenneth's activities during a single night, in Scott's *The Talisman* (chs. 12–14). King Richard's, that same night (ch. 15), rate only a page ([1825] 1920, 163). The contrast is blatant since the *parallel phases* (§1.5) are adjacent, and the knight's dereliction of duty appears all the sharper.

Alternative realizations of isotopic material in the same medium offer particular contrasts of tempi, as versions of the Synoptic Gospels demonstrate. Realizations in different media, such as film and operatic adaptations of Shakespeare, can produce even more radical changes. Later reworkings by the same hand can involve large-scale sequential rearrangement. Scott Fitzgerald's revision of *Tender Is the Night* (1934; 1951), and Dickens's reading versions of his own novels result in dramatically heightened tempi. Gottfried Keller's second version of *Der grüne Heinrich* (1855; 1880) involves a virtual doubling of chapters, new narrative gaps and continuities, resulting in livelier tempi.

Certain works, too, carry invisible but critically agreed indications of pace. Flaubert's *Salammbô* (1862) and Eliot's *Adam Bede* (1859), for example, might be marked as *lento*. Deviations within such novels, therefore, are especially striking. In Eliot's leisurely "pastoral," the norms of relatively long paragraphs and chapters are rudely interrupted at chapter 47 ("The Last Moment"). Shortest by far, visually shrunk to a single page of nine paragraphs, the chapter conveys at its close, an unexpected outcome for the heroine:

> But it was not a shout of execration—not a yell of exultant cruelty.
> It was a shout of sudden excitement at the appearance of a horseman cleaving the crowd at full gallop. The horse is hot and distressed, but answers to the desperate spurring; the rider looks as if his eyes were glazed by madness, and he saw nothing but what was unseen by others. See, he has something in his hand—he is holding it up as if it were a signal.
> The Sheriff knows him: it is Arthur Donnithorne, carrying in his hand the hard-won release from death. (Eliot 1981, 507)

In this largely iconic extract (DT = ST), dominated by a narratorial perspective which shifts from negative to positive, interpretation yields to actualization. Graphic present tense and direct second-person apostrophe to the reader, reach a climax in a transfer of focalization to the character who identifies Hetty's "rescuer."

Far more common than temporary exceptions to broad markings, are local shifts from ambient speeds, often to signal new material. The opening four chapters of Turgenev's *Virgin Soil* embrace a single day, as *immediate ties* between chapters underline. In the final sentence of chapter 4, however, a sudden acceleration of pace indicates the end of this first narrative phase, set in St. Petersburg: "During the space of an hour Nejdanov listened to the wise, courteous, patronising speeches of his host, received a hundred roubles, and ten days later was leaning back in the plush seat of a reserved, first-class compartment . . . being borne along to Moscow" (Turgenev [1877] 1969, 31). Shifting within a single sentence, from the summary of an hour's conversation, to an ellipsis of ten days, followed by the singulative focus on a specific day, the extract functions to remove the hero as rapidly as possible from one location to another. As narratorial report, it is noniconic, with story-time variably exceeding discourse-time (ST>DT). It provides a sharp contrast with the time coverage hitherto, and invites comparison with the treatment of other determinate periods in the novel overall.

Theodor Fontane's journalistic skills inform a deft transition in *Effi Briest*, from an account of the heroine's sleigh-ride with her admirer (ch. 19), to a new chapter, whose opening sentence telescopes a reference to Effi's arrival and her husband's reactions the following day (20i). In the same syntactic unit, therefore, an iconic report by the narrator (ST=DT) couched in implicit and explicit past perfect forms, is combined with summary (ST>DT), and a shift to internal focalizer. An effect of speed results here from *not* following the usual custom of terminating the events of one day at chapter end, but instead continuing them into the next chapter, by means of an *immediate tie* and radical contraction of the nocturnal gap: "Innstetten, der Effi, als er sie aus dem Schlitten hob, scharf beobachtet, aber doch ein Sprechen über die sonderbare Fahrt zu zweien vermieden hatte, war am anderen Morgen früh auf und suchte seiner Verstimmung, die noch nachwirkte, so gut es ging Herr zu werden."[33] (Fontane [1894] 1963a, 162).

Contraction in time, together with a drastic reduction in scale, produces the micronarrative known as *mise en abyme*, of which the dumb show in *Hamlet* provides a classic model.[34] The device, with its powers of high-speed analeptic review or proleptic vision, incorporates, like Bakhtin's chronotope, "congealed time" (Morson and Emerson 1990, 374). At the outset of *Persuasion* (1818), the Elliot family's entry in the Baronetage serves as a vivid time capsule, which summarizes past events and telegraphs future concerns.

By contrast with this change from rapid review to regular pace, the reverse obtains, where narratives are affected by alternations of frequency.[35] A sudden shift of tempo, for instance, at the end of chapter 68 in Eliot's *Romola*, may be attributed to the movement from singulative to iterative mode. From a relatively slow and intensive focus on Romola's awakening in a boat and aiding the plague-stricken families, the final three paragraphs recount how the heroine, over many months, attains legendary status (Eliot [1863] 1980, 649).

If readers feel dissatisfaction at being denied further details of these latter events, the reason may be entirely pragmatic: the need in *Romola*, to accelerate narrative pace in response to the commercial demands of serialization. Elsewhere, grounds of probability dictate that a single book (bk. 4) in *Adam Bede* covers seven months, simply to suggest the passage of Hetty's pregnancy, while another of the same length (bk. 2) accounts for a mere two days. Similar demands for acceleration are imposed on *Effi Briest*, where the first twenty-four chapters extend over two years, but chapter 25 then consumes a further four years, so as to present Instetten with his dilemma of a time limit for revenge on Crampas.

With serialization, extratextual factors of historical and cultural production come into play. Victorian readers, whose first encounter with a novel often took place through periodical installments, are affected by this mode. It generates broken reading rhythms, encourages forced climaxes and speeding-up of tempi, in order to maintain curiosity across serial-gaps. The popularity of multinarratives such as Wilkie Collins's *The Woman in White* (1860), promotes in contemporary readers an awareness of variable speeds, through accounts by different witnesses. A reader today contrasts Collins's leisurely overall pace with the more dynamic tempi of twentieth-century detective fiction.

Particular genres are often associated with particular motifs and features. In poetry, elegy and Pindaric ode project opposite notions of pace; in prose fiction, the Gothic novel suggests urgent propulsion, and the arousal of emotion in readers. In Horace Walpole's prototype, the forward tempo of events is conveyed by a virtually seamless continuation across chapter boundaries, especially notable in a short narrative with so few divisions:

> . . . a brazen trumpet . . . was suddenly sounded. At the same instant the sable plumes on the enchanted helmet, which still remained at the other end of the court, were tempestuously agitated, and nodded thrice, as if bowed by some invisible wearer.
> ### Chapter 3
> Manfred's heart misgave him when he beheld the plumage on the miraculous casque shaken in concert with the sounding of the brazen trumpet. (Walpole [1764] 1978, 92–93)

Here, isotopic material at either side of the unit divide, foregrounds a shift of perspective from narrator to Manfred, as an *immediate tie* fuses report with character reaction in a preserialization manner. Though subtle lexical modifications are apparent, the passage remains iconic (ST = DT), with textual time enacting fictional reality.

In handling tempo, Günther Müller's approach, of page/time correlation, has the virtues of clarity and precision. As he himself points out, however, to note that an evening covers a given number of pages in a given chapter has little value per se, but the observation that a whole winter elapses in the next chapter, raises issues of detailed versus cursory treatment, dense versus loose linkages (Müller 1950, 20). His analysis of Conrad Ferdinand Meyer's *Jürg Jenatsch* (1876), whose events span nearly as many years, but at one-quarter the length of bildungsromane by Keller and Stifter, shows how the bulk of its pages focuses on a mere two weeks. These are drawn from the beginning and end of the eighteen-year period, and Meyer has simplified and reorganized actual historical happenings to fit this grouping (Müller 1950, 12–14).

Such studies encourage the emergence of broad narrative types. They range from "front-loaded" examples, whose opening sections extensively mine the first day's events, then gradually telescope subsequent periods (Werfel's *The Song of Bernadette*, Mann's *The Magic Mountain*); a type that alternates between concentrated and loose treatment, focus and flux (Goethe's *Wilhelm Meister*, Hemingway's *For Whom the Bell Tolls*); to another type, containing little action at the start (Bennett's *The Old Wives' Tale*, Jacobsen's *Niels Lyhne*). By intertextual comparison of temporal ratios, moreover, works otherwise dissimilar can appear in surprising company.

Eliot's *Silas Marner* thus shares nearly four decades with Hesse's *Magister Ludi*, but at one-quarter its length; Greene's *The Power and the Glory* and Balzac's *Père Goriot* alike in time cover, focus and bulk; similar tripartite proportions in the near-contemporary but thematically unrelated *Dorian Gray* of Wilde, and Fontane's *Stine* (Müller 1953, 117–18). Müller's temporal profiles justify the wealth of his statistical groundwork, though his approach is unsuited to Modernist novels of inner experience (Jauss 1955, 16). In lesser hands, too, as Bal (1985, 69) recognizes, the danger becomes one of sterile line counting, when relevance to other matters, such as interpretation, analysis of how the reader's attention is patterned, and the use of data to make comparisons, are all neglected.[36]

For some critics, tempi can express deepseated attitudes. In *Great Expectations*, "shockingly abrupt accelerations" project a nonnaturalistic absurd world; in *Wuthering Heights*, the "pace of assault" represents the eruption of a nonhuman Otherworld of excess (Van Ghent 1953, 173–75). To one of the most creative of film directors, the account of Smithfield market in *Oliver Twist* (ch. 21), offers swift transitions between visual and aural, detail and panorama, as well as marked tempo changes from evocations of a slow dawn to bustling commercial activity (Eisenstein 1951, 214–16).

Deceleration of pace, by contrast, is vital to convey any sense of Fanny's desperate five-hour crawl along the Casterbridge highway in *Far from the Madding Crowd* (Gregor 1980, 101), or of Verloc's death in *The Secret Agent*, where Conrad resorts to a hypnotic, filmic slow-motion, shifts of perspective and motivic repetition (Stallman 1970, 124). In Richardson's *Clarissa*, the pace of life is retarded by the novel's sheer bulk, the time it takes to read it, the constant epistolary shifts involving the multiple viewing of events, in the repetition of which time ceases almost wholly to progress (Grabo 1928, 218–19).

In the set, events: fictional time: textual extent, critics divide according to the relative weight they place on each element. The Müller camp take a macronarrative view in their concern for the last two. Other critics are swayed by the quality and number of events, or moves (Pavel 1985, 65), the element of frequency being especially relevant in thriller fiction and comedy. Another major factor in the discussion of tempo, however, has to do with the notion of continuity, detailed in §1.5. An important point is raised by Toolan, when he argues for a view of pace, as "the rapidity of the telling of what does get told" (1988, 57).

Thus, he downplays the role of ellipsis as a spatiotemporal gap, seeming to discount the value of textual blanks and omissions, which, as "intervals of silence" promote rhythmical interplay (Walker 1984, 231), create dynamism, force readers to establish their own connections, mark off schemata and perspectives (Iser 1971, 285; 1978, 183). Such breaks, however, either within or between units, have been purposely inserted by authors. The fact that events flow uninterruptedly from one chapter to the next, or that intervals of two hours, two days, two months occur, or that earlier, parallel, simultaneous phases are presented in the new chapter, must inevitably affect tempo and continuity, as well as the notion of sequential dynamics itself.

The role of tempo in both fiction and music furthers the relevance of music as a paradigm. It is Mann's narrator in *Der Zauberberg [The Magic Mountain]*, who notes that both are manifest only as a succession in time, and, as such, lack the full-bodied presence of the plastic arts: "ebenfalls (und anders als das auf einmal leuchtend gegenwärtige und nur als Körper an die Zeit gebundene Werk der bildenden Kunst) nur als ein Nacheinander, nicht anders denn als ein Ablaufendes sich zu geben weiss, und selbst wenn sie versuchen sollte, in jedem Augenblick ganz zu sein, der Zeit zu ihrer Erscheinung bedarf"[37] (Mann [1924] 1974b, 748). Hillis Miller, too, speaks of the structure of a novel as a musical design, and any given passage as a moment in an ongoing movement, which draws meaning "from its multiple temporal relations to what precedes and follows" (1968, 6).

One objection to applying exclusively the concept of spatial form to fiction, indeed, is the sense, as in music, that meaning is created, and new centers are constituted, by virtue of the very incompleteness of the pattern. Even the term "structure" itself seems misleading with respect to fiction, and traditional analogies with architecture appear mistaken. Like music, the novel "is conceived in time. Its essence is rhythm. The thing is not perceived as a whole in one view. It moves sequentially, from moment to moment" (Grabo 1928, 227). To view reading as an experience that happens in time, and involves a processing of texts, also sponsors claims of the mimetic force of sequencing itself (Leech and Short 1981, 236).

According to Milan Kundera, contrasts in tempi represent some of his earliest novelistic ideas. He equates chapters with musical measures, parts with movements, and analyzes his own *Life Is Elsewhere* (1973), in terms of relations between the length of each part, its constituent chapters and pages, and the duration of narrated events (1988, 87–89). If Kundera is unusual, by musical training and sensitivity, in his high evaluation and open celebration of tempo, Barthes too acknowledges its value, when, in S/Z, he compares the space of the literary text to a musical score.

In a diagram, or polyphonic table, he presents a visual display of how his five semiotic codes organize the text (1970, 36). The student of tempo, we propose, might process fictional texts as the member of a chamber ensemble might scan a musical score: responsive at every level to all the varied nuances of rhythmic, melodic and harmonic effects from the other performers of the work. Offering a paradigm for fiction, music also supplies an appropriate coda to the topic of tempo, at the same time as tempo preludes the topic of continuity.

CONTINUITY RELATIONS AND CATEGORIES OF TRANSITION

> When a man is telling a story in the strange way I do mine, he
> is obliged continually to be going backwards and forwards to

keep all tight together in the reader's fancy—which, for my own
part, if I did not take heed to do more than at first, there is so
much unfixed and equivocal matter starting up, with so many
breaks and gaps in it.
—Lawrence Sterne, *Tristram Shandy*

Continuity as Narrative Principle

In fiction, as in life, a set of events is rarely perceived and convincingly rendered as a symmetrical unit, neatly occupying a delimited frame. Its germination can usually be traced before, and its
consequences felt after the fixed confines of a chapter, or day.
Some picaresque novels, in which a specific episode exactly fits its
containing chapter, suggest exceptions to the rule, but may still
omit material felt necessary by the reader for a larger understanding.

To define continuity as "connectedness; unbroken succession;
logical sequence . . . uninterrupted duration" (*OED* 1993), as
"union without a break or interval" (*Cassell* 1989), means that absolute observance throughout fictional texts is scarcely feasible.[38]
Artistic experiments elsewhere: Andy Warhol's eight-hour film *Em-
pire* (1964), with its enormous single "take," or John Cage's composition 4' 33" (1952), opening its brief span to all ambient sounds,
supply extremes of continuity, whereby real time matches on-
screen time, or replaces the time of scored musical events.

The notion of continuity has often seemed a sine qua non of narrative, a condition affording readers a maximum sense of a text's
cohesion. It is the "one quality we expect of all writing" (Lodge
1979, 231), for which the human need is so strong, "that a man
will find some principle of order in any random sequence" (Miller
1978, 375). According to action theory, a compound event, made
up of several events linearly ordered but perceived or conceived at
a certain level of description as one event, is called continuous, if
the final stages of component events are identical with the initial
states of the following component events (van Dijk 1977, 169–70).

To illustrate: the event of "crashing" compounds the ideas of
"moving" and "breaking" and is continuous, whereas the event of
"thunder" may be discontinuous, as a result of temporal gaps between its component events. In terms of Roman Jakobson's view
of metaphor and metonymy as the essentially binary operations of
language, the former is linked to the paradigmatic axis of selection,
the latter to the syntagmatic axis of combination (Jakobson 1971).
Continuity, therefore, relates to the second of the two poles. Met-
onymic writing, best exemplified by realistic fiction, displays "a very

obvious and readily intelligible kind of continuity based on spatio-temporal contiguities" (Lodge 1979, 231).

Readers who expect continuity, also expect, paradoxically, that the text will "resist and surprise . . . create difficulties and delays in discovering the coherence, in recognizing the frames relevant to it" (Perry 1979, 50 n). Applying perception theory to the arts in general, results in the equation of frustrated expectancy with discontinuity. Relations among different arts, which may set up quite different expectancies in the perceiver, can bear fruit when their separate discontinuities are compared. By contrast with most human activity, which is normally rewarded for following rules and offering a continuity of experience, the artist may be concerned with the very opposite. Hence, the perceiver's role is to be aware of "the disparity between expected and experienced configuration" (Peckham 1967, 220). Various subcategories of discontinuity (implicit, internal, modal, external) can be applied, to demonstrate the adaptational and disorientative function of art within different media and historical periods (314).

Diachronically, continuity as a Western convention in the represented world of fiction, has been generally observed up to the late nineteenth century.[39] The dislodgment of the principle of transition by newer practices of juxtaposition and simultanism (Shattuck 1959, 256–70), of "dialectical montage" (Spiegel 1976, 173), fragmentation (Josipovici 1977, 124–39) and "radical parataxis" (Hayman 1987, 151), has, since then, wrought inevitable changes. In Postmodernist fiction, especially, discontinuity has taken on a physical dimension: brief chapters or paragraphs become independent units surrounded by blank space, shaped or schizoid texts may be reinforced by alternative orders of reading (McHale 1987, 181–93). Even narrative discontinuity, however, is entirely a question of degree. The reminder, from a Postmodernist practitioner and critic, is salutary: "Only the simplest fairy-tale or the most elementary narrative forms are wholly continuous, and the novel has been playing with time and space shifts and discontinuous moments for a long time" (Brooke-Rose 1983, 357).

The use of natural language, rather than, for instance, a movie camera, means that the notion of continuity in fiction has at best only conventional force. Even where dialogue serves as a quasi-isochronic element, its treatment differs from film or stage practice. Thus, a general narratorial aim is to convey to the reader a sense that, although new events may have intervened, no vital stretches of time have gone unmentioned. Since few writers (or directors) aspire to rival the completeness (to put it no higher) of Warhol's visual coverage, they necessarily make selections and adjustments in what they present. The implied diegetic events, at the level of the signified, appear to be continuous, though, at the level of the signifier, they may be evoked intermittently, in dislocated or in fragmentary guise.

It is at junctures where narrative units begin and end, that issues of continuity, like those of division, are most sharply focused. At such hinge-points, a narrator may explicitly draw attention to the status of events in adjacent chapters, or invite inferences from the reader. Developments and shifts of all kinds can obviously be introduced into the central portions of chapters, which may comprise crucial subunits, graphologically distinct one from another, and establishing a variety of relations. The larger divisions, at chapter end and chapter start, will, however, receive priority here, by an analysis of different categories of transition, marking the passage between narrative units.

Three broad types of sequential combination have been classified by Tzvetan Todorov (1981, 52–53) as *embedding* (one story enclosed inside another), *linking* (juxtaposition of different actions), and *alternation* (moving back and forth between stories). The present concern is with the closer detail of such combinations, of relations between events registered in the final segment of one chapter, and in the initial segment of the following chapter. That relationship may appear in quite another light, when adjacent chapters as a whole, and different segments of those chapters are considered.

For convenience of analysis, each chapter can be decomposed into three broad segments: *initial (i)*, *medial (m)*, and *final (f)*, necessarily approximate and flexible. Initial and final segments frequently correspond to opening and closing paragraph(s), but the normative transition between chapters comprises the contiguous relationship of $f \rightarrow i$. In some texts, chapter-segments must be further subdivided, into first *(i1, f1)*, and second *(i2, f2)* instances, so as to track continuity with greater precision.

For the novel as a genre, one of the most common temporal gaps between chapters is one embracing from several minutes up to several hours: *proximate continuous phase* or *proximate tie*. The briefest gap is represented by *immediate continuous phase* or *immediate tie*. An interval of up to twenty-four hours comprises a *(continuous phase with) nocturnal gap*. All three types of forward narrative movement may combine with others, to create the juxtaposed phases of a *continuity span*. Chapters linked by gaps exceeding a single night, move into areas of ever more distant, problematic continuity.

Determining the status of narrative sequences are temporal indices in the text. These may be presented early in the chapter, deliberately delayed, or suppressed. Each option affects the reader's capacity to identify the type of sequence, as, too, does their relative specificity.[40] Their position, especially, allows the formation of further subcategories of sequence. Essential also to confirm temporal succession, is the issue as to which sequences should be regarded as dominant, which subordinate. To isolate a central line, involves decisions about the status of particular characters and elements of plot, according to estimates of their overall significance, in addition to the amount of textual space they assume (Sternberg 1974, 45). The content of one chapter, for example, may be surveyed in relation to that of another, belonging to the temporally most advanced stage of action, measured from the narrative-Now (Chatman 1978, 63) or narrative instance (Brooke-Rose 1983, 328).

Fielding's strategy in *Tom Jones*, of interweaving the Tom and Sophia lines of action, is echoed on a smaller scale in Fowles's *FLW*. Sarah Woodruff features in far fewer chapters than Charles Smithson, and their narrative lines, even in the same chapter, are often kept separate. While she takes a single chapter (ch. 36; [1969] 1970, 217) to establish herself at Exeter, the nine subsequent chapters are given over to Charles's trip to London. In terms of chapter 36, the most advanced stage of action, chapters 37–45 as a unit are retrograde or *analeptic* (Genette 1972, 90–105). They bring Charles's line up to date, though to one another they relate by various types of continuous phase.

A later sequence (chs. 50–51), treating Charles's broken engagement to Ernestina, is internally continuous between the final segment of one chapter and the initial segment of the next (50f→51i). It is nonetheless analeptic with respect to the most advanced stage of action, represented at 49f by the secondary characters, Sam and Mary. Though the initial segment of chapter 10 narratorially amplifies a reference to Ware Commons at the close of chapter 9, the bulk of this chapter, however, evoking Charles's encounter with Sarah, involves analepsis: in its medial segment, it resumes material from the final segment of the last-but-one chapter (10m→8f). Such instances raise questions, about whether phases of linear movement should be defined in terms of chapter-segments rather than whole chapters; whether early sequences must be deemed normative, and the most advanced stage necessarily privileged; whether there can be sequences of equal overall importance and weight.

Though time is fundamental to a discussion of continuity, other factors too are highly relevant.[41] Apart from technical issues (cohesive ties, syntax, grammar), continuity in terms of theme and location, character and perspective is salient, since, on many occasions, these factors relegate temporality to the background. The reader of Tolstoy's *Anna Karenina*, for example, witnesses the reunion of heroine and husband at Petersburg (1.30f), only to encounter, across the chapter gap (1.31i), a switch of focalization, to Vronsky ([1877] 1973a, 119). An initial reversion to his own sleepless night, is followed by his reflections on that reunion, so that time and location prove continuous, and, thematically, Anna's relationship with Vronsky is to survive the textual division.

Eliot's *Adam Bede*, chapter 6, affords clear continuity of location, but delayed evidence of temporal and character continuity. The Rev. Irwine and Arthur Donnithorne ride over to Hall Farm, narratorially reported, at 5f, to be just visible in the distance ([1859] 1981, 114). Entitled "The Hall Farm," the next chapter generously surveys the house's architecture, history and domestic activities, before permitting the two riders to reenter the narrative near chapter end. In Alessandro Manzoni's *The Betrothed [I Promessi sposi]*, by contrast, a sequence of half-a-dozen chapters maintains temporal and character continuity, as it follows Renzo's escape from the police in Milan, to the inn at Gorgonzola. Locational continuity, however, is broken again at 17i ([1827] 1972, 316), as Renzo heads off at dusk for Venetian territory. The limit of the continuous phase itself is resolved by the appearance of analepsis at 18i.

Continuity and Focalization

As the above examples illustrate, the angle from which a narrative is presented may shift from one character to another (Tolstoy), be controlled by an authorial narrator (Eliot), or be fixed on the same figure (Manzoni), and a range of other options is available.[42] For reasons of technical precision, the term "point of view" has, since Genette, been largely replaced by *perspective* or *focalization*. This latter has been defined as the "triadic relation formed by the *narrating agent* (who narrates), the *focalizer* (who sees), and the *focalized* (what is being seen and, thus, narrated)." The relationship itself is based on "contiguity (the degree of proximity of narrator to focalizer to focalized), which, in turn, establishes relations of similarity (closeness or consonance) or opposition (distance or dissonance)" (Cohan and Shires 1988, 95) between those elements, at different points in a narration.

Mieke Bal (1985, 104–5; 109–10; 122) distinguishes between

the relatively biased and limited vision presented by a character in the *fabula:* character-bound focalization (CF), and that by an anonymous agent situated outside the *fabula:* external focalization (EF). The focalized may be a character, objects, landscapes or events; it can be "perceptible" or "nonperceptible," and the words of characters may be spoken (audible and perceptible to other characters) or unspoken (thoughts, internal monologues not perceptible to others). A narrator who does not figure in the *fabula,* and never refers explicitly to itself as a character, is described as external (EN), whereas the "I" identified with a character in the *fabula* which it itself narrates, is character-bound (CN).

In a diagrammatic summary of the poetics of point of view, encompassing the status of the narrative voice, modes of contact and narrative stance, Susan Lanser situates focalization within the psychological aspect of stance (1981, 224; Fig. 21). Supplementing Genette's distinction between fixed, variable and multiple types of focalization (1972, 206–7), Shlomith Rimmon-Kenan (1983, 77–82) broadens the debate to include perceptual (spatial and temporal), psychological (cognitive and emotive) and ideological facets, which may concur, but may also belong to different focalizers.

Citing the example of film, where footage is photographed from various angles, and then edited into a temporally linear series of shots, Cohan and Shires convincingly demonstrate, by dissecting a chapter of *Pride and Prejudice*, how a continuous discourse is produced from segments projecting plural points of view, in rapid shifts between narrator, focalizer and focalized. The analysis suggests the value of considering narrative as a "syntagmatic organization of focalizing segments placed in contiguous relation to each other" (1988, 103). Elsewhere, the same critics associate focalization with sequentiality, by noting how, even if only indirectly, temporal order, frequency and duration display a narrating agency. Pause, slow-down and summary, in particular, stress narration over story, whereas ellipsis and scene do the opposite, though not effacing all signs of narrational mediation (89).

At the hinge-points of chapter end and chapter start, issues of focalization as well as continuity are most prominently accentuated. The reader's expectation of new material at the opening of a new narrative unit may also include a fresh narrator or focalizer. From external focalization of events in one chapter, for example, the narrative may shift to character-bound focalization in the next, as a detached account gives way to subjective memories, the most advanced stage of action to an analeptic phase, either internal or external to the starting point. There is no requirement, however, beyond that moment of transition, for the focalizing segments to be consistent or extensive, and the bulk of each chapter may be dominated by different relationships of sequence and focalization.

The choice of focalizer clearly has implications for narrative temporality. Whereas external focalization, for instance, can range over different time periods if the focalizer is unpersonified, it is limited to retrospection if tied to a character (Toolan 1988, 72), and an internal focalizer is restricted still further to the "present" of the characters (Uspensky 1973, 67; 113). Direct speech, close to the beginning of a spectrum running from mimetic to diegetic (narratorial) discourse (Lanser, 1981, 187; Fig. 11), may be associated with the self-expression of specific characters in the *fabula*. By placing this character-bound utterance, unmodified and unmediated by any narrator, at either limit of a chapter, its impact on the narrative transition is all the sharper, and challenges narratorial by mimetic authority. In terms of the overall narrative economy, the frequency, positioning and proportion of direct speech, as opposed to other forms of discourse, can affect both focalization and temporal continuity.

If focalization or point of view, "conditions and codetermines the reader's response to the text" (Lanser 16), the type of time shifts familiar in fiction from Conrad onwards, and which manipulate the temporal progression of events, provide "contrasting viewpoints" (Lothe 1989, 205) of equal importance, so that new focalizing segments frequently correspond to new sequential phases. The handling of narrative tempo has also been taken to offer an index of a narrator's psychological and ideological stance, by suggesting "what he or she finds important enough to present in depth" (Lanser 201). Citing panoramic or simultaneous views by an external narrator-focalizer as illustrations of the perceptual facet of focalization, Rimmon-Kenan (1983, 77) is concerned with the spatial coordinate, but the temporal co-ordinate is no less involved, when it is represented by simultaneous phase, one of the categories of transition.[43]

By contrast with psychological and ideological facets, perceptual focalizing, whether spatial or temporal, does not evaluate, but states the facts about the when and where of what is witnessed (Toolan 1988, 74). The potential here for a mere compilation of data, with little regard for its function and operation, is evident, so that the linkages between focalization and temporality traced out above, reinforce the need to set continuity relations in their larger context. Though the role of human agency is more apparent in focalization, it is critical too in sequential dynamics, and the interdependence of narrative elements serves as a useful reminder that any tendency toward formal categories and abstractions in the analysis of continuity, is a relative rather than absolute one.

Types of Continuous Phase

IMMEDIATE TIE

As the briefest type of continuous phase in terms of its transitional gap, the *immediate tie* is also, in many ways, the most significant. The notion of immediacy itself, at best relative, will be taken to imply a reduction close to zero in the degree of temporal ellipsis between narrative units. Such minimal separation of material reinforces in the reader a sense of linear impetus; the customary pause allowed by a formal division seems inadequate to arrest the force of fictional events. A comparison with enjambement in poetry may be apposite. Despite formal allocation of material into separate lines of verse, the natural or logical flow of ideas and feelings quickly compels the reader across graphological bounds.

A contrast with breaks in drama may be instructive. Only rarely, for instance, does the action on stage at the start of a new act or scene, take up immediately the juncture reached by the action at curtain fall of the previous set or scene. The physical or metaphorical curtain thus implies an interval of proximate phase, at least. In prose fiction, the presence of *minimum retards*, such as chapter titles, summaries, spatial blanks, or prefatory epigraphs, means, however, that even chapters of immediate continuity cannot, in practice, be linked more tightly together than these "retards" permit. With epigraphs, particularly, a tradition associated with Scott, Stendhal, and George Eliot often involves poetic format and allusive richness, thereby interrupting or diverting from the flow of events.

A possible test for immediate continuity might be to rewrite material, omitting epigraphs and chapter divisions, yet to avoid any unsteady or jerky effect. Two deft, paratactic transitions, from Meredith's *The Egoist* ([1879] 1968, 457–58), and Hardy's *Jude the Obscure* ([1896] 1975b, 396–67), are thematically similar. Both concern meetings, and both suggest the arbitrary character of formal breaks, which the fluency of events here calls into question:

[Clara] approached.   (37f)
They met; Vernon soon left them.   (38i)

Types of Continuous Phase	Abbreviated Forms	Examples
Immediate Tie	ICP	LE [7f➡8i]
Narratorial Immediate Tie	NICP	LN [7f➡8i] (ellipsis close to zero)
Proximate Tie	pCP	7f➡8i (ellipsis of several minutes to several hours)
Nocturnal Gap	nCP	7f➡8i (ellipsis of up to 24 hours including nocturnal gap)
Distant Continuity/Discontinuity		7f➡8i (ellipsis over 24 hours)
Continuity Span		7f➡8i➡8f➡9i etc.
Immediate Continuity Span		each ellipsis close to zero
Narratorial Continuity Span		linkage via narrator rather than events
Continuity via Events		LE➡LE
Continuity via Narrator		LN➡LN
Mixed Continuity		LE➡LN or LN➡LE
Delayed Continuity	d	as in pCP(d) , where confirmation of proximate gap is delayed
Internal Proleptic Phase or Tie	iPRO	7f➡8i (where 8i:7f is continuous phase)
Explicit/Implicit		
Alternate Proleptic Phase	ALPRO	7f➡9i (where 9i:7f is alternate phase)
External Proleptic Phase	ePRO	7f➡x (beyond narrative terminus)
Explicit/Implicit		
Major Parallel Phase	PAR	8i‖7i
Minor Parallel Phase	par	8i‖7m
Major Parallel Overlap	PAR+	8i‖7i 8m then exceeds limit of
Minor Parallel Overlap	par+	8i‖7m last forward phase at 7f
Progressive Simultaneous Phase	SIM (p)	8i‖7f; 8i➡8f
Nonprogressive Simultaneous Phase	SIM (n)	8i‖7f; 8i➡8m
External Analeptic Phase	eAN	}
Delayed	eAN (d)	} 8i➡y (anterior to starting-point)
Narratorial	NeAN	}
Internal Analeptic Phase	iAN	8i➡4f
Narratorial	NiAN	}
Immediate	IiAN	} 8i➡7m
Narratorial Immediate	NIiAN	}
External Analeptic Overlap	eAN+	8i➡y }
Internal Analeptic Overlap	iAN+	8i➡4f } 8m then exceeds
Narratorial	NiAN+	8i➡7m } limit of last forward
Immediate	IiAN+	8i➡7m } phase at 7f
Narratorial Immediate	NIiAN+	8i➡7m }
Alternate Phase	ALP	8i➡6f
Narratorial	NALP	8i➡6f
Immediate	IALP	8i➡6f
Narratorial Immediate	NIALP	8i➡6f
Delayed	ALP (d)	8i➡6f
Delayed Immediate	IALP (d)	8i➡6f

In the examples above, segments of chapters 7 and 8 serve as starting points for classification of categories of transition. i= initial; m= medial; f= final segments of chapters; i1, i2, etc. as subdivisions of chapter-segments. Other delayed, false, and quasiversions of the above categories can appear across a range of texts. LE= level of events or focalized object; LN= level of narrator.

Figure 1.2   Categories of Transition

> [Jude] did not reach Christminster till ten o'clock.   (6.8f)
> On the platform stood Arabella. She looked him up and down.   (6.9i)

The terse, anaphoric style of these examples, and the direct succession of narrated events that the minimal chapter-gaps dramatize, obviate any need for temporal adverbials at chapter start, of the sort employed to announce an immediate tie.[44]

Taking a single temporal index, and not the whole context, into account, may, however, mislead the reader into false attribution. Esther Summerson, in Dickens's *Bleak House* ([1853] 1996, 387), by using a past perfect form, implies an extended rather than immediate interval: "As soon as Richard and I had held the conversation, of which I have given an account, Richard communicated the state of his mind to Mr. Jarndyce." (24i). In a writer such as D. H. Lawrence, whose *Sons and Lovers* and *The Rainbow* notably lack any immediate ties, even a chapter-start event marking the reaction of one couple to the departure of another, proves not to be direct but delayed. Thus, in *Women in Love* ([1920] 1967, 496): "When Ursula and Birkin were gone, Gudrun felt herself free in her contest with Gerald. As they grew more used to each other" (30i).

Anaphora, likewise, may not guarantee immediate continuity, since its coupling with a particular verb can suggest an iterative process, stretching over a considerable period. The openings of successive chapters in the first version of Keller's *Der grüne Heinrich* make this point: "Er verschwieg dies sorgsam vor seiner Mutter" (4.5i; [1855] 1926, 19.95); "Als er solchergestalt diese Dinge betrachtete" (4.6i; 19.112)[45] By choice of verb, a narrator may leave insufficient data on which to decide the temporal status of a new chapter. In Trollope's *Orley Farm* ([1862] 1993, 76), for instance, the period of elation remains vague: "Though Mr. Dockwrath was somewhat elated by this invitation to lunch, he was also somewhat abashed by it" (8i). In Meredith's *Beauchamp's Career* ([1876] 1913, 362), the hero's response to his uncle's refusal of funds may, or may not, be immediate, depending on the reader's interpretation of the verb's connotative force:

> ... his [uncle's] head assumed a droll interrogative fixity, with an air of "What next?"   (38f)
> Beauchamp quitted the house without answering as to what next ...
>   (39i)

Ultimately, it may be argued, if the sequential status of a new chapter cannot be easily determined by the reader, it is unlikely to be crucial to the narrative's overall economy, since the narrator freely opts either for precision or imprecision. The use of immediate continuity, in any case, broaches the issue of narrative articulation, in a paradoxical movement that forges semantic links, even as it creates physical divides. Clearly, the length of particular chapters within the totality of the work is involved, while decisions about where breaks are to occur must inevitably affect the narrative's rhythms. In essence, an immediate tie foregrounds material by lending it a position of high visibility, as new text replaces the blank space between chapters, yet creates a bridge back to the last segment.

Single instances of immediate ties, as opposed to a continuity span comprising juxtaposed chapters, bring sudden focus upon significant events. The solitary example in fourteen chapters of Spark's *Symposium* (12i; 1991, 151), reinforces its effectiveness. When Margaret sticks a pin in her list of marriage candidates (11f), and Damien's name emerges (12i), the immediate tie acts as an unobtrusive yet subtle herald of a crucial encounter. A meticulous James, rarely using immediate continuity in *The Golden Bowl*, foregrounds, by this means, the pivotal quality of chapter 33 ([1904] 1983, 411). Maggie Verver's revelation there to Fanny Assingham, that Charlotte and Amerigo were formerly lovers, leads to Fanny's shattering the bowl as the Prince enters. The event occurs in what is, pointedly, the longest chapter of the novel.

In *The Ambassadors*, similarly, the key scene in which Strether is suddenly arrested by the sight of Chad and Mme. de Vionnet together on the river, comprises two chapters (11.3–4) bound by another rare immediate tie ([1903] 1986a, 460–61). On a different river, Maggie Tulliver and Stephen Guest appear no less compromised. The episode is marked both by its dramatic quality, and its position at the close of the penultimate book of Eliot's *The Mill on the Floss* ([1860] 1985, 596). In a novel featuring indeterminate chapter lapses and only three immediate ties in fifty-eight chapters, this scene accounts for one such tie (6.13–14). As with so many narrative features, their rarity, and resulting prominence is obvious only in retrospect, and the value of rereading, as a narrative strategy, is reiterated.

Lexical repetition frequently serves to confirm or underline the sequential status of chapters. Thus, a closing allusion in Dickens's *Dombey and Son* ([1848] 1982, 359), to the scene at Leamington Spa where Mr. Dombey "walked out with the Major arm-in-arm" (20f), is echoed, if in reverse order, at 21i. Direct continuity of action is thereby confirmed: "The Major . . . walked arm-in-arm with

Mr. Dombey." Another immediate tie can have punning and meta-phorical potential. Graf Botho's thoughts, in Fontane's *Irrungen Wirrungen* ([1887] 1963c, 455–56), as he burns Lene's letters: "Alles Asche. Und *doch* gebunden" (22f), are directly resumed at chapter start: "Botho sah in die Asche. Wie wenig und wie viel" (23i), and the poignancy of her loss is brought home.[46]

The early repetition of a name, so soon after its owner's appear-ance, can accentuate importance. When Mann's *Buddenbrooks* 4.5f ([1902] 1974a, 138) closes with "und Herr Kesselmeyer trat ein," immediately succeeded at 4.6i by "Herr Kesselmeyer kam als Hausfreund unangemeldet . . . blieb an der Türe stehen," the reader is half-prepared for the banker's exposé of Grünlich's fi-nances, and Tony's first marital disaster.[47] In *Anna Karenina* ([1877] 1973a, 742), lexical repetition seems to annul the spatial and temporal gaps that must inevitably exist, but which, in the con-text, are immaterial. A chapter-end summary: "[Levin] told him to drive to the doctor's" (7.13f), is succeeded by a chapter-start sug-gestion of immediate continuity, with driving-time glossed over: "The doctor was not yet up" (7.14i).

When chapter-end speech directly recurs, if minimally modified, at chapter start, the impression is that of words percolating the lis-tener's consciousness, even as the outward response is swift. In Scott's *Kenilworth* ([1821] 1993, 352), for instance, the closing whisper from an unknown voice, " 'I do desire some instant confer-ence with you,' " (3.12f), becomes revised memorially, at 3.13i, as " 'I desire some conference with you.' The words were simple in themselves, but Lord Leicester . . . turned hastily round. . . . There was nothing remarkable in the speaker's appearance."

Immediate ties often convey instant reactions to events, and may take either a mental or physical form. Thus, Frédéric Moreau's first thoughts, in Flaubert's *L'Education sentimentale* (1869):

> Ruiné, dépouillé, perdu!
> Il était resté sur le banc, comme étourdi par une commotion.[48]
>
> (1.6i; 1965, 114)

Frédéric's later, enraged response to news of his uncle's inheri-tance ("Quand il fut à sa place, dans le coupé . . . il sentit une ivresse le submerger" [2.1i; 125]),[49] has special stress, since imme-diate continuity, rather than temporal ellipsis, binds parts one and two of a novel otherwise notable for its discontinuous movement.

This kind of semantic bridge, not merely over chapter but also part divisions, affects overall narrative rhythms. It runs counter to reader expectations that sequences, even if they flow across chapter boundaries, will terminate at the larger-scale breaks. Flaubert's subversion of the principle finds echo in Hardy's *Tess of the D'Urbervilles*. By raising the possibility that the preacher in the barn at 44f is Tess's seducer, the narrator brings Phase the Fifth to a dramatic close, but allows the shock upon Tess of the rencounter with Alec d'Urberville to spill over to the next chapter, which also initiates Phase the Sixth ([1891] 1975e, 330).

Rather than reserve for a new chapter another critical meeting, between Hester Prynne and Roger Chillingworth in *The Scarlet Letter*, Hawthorne unexpectedly commences the episode in the final sentence of chapter 13 ([1850] 1982, 185). It then proceeds, via immediate continuity, into chapter 14, as if to stress a depth of emotion exceeding normal articulation, and so requiring an allotment that questions traditionally rigid compartments.

A further function of immediate continuity is to mark transitions into embedded material. With a chapter entitled "Weiterträumen," following the hero's relapse into slumber at previous chapter end, the onset of dream and change of possible world is signalled in Keller's *Der grüne Heinrich* 4.7 ([1880] 1961, 502). Within a novel, characters frequently present subworlds of their own, and the conventional chapter gap is one of immediate continuity. Turgenev, in *Fathers and Sons* ([1862] 1975, 99), also includes *proleptic phase* for the story of Pavel Petrovich: "And Arkady proceeded to relate his uncle's story. Which the reader will find in the following chapter" (6f).

In examples from *Great Expectations* (41f; [1861] 1973, 360) and *A Tale of Two Cities* (3.9f; [1859] 1975, 348), Dickens employs the *cataphoric* formula of "what follows" and "as follows," to introduce direct speech and report across chapter divisions. Only considerations of chapter length, discouraging prolixity and consequent imbalance, opt here against the use of colons and continuation within the same, rather than new chapters. Written documents of various kinds may be introduced via immediate ties, as is Werner's letter to the hero, announcing his father's death, in Goethe's *Wilhelm Meister* 5.2 ([1795] 1964, 230). Other letters, such as Helen Schlegel's to her sister Margaret in chapter 1 of Forster's *Howards End*, are immediately succeeded by recipient reactions (2i; [1910] 1967, 8). With the latest note (1f), there is an acute sense of its being perused by character and reader simultaneously, the narrator having virtually closed the gap between narrated past and narrative instance.

In Sterne's hands, little that is conventional escapes deflation; in

Yorick's, even immediate continuity becomes piquant eroticism, as he applies himself dexterously, in *A Sentimental Journey* ([1768] 1986, 75), to the Grisset's artery: "I had counted twenty pulsations, and was going on fast towards the fortieth, when her husband coming unexpected from a back parlour into the shop, put me a little out in my reckoning." (34i).

Part of the humorous legacy from Sterne is inherited by Lewis Carroll, who adopts, in *Through the Looking-Glass* ([1871] 1947, 185–86), similar graphological tactics of immediate transition to those of *Tristram Shandy* 2.15 ([1767] 1967, 135–56):

> . . . in another moment [Alice] recovered herself, feeling sure they must
> be —— (3f)
>
> TWEEDLEDUM AND TWEEDLEDEE
> (CHAPTER IV)
> They were standing under a tree . . . (4i)

The chapters of *Alice in Wonderland* (1865) are linked almost entirely by immediate ties, suggesting the uninterrupted flow of dream, with an understandable absence of nocturnal breaks, and ellipses being relegated to intrachapter gaps. Other works vary in their practice.

Immediate continuity proves effective, for instance, in the Gothic context of Walpole's *The Castle of Otranto*, in Godwin's psychological novel *Caleb Williams*, in the Romantic melodrama of Hugo's *Les Misérables,* and in detective fiction such as Collins's *The Moonstone*, where serial techniques serve, additionally, to heighten tension. In Eliot's *Daniel Deronda* and *Middlemarch*, it is virtually confined to scenes involving letters, and in another large-scale depiction of society, Thackeray's *Vanity Fair*, to revelation and reunion. In novels of the episodic bildungsroman tradition (Mörike's *Maler Nolten*, Stifter's *Nachsommer*), as well as in much of Zola and Lawrence, immediate continuity is rarely found. Neither Radcliffe's *The Mysteries of Udolpho*, with its nocturnal rhythms, nor Ludwig's *Zwischen Himmel und Erde*, with its self-contained scenes of Poetic Realism, contains a single example.

Its presence in a range of other works markedly declines after initial stages: the first book in Mann's *Buddenbrooks*, the first half of Gaskell's *North and South* and Goethe's *Wilhelm Meister*, the first volume of Eliot's *Romola*, the opening shorebound chapters of Melville's *Moby-Dick*. Thereafter, reduced appearances of immediate ties suggest the notion of a growing loss of unity and cohesion. In Stendhal's *Le Rouge et le Noir* and Bennett's *The Old Wives'*

Tale, Dickens's *Dombey and Son,* and Trollope's *Barchester Towers,* its application is selective, and directs attention only to key events. In Meredith's *Beauchamp's Career* and *Diana of the Crossways,* for instance, immediate ties are restricted to meetings between lovers actual or prospective. The interchangeable nature of chapters in Huysmans's *À Rebours [Against Nature]* and Kafka's *Der Prozess [The Trial],* by contrast, means that notions of linear movement and accelerated transition, as manifest in immediate ties, have little place, and that narrative interest lies elsewhere.

PROXIMATE TIE
NOCTURNAL GAP

Taken together, *proximate* and *nocturnal* phases represent the most common type of forward movement in fiction. The two phases occupy an area demarcated on the one hand by *immediate,* on the other hand by *distant continuity,* between the extremes of Carroll's *Alice* and Scott's *Ivanhoe,* where immediate ties overwhelmingly prevail, and Woolf's *Orlando,* where intrachapter transitions embrace centuries. It is useful to compare in the same work, the proportions of proximate, nocturnal and immediate phases, as a broad measure of continuity.[50]

Where relatively precise indices are given, distinctions between immediate and proximate phases can be easily drawn. Some chapter starts mark temporal gaps without preamble, as in chapter 6 of Lawrence's *Women in Love* ([1920] 1967, 68): "They met again in the café several hours later." Other intervals are ambiguous, as with the heroine's fainting fit at the end of chapter 2 of *Jane Eyre.* The new chapter ([1847] 1978, 51) then recalls her first moments of consciousness: "The next thing I remember is waking up with a feeling as if I had had a frightful nightmare" (3i). Since it is still dark, the interval is likely to be proximate.

In *Oliver Twist* ([1838] 1978b, 360), Nancy is taken to a rendezvous with Rose Maylie: "Here [the man] left her, and retired" (39f). Verb tense, generalization and lack of specific index at the start of the next chapter, suggest a proximate rather than immediate gap: "The girl's life had been squandered in the streets, and among the most noisome of the stews and dens of London, but there was something of the woman's original nature left in her still; and when she heard a light step" (40i).

When characters review impressions made on them by recent scenes, moreover, as does the heroine's husband, in *Anna Karenina* 4.17 ([1877] 1973a, 434), after Dolly's exhortations about forgiveness, the sequential status is again uncertain. Given the need for ample reflection, it may, once more, be allotted to proximate phase. The response of lovers, similarly, tends to be lingering and repetitive. Thus, the same proximate phase applies both to Jude's mulling all night long over Sue's confession, in Hardy's *Jude the Obscure* 4.3i ([1896] 1975b, 233), and to Heinrich's fixation with Dorothea's singing, in the first version of Keller's *Der grüne Heinrich* 4.13i ([1855] 1926, 4.271). Proximate phase also accompanies the heroine's wavering, in chapter 10, helpfully entitled "The Conflict of the Night," of Meredith's *Diana of the Crossways* ([1885] 1922, 113), between the three rival claims of husband, Redworth, and the idea of freedom.

Nocturnal phases are recognized by such formulae as "next day," "the following morning," "on the morrow."[51] In some cases, however, they may extend to the evening or night of the next day, before the notion of continuity begins to lose its hold. One danger in the overuse of nocturnal phase is a resultant monotony of rhythm, with a predictable stop/start pattern between chapters. Thus, in Radcliffe's *The Mysteries of Udolpho* (1794), over half the total chapters, and two of the three transitions between books, are composed of nocturnal gaps. These convey the heroine's regularity of repose, with longer ellipses being placed *within* chapters. Not surprisingly, Austen's *Northanger Abbey* (1818), which partly parodies *Udolpho*, reproduces a similar rhythm of chapters divided by gaps of a single night. Overall, nearly one in three of its chapters shows nocturnal phase.

A degree of invention is valuable, to confirm the sequential status of a new chapter, but without resorting to stock phrases. The passage of night hours, therefore, may be conveyed in a variety of ways, projecting narratorial attitudes.[52] By also advancing to previous chapter end a scene that commences the following morning or day, and would normally be expected to appear at chapter start, a tightening of rhythm, and a mild rebuff, at least, to reader assumptions, is registered. The transition to a new chapter is affected, so that a nocturnal phase is now replaced by one that is immediate or proximate. Appearing as early as Homer's *Odyssey*, where an epic hero, after escaping from Polyphemus, embarks at dawn, in the final segment of book 9, the device recurs in as different a work as Dostoyevsky's *The Devils* ([1872] 1977, 159). Here, the events of a crucial Sunday begin in the last chapter of a section (1.4.7), and flow uninterrupted to the end of the next.

Ambiguity often enters, when discrete actions are combined in a single initial utterance. Thus, Marcell, at the end of chapter 15 of

Fontane's *Frau Jenny Treibel*, promises his uncle to write to Corinna. Then, at new chapter start (16i; [1892] 1963b, 468): "Und Marcell schrieb wirklich, und am andern Morgen lagen zwei an Corinna adressierte Briefe auf dem Frühstückstisch"[53] The letter-writing itself, in the evening, represents a proximate gap between what precedes it, though the stress on the finished epistles, in the morning, makes the nocturnal gap a more relevant one in the context of chapter 16 as a whole.

When a given grammatical item frequently appears, as does a present verb tense in *Bleak House*, the reader needs contextual data (Inspector Bucket's meeting with Sir Leicester in the foregoing ch. 53), to ascertain that 54i is in fact separated by a nocturnal interval ([1853] 1996, 816). Stylistic concision and dexterity can enable a scene to shift effortlessly from immediate to nocturnal phase. In *Effi Briest* (20i; [1894] 1963a, 162), Fontane records, in a relative clause, the instant reaction of Effi's husband to her afternoon sleighride with Major Crampas, only to accelerate over the night hours, and to take up within the same sentence Innstetten's matutinal activities.

DISTANT CONTINUITY / DISCONTINUITY

Beyond the bounds of nocturnal phase lie intervals of several days, weeks, or longer, allowing narratives to advance with least hindrance toward new developments. Such chapter gaps may either be precisely measured or left indeterminate, overt or covert, announced on site or in retrospect. They feature in many works of fiction, even if the issue of sequential status is not easy to resolve. Considerations of theme, location and character, as well as time, need to be weighed up by readers, in deciding where to situate a text along a cline from distant continuity to discontinuity. Though the physical space separating graphic units remains identical, the semantic linkages may become so tenuous as to compel a verdict of discontinuity.

An insistence on similar factors within successive units, can mask the sharp dissimilarity of other factors. In Hardy's *The Mayor of Casterbridge* ([1886] 1975c, 52), chapter 3 resumes the initial venue of Weydon-Priors, and reintroduces Susan Henchard and her daughter from chapter 1. Only the revelation of a nineteen-year interval suggests the scale of change that has occurred. The chief events of that interval appear to be telescoped into a two-page summary at 4m (56–58). It is not for another fifteen chapters (19m; 146), however, that the reader perceives that even such slender threads of continuity are spurious. *Paralipsis,* a dramatic gap omitted by the narrator (Genette 1972, 93), has been used to withhold vital details from protagonist and reader alike. Thus, the daughter who returns with her mother to the village of the wife-sale, proves to be the sailor's, not Michael Henchard's offspring.

If Hardy's exposition here is linear but selective, entailing subsequent analepsis to complete its account, the corresponding section of another work offers a different kind of discontinuity. Even before Dickens's *Our Mutual Friend* gets underway, an opening key of mystery is intensified and the reader disorientated. A succession of chapters brings new sets of characters seemingly contrasted with each other, barely connected with the initial plot and time-frame. No concessions, moreover, are made to readers of the serialized version. At the start of the second monthly part (ch. 5), they encounter fresh characters in Silas Wegg and Noddy Boffin ([1865] 1988, 87). As expository material, the "disjunctive tactics" (Knoepflmacher 1971, 139) of these opening chapters project a polyphonic density scarcely rivalled elsewhere in Dickens, and richly diffusing narrative tension.

In the development section of another novel, a crucial event takes characters and readers by surprise. At the end of chapter 10, in Forster's *Howard's End*, Mrs. Wilcox leaves King's Cross Station with her family. Chapter 11 begins with a seemingly total topic change: "The funeral was over. The carriages had rolled away through the soft mud, and only the poor remained" ([1910] 1967, 83). Only slowly does the reader grasp that chapter end and chapter start are homodiegetic, relating to the same figure. This realization clarifies the initial ambiguity as to the temporal relations between the two chapters. The events prove to be consecutive, but the intentional fracture of continuity and the playfully clipped opening in the *syuzhet,* masking an ellipsis of several days in the *fabula,* show narratorial preference for the consequences over the circumstances of Mrs. Wilcox's death.[54]

CONTINUITY SPANS

Any multiple appearance of narrative devices clearly adds to their degree of impact upon the reader. Such is the case with *continuity spans,* groupings of continuous phase units. Where two chapters linked by any type of continuity are joined by a third, directly contiguous, a minimum span is established. Its beginning, therefore, is the earliest point, its end the latest point at which a gap of no longer than a day, that is, a nocturnal phase, can be marked. Intrachapter ellipses may obviously occur, but provided these are specified, the span is not interrupted, even if its overall impact may be reduced. In part, this can also be due to the number and combination of the juxtaposed phases from which it is composed. A span of mixed types is bound to function differently from one entirely made up of immediate ties. For novels as early as Cervantes's *Don Quixote*, and as crucial to Modernism as Conrad's *Lord Jim*, continuity spans play important roles.

Broadly, their effect is to unify individual episodes from separate chapters, even separate volumes or parts of a work. Such spans project a sense of irreversible movement, by the refusal to terminate an episode at chapter end, but rather to establish a new overall rhythm, by allowing it to flow across the expected boundary. In music, the *sostenuto* direction offers perhaps the closest analogy. By comparison with the more leisurely type of span, punctuated by intervals ranging from several hours but no longer than a single night, the immediate version expresses greater force and keener tension. Its feeling of urgency and expansive flow eliminates any pause, at chapter end, for steady thought, insisting on the pressure of events across a considerable stretch of text and reading-time.

Nearly all fifty-two chapters in book 1 of *Don Quixote*, the majority linked by immediate ties, make up a single continuity span. By confining ellipses *within* chapters, and allowing embedded tales to exceed chapter boundaries, the narrator suggests a restless momentum. The succession of experiences by the knight and others is intensified, because telescoped by mode of presentation. In ten of the brief chapters of Voltaire's *Candide,* similarly, a span of immediate ties, including two embedded stories, deftly translates the hero over an even greater stretch of time and space, from Portugal to Paraguay.

Personal histories are frequently articulated as continuity spans, with breaks being introduced, so as not to overinflate the chapter unit. Smollett's "Memoirs of a Lady of Quality" in *Peregrine Pickle* ([1751] 1983, 432–539) shows the destabilizing result of such inflation. The (nonfictional) story of Lady Vane (ch. 88) extends to well over fifteen times the average length of the other (fictional) chapters.

Continuity spans elsewhere are more carefully proportioned in terms of significance. Goethe's hero recounts his history to Mariane early in *Wilhelm Meister* (1.4→8); Fielding distributes accounts by the Man of the Hill (8.11→15) and Mrs. Fitzpatrick (11.4→7) across consecutive chapters of *Tom Jones*. In *Amelia*, he has Booth and Miss Matthew exchange their life stories in prison, over a span of no fewer than twenty-seven chapters (1.6→4.1). When the criminal Vautrin, disguised as the Canon of Toledo, converses at length with the hero Lucien, in Balzac's *Illusions perdues* (3.31→35), the implied *fabula* is unbroken. The *syuzhet*, by contrast, is divided into a sequence linked by immediate ties. In Conrad's *Lord Jim*, Marlow's account runs with barely a break for a span of thirty chapters (chs. 5→35), though the continuity of transitions belies pendular movements by the narrator.

As an expositional tactic, some novels use continuity as a "front-loading" technique. This often produces the effect of an establishing shot in film, whereby the relations of characters and setting are clearly framed from the first. In Turgenev's *Fathers and Sons*, for example, an opening sequence of four chapters is linked by immediate continuity. It "places" Arkady and his friend Bazarov at the estate of Marino, and dates the scene exactly on 20 May 1859. Hugo, likewise, begins his *Notre-Dame de Paris* with specific dating, then devotes the whole of his first book, unified by immediate span, to the characters and mood in the Palais de Justice on that 6 January 1482. Eliot, in two immediate spans at the start of her own historical novel, *Romola,* follows Tito's ambitious progress through Florentine society up to his marriage at Easter 1493. Thereafter, a marked decline in the number of immediate, and of all spans, projects the disintegrating effects of a flawed, egotistic figure.

Hardy's goal, in the continuity span that pervades the first six chapters of *The Return of the Native*, is to evoke the magnetic influence that Egdon Heath will exercise over events. In Scott's *Ivanhoe*, the first eleven chapters are divided almost equally into two immediate spans. These focus on the two venues of Rotherwood and Ashby, critical for the narrative as a whole. The appearance of an immediate span can also point up a contrast with ensuing events, acting as negative exposition. Thus, the account of the Hales's last days at Helstone, in Gaskell's *North and South* (chs. 2→5), takes on in retrospect, once the family has removed northwards, an irretrievably elegiac quality. Dostoyevsky, as if to anticipate extensive usage, gives over the first part of *The Idiot* to a succession of fourteen chapters of immediate ties, which shuttle Prince Myshkin, in the course of a single day, between the key society venues of Petersburg.

With episodes of suspense or crisis, the narrator can expand the chapter(s) beyond average length, or divide the sequence into units marked by immediate transitions, so as not to slacken overall pace. Such is the frequent practice with adventure-fiction. Such, too, the method adopted by a variety of texts, to convey the excitement of events. An escape from a convent forms only part of a longer span of immediate continuity in Maturin's Gothic *Melmoth the Wanderer* (2.7→3.13). The physical violence of the workers' attack on a mill, in another immediate span, in *North and South* (chs. 19→23), has clear ramifications for the emotional relationship of Thornton and Margaret Hale.

An attack by bandits, in *Wilhelm Meister* (4.4→8), is similarly articulated, and, on a larger scale, a Russian assault on French forces near Shamshevo, in *War and Peace* (14.4→11), gains much of its impact on the reader from being presented as an immediate span. The attempted burglary at Chertsey, in *Oliver Twist* (chs. 20→22), which occupies a single period-installment, and the heroine's desperate search for an eyewitness, in *Mary Barton* (chs. 21→28), which is broken only by a nocturnal gap at 26i, and culminates in an Irish Sea chase, likewise render suspense through immediate spans.

Lengthy mixed spans of a dozen or so chapters feature in Meredith's *The Egoist* (chs. 27→39), to carry forward the action from Clara Middleton's attempted flight from Patterne Hall, to Sir Willoughby's midnight rendezvous with Laetitia Dale; in *War and Peace* (8.7→18), to track Natasha's emotional conflict, and her attempted abduction by Anatole Kuragin. Similar mixed spans, in Eliot's *Felix Holt* (chs. 14→22), record a less tense sequence of events, via nocturnal and proximate ties, triggered off by discovery of Debarry's pocket-book. Narrative brevity, rather than length, can often serve to highlight the tight proximity of material.

A fleeting central chapter in a minimal span of immediate continuity, may introduce a lightness of rhythm and draw a triad together. When Margaret barricades herself in with her pregnant sister Helen, in Forster's *Howard's End* (chs. 35→37), the narrator suggests their strong attachment by making the chapters into an immediate span, so that a unifying mood overflows from one chapter to the next. The very concision of chapter 36, central chapter of the span, and one-third the length of the novel's average chapter, also reinforces the compressed tension.

In Scott's *Kenilworth* (chs. 27→29), the brevity of the encounter between Edmund Tressilian and Michael Lambourne, is graphologically suggested by a chapter of scarcely two pages, less than one-fifth of that novel's average. Tressilian's forbearance toward Lambourne, in the central chapter of this immediate span, is shown to be directly coloured by his recent interview with Amy Robsart (ch. 27).

Elsewhere, the motif of courtroom trial represents a natural arena for dramatic expression, encouraging the use of immediate spans to maximize the impact of isotopic or associated material. Valjean's trial (*Les Misérables*, chs. 1.7.9→11), those of Rebecca (*Ivanhoe* [chs. 35→38]) and Effie (*Heart of Midlothian* [chs. 21→23]), the deliberate thematic duplication in *A Tale of Two Cities* of Darnay at the Old Bailey (2.2→4) and at the Revolutionary Tribunal (3.9→11) offer striking examples. In *The Brothers Karamazov*, furthermore, Dmitri's trial involves an immediate span of twelve chapters, which comprise the whole of the last book, bringing the novel to an intense climax.

The outwardly climactic points of *Madame Bovary* (3.7→10), and *Anna Karenina* (7.26→31), are registered in the suicides of their heroines. In both cases, the sequences employ immediate spans. In *Tom Jones*, the dénouement (18.3→9) uses the same type of spans to uncover Tom's origins. Jane Austen, in the final stages of her novels, resolves the emotional fate of two heroines, by inducing proposals from Knightley (*Emma* [chs. 46→51]) and Wentworth (*Persuasion* [chs. 19→23]). Mixed continuity spans mark these culminations, with immediate ties predominant.

FALSE CONTINUITY

A chapter start that promises to resume events from the foregoing chapter, but that, in practice, proves deceptive, exemplifies *false continuity*. This intentional asymmetry adopts various forms and techniques, but nearly always results in dashing reader expectations. Of the three main types of mismatch: *temporal, characterological*, and *locational*, the first is generally the most crucial, though it frequently combines with the others. In Lindsay Clarke's *The Chymical Wedding* (1989), where chapters consistently alternate between nineteenth-century and twentieth-century plots, the reader gradually becomes alert, by rhythmic regularity, to the switch at chapter start. Having left Louisa Agnew penning her manuscript at Decoy Lodge in November 1848 (6f), the new chapter begins: "The door of the Decoy Lodge opened at my second knock" (7i; 1990, 153). The location is identical, but the possessive pronoun betrays the return to Alex Darken in the 1980s, nearly a century and a half distant.

Henry Green also, in *Living*, makes frequent intrachapter use of personal pronouns (9i; [1929] 1979, 283), so that the reader tends to draw false anaphoric inferences to Hannah Glossop, or to Lily. In Fowles's *FLW*, interchapter anaphora serves to tease readers. A closing reference to Sarah (19f), gives way to a new chapter: "She stood obliquely in the shadows" (20i; [1969] 1970, 133): immediate continuity, parallel phase, or dream-projection? Only with details, in the third sentence, of brilliant weather, is the falseness of such assumptions clarified, and the chapter as a whole revealed as an ellipsis of two days. The temporal and locational mismatch of the transition resonates, too, in a sharp clash of epigraphs. Tennyson's *In Memoriam* (1850) is coupled with an account of Kennedy's death (Manchester 1967), period of story with period of writing.

One of the most striking examples of temporal mismatch occurs in George Moore's *Evelyn Innes* (1898). After her singing trial with Madame Savelli, the heroine plans the future with her lover Owen at their Paris hotel, and, eyes aching with sleep, she "laid her face on the pillow where his had lain" (11f; 1898, 148). The new chapter involves lexical repetition, hinting at immediate or proximate continuity: "As she lay between sleeping and waking . . . shadows of sleep fell, and in her dream there appeared two Tristans" (12i; 149). Memories of Dulwich blend with longings to play Isolde. Past perfect allusions to Savelli and Owen yield to her maid's knocking on the door, to remind her that, "she wanted to go for a long drive to the other end of London before she went to rehearsal" (151).

Since earlier chapters have shown Evelyn's projections into the future, including a vision of France in chapter 9, the reader assumes that chapter 12 is a further projection. References to maid and London, however, and use of the past perfect form provide clues. Only gradually, by mention of a reunion with Owen in Venice, "nearly four years ago," (156), and, on the penultimate page of the chapter, to their "six years of *liaison*" (166), is the chapter gap (11f→12i), and the radical nature of the temporal and locational mismatch finally resolved.

False continuity of a different temporal order occurs, when the expected elaboration of a scene is succeeded at chapter start, by a brief, or merely generalized review covering an extensive period of time. Thus, the singulative focus at the close of a chapter detailing Jane Eyre's arrival at Thornfield Hall: "We found dinner ready, and waiting for us in Mrs. Fairfax's room" (Brontë 11f; [1847] 1978, 139), contrasts with the iterative summary announcing the new chapter: "The promise of a smooth career, which my first calm introduction to Thornfield Hall seemed to pledge, was not belied on a longer acquaintance with the place and its inmates" (12i; 140). In film terms, the camera pulls back from a closeup, to a panoramic or long shot.

Narratorial play at the reader's expense, is frequently indulged in by Dickens, and can take the form of overtly deflating assumptions.

At a point of natural suspense in *Martin Chuzzlewit* (1844) comes a loud knocking on Pecksniff's door (20f). Lexical repetition at new chapter start (21i), with its suggestion of immediate or proximate continuity, is quickly robbed of even analogical potential. The mismatch here involves all three main types. Even the identity of the person knocking, moreover, is withheld for a further three chapters: "The knocking at Mr. Pecksniff's door, though loud enough, bore no resemblance whatever to the noise of an American railway train at full speed. It may be well to begin the present chapter with this frank admission, lest the reader should imagine that the sounds now deafening this history's ears have any connexion with the knocker on Mr. Pecksniff's door" (21i; 1986, 405–6).

If the linkage is spurious since the signifieds differ, in another instance the implied continuity relies on the identity of verbal signifiers. In *Oliver Twist,* the hero loses consciousness after the burglary: "a cold deadly feeling crept over the boy's heart; and he saw or heard no more" (22f; [1838] 1978b, 215). A new chapter repeats the epithet: "The night was bitter cold. The snow lay on the ground" (23i). Only with the reference to Mrs. Corney, in the second paragraph, does it become evident, however, that the coldness is not bodily but climatic, that the mismatch is triple, the relationship of chapters purely associative. The whole temporal status of chapter 23 remains indeterminate. Characterological and locational continuity is highly tenuous, Mrs. Corney being matron of Oliver's first workhouse. His narrative line is suspended for another six chapters, or two complete monthly installments.

A wakeful Esther, in Eliot's *Felix Holt,* catches a sound outside the door, and a quasi-Gothic climax threatens: "in the dim light of the corridor, where the glass above seemed to make a glimmering sky, she saw Mrs. Transome's tall figure pacing slowly, with her cheek upon her hand" (49f; [1866] 1972, 593). At 50i, however, the narrative reverts to the point reached at 48f, when Esther's lover Harold asks her about his father. The outcome of Mrs. Transome's pacing is not resumed until 50m: "Mrs Transome was walking towards the door when it opened. . . . In an instant Mrs. Transome felt Esther's arm round her neck" (596). Here, the mismatch is only temporary, serving to postpone briefly the reader's curiosity.

In other cases, temporal mismatch points to the noncoincidence of syntactic and semantic links across chapters. In a series of three sentences: "She should rather have prayed? But she believed she was praying. And now she was sleeping" (Fowles [1969] 1970, 195–96), the last, a terse sentence-paragraph, is actually the start of a new chapter, in Fowles's *FLW*. By connective, and identical subject, a relationship of immediate continuity is indicated, but the very next sentence overturns this notion. The chapter shifts from Sarah, dismissed by her employer, weeping by her bed (30f), to Charles's sight of her sleeping in the barn (31i), a scene directly continued from 29f. This makes the chapter's relationship not forward continuous, but analeptic.

Hardly four pages later, in the next chapter gap, comes false continuity resulting from mismatch of character. At a tantalizing moment, as the couple embrace in the barn, Charles suddenly breaks away: "he turned and rushed through the door—into yet another horror. It was not Doctor Grogan" (31f; 200). This negative identification is followed by an epigraph for the new chapter, taken from Hardy's poem "The Musical Box":

> And her, white-muslined, waiting there
> In the porch with high-expectant heart . . .
>
> (200)

The image evoked by these lines is then supplemented by an immediate allusion to Charles's fiancée, which the reader takes to be a positive identification: "Ernestina had, that previous night, not been able to sleep" (32i; 200). In relation to the events in the barn, her actions are analeptic. That she is not in fact the intruder, only becomes less likely by 32f, to be finally quashed at 33i. Fowles's exercise in ironic bathos, by resort to mismatch of character, continues his pastiche of Victorian serial publication.

In *The Mayor of Casterbridge*, Hardy, too, employs the same technique of false continuity, though on informational grounds. Thus, an error at 22f: "Lucetta flung back the curtain with a nervous greeting. The man before her was not Henchard" ([1886] 1975c, 174), gives way, at new chapter start, to detail of the newcomer's appearance and mutual reactions, before he is identified, in the sixth paragraph (175), as Farfrae. Eliot, in *The Mill on the Floss* (6.10), deliberately chooses to avoid a melodramatic close, by positioning a negative identification a page before, rather than at the chapter limit. Maggie, expecting Stephen Guest, hears the doorbell ring. The visitor "seated himself by her on the garden chair. It was not Stephen. 'We can just catch the tips of the Scotch firs, Maggie, from this seat,' said Philip" ([1860] 1985, 563).

Their brief reunion, of little more than a page, closes the chapter. Four days, and another page elapse, before Stephen himself finally makes an appearance (6.11). By introducing another scene in a penultimate paragraph, preempting the start of a singulative event from chapter start to chapter end, melodramatic suspense, together with false continuity, is again prevented. At home one afternoon, Mrs. Transome hears somebody approaching: "it was not quick enough to be her son's step, and besides, Harold was away at Duffield. It was Mr. Jermyn's" (8f; [1866] 1972, 199). With uncertainty banished, the new chapter of Eliot's *Felix Holt* proceeds smoothly, via immediate continuity, into a conversation between the couple.

NARRATORIAL AND MIXED CONTINUITY

Among factors affecting continuity, is focalization, in particular the relative prominence assumed either by the focalized object or events, or by the narrator, at chapter end and chapter start. It may often be problematic as to which predominates, and a spectrum of intermediate positions has to be established. Between two chapters, transitions may be broadly expressed as focalized to focalized ("She fell asleep almost at once" // "Belinda woke up early next day"), or as narrator to narrator ("Let us leave her now to blissful dreams, as we speculate" // "Before we return to our doughty heroine"). A *mixed grouping* involves a shift at chapter start, from focalized to narrator, or narrator to focalized.

Chapters linked by the relative prominence of narrator rather than events, stress *narratorial continuity*. First-person and autobiographical narratives are special cases, since all constituent parts, including chapter transitions, are narratorial. This obtains as much for Proust's Marcel, as for Achebe's Odili in *A Man of the People*, even where the narratorial voice is partially suppressed or deemphasized, to the extent that the reader often tends to forget the directing framework.

In *Tristram Shandy*, admittedly, that voice rarely loses its omnipresent verve. Even in this model of first-person fiction, nonetheless, it does not sound with the same intensity, nor intrude with identical frequency in all chapters. Though the heroine Lucy Snowe ensures narratorial continuity throughout Charlotte Brontë's *Villette*, chapter links are still reinforced by anaphora and connective: "It was so, for God saw that it was good" (37f; [1853] 1962, 480) // "But it is not so for all" (38i). The kind of authorial narrator employed by Fielding, Thackeray, and Trollope, is, by contrast, a nonparticipant, and self-consciously regulates the material. In *Barchester Towers*: "Mr. Slope, however, on his first introduction must not be brought before the public at the tail of a chapter"

(3f; [1857] 1981, 20)// "Of the Rev. Mr. Slope's parentage I am not able to say much." (4i; 21).

It is rarely possible, in practice, to estimate the immediacy or otherwise of any lapse in narratorial continuity of recital between one chapter and the next. On occasion, there may be a suggestion of delay in continuation of the account, as in Rushdie's *Midnight's Children*. At 2i, the narrator Saleem introduces a second plot line, the relationship with his critical narratee Padma. He refers to a "narrative which I left yesterday hanging in mid-air" ([1981] 1982, 24), underlining the crucial oral component of the novel.

In the context of a first-person bildungsroman, a notion of spiritual growth is usually attended by subjective reflections. These may extend to comments on the notations themselves, and their evidence of a change in character. The artist-protagonist of Keller's second version of *Der grüne Heinrich*, therefore, looks back over a writing-gap between chapters, and sees a different person: "Wie lange ist es her, seit ich das Vorstehende geschrieben habe. Ich bin kaum derselbe Mensch, meine Handschrift hat sich längst verändert" (3.9i; [1880] 1961, 319).[55]

Mixed continuity, generally more common than pure narratorial, shifts between chapters, to place greater weight either upon events or narrator. The category often appears in texts which insist on narratorial control, and use the opening and closing segments of chapters strategically to reinforce that power. At the same time, such shifts offer variety in presentation, and create fresh adjustments of distance between *fabula* and *syuzhet*. Generalizations on the human state can be foregrounded, by positioning at either side of narrative divisions. After Boldwood has bared his soul to Bathsheba, in Hardy's *Far from the Madding Crowd*, a final sentence broadens her "fearful joy" into one applicable to all womankind: "The facility with which even the most timid women sometimes acquire a relish for the dreadful when that is amalgamated with a little triumph, is marvellous" (23f; [1874] 1975a, 181). Her contrastive encounter with Troy closely follows, so that the transition of 23f→24i is from narrator to events.

A page-length elegy from the narrator at the close of chapter 52 in *Adam Bede*, provides a far more substantial instance of the same mixed continuity. The tone is unmistakable, as it laments what has passed: "Fine old Leisure! Do not be severe upon him, and judge him by our modern standard: he never went to Exeter Hall, or heard a popular preacher, or read *Tracts for the Times* or *Sartor Resartus*" ([1859] 1981, 558). From this elevation, Adam's mere journeying home, at the start of the next chapter, must inevitably seem anticlimactic. This kind of shift, however, expresses the narrator's desire to summarize developments and indicate directions, to offer points of meditation before new material (here, the scene of the harvest supper in ch. 53) is broached.

Despite the importance of these examples, the opposite shift, from events to narrator, is by far the most frequent. Since Scott, at least, the graphological gap seems to validate a regular pattern, whereby a newcomer announced at chapter end (f), is presented in detail at chapter start (i1), before being set in motion (i2, or m). At the close of chapter 9 in *The Fair Maid of Perth*, "a gentleman usher announced the Duke of Albany" ([1828] 1969, 116); at chapter start, "The Duke of Albany was, like his royal brother, named Robert" (10i; 116). Two paragraphs of biographical detail later, the action unfreezes: "At the Duke's entrance the Prior . . . respectfully withdrew" (117).

With an authorial narrator as ubiquitous as Thackeray's in *Vanity Fair*, it is natural that the arrival of the Crawleys in Curzon Street, at chapter end (36f), should cause the new chapter to be entitled "The Subject Continued," and inspire its strongly narratorial coloring: "In the first place, and as a matter of the greatest necessity, we are bound to describe how a house may be got for nothing a year" (37i; [1848] 1950, 380). A similar type of narrator, in Trollope's *Orley Farm*, conveys a similar sense of control at chapter start, by exploiting lexical repetition in a serial-break manner. Chapter-end statement ("But going to Leicestershire this winter was out of the question" [3f; [1862] 1993, 34]), gives way to shrewd reformulation at chapter start, producing a sting in the tail ("Going to Leicestershire was quite out of the question for young Orme at this period of his life, but going to London unfortunately was not so" [4i; 34]).

In a move reminiscent of Denis Diderot's authorial narrator in *Jacques le Fataliste* (1773), Wilhelm Raabe's, in *Abu Telfan* (1868), offers the reader a choice of narrative routes. At 33f, the focalized Frau Claudine sits quietly, listening to footsteps approaching and departing. At 34i, the narrator ironically repeats the idea, which then triggers off separate options for the reader: "Auch wir sitzen und lauschen einen Augenblick den Fusstritten, die sich entfernen, und denen, die sich nähern; denn wir haben nunmehr zwei Wege vor uns, auf welchen wir dieses Mal das Ziel unserer Wanderschaft zu erreichen vermögen" (1980, 347).[56]

While Raabe playfully exploits narratorial control, Dickens makes use of a similar transition from events to narrator, to make associative linkage, and advance the narrative in a different way. A peripheral allusion at chapter end to a church service after Miss Charity's leaving home, in *Martin Chuzzlewit* (30f), is taken up by a self-conscious narrator at chapter start. This reiteration allows more than a week to slip by in the *fabula*, before presentation in the *syuzhet* of Pecksniff's eavesdropping on Tom and Mary Graham, in another church. Thus, at 31i: "The closing words of the last chapter lead naturally to the commencement of this, its successor; for it has to do with a church. With the church, so often mentioned heretofore, in which Tom Pinch played the organ for nothing. One sultry afternoon" ([1844] 1986, 556).

Though Eliot's novels contain frequent reminders of narratorial presence, the opening paragraph of *The Mill on the Floss* 5.4, is particularly striking. An apostrophe to the reader accompanies careful scene-setting and graphic present tense, by way of preparation for another meeting between Maggie and Philip: "Early in the following April, nearly a year after that dubious parting you have just witnessed, you may, if you like, again see Maggie entering the Red Deeps through the group of Scotch firs. But it is early afternoon" (5.4i; [1860] 1985, 432). Here, the authorial narrator, doubling as critic, actually draws attention to the divergence between *fabula* and *syuzhet*, to the large gap in terms of focalized events ("nearly a year after"), and the minimal lapse ("just witnessed"), from 5.3f→5.4i, in narratorial terms.

DELAYED PRESENTATION

One common feature of categories of transition is *delayed presentation*. The late appearance in the text of temporal data, holds back the reader's determination of the sequential status of succeeding chapters. Opening paragraphs may often take the form of narratorial statements, and the focalized events may be resumed only afterwards, so that the shift occasions a delay, suggesting the passage of time in the narrative. By withholding for several sentences, paragraphs, or pages, any temporal confirmation, the text can cause the reader fruitful uncertainty or disorientation, arouse curiosity, and increase suspense. It can also satisfy the need for background detail, deliberately block the flow of action, or simply bare the narratorial hand.

In many cases, the use of delayed presentation seems so conventional and automatized, as to be overlooked. When a description of Anna Sergeyevna's country house occupies the first paragraph of chapter 16 in Turgenev's *Fathers and Sons* ([1862] 1975, 156), and the second records the arrival of Arkady and Bazarov, confirmation of the chapter's status of proximate phase is only minimally held back. Ten chapters further on (274–75), another opening paragraph deals with Odintsov's garden "portico," where Arkady and Katya, in the second paragraph, are discovered, so that the nocturnal transition between 25f and 26i is again only briefly obscured.

Classic realism, from Balzac on, tends to rely on solid specification of setting, before the entry of characters and events. In *Illusions perdues*, however, Balzac ushers his characters across the threshold at 2.17f, records their dialogue at new chapter start, to suggest its status of immediate continuity, then describes dining room and dress ([1843] 1961, 351–52). Fontane, conversely, in his *Frau Jenny Treibel*, has his loquacious guests passing through the doors at 2f, then gives over the first page of 3i ([1892] 1963b, 314) to details of the Treibels' dining room, thus postponing resumption of events.

On a terse note, Hardy closes chapter 46 of *The Woodlanders*, by crystallizing into a dramatic, monosyllabic sentence-paragraph the means of Tim Tangs's revenge on Fitzpiers: "It was a man-trap" ([1887] 1975f, 359). In the following chapter, however, the first five paragraphs depart completely from the specific cobwebbed model unearthed by Tangs, to offer a general excursus on the history, varieties and local uses of man-traps. Only then does the action resume, with immediate continuation from the juncture reached at 46f: "As soon as he had examined the trap . . . he shouldered it without more ado." (361).

At least, in all these instances of delayed presentation, of *immediate* and *proximate ties*, and *nocturnal gap*, the degrees of delay in establishing sequential status are not excessive. In chapter 13 of Raabe's *Abu Telfan* ([1868] 1980, 129), however, a historical preamble on the German *Residenzstadt* occupies three-quarters of the chapter, before any temporal index appears. The delay is partly motivated by the fact, that more than a year has elapsed since the reader's last encounter with Leonhard Hagebucher, and the synopsis clearly serves to speed the passage of time.

Stretches of dialogue, as well as description, help to postpone confirmation of a chapter's status. By opening with direct speech, the text plunges the reader in medias res, and characters are apparently freed from narratorial control, which only makes itself felt with the first temporal index. Typical of the way in which exchanges at chapter start tend to gloss over temporal gaps, and promote more gradual transitions, are the four "turns" that divert attention from the passage of several weeks in Zola's *Germinal* 3.4i ([1885] 1968, 185), the six "turns" that cover a similar period in

Hardy's *Jude* 3.2i ([1896] 1975b, 156), or the unspecified gap concealed by chapter-start dialogue in Conrad's *The Secret Agent*, 3i ([1907] 1980, 42).

Overuse of delayed presentation, even with phases other than forward continuous, runs the same danger of monotony and predictability as does the excessive use of any narrative feature. In a crime novel such as James Melville's *A Haiku for Hanae* (1990), delayed presentation features in well over half its chapters, with the voice of its detective prominent in one-third, contributing to an overall sequential mannerism.

In certain printed editions, there may even be ambiguity at chapter start about the type of discourse involved. After chapter-end dialogue between Sidney Kirkwood and John Hewett, in Gissing's *The Nether World* (22f), the new chapter employs identical speech-marks (23i; [1889] 1973, 200). Not until nineteen lines later, does it become clear that the discourse is not speech or thought, rather a letter, involving not Kirkwood or Hewett, but two quite different correspondents. Delayed presentation may also occur at chapter end, so that it is necessary to refer to continuity between subsegments. At 1.1f, the young title-figure of *Jude the Obscure* ([1896] 1975b, 35) is seen at Marygreen, carrying buckets of water (f1), but the final paragraph is then devoted to an account of the village (f2). The new chapter immediately resumes Jude's porterage, so that the continuity runs 1.1f1→1.2i.

A double delay, by reason of narratorial explanations at both chapter end and chapter start, features in Voltaire's *Candide* ([1759] 1968, 129–30). Subsegments are again involved, continuity of events running 8f1→9i2, of narrator, 8f2→9i1. In *The Secret Agent* ([1907] 1980, 90–98), the Assistant Commissioner's inward reflections on Michaelis help to bridge chapters, and delay for over eight pages any confirmation of immediate continuity (5f1→6m). A span of three consecutive delayed presentations, in Meredith's *Richard Feverel* (chs. 27→29), further intensifies effects of ironic distance and playful obliqueness. At 29i ([1859] 1984, 276), especially, the opening allusion to Caesar's crossing the Rubicon remains enigmatic, until a less tangential analogy is drawn with the hero's imminent marriage.

Proleptic Phase

> What I have to inform you comes, I own, a little out of its due
> course;—for it should have been told a hundred and fifty pages
> ago, but that I foresaw then 'twould come in pat hereafter, and

> be of more advantage here than elsewhere.—Writers had need
> look before them to keep up the spirit and connection of what
> they have in hand.
>
>   —Lawrence Sterne, *A Sentimental Journey*

Anticipatory or *proleptic phase*, like other types of continuous phase, is part of forward narrative sequence. In Western tradition, it appears much less common than analepsis (Genette 1972, 105). Less attention has generally been paid to prolepsis, since its onset and divergence from linear practice may often go unremarked. Allusions to future events, either within or beyond the text, can be positioned at virtually any point, but proleptic phase as such belongs more properly to the closing segments of narrative units. *Analeptic phases*, by contrast, usually feature in initial segments, at junctures of relatively higher visibility.

The interlocking of chapter-end anticipation and chapter-start retrospective, has been termed *Hakenstil* (Lämmert 1955, 171). Replacing a narrative standstill by a pause for breath, it may predict the course of events or merely announce venue and intent. Most importantly, it levels out breaks into transitions, and has close affinities with telegraphing in film. Since autobiography and first-person narrative offer retrospective accounts, the narrator is already aware of an ordered sequence. Proleptic phase can thus indicate how one incident led to another, or underline the future relevance of specific events. It serves other purposes, too, but its use hints at a narratorial desire to interrupt, however fleetingly, the flow of action, in order to insert a divisional marker for the reader.

The issue is one of relative viewpoint. Looking ahead from the final segments of chapters 29, 31, 37, and 51 in Fowles's *FLW* suggests their proleptic character, with their narrative expectations being fulfilled respectively in chapters 31, 33, 38, and 53. Looking back from the initial segments of these chapters, the relationship of 38:37 is (proximate) continuous phase, that of 31:29, 33:31, and 53:51 is analeptic. In normal reading, however, determination of a chapter's status often requires little more than turning back a page, or applying data already known.

With proleptic phase, the process may be one-way: proof of fulfillment lying somewhere ahead in the text, and not easily accessible. Ideally completed by relating the foreshadowed to its foreshadowing, the interaction frequently does not occur. The dynamic motion back-and-forth typical of other phases, is absent, and proleptic phase as a whole accorded a lower value. It comprises two main categories, *internal*, and *external*; the former, in turn, may be subdivided into *explicit* and *implicit* types.

Explicit internal prolepsis is specific as to its expected locus, and confined within the main narrative. Early in *Don Quixote* ([1615] 1965, 41), the hero's chapter-end resolve to be knighted (1.2f), anticipates the title-summary and content of the next chapter. That the later episode of the suspended swords of knight and Basque is not destined for oblivion, is confirmed at 1.8f (75), with a conclusion promised, and then realized in 1.9. Advance notice of the sonnets recited in 1.40 is given by Don Pedro's brother at 1.39f (352), exemplifying at chapter end a common type of prolepsis involving letters and documents.

Implicit internal prolepsis lacks any specifics of expected locus or distribution. Its advance notification may encompass, as does the paragraph-length summary by Dame Gossip of characters and events in Meredith's *The Amazing Marriage*, "a few touches" of "excitement" to come (3f; [1895] 1896, 34–5). It may forewarn, as does Balzac in *Ursule Mirouët* (1.2i; [1841] 1965, 464), about the content of current and following chapters, here anterior to the novel's starting point. Very often, if a single event is anticipated, its nature remains studiously vague. Thus, the allusions to the "unexpected incident" affecting Lavretsky, in Turgenev's *A House of Gentlefolk* (15f; [1858] 1970, 49), or the "etwas Fürchterliches"[57] involving Tony, in Mann's *Buddenbrooks* (6.8f; [1902] 1974a, 252).

On another occasion, a literal announcement by a character within the narrative brings immediate continuity, though prolepsis, by itself, does not guarantee this. A preemptive start to a scene, at chapter end, in Gaskell's *North and South* : "[Margaret] was busy preparing her board one morning, when Sarah . . . threw wide open the drawing-room door, and announced, 'Mr. Henry Lennox' " (2f; [1855] 1982, 53), sponsors, at chapter start, a direct realization of wishes: " 'Mr Henry Lennox.' Margaret had been thinking of him only a moment before" (3i; 54).

If an event, foreshadowed by chapter-end prolepsis, directly features at new chapter start, it need not imply an equally brief succession in narrative time. The "foreign tour" proposed in the last words of chapter 61 in *Vanity Fair* ([1848] 1950, 646), takes several weeks, elided in the chapter break, to materialize (62i). With part-publication, the advance hints at serial break, to sustain the reader's interest, may entail a month of calendar time, before their relevance can be appreciated. Miss Nickleby's undeceiving cannot in actuality be revealed *sooner* than Dickens's next instalment of *Nicholas Nickelby*: "Poor Kate! she little thought how weak her consolation was, and how soon she would be undeceived" (17f;

[1839] 1985a, 285). Prolepsis may aim at even longer-term events. Less than two-thirds through Turgenev's *Virgin Soil*, the "grateful glance Mariana fixed on [Solomin] . . . set him thinking" (24f; [1877] 1969, 190). The possibility of future links is only finally borne out in the novel's coda.

When events anticipated by prolepsis, appear not in the following, but in the next-but-one chapter, we may posit a subcategory of *alternate proleptic phase*. Fowles's *FLW* (chs. 29, 31, 51) offers illustrations, together with the deliberate artifice of a chapter first resolving (31i) an earlier prolepsis (29f), then, by negative identification at chapter end (31f), anticipating another resolution (33i), as the couple in the barn are interrupted, not by Dr. Grogan, but by Sam and Mary. On a larger scale, Fowles's novel also demonstrates a mixed type, of *quasiprolepsis*.[58] Thus, Charles's experiences on his return to Lyme Regis (43m→44f), are only disclosed retrospectively (45i) to be fantasy projections, designed to tease reader credulity: "the last few pages you have read are not what happened, but what he spent the hours between London and Exeter imagining might happen" ([1969] 1970, 266).

External prolepsis, the second main category, less important and frequent, points beyond the temporal bounds of the fiction. An *explicit* type, illustrated by Sterne, alludes in *Tristram Shandy* 1.13 ([1767] 1967, 64) to a nonexistent volume 20, and in chapter 36 ["The Translation—Paris"] of *A Sentimental Journey* ([1768] 1986, 79) to a concert at Milan, never detailed, since Yorick's narrative never advances that far. As for *trials* at Milan, an account is promised by the narrator of Manzoni's *The Betrothed* (32f) for inclusion in another work. This turns out ([1827] 1972, 604 n) to be Manzoni's own *Storia della colonna infame* of 1842. In Clarke's *The Chymical Wedding* ([1989] 1990), events alternate between the 1840s and 1980s, so that the outcome of the Victorian plot is made explicit in the later plot, with which it has close affinities. In turn, its link with the earlier Agnews is one of external analepsis.

A combination of simple present for the narrative-Now, and future tense for eyewitnesses, in Spark's *The Driver's Seat* ([1970] 1974), offers an unusual type of prolepsis. The novel's ending coincides with Lise's murder, but its consequences have already been indicated. An *implicit* type of *external prolepsis*, unspecific about future locus or distribution, may be instanced by allusions in component novels of Balzac's *La Comédie Humaine*, to further appearances by his recurrent cast. In Trollope's *Can You Forgive Her?* ([1864] 1986, 793), both reader and narrator bid farewell to Burgo

Fitzgerald (76f), as unaware at that time as its author, that Burgo is to return later, in *The Duke's Children* of 1880.

Parallel Phase

> The special train left the siding in Kroonstad a couple of hours before dawn on Tuesday 30 May.
> —Thomas Pakenham, *The Boer War*

> That same dawn that found Kruger's special train steaming south to Bloemfontein found a second special, flying two Union Jacks beside the cow-catcher, steaming north to the same destination.
> —Pakenham

By contrast with forward narrative phases, *parallel phase* is particularly affected by conventions of typesetting and consecutive page layout. It has to be placed *after* a given sequence, though on the level of events, the reader is meant to assume it occurs *parallel* with that sequence. Unusual cases such as Alasdair Gray's *Lanark* ([1981] 1985a), with graphological patterns and marginal commentaries, or Jacques Derrida's cross-generic *Glas* (1974), with interplay of topics and typefaces, and columns like split-screen film, only reinforce the general rule.

Thus, the phase involves reversion from the point reached at previous sequence or chapter end. The narrator aims to provide background for the reader, to suggest unsuspected analogies and contrasts among figures already introduced, rather than to advance events. This new phase begins at a specified or indeterminate juncture before the end of the previous sequence, but if the parallel phase antedates the start of that sequence, then analepsis results. Any sequence, it should be recalled, may extend beyond, as well as occupy less space than a single chapter. In addition, it may be relevant to contrast the length of adjoining sequences, their page/time ratios, and their coordinate, or subordinate status. Parallel phase itself may be divided into *major* and *minor* types.

Where heterodiegetic action, or a set of events recorded at the beginning of one chapter coincides with that at the beginning of the preceding chapter or sequence, a *major parallel phase* exists. In its pure state: two sequences whose temporal beginnings and ends exactly correspond, examples are rare, since such symmetrical twinning is highly factitious. Hardy, sometimes accused of overly architectonic form, offers a condensed version. In a single chapter of *Far from the Madding Crowd*, he assigns separate sections to

Bathsheba and her suitors. Aptly entitled "Converging Courses," chapter 52 ([1874] 1975a, 361) focuses on each character in turn, as, in their different venues, they dress for Boldwood's Christmas-Eve party. Direct speech then unifies all their second appearances. Even here, with sections of similar length, however, there is no pretence of identical time coverage, which would only connote mechanical pedantry.

Elsewhere, major parallel phase can align developments with main characters, such as Esther (22i) and Philip Debarry (23i), in Eliot's *Felix Holt*. It can bring together, in successive chapters, two female leads: Romola (49i) and Tessa (50i), in *Romola*. Though chapter starts may coincide, overall chapter relationships may differ. The initial paragraph of chapter 8 in Fowles's *FLW* : "Sam's had not been the only dark face in Lyme that morning. Ernestina had woken in a mood" (1970, 41), temporally matches that of chapter 7: "The morning, when Sam drew the curtains, flooded in upon Charles" (36). This parallel phase, however, remains partial and brief. Charles reaches Ernestina's house by the fourth sentence of 8i, thus continuing, by proximate tie, the material of 7m. More precisely, the sequential status must be designated as $8i1\|7i$, and $8i2 \rightarrow 7m$, illustrating again the need for subdividing chapter-segments.

Where action coincides with that within, but not at the beginning of the previous chapter or sequence, a *minor parallel phase* exists. This type, as indicated, is more prevalent than the major version. In a multiplot novel, such as *Vanity Fair*, an authorial narrator must track to and fro in order to follow different groups of characters. The reduced circumstances of the widowed Amelia and her son at Christmas (46i; [1848] 1950, 474), are contrasted, by use of parallel phase, with the society world of Becky and Rawdon at the same season (45m).

In Gaskell's *Mary Barton*, the narrator juxtaposes the genteel setting of the Carsons' home, with the Bartons' more humble abode (17m): "I must go back an hour or two before Mary, and her friends, parted for the night. It might be about eight o'clock that evening, and the three Miss Carsons" (18i; [1848] 1983, 254). During the same chapter, significantly, the thematic linkage between the two families grows closer, with the report of Harry Carson's murder.

Social divides in *Gründerzeit* Berlin motivate the piquant application of parallel phase in Fontane's *Frau Jenny Treibel*, for accounts of two very different dinners, at the Treibels' (4m), and Professor Schmidt's: "Um dieselbe Stunde, wo man sich bei

Treibels vom Diner erhob, begann Professor Schmidts 'Abend' "
(6i; [1892] 1963b, 346).⁵⁹ Parallel segments in the same chapters
then record his family's differing views of Leopold Treibel (ch. 8),
and the gossip of the promenading pairs around the lake at Halensee (ch. 10).

Where a sequence extends longer than a single chapter, as in
Oliver Twist, the parallel phase may temporally couple episodes
many pages apart. Thus, chapters 39–41 make up a serial installment, with revelations about the young hero. In the new part (42i),
different characters (the Claypoles) are introduced, explicitly parallel with the stage reached at 39m: "Upon the night when Nancy,
having lulled Mr Sikes to sleep, hurried on her self-imposed mission to Rose Maylie, there advanced towards London, by the Great
North Road, two persons" ([1838] 1978, 376).

A striking, multiple use of minor parallel phase occurs in three
successive chapters of Scott's *Ivanhoe*. Led into separate cells at
Torquilstone Castle (21m), the reactions of Isaac (ch. 22), Rowena
(ch. 23), and Rebecca (ch. 24) are all keyed in to the identical horn
blasts sounded at 21f ([1819] 1987, 251). These predetermine the
parallel articulation and closure of all three chapters.

In *The Return of the Native* 5.5→7 ([1878] 1975d, 341–59),
Hardy turns to parallel phase, in three more successive chapters,
to record separately the activities of his protagonists on the key
nights of 5 and 6 November. By insisting on temporal parallels
throughout, the narrator exploits ironic contrasts between the apparent independence and actual interdependence of Eustacia,
Wildeve, Clym, and Thomasin. He thereby prepares for the inevitability of the catastrophe in the book's last chapter (5.9). With a different novel, offering three possible endings, parallel phase serves
to mark off diverging, rather than converging destinies. Thus, the
medial segment of the last chapter of Fowles's *FLW* (61m; [1969]
1970, 362) supplies an alternative course to that at an identical
juncture of 60m, relating to the *same* rather than *different* characters. As if to stress the favored status of the second and third versions, the minor parallel phase at 61m exactly reproduces the
paragraph at 60m, in contrast to the single line reiterated by 45m
from 43m, prelude to the novel's first ending.

PARALLEL OVERLAP

Two subcategories of parallel phase are represented by *major* and
minor overlaps. The *major* version occurs when a phase temporally
exceeds the limit of the last forward phase or most recent action.

Instead of simply updating a given sequence, a new, more advanced date is established. The process of overlapping also becomes one of surpassing, as the reader is carried forward by the momentum of fresh events. Early in *Tom Jones*, the opening of 1.8 exactly matches the time juncture of 1.7, when Bridget and Deborah eavesdrop on Allworthy's interrogation of Jenny Jones. By the third paragraph of 1.8, however, both listeners start to react to the completed scene ([1749] 1963, 47), and the chapter, now a major overlap, continues their dialogue.

An overlap may also appear later in a chapter. Thus, the action in Meredith's *The Egoist* involving Clara (41i; [1879] 1968, 483), runs parallel to Sir Willoughby's midnight offer to Laetitia (40i). At 41m, the Clara line then goes beyond that reached by breakfast-time at 40f, resulting in a major overlap.

Parallel phase may assume a summarizing, generalizing tendency, if it commences at an identical juncture, but eschews detail and singulative event. This is Mann's approach in *Buddenbrooks* 5.3i ([1902] 1974a, 182). He reverts to the concrete arrival of an errant brother (5.2i), but then moves to Thomas's mental review of Christian during the first few days and week, in 5.3i. The match of initial segments may take a different form. *The Pickwick Papers* 36i1 ([1837] 1983, 594) deals with the daily round of the Pump-Room at Bath, before introducing its hero at 36i2, on the evening of an eventful day. Sam Weller's activities on that same day, however, are detailed from morning on (37i), then overlap the previous phase by advancing the action to the next day, when Pickwick reports on Winkle's adventure with the sedan chair.

Here, secondary and main narratives fuse, but a resort to parallel phase accentuates the issue of narrative priorities. In chapter 42 of *Felix Holt* ([1866] 1972, 510), the Jermyn plot line exceeds that of Esther and results in parallel overlap, but raises the problem of a dominant line. From chapter 40 on, the Transomes also compete with Esther and Jermyn, though Mrs Transome herself has been absent between chapters 10 and 34. Felix himself only exacerbates the difficulties, being in gaol at this stage, and absent for thirteen whole chapters (chs. 33→45).

Minor parallel overlap, like minor parallel phase in general, is far more common than its major counterpart. It offers greater flexibility in choice of entry point for the parallel segment. By matching the medial or final, rather than initial segment of a previous sequence, it stays closer, in terms of pages or reader-memory, to the new phase. Occurring at a point *within*, but not at the start of the previous sequence, minor overlap then exceeds the terminal limit of that sequence. Just prior to Jem Wilson's trial for murder, at the end of chapter 31 in *Mary Barton* (Gaskell [1848] 1983, 380), Mary has watched all night for change in the weather, and with it Will's return, until a melodramatic crimson dawn appears. At 32i, Carson's ordeal as the victim's father, at identical points in time, underlines parallel anxieties, before an overlap takes forward the action into the trial itself (32m).

Such relative specificity and textual closeness of the parallel phase is elsewhere lacking. In Turgenev's *Fathers and Sons*, for instance, the action at 25i ([1862] 1975, 253), on Anna Sergeyevna's estate, is set at an indeterminate period during the time covered in chapter 23, before Bazarov's return from his duel with Pavel Petrovich means a minor parallel overlap. Sue's note to her cousin, given verbatim in *Jude* 4.5i ([1896] 1975b, 252), is a day old, from a period during which "some days passed" at 4.4m (248). Her trip to the station, evoked directly afterwards, parallels Phillotson's reactions to her departure at 4.4f. This double parallelism then gives way, at 4.5m, to the meeting with Jude proposed in that note, so that the overlap is completed.

Delayed presentation of the phase also occurs in *Jude*, briefly obscuring the status of 3.3i. By the end of the first paragraph (160), however, the focus has shifted from a survey of the Training School, to the scene there on the evening spent by Sue and Jude at the shepherd's cottage (3.2f1). Her return to the school (3.2f2) is again recorded at 3.3m, before the ensuing reprimand and flight signals a minor parallel overlap.

An instance in *Anna Karenina* begins, unusually, in mid-chapter, only to continue into the next. Vronsky's perspective on the disastrous officers' steeplechase (2.25), is exchanged for Anna's at 2.28m, and her "version" of the events is carried via immediate continuity into 2.29 ([1877] 1973a, 229). This surpasses the limit of the Vronsky action, to become another overlap. Hardy's *The Woodlanders* contains a wealth of such phases, including many intrachapter examples, but the most sustained case appears in *The Return of the Native*, with a span of three successive chapters unified by minor parallel overlap.

Each resumes a sequence from within a previous chapter, now overtaken by other events: "[Clym] in the meantime had aroused himself from sleep" (4.7i; [1878] 1975d, 297), a phase parallel with 4.6m, before the intervening actions of Wildeve's leaving Eustacia's cottage, and Clym's mother, denied entrance, making her way home. At 4.8i, similarly: "In the meantime Eustacia, left alone in her cottage at Alderworth" (304), a phase parallel with 4.7m, before Clym's discovery of his mother, stung by an adder. Following a chapter (4.4) in which brief sections run parallel with and overlap their predecessors, the last chapters of book 4 occupy a single day. That day's climax is dramatically reinforced by the interlocking technique of parallel overlap, projecting the enmeshed density and accelerating tempo of events overtaking human relations.

Simultaneous Phase

> A ce moment, ce soleil se voyait aussi là-bas, en Bretagne, où midi allait sonner. . . .
> En Islande, où c'était le matin, il paraissait aussi, à cette même minute de mort. . . .
> Au moment . . . où le soleil équatorial disparut tout à fait dans les eaux dorées.
>
> [. . . At that moment, this same sun was visible over there in Brittany, where midday was about to strike. . . . In Iceland, where it was morning, it also appeared at this very same instant of death. . . .
> At the moment . . . when the sun at the equator completely sank beneath the golden waters.]
>
> —Pierre Loti, *Pêcheur d'Islande*

Where the start of a narrative phase coincides with the end of a previous sequence, but heterodiegetic characters or events are featured, a *simultaneous phase* exists. In drama, we might cite the use of teichoscopy and multilevel action, and in film, the exploitation of split-screen and deep-focus techniques. Allusions in fiction to elements of the previous sequence can vary from explicit to minimal, as the new phase moves time forward. Often, by switch of focus, the use of simultaneous phase increases suspense by fastening upon another, sometimes less vital line of action, while implying that the central narrative line continues, though unremarked upon, in the background.

With the discriminating James, a reader is reminded, however, that conversations recorded on the page do not simply vanish in the story, rather that fresh interests emerge. Thus, the discussion between Isabel and Osmond, at the close of chapter 24 in *The Portrait of a Lady*, yields, at 25i, to another: "While this sufficiently intimate colloquy (prolonged for some time after we cease to follow it) went forward Madame Merle and her companion . . . had begun to exchange remarks" ([1881] 1991, 288).

Often, the new phase involves change of character and setting, despite a common theme. The co-occurrence may be lexically stressed at chapter start, as in Radcliffe's *The Italian*: "While the Marchesa and the Monk were thus meditating conspiracies against Ellena, she was still in the Ursuline convent" (2.5i; [1797] 1971, 179). Though Grandcourt, in Eliot's *Daniel Deronda*, has last appeared in chapter 25, and references to him are made in chapter 26, dominated by Gwendolen and Mrs. Davilow, the reader, via simultaneous phase, is not allowed to forget him. At 27i, as if to anticipate his entry later in the chapter, Gwendolen herself takes a syntactical second place: "While Grandcourt on his beautiful black Yarico, the groom behind him on Criterion, was taking the pleasant ride from Diplow to Offendene, Gwendolen was seated before the mirror" ([1876] 1978, 340).

In Hugo's *Les Misérables*, the presence of simultaneous phase is clear: "Cependant, en ce moment-là même, Fantine était dans la joie"[60] (1.7.6i; [1862] 1957, 1.305), the girl being sandwiched between chapters involving Valjean. The use of "meanwhile" in English, however, is not unambiguous in designating a simultaneous phase, since it may also introduce a parallel phase. With Gaskell's *North and South*, the shift from news of Margaret's legacy (ch. 49), to the Thornton plot line: "Meanwhile at Milton the chimneys smoked" (50i; [1855] 1982, 510) prepares for news of misfortune, and the chapter's iterative status also suggests simultaneous phase.

In Hardy's *The Woodlanders*, however, the same time index, combined with a past perfect verb, marks a parallel phase, reverting to action at 5m: "Meanwhile Winterborne and Grace Melbury had also undergone their little experiences. As he drove off with her out of the town" (6i; [1887] 1975f, 72). The couple's ride precisely matches that of Marty South and Mrs. Charmond, as far as Little Hintock (6m‖5f). Here, "these people with converging destinies" (75), in Hardy's pointed phrase, finally part. Giles himself stays only briefly at the Melburys', but a section switching back to the timber-merchant's "in the meantime" (76) reports on the family's conversation in a genuine simultaneous phase.

Two subdivisions, *progressive* and *nonprogressive*, refer basically to the length and importance of the phase, with the latter type usually represented at medial, rather than initial junctures. The new line of action is not developed in the *nonprogressive* type, but often serves as diversionary interlude, with a shift of tone, before the central narrative line returns. In one of the numerous brief chapter sections of H. G. Wells's *Mr. Britling Sees It Through*, for example, a monologue is interrupted at 2.5f by a new section. This uses simultaneous phase to contrast the small world with the large: "And indeed at the very moment when Mr. Britling was saying these words, in Sarajevo in Bosnia, where the hour was somewhat later, men whispered together" (2.6i; [1916] 1969, 49). The nine-line section complete, attention reverts to suppertime at the Dower House.

Both Günter Grass and Salman Rushdie demonstrate nonprogressive simultaneous phase, matching events on the personal, fictional level with those on the public, historical level (Ireland 1990, 356). Oskar Matzerath's linkages, in *Die Blechtrommel* (1963), tend to be inconsequential and irreverent, with larger issues constantly devalued; Saleem Sinai's, in *Midnight's Children* (1981), more frequent and central, legacy of the co-occurrence of his own birth and India's Independence.

Nonprogressive simultaneous phase within chapters often involves shared auditory signals, to indicate co-occurring perception by different figures. A transition between Louisa Agnew in her room, and her father in the library, in chapter 2 of *The Chymical Wedding*, is eased by both hearing, at the same time, horses' hooves in the drive (Clarke [1989] 1990, 29). Church clocks striking in the small hours sponsor another intrachapter shift, in *Jude* 2.3, from Sue in one suburb of Christminster, to her cousin in the same city (Hardy [1896] 1975b, 118–19).

Since *progressive simultaneous phase* introduces a new line of action at chapter start, which then continues to the end of a sequence or chapter, it represents a more comprehensive version. For the serial publication of *Romola*, Eliot resorts to the phase in the final chapter of the penultimate part (ch. 67; [1863] 1980, 633), which reaches its climax with the deaths of Baldassare and Tito. Dickens makes untypical use of simultaneous phase, by contrasting the activities of separate social groups on a given morning. In *Our Mutual Friend*, "up came the sun" refers, at 3.11f, to the superficially decent Bradley Headstone; at 3.12i, to the superficially brightened Lammles ([1865] 1988, 618).

At the start of *The Return of the Native* 5.8, Hardy again makes readers aware of separate, but co-occurring plot lines. Ominously foreshadowing a concatenation of events, to climax in the deaths of Eustacia and Wildeve in the next chapter, three different lines, of Susan Nonsuch, resumed from 5.7f, Eustacia from 5.7m, and Clym from 5.6m, are held in a single, tenuous view. The effect of this triple superimposition is like the *stretto* passage of a fugue: "While the effigy of Eustacia was melting to nothing, and the fair woman herself was standing on Rainbarrow, her soul in an abyss of desolation seldom plumbed by one so young, Yeobright sat lonely at Blooms-End" (5.8i; [1878] 1975d, 360).

With simultaneous phase, as with most other sequential types, deceptively authentic forms exist. In Conrad's case, the reader may be wary of jumping to conclusions, or employing conventional logic. Since an account of the storm has been consigned to the gap between chapters 5 and 6 of *Typhoon* (1903), the reader is curious to learn of MacWhirr's subsequent epistle: "The hammering and banging of the needful repairs did not disturb Captain MacWhirr. The steward found in the letter he wrote, in a tidy chart-room, passages of such absorbing interest that twice he was nearly caught in the act. But Mrs. MacWhirr, in the drawing-room of the forty-pound house, stifled a yawn—perhaps out of self-respect—for she was alone." (1991, 197).

Syntactic linkage, balanced adverbial phrases and contrasting responses, all within a brief paragraph, suggest simultaneous events. It gradually becomes clear, however, that Mrs. MacWhirr is reading in England the same letter that so absorbs the steward in Fu-chau. To reinforce the reader's disorientation, the steward's exchange with the cook is directly juxtaposed to Mrs. MacWhirr's further skimming over her husband's letter (198). A later reference to newspaper reports of the typhoon two months ago (200), finally establishes the sequential status as that of *false simultaneity*, stylistically abetted by syntactic proximity, and narratively by delayed presentation of temporal data.

Analeptic Phase

> Retournons en arrière, c'est un des droits du narrateur.
>
> [Let us retrace our steps, that being one of the narrator's prerogatives.]
> —Victor Hugo, *Les Misérables*

When the linear impetus of forward phase is checked by a new sequence, which antedates the start of the previous sequence, an *analeptic phase* results. Genette's relatively neutral designation has been adopted, rather than the more familiar "flashback,"[61] with its ambiguous connotations. Analepsis signals the retrospective evocation of an event, and its divisions of *external*, *internal*, and *mixed*, in reference to a work's starting point. The notion of an originating moment or primary story-time, however, is itself by no means unproblematic (Bal 1985, 57; Tambling 1991, 15–16). Since our discussion essentially concerns chapter-to-chapter transitions in a single text, rather than the large-scale sweep of Proust's multivolume work, which is analyzed by Genette, narrative divisions invite further refinement and modification.

The inception of an analeptic phase need not imply a break of narrative continuity. Where the action is homodiegetic, the new segment or chapter resumes those semic and proairetic interests, but relocates them in order of chronology. By this retrograde motion, narrative elements hitherto unmentioned or unelaborated take on the role of motivations or causes, which help to explain or elucidate the most recent stage of events. Where the action is heterodiegetic, continuity involving secondary characters need not be severed by relocation, but the arrival of new characters tends, at their point of introduction, to have an effect of discontinuity.

The fact that new characters make their appearance in an analeptic phase, does, however, suggest the relevance of their temporal relationship. It also hints that their linkage to the main narrative may subsequently prove more than merely tenuous. They may, indeed, come to constitute the main narrative itself. In the opening chapters of *Our Mutual Friend*, Dickens provides a set of counter-examples, in which the marked lack of temporal indices seems to underscore the complete separation from one another of new plots and characters. This lack reinforces the principle of contrast, and raises in readers' minds the very issue of the identity of the main narrative.

It is at such hinge-points as chapter starts, that analeptic, like forward phases, are normally found. Some texts may subdivide chapters, using typographical gaps to project temporal ellipses. In Turgenev's *Fathers and Sons*, double-spacings appear in medial segments of chapters to mark new phases. These range from immediate (8m) to nocturnal continuity (26m), from external analeptic (8m) to parallel phase (22m). By far the favorite position for analeptic phase is as initial segment. Here, the shift away from forward movement can be most clearly registered, if reversion has not already been anticipated at previous chapter end. When analeptic phase functions to unmask an enigma or mystery, it might well occupy a pre-final position, as in *Daniel Deronda* or *Jane Eyre*. Deronda's origins or Rochester's history, at respective three-quarter points of the novels, result in alternative courses for narrative or heroine. In the tradition of *Tom Jones* and *Oliver Twist*, secrets may be preserved until a final stage, to be revealed as *external* analeptic phases. *Great Expectations*, by contrast, at its close, exemplifies the *internal* form. Pip's identification of his benefactor can also be viewed as *paralipsis*, since from the outset, on grounds of narrative suspense, Pip-as-narrator withholds Magwitch's name.

If analepsis occurs early in a text, it is almost always external, as so little material will have been presented. It may likewise convey a sense that the sooner preliminaries can be discharged, the more quickly the main narrative can be broached. Henceforth, no turning back becomes a literal motto for works that, an initial reversion apart, scarcely deviate again from linearity. Despite the disjointed movement of Flaubert's *L'Education sentimentale*, for instance, the only significant retrograde phase belongs to 1.2 ([1869] 1965, 30). The brief account of Charles Deslauriers's father from 1818 onwards, soon gives way to the dated starting point of 1840.

Scarcely begun, Fontane's *Unwiederbringlich* almost immediately moves back seventeen years, in a retrospective of Holk's marriage. This crosses the first chapter gap ([1891] 1963d, 571), before the narrative instance of 1859 is reestablished, and the action goes unswervingly forward. With Flaubert and Fontane, analepsis at so early a juncture only underscores the fact, that it represents the sole example in each novel.

Different grounds prompt other analeptic positioning. The rarity of the phase in James's *Portrait of a Lady* (1881), makes its presence especially revealing. Thus, details of Isabel Archer (ch. 4), Ralph Touchett (ch. 5) and Caspar Goodwood (ch. 13) are sketched in at medial segments of those chapters, as if to avoid the convention of chapter-start portraiture or retrogression. Another biographer, in *Der Landvogt von Greifensee* (1877), Keller's framework *novelle*, organizes Salomon Landolt's five love affairs in chronological succession, though all are external analepses in relation to the opening scene.

Such an arrangement promotes clarity and orderliness: "Wir wollen die Geschichten nacherzählen, jedoch alles ordentlich einteilen, abrunden und für unser Verständnis einrichten"[62] (1944, 170). By contrast, analepsis may be virtually absent until a work's final chapters. It is then that Scott, precinematically, leads up to the climax of *Guy Mannering*, by switching back and forth between the Mannering and Bertram plots, before both fuse in the culminating chapter 50 ([1815] 1968, 358).

As well as textual position, the temporal and spatial extent of analeptic phase merits attention. By "amplitude," however, Genette refers to the level of events, the "durée d'histoire" (Genette 1972, 89), rather than level of presentation, just as "portée" connotes the temporal reach of the anachrony from the most recent narrative. The proportion of chapter or total work which analepsis occupies, is, nonetheless, a significant factor in determining narrative momentum and rhythm. When the reversion is considerable in scale, it may imply the sheer weight that past events exert over present, as Proust attests. Tiny, by comparison, Theodor Storm's *Immensee* (1851), as a framework *novelle*, shows no less, in its own ratios of forward to retrograde movement (1:16), the overwhelming force of lyrical and elegiac feeling engendered by the past.

In a microsequential example of analeptic phase, Ambrosio's designs on Antonia, in Matthew Lewis's *The Monk* 2.4i ([1796] 1973, 256), resume from the penultimate subsegment of the previous chapter (2.3f1), since the closing subsegment, 2.3f2, records her reactions to his visit. Both Lemm and Lisa have single chapters devoted to their careers, in Turgenev's *A House of Gentlefolk*, whereas the lengthy treatment, by external analepsis, of Lavretsky, takes up nine successive chapters (chs. 8→16; [1858] 1970, 23–53). These far exceed the framework of the opening section, to create an expository imbalance.

Eliot's strategy in *Daniel Deronda* (1876) is to devote the first quarter of a much longer novel to large-scale exposition. Bridging the interval of eighteen chapters, between Gwendolen's return from Leubronn and arrival back in Offendene, two external analepses convey the year-long relations of Grandcourt and herself (chs. 3–14), another the history of Deronda from boyhood on (chs. 16–20). Balzac's approach in *Ursule Mirouët* is similar, but proportionately more substantial. Opening on a Sunday in 1829, he early announces "une espèce d'intitulé d'inventaire"[63] (1.2i; [1841] 1965, 464), and proceeds to a historical review of the eighteenth century and of Ursule's origins. Only with Savinien's arrival at the end of part 1 is the exposition concluded, though the novel is already half over.

In multiplot novels, the general function of analeptic phase is to revert to stages at which a plot line was suspended by the entry of other characters or events, and to resume that line. The frequency of such returns, in so commanding a generic model as *War and Peace*, foregrounds the role of specific figures. At various points, the narrative moves back to take up the fortunes of Natasha, Prince Andrei or Petya, but it is Pierre Bezuhov who, in nearly twenty instances, ranging from a chapter up to the whole of book 2, part 4, becomes the focus of analepsis, testifying to his central role in a complex interweave. The reader's sense of narrative density is not only affected by expansiveness, but also by sequential contrast.

Close proximity of different types of phase in the space of a few chapters, can help to reproduce the momentum of distinct, interlocked events. On the Friday preceding Jem's trial, Gaskell's *Mary Barton* follows a parallel phase with three successive analepses of varying types (chs. 18–21). These suggest the contrasting activities of the Carsons, Mary, Job and Esther, and update each plot line, before an immediate span accelerates events toward the fatal Tuesday in court. Fielding too, in preparing for the dénouement of *Tom Jones*, makes use of sequential variety in his penultimate book 17. By alternating between types of analeptic and proximate phase, he distributes the action between Sophia, and incarcerated Tom.

The inclusion of documents, especially letters, within the narrative, can subtly dislocate forward movement, by directing attention back to past actions which impinge on present situations. With Richardson or Laclos, epistolary conventions represent the norms that readers adjust to and assimilate, but their combination with other forms of discourse often introduces greater complexity.[64] Since few letters in fiction are usually written and perused as rapidly as is Captain Wentworth's by Anne Elliot, in Austen's *Persuasion* 2.11 ([1818] 1971b, 441–42), the discrete periods of epistolary composition, despatch, receipt and reaction deserve consideration.

An incident can be as minimal and seemingly commonplace, as in Trollope's *The Warden*: "The evening before [the warden] went he wrote a note to the Archdeacon" (16i2; [1855] 1973, 150). It may entail narrative loops back and forth, to ascertain a particular exchange, as with Vavasor's letters to Alice, her feelings and replies, in Trollope's *Can You Forgive Her?* ([1864] 1986, 331–56). Rendered by textual position (30m→31i→32i→30f/32f1→32f3→32m), the series suggests how analepsis, in so reliable a linearist as Trollope, can project emotional fluctuations through temporal sequence.

With analeptic phase, the sequential status of chapter-segment and chapter-whole comes into clear focus, where the narrative engages more than a single character. Both Arthur Donnithorne and the Rev. Irwine enter Hall Farm at 6i in *Adam Bede*, but at 6m attention switches to Arthur and Hetty, continuing with them up to 7f, when the former leaves the dairy. Irwine and Dinah then feature at 8i, in an analeptic phase which directly resumes from 6m. The two plot lines converge again at 8m, with an almost verbatim repetition of 7f: "Captain Donnithorne . . . came out of the dairy" ([1859] 1981, 137–38). As a whole, chapter 8 seems a delayed presentation of immediate continuity. That status depends on whether our perspective is that of strict contiguity of chapter start to chapter end (8i:7f), or of chapter–whole in relation to previous chapters, and as corollary to the bifurcation of narrative lines at 6m.

In an example from *War and Peace*, that division of interest relates to the same character, but in separate terms of recounted experience, and of physical presence. At 3.3.31f, Natasha tends the wounded Andrei after the Battle of Borodino: "He smiled and held out his hand to her" ([1869] 1973b, 1087). The initial segment of the new chapter, via internal analepsis, returns to the battlefield, until, in its medial segment, the point reached at 3.3.31f is immediately resumed after the opening delay: "Prince Andrei fetched a sigh of relief, smiled and held out his hand" (3.3.32m; 1091). This dual or ambivalent status is echoed in other works, which may combine different phases, such as nocturnal and analeptic.

Chapter 36 of Turgenev's *Virgin Soil* ([1877] 1969, 294) takes up after a night's lapse the concerns of Mariana and Nejdanov from 33f, continues 34m in temporal terms, but discontinues the plot line of Sipiagin and Paklin from the close of chapter 35. Essentially, the whole issue of sequential status here has to do with different types of continuity: the first dealing in absolute terms of clock, calendar and public time; the second, in relative terms of continuity in character appearance. These dual functions complicate as well as enrich works of fiction.

Bifurcation of narrative lines is taken further in *Anna Karenina*, where the priority of the most advanced temporal action frames no fewer than three separate but interconnected analeptic phases. Levin's epiphanic glimpse of Kitty after his night on the haycock (3.12), gives way to eleven chapters which resume events at the steeplechase, before the frame closes with Levin's considered reflection of life (3.24; [1877] 1973a, 300–346). In those chapters, the varied reactions of Karenin (3.13→14), Anna (3.15→18) and Vronsky (3.19→21), to the calamitous fall of Frou-Frou and its rider, are continued from book 2. Its aftermath is then recorded in meetings between Anna and her lover (3.22), and husband (3.23). All the enframed chapters, though successive in relation to one another, remain analeptic in relation to the most advanced action, represented by Levin.

Another instance of internal analepsis, though less involved than Tolstoy's trifurcation, relates to the segment of a chapter which is itself analeptic, measured from the most recent narrative. In an English multiplot novel, Thackeray regresses nine chapters, to continue Becky Sharp's adventures in chapter 64 of *Vanity Fair*, only to comment in its medial segment, that by mentioning her life in Florence, "we are advancing matters" ([1848] 1950, 674). The following eight pages then retrograde, in order to update her history.

By contrast with this doubling, exemplifying *internal analepsis within internal analepsis*, Manzoni establishes the episode of Lucia at the monastery as most advanced stage, in *The Betrothed*

(9i; [1827] 1972, 166). This subsequently frames an external analeptic account of nun Gertrude's history, continuing, via proximate phase, into the new chapter (9m→10m). In relative terms, chapter end (9f) and chapter start (10i) are unified by their treatment of the same character; in absolute terms, the account is analeptic to the scene at 9i.

While the temporal distance from the most advanced stage of narrative, ranges from external to an immediate form of internal analepsis (whereby an earlier sequence is resumed as if ignoring the presence of intervening chapters), a scale of relative precision may be introduced. From *Don Quixote* onwards, authorial narrators variously underline the analeptic movement. Fielding, in *Tom Jones* 10.8, by chapter title ("In Which the History Goes Backward"), and specific text reference: "Before we proceed any farther in our history, it may be proper to look a little back in order to account for the extraordinary appearance of Sophia and her father at the inn at Upton. The reader may be pleased to remember that in the ninth chapter of the seventh book" ([1749] 1963, 467).

Sterne, motivated more by wit, is even more detailed in *Tristram Shandy* 3.31, alluding to the "fifty-second page of the second volume of this book of books" ([1767] 1967, 225). Scott seems more genuinely informative, pointing out in *The Heart of Midlothian*, that "our history unites itself with that part of the narrative which broke off at the end of the fifteenth chapter" (18i; [1818] 1954, 194).

In a novel such as *The Old Curiosity Shop*, published by installments, and with interwoven plot lines, Dickens feels his responsibility to readers. He makes explicit allusion, at the start of chapter 38, to Kit's absence for the last fifteen chapters ([1841] 1985b, 362). In another exact allusion, at the three-quarter point of *Virgin Soil*, Turgenev not only stresses narratorial self-consciousness and challenges the reader's acuity, but also raises the issue of development and progress in the narrative thus far: "A few moments later Mashurina appeared in the doorway, in the same dress in which we saw her at the beginning of the first chapter" (30f; [1877] 1969, 248).

Two illustrations from Trollope's *Can You Forgive Her?* convey differing degrees of specificity. The first enables the reader to discover easily a textual occasion: "Early in that conversation which Mr Vavasor had with his daughter, and which was recorded a few pages back" (36i; [1864] 1986, 385). The second, in many ways more typical of fiction in general, is far less precise, alluding merely to an earlier period during which other events co-occurred: "We must go back for a few pages to scenes which happened in London during this summer" (71i; 734).

ALTERNATE PHASE

While instances of internal analepsis generally exceed external, one reason may be the common occurrence of a sequence which resumes events from the last-but-one, or occasionally from the third previous chapter. This special category is *alternate phase*. Often a succession of such phases appears, interweaving separate plot lines, but at relatively close proximity and at regular intervals. The notion of symmetry in the use of alternate phase may be extended to entire works.

E. T. A. Hoffmann's novel *Kater Murr* (1821) is exemplary, in its alternation between the sectional units of the tomcat's autobiography, semantically and syntactically continuous, and Kreisler's biography, fragmentary and disjointed, having served the feline vandal as pad and blotter. Breaks in this *Doppelroman* produce a range of ironic effects, with sudden suspensions and comical contrasts of theme, resulting from the jagged transitions from one narrative section to the next.

With multiplot novels, alternate phase may shift narrative interest between various participants, after they have been observed together as a group, and have then gone their separate ways. In Trollope's *Barchester Towers*, the lengthy and crucial Ullathorne party ([1857] 1981, 318–86) is one such assembly, so that further developments in the Eleanor (42f→44i), and Stanhope plot lines (42f→45i) date from that event. Even in early chapters, a title-figure is not guaranteed unwavering attention. In *Adam Bede*, the hero's progress is soon broken by chapter 3, devoted to Dinah and Seth ([1859] 1981, 77), so that Adam's course runs 2f→4i.

Other instances of alternate phase interrupt a lengthy sequence by returning to another set of events, thereby ensuring variety and suggesting continued activity at different levels. In *Tom Jones* 8.2 ([1749] 1963, 342), Fielding resumes a narrative from the final chapter of the previous book (7.15), since the opening of book 8 contains the customary essay by an authorial narrator. His counterpart in Fowles's *FLW* offers *narratorial alternate phase*. He reassesses the heroine (9i; [1969] 1970, 46), at a gap of three chapters from his explanation as to why Sarah became Mrs. Poulteney's companion (6f).

In some cases, a sequence may resume so directly from the point at which an earlier sequence left off, that a separate category of *im-*

mediate alternate phase operates. Its effect is one of tautness; the length or novelty of an intervening chapter often functions as a comparative rest or contrast of pace, before a more dramatic plot line is continued. A cliffhanging close to Hugo's *Notre-Dame de Paris* (10.7f), sees Quasimodo's vain search for Esmeralda: "Lorsqu'il entra dans la cellule, il la trouva vide"[65] ([1831] 1959, 521). This is followed, across the book divide, by the longest chapter of the novel, which employs normal alternate phase (11.1→10.6), to record how the poet Gringoire has "rescued" the gypsy-girl. In the next chapter, an immediate alternate phase directly resumes the hunchback's plot line from 10.7: "Quand Quasimodo vit que la cellule était vide"[66] (11.2; 557), initiating developments which culminate in Claude Frollo's plunge to his death.

A *narratorial* version of *immediate alternate phase* appears in Dickens's *Nicholas Nickleby*. This example shows a self-conscious precision, as well as affording help to the reader at the start of a new periodical installment. The sequence at 56i is directly resumed from 54f: "The course which these adventures shape out for themselves and imperatively call upon the historian to observe, now demands that they should revert to the point they attained previous to the commencement of the last chapter" ([1839] 1985a, 832). Here, the allusion is to the aftermath of Bray's death and Madeline's removal by Nicholas.

Further subcategories include *delayed* versions of *alternate* and *immediate alternate phase*. As with forward phases, readers are made uncertain at chapter start about exact sequential relations with previous chapters. Five paragraphs, for instance, detailing places of refuge in medieval France, must elapse before Hugo allows his hunchback to bring Esmeralda to the Cathedral cell (9.2→8.6; [1831] 1959, 418).

ANALEPTIC OVERLAP

When a phase returns to a juncture after the narrative starting-point, but prior to the previous chapter, then exceeds the temporal limit of the most advanced stage, an *internal analeptic overlap* occurs. Such leapfrogging or advance by initial reversion, hints that a plot line is significant by virtue of its overtaking competitors, and then, by its own impetus, taking on the status of leader. Chapter 11 of Iris Murdoch's *The Sandcastle* ([1957] 1972, 184) ends as Nan runs away, surprising both her husband and Rain. 12i returns to a period anterior to 11i, traces the source of Nan's suspicions, but then follows her flight to Tim Burke and her emotional return home. Her plot line proceeds, therefore, beyond that of Mor and Rain, and establishes itself as the most advanced.

Three successive overlaps, in Gaskell's *Mary Barton*, register the increasingly frantic tempo of events on the weekend before Jem's trial. Mary's sense of urgency is conveyed by making her plot line at 19i into an *immediate analeptic overlap* : "I left Mary, on that same Thursday night" ([1848] 1983, 267). Directly resuming her activity from 17f, this surpasses the Carsons's line in chapter 18, as if to stress that acquittal of the accused will be determined by the heroine's energy and efforts alone.

External analeptic overlap, like Genette's *mixed analepsis*, begins prior to and continues after the original starting point. It then, by contrast, goes on to exceed the most forward stage of the narrative, and in its sweeping movement, has large dramatic force, particularly when concentrated within the tight limits of a framework *novelle*. Thus, a grandmother's rambling tale of youthful love and tragedy in the past, becomes suddenly relevant to the narrative instance in Brentano's *Kasperl und Annerl*. Still incomplete, the tale's closure lies within the present hour, when it emerges that execution awaits Annerl ([1817] 1970, 369), a fate that desperate steps by the outer-frame narrator fail to prevent.

Hardy's *Mayor of Casterbridge*, by contrast, offers the less intense *narratorial internal overlap*. Following Henchard's surprise (21f), that his stepdaughter is leaving him so soon, and for Lucetta's High-Place Hall, of all places, the narrator opens a new chapter by motivating the mayor's puzzlement: "We go back for a moment to the preceding night, to account for Henchard's attitude" (22i; [1886] 1975c, 166). Thereafter, those reasons presented, a further note to him from Lucetta indicates that the Henchard plot line has overtaken that of Elizabeth-Jane, and become the most advanced stage.

From categories of transition, however, we now shift to a series of specific case studies (§2.1–4), in which these same categories and other aspects of temporal and continuity relations find detailed application.

2

Practice: Four Case Studies of Sequential Dynamics

IN THE CASE STUDIES THAT FOLLOW, VARIOUS ASPECTS OF SEQUENTIAL dynamics are explored in texts from the early nineteenth to the late twentieth century. Jane Austen's last novel represents a "classic" work by a canonic English author, which can nonetheless benefit from being viewed from a sequential perspective. Nearly a century later, Natsume Sōseki, a Japanese novelist with as high a rank in his own country, produces a work organized around a key sequential device, allying his novel with international currents.

A French-African work by the Ivoirian novelist Ahmadou Kourouma in the 1970s, which has taken on key status in its own region and national culture, fosters analogies of technical and thematic interplay. One of the best-known English novels of the 1980s, by Graham Swift, finally, involves considerable complexities of transition and articulation, which expand and enrich taxonomic boundaries.

TEMPORALITY AS PLOT: JANE AUSTEN, *PERSUASION*

> But seven years I suppose are enough to change every pore of
> one's skin, & every feeling of one's mind.
> —Jane Austen, *Letters*

Gladly yielding his charge to the care of a willing escort, Charles Musgrove hurries off to the gunsmith's, while Captain Wentworth and Anne Elliot withdraw to a quiet path. Here, in an untypically complex statement for Jane Austen, it is noted that, "the power of conversation would make the present hour a blessing indeed; and prepare for it all the immortality which the happiest recollections of their own future lives could bestow" ([1818] 1971b, 444). With privileged hindsight, the narrator can confirm, as hero and heroine

125

cannot, the enduring impact of the moment, projecting it beyond the writing-Now, and suggesting by fusion of time planes its climactic centrality in the novel.

This explicit illustration from the penultimate chapter (2.11) of *Persuasion*, hints at what is implicit throughout. The force of time (Duffy 1954), its losses and gains (Wilhelm 1979, 91), its effects on ideolects of speech and thought (Burrows 1987, 211), and a prevailing sense of the past (Wolfe 1971) help account for the novel's atmosphere and appeal. Austen's last complete work is also the only one with a plot involving "considerable temporal complexity" (Kroeber 1971, 79). Its climax, and *Persuasion* as a whole, can be examined from the manner in which its temporal, as well as its plot elements develop.

Determinacy

One way of identifying temporal data is to conceive a scale that modulates from *specific* to *indeterminate*. Along it, a given item finds a place appropriate to its own relative degree of precision. From the unparticularized "one day," to the highly discrete "on Monday 13 July 1814 at 8.30 A.M.," a series of gradually more informative statements can be constructed. Not only *temporal locus*: the juncture at which a narrative sequence begins, but also *temporal lapse*: the interval preceding or succeeding another sequence ("shortly after"—"several days after"—"five days after"), and *temporal accumulation* ("young"—"in her twenties"—"twenty-seven years old") allow this relative determinacy.

Further distinctions can be made between *direct* and *indirect specific* data; the sole indication of month in *Persuasion* 1.3, is to quarter sessions at Taunton. Seemingly obscure, the allusion identifies a period in June. *External* and *internal specific* data can be separated. Events in Austen frequently relate not to clock or calendar time, but to other events such as visits, balls, dinners, parties, internal to the narrative. Specific internal reference, common since Cervantes, whereby a narrator indicates a particular chapter or page, is, however, rare in Austen. Other distinctions, between *recurrent* and *nonrecurrent* aspects, may contrast the annual return of a month and season, with the unique appearance of a dated year and a historical event.

In its first paragraph, *Persuasion* contains the time capsule of the Elliot family's entry in the Baronetage: a laconic documentation of Sir Walter's offspring, and mirror of his vanity. By including the detail of a "still-born son, November 5, 1789," Austen's attention to minutiae is early evident. This date hints at the frustrated desire for a successor, motivates the presence of the heir-presumptive Mr. Elliot, and prefigures the acquisition in Captain Frederick Wentworth of a son-surrogate as the result of events in another November, twenty-five years later. Without the temporal locus of 1.1 as "the summer of 1814," (232), however, the force of this specificity of births, marriages, and deaths would be largely lost.

The locus of the crucial 1.4 as "the summer of 1806" (247) is then similarly determined, so that temporal underscore motivic parallels. By far the most explicit markers are in 1.6 and 2.6: 29 September as the Crofts' arrival at Kellynch, 1 February, Mary's letter about Louisa and Benwick's engagement. Symmetrically positioned at the exact quarter and three-quarter stages of the novel, each chapter anticipates Wentworth's immediate arrival, via a sister (Mrs. Croft) and a supposed fiancée (Louisa). Apart from references to November (1.10,11) and Christmas holidays (2.2), the above are the sole explicit dates of the novel. Their sparse though strategic distribution means that most chapters depend on these few loci for their temporal bearings, and relate to these fixed points concomitantly, prospectively or retrospectively.[1]

Specific data of temporal locus and lapse can be represented by rhetorical reiterations, which appear where present-time markers are weak and earlier time-levels predominate. The example of the thirteen years since Lady Elliot's death and Elizabeth's assumption of her mother's role (1.1), rehearses from the outset the passage of time and its disappointments, while hinting at the possible fate of the second unmarried daughter. In 1.4, tracing the episode of 1806, Anne's age at that time is thrice repeated, before returning subtly modified: "Anne, at seven and twenty, thought very differently from what she had been made to think at nineteen" (250).

Her first meeting with Frederick is viewed largely through her own impressions, and lexical repetition reveals an agitation despite herself: " 'It is over! it is over!' she repeated to herself again, and again, in nervous gratitude. 'The worst is over!' . . . Eight years, almost eight years had passed, since all had been given up. . . . What might not eight years do? . . . Alas! with all her reasonings, she found, that to retentive feelings eight years may be little more than nothing" (278–79). Barely two pages later, in an account of their first evening, the counterpoint of past and present is reinforced by triple reference to the year of their engagement. Characteristically, the final specific reiteration, thrice alluding to the last hour of the concert (2.8), conveys Anne's impatience for a further exchange with him, but now refers to future rather than past, hope rather than sorrow.

In terms of temporal accumulation, it is more essential than in any other Austen novel to know the heroine's precise age. A biographical hypothesis of Jane Austen's own broken romance around 1802 at the age of twenty-seven, has been linked with the identical age of Charlotte Lucas on her engagement to Mr. Collins (Litz 1976, 229). Marianne Dashwood in *Sense and Sensibility*, solemnly disclaims the pretensions of such "advanced" years: " 'A woman of seven and twenty . . . can never hope to feel or inspire affection again. . . . [Any marriage] would be a compact of convenience . . . a commercial exchange' " ([1811] 1970c, 32).

Anne's "danger" is apparent from the first, whereas the ages of Frederick and Elliot, being less critical, are delayed until the second volume. The reader's knowledge that she is the oldest as well as the last of Austen's heroines, allows comparative measurement of her emotional maturity. A running counterpoint, emphasized by rhetorical reiteration, of the eight years' lapse since the broken courtship at nineteen, adds to *Persuasion* a dimension lacking in Austen's other novels.[2] Her specific dating of its action is again unique. This distinction (direct/external/nonrecurrent), as opposed to the allusions to quarter sessions (indirect/external/recurrent) and the "peace" (indirect/external/nonrecurrent), has several motivations.

Historically, by occupying a calendar period between June 1814 and February 1815, the novel unrolls in the hiatus of military activity between Napoleon's exile to Elba, and his return to France. This fortuitous lull affords Austen's naval men their shore leave during which to secure wives, and lends credibility to their novelistic presence. By specifying a year, the deaths of Fanny Harville and Mr. Smith in 1813, and that of Mrs. Elliot earlier in 1814, gain in temporal relief. Future debates on the use of particular years' calendars are also thoughtfully avoided.[3] Austen's writing-Now, barely twelve months' remove from the fictional events she chronicles, enables her to suggest an unusual sense of tension. This is heightened by resort to a present tense in the closing chapter, to vague apprehensions of "the dread of a future war" and "the tax of quick alarm" (455), in a projected period into which she herself was not to survive.[4]

Ordering

Only *Persuasion* diverges significantly from the relatively unelaborated linearity of Austen's other novels.[5] Its key episode and thematic trigger is prenarrative, anterior to the starting point of summer 1814 (1.1). No hint of the broken engagement in 1806 occurs until 1.4, so that its brief account carries special force. This constitutes a major *analepsis*, semantically and in the accelerated effect of its *page/time ratio*. The account gains expressiveness by its role as a confidence exchanged between narrator and reader. It is the incomplete reverberations from this dated prenarrative episode that govern the arrangement of the text, and finally bring it to completion.

Another major analepsis occurs at an identical juncture measured from the end of the novel (2.9). Here, Mrs. Smith's disclosure of Elliot's infamy must be seen as major in its decelerated page/time ratio, rather than semantically. In the climactic 2.11, *internal* and *external* analepses combine in a major return that balances narrative paraphrase with direct speech, paginal/temporal with semantic importance. Elsewhere in Austen, analepsis is nearly always internal.

Persuasion is unusual, therefore, not only in its strategic use of external analepsis to highlight the binding force of the past, but also in its impulse to recapture or re-create the emotions of that past. The seeming paradox of forging a narrative future out of a prenarrative past, can be linguistically charted in the microcosm of protagonist reactions. With much of the novel seen from Anne's perspective, the reader penetrates her inner workings in a way not permitted with Wentworth.[6]

The completion in 2.11 of the couple's emotional exchange, however, has been prefigured in the major analepsis of 1.4, where a narrative paraphrase by its very ambiguity covers the situation to date and, proleptically, that at the close. Such a *synopsis-sentence* (Fowler 1977, 23) reflects in its ordering of clauses and phrases, the temporal and causal sequence of the whole text of the novel: "She had been forced into prudence in her youth, she learned romance as she grew older—the natural sequel of an unnatural beginning" (251).

As micronarrative, the past perfect tense and passive voice, the denotation of outside pressure and ironic connotation of prescribed accommodation in the first clause, summarize the content of the chapter, and posit its relationship to the time plane of surrounding chapters. The second clause restates the same paradox of future sought in past, and encapsulates Anne's lot for the remaining twenty chapters, which couple temporal progress with emotional growth. Through chiasmus, the proposition—the reversal of usual sequence from romance to prudence—receives further linguistic stress. The whole novel can be seen to embody the "natural sequel" of which the analeptic 1.4 represents the "unnatural beginning."

Continuity

In comparative terms, *Persuasion* has by far the smallest total of *continuous phases* (whether immediate, proximate, or nocturnal), the smallest percentage relative to its chapters, the fewest *continuity spans*. Its largest span and most extensive page coverage of a single day are likewise dwarfed by other novels of Austen.[7] The small scale of *Persuasion*, however, must again be recalled. Thus, its single-day coverage represents a higher proportion of the total novel than in *Emma*. Its longest day takes in the exposé of Elliot, and Anne's reactions during the critical final period; that in *Emma*, the exposé of only the first of its heroine's self-deceptions.

The internal distribution and relationship to content of continuous phases need also to be considered. In *Persuasion*, the six-chapter span includes the only *simultaneous* phase in Austen, thus pointing up the increasing momentum of events, and it constitutes the novel's whole final section (2.6–11). Its seventy-three pages, almost one-third of the total, are exceeded only by the eighty-eight pages of the eleven-chapter span in *Northanger Abbey* (1.6–2.1). This, unlike the span in *Persuasion*, does not account for the tension of the climax, but only the mechanical sequence of social engagements. Few in number, the *continuity ties* in *Persuasion* are strategically disposed, signaling the more fluent motions and gathering impetus of the novel's second half, by spanning volumes one and two, as well as the third and fourth quarters.[8] The page spans of the four juxtaposed phases reflect, furthermore, the relative importance of their content.[9]

In terms of *chapter ellipsis*, the gaps of a single night dividing 1.10–15 of *Northanger Abbey* have a regularity that threatens to become tedious. By contrast, the sudden arrival and equally sudden departure of Willoughby, in *Sense and Sensibility* (3.8) are dramatically accentuated by reducing the degree of ellipsis between 3.7–8 and 3.8–9 close to zero. The overall pattern of such *immediate transitions* in *Sense and Sensibility* reveals a gradual increase between volumes, from 1 to 3 to 5; in *Northanger Abbey* and *Persuasion*, similarly, 1 to 3. A dramatic, *narratorial transition*, however, announces the crucial analepsis (1.4) in *Persuasion:*

. . . as she walked along a favourite grove, [Anne] said, with a gentle sigh, "a few months more, and *he*, perhaps, may be walking here." (1.3; 247)

Chapter IV

He was not Mr. Wentworth, the former curate of Monkford . . . but a captain Frederick Wentworth, his brother, who . . . had come into Somersetshire, in the summer of 1806. (1.4; 247)

Each quarter of the novel shows a steady growth in the degree and frequency of *determinate* chapter ellipsis, projecting a steady increase in the number and closeness of significant events. Of the five ellipses prior to the last chapter of the final quarter, all are explicitly determinate. The gathering concentration of the elliptical rhythm: night/several hours/night/immediately/ night, temporally articulates the narrative events culminating in 2.11. Here, the technical features of the final continuous phase and the last specific ellipsis coincide, to reinforce Austen's thematic resolution of the novel: "for the first time she was constructing a dramatic and emotional climax, an intensification of the heroine's experience, achieved suddenly, and in circumstances that affect her whole future" (Southam 1964, 92).

Tempo

An appreciation of narrative *tempo* presupposes a notion of the scale of a work. Shifts within a long novel, for instance, differ proportionately in significance from those in a short story. The mere 228 pages of *Persuasion* directly reverse the trend for each successive Austen novel to increase in size.[10] One corollary, is that its two longest chapters extend to twice the average for Austen, and are her longest. Such expansive articulation of narrative units has to be seen in the context of the comparatively brief compass of *Persuasion* as a whole.

Since its time span of eight months represents Austen's norm, the average number of weeks occupied by each chapter is proportionately the highest, nearly twice that of *Emma* and three times that of *Northanger Abbey*. It is against this background that the remarkable deceleration of pace in the closing chapters of *Persuasion*, corresponding to the force of events, needs to be judged. Even allowing for the indeterminacy of time spans, it is evident that four of the six novels lay greatest weight, in terms of slackening *page/ time ratios*, on their final volumes, so that narrative climax and temporal expansiveness coincide.

In her last completed novel, Jane Austen almost doubles the ratio of pages to week between volumes 1 and 2.[11] *Persuasion* falls conveniently into four equal parts, each of six chapters; their page/week ratios are striking: 45:14; 60:6; 50:12; 73:1.5. The final quarter, by far the longest, thus accounts for ten days in its seventy-three pages, making it temporally the most densely compact sequence in Austen, to match its narrative status as the most emotionally charged resolution in her work.

A strong argument for seeing *Persuasion* as quadripartite, is the pivotal role of the sixth, twelfth, and eighteenth chapters. These occupy, up to the three-quarter mark, the greatest narrative space, and fittingly close each part. Chapters 2.9–11 in the fourth quarter contain the longest adjacent span (53 pp.), nearly one-quarter of the total, as well as Austen's longest individual chapter (19 pp.). In view of the redundancy of Mrs. Smith's evidence (2.9), and of a suggestion that the new final paragraph of the novel hints at the writer's own uneasiness about that figure's role (Southam 1964, 97), it might be surmised that later revisions would have shortened the chapter, and retained the more dramatic, climactic 2.11 as longest.

Aside from fluctuations in sheer chapter length and in the allotment of narrative time to particular divisions, there are necessarily variations of narrative space to account for identical units of time. By examining comparable segments, tendencies of temporal expansion or contraction can foreground underlying narrative concerns. The single evening spent by Anne attending Mary's sick child, takes up 3.5 paragraphs (1.7); her first evening in Wentworth's company, topic of the next chapter (1.8), swells to 9.5 pages; the interview and insights of the concert evening stretch chapter 2.8 to 10 pages.

With the unit of a week, an effect of progressive temporal expansion is even more patent. A solitary paragraph crystallizes the melancholy week spent by Anne at Kellynch Lodge (1.5). An expectant week, with the retarding moment of little Charles's fall, occupies six pages of 1.7, before Frederick's brief appearance and Anne's reaction mark a sudden change of pace. Another week, embracing a fall and its consequences, takes up almost four times as many pages (23 pp.) and two whole chapters (1.12–2.1). The novel's final ten days bring the movement of narrative and temporal expansion to a culmination, by allocating no fewer than sixty-nine pages (2.7–11) to the preparation and realization of the couple's reunion.

Even isolated spans elastically alternate from extensive flux to intensive focus. The "few minutes" of Frederick's first appearance at

Uppercross Cottage (1.7), and of his intervention on Anne's behalf (1.9), the eventful hour on the Lower Cobb (1.12) represent such sudden movements of temporal intensity. At such junctures, the page/time ratio assumes immediate relevance. If Anne's reference to the "last ten minutes" of her interview with Wentworth at the concert is taken literally (2.8), the span would virtually be the densest in all Austen,[12] its compression being externally motivated by the demands of a public, social occasion. In the climax of 2.11, by contrast, there are no temporal restrictions on the lovers' meeting. A heightened tempo must be inferred from the statement, that Anne's eyes "devoured" Frederick's letter. Their subsequent walk takes place in a literal flux of circumambient activity, of which both are as unconscious as of the flux of time.

While dialogue offers the closest model of a metronomic norm, it is by contrasting the length, frequency, and distribution of speech segments with those of other forms of discourse, that some notion of *relative isochrony* results. In Austen's six novels, dialogue accounts for a little less than half (44 percent) of the total; in *Emma*, the proportion reaches 53 percent, but drops in *Persuasion* to a low of 35 percent. Her last novel obviously lacks its irrepressible Miss Bates and its talkative Emma. The accent is now displaced from idyllic to elegiac. Continuous transcript yields to dialogue with narrative interpolation; the action of memory in a more sensitive and already mature heroine ensures that the interior vision predominates.

Because indirect speech and free indirect style convey more authentically Anne's character, direct speech occurs more rarely than in previous novels. This fact reinforces a thematic concern with the relationship of two time planes, rather than the attempt to dramatize a single time plane by shortening the gap between text and clock-time to *near-isochrony*. It is also appropriate that *Persuasion* has only a single instance of dialogue at chapter start (compared with three in *Emma* and *Sense and Sensibility*), and three examples at chapter end (compared with ten). Equally fitting, however, in this most reflective of Austen's novels, is the fact that *Persuasion* has three chapters, more than in any other work, which close with *unmediated thought:* the heroine's in 1.3 and 2.8, the hero's in 1.7.

Despite the purely narrative mode of the final epilogue-chapter (2.12), the last quarter has the highest proportion of dialogue (48 percent) in the novel. Thus, it completes a constant pattern of increase from quarter to quarter.[13] It includes not only the chapter with the highest proportion of direct speech (1.9: 75 percent), but also the most sustained span of chapters employing dialogue

(1.9–11: 75, 38, and 54 percent, respectively), particularly striking in the light of the humble overall proportion for *Persuasion* vis-à-vis the other novels.

These three chapters, which bind Mrs. Smith's revelations to Anne with the rapprochement between Anne and Frederick, suggest by their high proportion of speech, how the characters themselves take command of the narrative, and the narrator retires behind Anne's inner vision. If the linkage between the near-isochrony of dialogue and the dramatic intensification of the present is a valid one, the high speech levels of 2.9–11 faithfully render the novel's thematic development.

This proceeds from an early alternation of past and present, marked by low occurrence of speech, to the later stages of its climax, when time planes converge and then fuse, while emotional directness all but annuls temporal awareness. In her rewriting of this episode, Jane Austen significantly changed the first manuscript's reported speech into direct speech, thus heightening the vehemence of Wentworth's self-condemnation (Southam 1964, 91). She also reinforces the larger implications of isochrony.

TECHNICAL/FORMAL TEMPORALITY

Most fiction uses past or preterite tense as narrative norm, so that the writing present or *narrative instance* (Brooke-Rose 1977, 528–31) is situated at a temporal remove from the events recorded. This *ulterior* type (Genette 1972, 228–38) can, however, exploit the convergence between the narrative and the *act of narration*. At various junctures, the preterite norm favored by Austen is interrupted by brief present-tense, "atemporal" statements that question "universal truths" or serve as moral *pointes*. Two larger occasions stand out.

The account of the party's arrival at Lyme (1.11; 311–12) abruptly shifts in mid-sentence from past to present, specific afternoon to general prospect, as the charms of the surrounding area are dwelt on in two unusually long enumerative sentences. A transient out-of-season visit becomes a permanent topography evoked through a roving all-season optic; a desolate town gives way to a lyrical eulogy delivered, in the heroine's stead, by an informed and sensitive narrator. Even landscape features seem anthropomorphized, and the age-old spectacle at Pinny likewise preserves its freshness through the use of present-tense verbs.

On the second occasion of *tense deviance*, two figures become detached from the group in the final summing-up. Whereas the other figures' subsequent careers are couched in the past tense, those of Elizabeth and Mrs. Clay are not. By suggesting their extra-fictional survival, the narrator intimates close acquaintance and a permanent existence analogous with that of landscape.

As the least sympathetic characters, they remain warnings of others' fates. By adopting a pose of nonomniscience, and so refusing to "complete" their happiness, the narrator maturely balances bliss with pathos at the close. The subtlety of taking leave, in the present tense, from Elizabeth especially, becomes all the more striking, when the reader recalls her dire marital situation in the first chapter. Outside the circle of happiness in the final chapter,[14] she underlines a latent sense of gravity: "It is a stately dance on the lawn—but all around there are the dark trees, the shadows. And if you do not dance well, if you have not been able, by the end of the day, to secure a permanent partner with whom to walk off the lawn, you are left, when the sun sets, alone amid the shadows. We are never allowed to forget that possibility, never allowed to forget what a serious business this dancing is" (Daiches 1948, 115).

Tense deviance of a different kind applies to *embedded narrative*, often epistolary or documentary. Of the three letters incorporated in the novel, the third, penned by Wentworth to Anne (2.11), is the only one whose import could have been conveyed in a more direct form of discourse, yet its indirect avowal matches that of Anne in her spirited exchange with Harville. By comparison with earlier letters, its contents are expected, it is perused the most rapidly ("her eyes devoured" [2.11; 441]), its effects prove the most overpowering and durable. It shows the briefest interval between composition and presentation, barely a minute: "She had only time, however, to move closer to the table where he had been writing, when footsteps were heard returning; the door opened; it was himself" (440–41).

This telescoped interval not only projects the degree of present emotional intensity, but also matches the narrative's gathering momentum, as expressed by the temporal remove of the novel's epistolary insertions (several days to twelve years to one minute). It prepares participants and readers, in addition, for the couple's subsequent meeting (444). Here, the linguistic fusion of time planes corresponds to the expressive fusion of human wills.

THEMATIC TEMPORALITY

Though all fiction variously allows scrutiny of such technical and formal features, not all relies to the same extent on the characters' level of temporal consciousness. Lady Russell's remark about Elliot's desire for reconciliation: "Time will explain" (2.4; 357), may be adopted for *Persuasion* as a whole. Mary has too much of it; her husband trifles his away. Sir Walter happily observes its ravages everywhere but in himself and his favorite daughter. Elizabeth, despite this reassurance, sadly notes its relentless course, which for Anne has left Wentworth unaltered, but has destroyed her own bloom.[15] The physical effects of time, however, differ from its inner residue, so that an individual's apprehension of its passage has a psychological rather than objective basis.

For Anne, the force of time in 1814 has softened but not eradicated memories of 1806, which, in its pastness, dominates both her and the novel. Her own efforts to rationalize a new situation lack conviction, when she argues the absurdity of resuming, "the agitation which such an interval had banished into distance and indistinctness!" (1.7; 278–79). Despite this distance with its intervening events and changes, the strength of Anne's emotional attachment remains scarcely diminished, since "with all her reasonings, she found, that to retentive feelings eight years may be little more than nothing" (1.7; 279). Aptly enough, Wentworth lexically varies this idea in his climactic confession, to justify his presence in Bath: "It was possible that you might retain the feelings of the past, as I did" (2.11; 447–48).

The essential pastness of the novel, the implications of an eight-and-a-half-year span between first meeting and successful engagement, may be usefully contrasted with the comedy in *Pride and Prejudice*. Mr. Collins makes an offer to Elizabeth Bennet after only two days' stay, and is accepted by Charlotte only two days later. Recalling the pathos of Elizabeth Elliot's unmarried state, a similar sense of latent gravity, of loss and waste, pervades Wentworth's realization that his pride in not soliciting Anne in 1808, led to "six years of separation and suffering" (2.11). Anne herself reflects, that the period since their broken engagement includes "nearly a third part of her own life" (1.7).

Temporal consciousness by the characters extends from personal experience to historical observation. Benwick's enthusiasm for the poetic richness of the "present age" (1.11), relates specifically to Byron and Scott in the 1810s. Anne's sensitivity to the recurrent seasons is checked by timely ironic intervention from the narrator: "the ploughs at work, and the fresh-made path spoke the farmer, counteracting the sweets of poetic despondence, and meaning to have spring again" (1.10; 301). Comparisons between old and new generations of Musgroves are likewise narratorial, as is the lyrical account of the landscape at Pinny: sobering reminder of time's enormous stretch and influence from prehistory on.

Since characters and narrator are encoded in the text, its title alone remains outside, and subject to the author's level of temporal consciousness. Despite the various types of "persuasion" that operate in the novel, its titular elevation is felicitous (Orange 1989, 63). Etymologically, its root suggests the idea of advising, recommending, urging as desirable, while its prefix alludes to the process taking place over an extended period of time, and also thoroughly, to completion. The relevance of title to novel scarcely needs elaboration; the relevance of temporality to both may bear rehearsal, since the climax of *Persuasion* in the penultimate chapter can, as demonstrated, be as well articulated on the basis of the development of its temporal elements, as of its narrative incidents.

Its point of greatest intensity, therefore, is gained on two separate fronts, only one of which is immediately transparent. That tension evident in the narrative account of events is rendered more effective, when the reader is made to feel a sense of accelerating rhythm (Cruickshank 1957, 141), in whose creation the novel's temporal elements conspire. In the final reunion of Anne and Wentworth, the movements of action and reaction, of outer event and inner debate coincide. Their future recollections of immortality will thus, in time, be assured.

Duplicated Micro-narrative: Natsume Sōseki, *Mon* [*The Gate*]

> It began when spring was just beginning to lift its head from under the foot of winter, and it was all over by the time the cherry blossoms had fallen and given way to fresh green leaves.
> —Natsume Sōseki, *Mon*

What Henry James called the "germ," Mikhail Bakhtin the "congealed event," and Jean Ricardou the "generative base" of a work of fiction, is represented in this single sentence from *Mon* [*The Gate*], by the Japanese novelist Natsume Sōseki (1867–1916). The same passage, moreover, illustrates the narrative device of *mise en abyme* to a more radical and literal, if less obvious, degree than usual. Its role in a novel outside the European tradition suggests its widespread relevance, as well as its contribution to the sequential dynamics of a given work.

Dating back in its practice as far as the Renaissance at least, the *mise en abyme* was identified as such by André Gide in the 1890s, and developed further by critics of the French New Novel in the 1960s and 1970s.[16] Referring to his partiality for thematic duplication, Gide contends that the device can illuminate a work and confirm its overall proportions ([1893] 1943, 44–45). As pictorial models, he names fifteenth-century Flemish canvases by Memling and Quentin Metzys, and especially *Las Meninas* by Velasquez, where mirrors afford a second, if distorting view of a scene. As literary models, Gide cites the play-within-a-play of *Hamlet*, marionette scenes in Goethe's *Wilhelm Meister*, and the inset romance in Poe's *The Fall of the House of Usher*.

For Gide, however, such models do not correspond as closely to the effects intended in his own works as·does an analogy from heraldry, whereby one escutcheon encloses a second, positioned at the heart-point (*en abyme*). It has since been shown that this inner coat-of-arms never exactly reproduces the outer by which it is subsumed (Morrissette 1971, 125–42), though Gide's formula, nonetheless, retains its value.[17] His brief discussion concludes with the claim that this effect of *inescutcheon* or *mise en abyme* is characteristic of the psychological novel.

Later commentators, especially on the *nouveau roman*, have favored approaches derived from structural semantics. Ricardou, for instance, sees the functions of the *mise en abyme* as narrative summary and enrichment (1967, 171–90; 1973, 47–75). Its roles may be antithetical or revelatory: challenging the narrative by acting as counterpoint, as vehicle for temporal sabotage (Poe's *Usher*), or revealing the narrative's own self-awareness (Robbe-Grillet's *Le Voyeur*).

Such roles may be subdivided into semantic operations of repetition, condensation, and anticipation. Ricardou's concern, and that of many *nouveaux romanciers*, is with the *mise en abyme* not simply as a hypodiegetic mirror of diegetic events, as a fragment foreshadowing the whole, but as its matrix. Thus, it functions as a model issuing directives for the production of the larger narrative, which then becomes the *mise en périphérie* of the micronarrative. In the extreme case of his own *La Prise de Constantinople* (1965), Ricardou uses the letters of his own name as generative base.

While, in practice, it is difficult to show that a *mise en abyme* actually preceded and generated the whole of a narrative, or that, alternatively, it developed later to provide an internal mirror of events, at least its functions in different contexts can be examined. Of Gide's two Anglophone examples, Shakespeare's tragedy has become a *locus classicus* of interior duplication. The play-within-a-play occupies the very center (3.3) of *Hamlet*, and in strict terms offers two mirrors rather than one of the larger events, since a dumb-show precedes and enacts the argument of "The Mouse-trap" itself.[18] In Poe's *Usher*, the text read aloud to Roderick apparently represents the *mise en abyme*, though an allegorical poem at the very center of the larger narrative offers, as in *Hamlet*, a further internal mirror.[19] The functions of the *mise en abyme* in Sōseki's novel are different again.

It is unlikely that "the first professional novelist in modern Japanese literature" (Yu 1969, 171), was aware of the procedure outlined by Gide. As perhaps the most important writer of the Meiji Restoration, when Japan, after centuries of isolation, was opened to the West, Sōseki was especially receptive to such influences. His stay in London, from 1900–1903, before his appointment at Tokyo Imperial University following Lafcadio Hearn, only reinforced an individualism unusual in his compatriots. Opposed to the literary naturalism prevalent in Japan, he moved toward an interest in the individual psyche.

It is to the category of psychological analysis that *Mon* (1910) and *Kokoro* (1914), best-known novel of his last period, belong. There is little evidence that Sōseki was acquainted with Freud (Doi 1976, 3; Yamanouchi 1978, 62), but his debts to William James and the notion of the "choosing activity of consciousness" have been noted (Sakuko 1975, 119–20). Beside Gide, the individualism of Sōseki seems comparatively modest, but they share an autobiographical bias and a common approach to the *mise en abyme*.

Mon [*The Gate*] is the third novel of Sōseki's first trilogy, and replaces the Hoffmannesque whimsy of *I Am a Cat* (1905) with a far more sober, even somber work, in which a young couple live out isolated and tedious lives in a gloomy quarter of Tokyo. There are only three major interruptions of the introverted existences of Sosuke and his wife Oyone: by Koroku, Sosuke's younger brother, by Yasui, his friend from student days, and by the landlord Sakai. Yasui is the most crucial figure, but makes only an "offstage" appearance in the penultimate chapter, a feature consistent with Sōseki's handling of his material.

It is Yasui's relationship to the couple, however, which forms the basis of the initial situation, though the decisive events lie outside and anterior to the primary narrative, as *external analepsis*. The vital facts concerning Sosuke and Oyone are not immediately broached, but, despite hints and enigmatic allusions, withheld until a point two-thirds of the way through. As in *Persuasion*, what precedes the narrative critically affects its characters, while the reader's ignorance of those events produces a parallel tension on another level. Control over what the reader is allowed to know, and when, blends with the couple's natural reticence to speculate in any detail about their past.

In the fourth of twenty-three chapters, the narrator surveys, in a *major analepsis*, Sosuke's life since student days. Not only are the listed facts necessarily selective, but a rereading supported by facts from later chapters exposes the archness and studied vagueness of such statements, that Sosuke "had had to leave the university, in circumstances which made it impossible for him to return home. From Kyoto he went directly to Hiroshima. . . . The two years or so . . . were spent in a hard struggle" (Sōseki 1975, 30–33).

Since the focalization is not that of a character's restricted vision, the narrative gaps must be *paralipses*, deliberate narratorial omissions, and the apparent aim is to tantalize the reader. This becomes still more evident in references, both metaphorical and hyperbolic, to Sosuke and Oyone suddenly finding themselves, "at the bottom of the deep dark pit of the past which they themselves had dug. The stain of their sin had besmeared their future" (35). By emotive language, the narrator's refusal to elaborate further on the nature of the "sin" is the more piquant.

It is not until nine chapters later, after the halfway point, in the second major analepsis, that additional facts emerge. Oyone's childless state is now seen (ch. 13) to be the result of events during pregnancy and birth, and not of a failure to conceive, as the reader has imagined hitherto. After her third child was stillborn, Oyone visited a fortune-teller, whose pronouncement stunned her: "You have done a terrible deed to another. This sin is still working itself out. That is why you can never have a child" (133).

The significance of the revelation is twofold. However obscurely, the couple's "sin" is directly related to their lack of heirs; the episode at the fortune-teller's, seemingly intended for reader alone, turns out to be a revelation to Sosuke, thus operating simultaneously at diegetic and extradiegetic levels. The notion of evasion and secrecy patent in the narrator, becomes reinforced when it appears in the chief protagonist.

While the synoptic fourth chapter makes passing allusion to the "sin," and the thirteenth records its consequences, the fourteenth promises, in the third major analepsis, to focus on this central event. A casual reference to Yasui gives way to an account of his secret companion, Oyone. The reader, already aware of the relationship between Oyone and Sosuke in the primary narrative, now follows their growing intimacy in this prenarrative sequence that withholds details of the "event." Only its reverberations are suggested in the subsequent sentences.

Metaphors and similes generalize and abstract any personal involvement: a "battle with life and death at stake," "like roasting green bamboo shoots," "a furious wind had blown up," "they were covered with dirt from head to foot" (152–53). Their wedding day coincides with abandonment by parents, relatives and friends. Sosuke resigns from university, and both isolate themselves from society. Once more recurs the image of a pit prepared for them by a cruel fate.

It is tempting to demystify the *mise en abyme* of the epigraph heading this case study, by citing Sōseki himself. Separating Eastern and Western concepts of love, he argues that, "we [orientals] regard love as important, but at the same time we always try to suppress it. If we fail to suppress it, we feel as if we have lost the dignity of an educated man. If we yield to the clamorous demands of passion, a sense of sin must inevitably follow" (Sakuko 1975, 114).

By transfer to *Mon*, it might be inferred that Sosuke and Oyone fail to suppress their passion and a sense of sin results. Though partially true, the account does no justice to the subtlety of Sōseki's novel, nor to a literary tradition dating back to the eleventh-century *Tale of Genji*, in which love is clearly not suppressed. Love scenes do not feature in Sōseki's work generally, but the narrative lacuna at the centre of *Mon*, constituting its *mise en abyme*, dramatizes essential concerns of the novel and significantly affects its sequential dynamics.

Novelistic examples of *paralipses* range from the "hole" in the action of Robbe-Grillet's *Le Voyeur*, to the seduction in Hardy's *Tess of the D'Urbervilles*, between sections entitled "The Maiden" and "The Maiden No More." Their counterpart in *Mon* relates, it must be assumed, to the liaison between the couple, though the epigraph merely marks the passage of time from the beginning of spring to the departure of the cherry blossoms. Remembering allusions to "pit," especially to the "deep dark pit of the past" (35), the reader is led to apply *mise en abyme* literally as well as heraldically.

The "abyss" or "gulf" becomes that into which the action of Sosuke and Oyone has plunged them. In *Mon*, the narrative device takes on the role of a purely verbal, narratorial utterance, by contrast with the guise of an artistic or literary model that it assumes in other fiction. The significance of its application here lies precisely in the narrator's silence about the central event. From this matrix extends a series of incidents dominating the whole narrative.

Sosuke and Oyone never discuss the central event, and scarcely mention the past, so that "at times it even seemed as if they had mutually agreed to avoid the subject" (34). When a conversation with Koroku touches on the topic of Manchuria, a look exchanged between Oyone and her husband leads to a sudden curtailment. In retrospect, the reader can appreciate the embarrassment caused by allusion to Yasui's place of exile. Even a visit to the dentist carries symbolic force, when an aching tooth turns out to have a dead core. To Sosuke, the words "evoked an image of the melancholy light of autumn" (59).

The six years between "the event" and its recapitulation, are shown as a period of sacrifice and hermitlike existence for the couple. By making the prenarrative chapters 4, 13, 14 the longest chapters, the manner in which past controls present is sharply dramatized. Within the crucial chapter 14 itself, a marked contrast of tempo is apparent between two specific segments. By correlating *page/time ratios*, it can be seen that Sosuke's first meeting with Oyone, lasting a bare few minutes, extends to nearly three pages (147–49), whereas the climax to the liaison, lasting some two months, is obliquely alluded to in the single epigraphic sentence that constitutes the *mise en abyme* (152). The contrast lies between an event fondly recalled and one buried in silence.

Such repression of uncomfortable facts by both main characters is echoed in the obfuscations of the narrator, and the detective-like organization of the narrative.[20] Recalling Gide's references to the psychological novel, and Sōseki's interest in the individual psyche, the dilemma of Sosuke and Oyone could be diagnosed as psychological blockage. As long as they blame fate, rather than recognize the "pit of the past" as a moral lapse on their part, there can be no freedom of conscience (Yu 1969, 98). Their shared suffering also entails, however, secrets kept from each other. Oyone bears alone the weight of the fortune-teller's prediction of childlessness, in a society that sets high store by offspring. Sosuke keeps from her a different secret, the impending arrival of the person whom both have betrayed.

The news about Yasui gives a pretext for continuing the analeptic sequence suspended after the *mise en abyme*: the effects of the central event on its chief victim, Yasui, his leaving university in mid-course, illness and flight to Manchuria. Sosuke's psychological torment almost assumes physical form, while the metaphorical storm invoked after the central event, is transferred to the actuality of fierce weather after Yasui's return. Conceding the failure of time to heal his wounds, recognizing his rootlessness, poverty of spirit, and self-centeredness, Sosuke attempts the path of Zen.

Just as the reader expected clarification in chapter 14, and met only with the silence of the *mise en abyme*, so too does Sosuke at the temple in Kamakura meet only with silence, instead of a gate to enlightenment. His preoccupation with Yasui, whose impending visit and past fate have also aroused expectancy in the reader, is intensified on his return home by his dread that Oyone has learned of the secret. Both Sosuke and the reader remain in suspense until the former forces himself to enquire about Yasui's whereabouts.

Any possibility of a dramatic encounter, however, is avoided by having Yasui depart before Sosuke's return, and allowing a conventional climax in the penultimate chapter to relapse into bathos. In the final third of *Mon*, furthermore, are four instances of *continuous phase*. Only two such linkages occur in the previous two-thirds, so that the sense of gathering concentration and insistent rhythm is obvious toward the close. All the more ironic, then, is the "betrayal" of what this technical feature promises, by the anticlimax of the narrative.

Sōseki's novel begins one Sunday in autumn, and ends on another Sunday in spring. The new season offers little hope for one who has so narrowly escaped public exposure and fears for the future: " 'But it will soon be winter again,' [Sosuke] said, as with downcast eyes he continued to cut his nails" (213). It can scarcely be accidental that the temporal span of the *macronarrative*, from autumn to spring, exactly duplicates that of the *micronarrative* produced by the *mise en abyme*.

Thus, the analeptic sequence in chapter 14 traces the relationship of Sosuke and Oyone, six years previously, from their introduction one Sunday in October, until their betrayal of Yasui in the following spring. While the *mise en abyme*, in Ricardou's terms, plays a revelatory role by generating the notion of silence and concealment, the micronarrative acts as a mirror which unceasingly reflects the past and its guilt, on the macronarrative set in the present. Gide's claim, that an internal duplication illuminates and confirms the overall structure of a work is here borne out, but *Mon* contains a further dimension not immediately apparent.

In chapter 3, the reference to Prince Ito's assassination (21) a few days before the narrative's starting point, precisely locates the action at the end of October 1909. The narrative must therefore conclude in the spring of 1910, when *Mon* itself was published. Thus, the act of writing coincides or is contiguous with the written narrative. Only on the final page, with its announcement of the arrival of spring, does this larger rubric of contemporaneity reveal itself, prompting the reader of the day to heightened identification with the fiction, as well as encouraging awareness of autobiographical projection.

Compared with *Kusa Makura* [*The Three-Cornered World* (1906)], *Mon* appears far more conservative in its exposition. His earlier "haiku-like novel" has indeed suggested links with the French New Novel (Janeiro 1970, 136), as its *chosiste* bias, strongly intertextual and self-reflexive traits hint. Its use of association in language and image also helps recall Sōseki's admiration for *Tristram Shandy*. More germane is the revelatory role of a painting, Sir John Millais's *Ophelia* (1852), to which reference is repeatedly made in connection with Onami, the girl at the inn where the artist-protagonist stays.

In a novel meager in plot or drama, often relapsing into a series of lyrical moods, Millais's canvas functions as a pictorial *mise en abyme*, an aesthetic construct which condenses motifs and ideas from the text as a whole. While the artwork looming largest in *Mon* is the family heirloom of a painted screen, whose sale testifies to the betrayal of a worthy past, the painting of *Ophelia* in *Kusa Makura* has a purely objective value as a mirror of intrinsic beauty.[21]

If aesthetic considerations are uppermost in this experimental work, Sōseki observes in *Mon* a dictum with echoes of Gide, that the organic unity of fiction should emerge from "psychological necessity" (Sakuko 1975, 259). *Kusa Makura* seems modern from a Western perspective, though its use of *mise en abyme* comes closest to Gide's original pictorial models; *Mon*, relatively traditional, though its use of *mise en abyme* is one of the most literal and radical anywhere, its central void affecting the sequential dynamics of the entire work. Both novels exploit Gide's narrative device, albeit unwittingly. They thereby substantiate its international application, as well as the claim, that Sōseki "accomplished what Meiji—indeed, modern Japan—has not yet fully succeeded in accomplishing. He in his own person created a synthesis of the East and the West" (Viglielmo 1964, 16).

LINEAL/LINEAR INTERPLAY:
AHMADOU KOUROUMA, *LES SOLEILS DES INDÉPENDANCES*

> The time is out of joint. O cursed spite,
> That ever I was born to set it right.
>
> —Shakespeare, *Hamlet*

For Prince Hamlet of Denmark, the chance remains to "set it right." For the Malinké Prince Fama of Horodougou, however, neither the will nor the ability any longer exists. The central figure of *Les soleils des Indépendances* (1970)[22] by the Ivoirian novelist Ahmadou Kourouma (1927–), senses with peculiar acuteness the out-of-joint relationship between himself and his age. In a prize-winning novel, widely acclaimed in particular for its mastery of African oral tradition,[23] temporality is crucial and is explored both in terms of sequence and consequence.

Although non-African critics have hitherto heeded them more, and non-African writers have experimented more with their possibilities, temporal issues affect all literature. In different cultures, modes of thought or systems of values influence attitudes to the practice of achrony or relative chronology in written and oral narrative,[24] while universal concepts which feature in Kourouma's novel, such as death and inheritance, survival and succession, can be treated in their temporal as well as thematic aspects.

In terms of historical distance or *external analepsis*, Fama's recollections of the establishment of his West African Doumbouya dynasty reach farthest back from the narrative starting point. Souleymane, its founder, caused Fama's birthplace of Togobala to grow prosperous, his progeny prodigious and vigorous. Later, Allah persuaded Bakary, a lineal descendant, to take power, even though the latter knew this to be unlawful. Like streams, it was prophesied, Bakary's heirs would become weaker and eventually die out, far from rivers and sea. Understanding that his line's extinction would coincide with the Last Judgment, however, Bakary precipitously interrupted the prophecy before it was completed. For Fama, this only confirms gloomy apprehensions that all conditions for the final catastrophe are now being fulfilled.

In strictly linear novels, this account of dynastic beginnings might well have graced the start of the narrative, in order to supply an epic backcloth. *Le devoir de violence* (1968), for example, by the Malian novelist Yambo Ouologuem, adopts this approach. The fact that Kourouma's account is withheld until a much later juncture suggests that the narrator consciously introduces it where it will operate with maximum effect, in terms of its sequential dynamics. Since a prophecy and its interpretation is involved, one whose ramifications touch the chief character most profoundly, the past assumes a key role within the present, serving not for purposes of factual consolidation, but as determinant.

Thus, the centrality of meaning in this dynastic survey is emphasized by its centrality of position: at a juncture précisely halfway through the novel (Kourouma 1970, 99–102). Geographically, Fama's recollections occur at Bindia, his wife, Salimata's, birthplace, and the overnight stop halfway between the coastal capital and Togobala. This recall of the prophecy made to Bakary is presented, therefore, at a critical point in the narrative, in a temporal and psychological limbo between past and future.

From this central vantage point in the second of the novel's three parts, we may gain a sense of orientation. Like the first part, the second commences with a death, a timeless event set in fictional time, on this occasion Fama's own cousin Lacina. Each succeeding death draws Fama closer to his physical and spiritual birthplace at Togobala, and to his own end. In the second part also, he is greeted at his mother's grave by the ominous sight of vultures tearing apart a dead dog. If the reader's expectations of symmetry are frustrated by the absence of death at the beginning of the third part, they are amply fulfilled later by the demise of Balla, one of Fama's two remaining followers, and at the close by Fama's own end. Stripped finally of titles and pretensions, his culminating act marks out the novel's circular progress from death to death, timelessness to timelessness. The process is unending, as the syntactically incomplete initial and closing sentences of the novel suggest.

Fama's course is not unremittingly downward. Lacina's death makes him tribal chief and brings the attractive inheritance of Mariam, one of his cousin's four wives. By contrast with his grotesque situation of princely beggar (11) in the first part, when he is reduced to "time-serving" as professional mourner, he might seem in the second part to enter an optimistic future. It is in this verb form that he thinks of Mariam. Salimata is now relegated to preterite and past perfect, while thoughts of earlier ambitions, frustrated by his father or Independence, are couched in the past conditional.

By contrast, however, with his prenarrative childhood to which repeated allusion is made, his prospects appear bleak. Here, more than anywhere, the pressure of time shows itself. The princely entourage of slaves, praise-singers, and concubines has now almost vanished from memory. Salimata's handsome young man has declined into a "chose usée et fatiguée comme une vieille calebasse ébréchée"[25] (55). When, in the middle of the second part, he reaches his native Togobala, the movement of time is concretized by images of a destitute baobab tree, a ruined settlement, a retinue of two old men.

What in theory should be the climax of the narrative and his career, assumption of the tribal chieftancy, amounts in practice to hollow insignificance: village, ancestry and tribe together, "ne valaient pas en Afrique un grain dans un sac de fonios"[26] (117). By the final chapter of the third part, Fama concedes the falsity of predictions by *marabouts* and soothsayers of his triumphant arrival in Togobala. Glimpses of white charger and escort decked in gold now belong only to dream. At the border of Côte des Ébènes and Nikinai, however, the realization that he is again in Horodougou territory summons up all his self-repressed memories: "tout lui appartenait ici, tout, même le fleuve qui coulait à ses pieds, le fleuve et les crocodiles sacrés"[27] (194–95). The latter, by a supreme irony, deliver the final coup de grâce to their master[28]: the bankrupt charisma of the past could not have been expressed with more bite.

Consistent with the nonlinear presentation of events, it is only in the third part that Fama's birthdate of 1905 is supplied. Equating a fictional Nikinai with an actual Guinea or Mali, this would imply that he has had no experience prior to French colonization and Independence. His memories of an idyllic childhood belong already, therefore, to an "unfree" period or have been mythologized. If significance is attached to this temporal detail, the reader's retrospective appreciation of the contrast between past and present becomes greatly modified.

As the Malinké phrase of the title indicates, the second era, a defined historical period, has been most decisive for Fama in separating him from his inheritance. Its pervasive intrusion upon the present is rendered all the more effectively, by combining the historical and abstract sense of "soleil" (era), with its tactile meaning. From the very beginning, at Koné's funeral, the two time planes of immediate feeling and past events coalesce: "le soleil des Indépendances maléfiques remplissait tout un côté du ciel, grillait, assoiffait l'univers"[29] (9). Despite its title, moreover, the novel studies the effects of Independence on an individual, rather than the political events as such. It is symptomatic that these are viewed analeptically.

Thus, the most graphic accounts of changes do not stem from Fama, as if to suggest his indifference toward and lack of contact with those events, but from fellow-travelers on the trip to Togobala. This takes place not at the beginning of the novel, but in its second part, emphasizing again the novel's nonlinear organization. Here, storytelling serves to inform the reader as well as to "kill" time, while the accounts illustrate a steady regression into the past, since they are followed by the Bakary episode. Fama's personal reward for opposing the colonizers has been the loss of his livelihood and rank in an unsentimental one-party state, to which, at the end of the second part, he must swear allegiance. The new order's omnipotence, patent by its lengthy reach into the private domain of dream, is amply demonstrated in the third part of the novel. Fama is arrested, imprisoned and sentenced for failing to report a dream warning Nakou, a suspected Malinké, of impending danger.

Soleils comprises patterns of parallels and contrasts bound up with the theme of time. Fama's two dreams in the third part, foreshadowing the future, prove in Nakou's case to be all too true; in Fama's own case, of triumphal entry to Togobala, all too false: a mere wish-dream. Of the portents in the second part, he is horrifyingly aware of the dead dog at the graveside, but unaware of the unprecedented appearance of midday clouds during *harmattan*. With this portent, the central part ominously closes. It thereby signals the dire effects of Fama's refusal to heed the advice of the fetish-priest Balla. The wetness of the capital brings nostalgia for the aridity of Horodougou, city for village, poverty for prosperity: present for past.

It is this contrast that concerns Salimata in the first part, two chapters of which are focalized through her. His slumbering unconsciousness contrasts with her wide-awake reflections and memories: unflattering comparisons between the past and present Fama, traumas of excision and rape, physical revulsion from men, and literally fruitless marriages. For Salimata, the *marabout* Abdoulaye appears vigorous and virile beside her seemingly sterile husband. For Fama, in the third part, his twenty years of marriage stretch out behind him with the same barrenness as the twenty years of imprisonment which lie in front of him. Such movements, backwards and forwards in narrative time, typify the novel's sequential dynamics.

Traditional institutions recklessly abandoned on Independence include fetish and sacrifice, which always served to ward off evil and reveal the future. Fama's own memories of Togobala's oracles of hyena and boa, which saved the village from a epidemic in 1919, suggest the vivid contrast in the novel's third part, between a specific personal past and an undated impersonal present. It is claimed that prophecies, portents, and dreams all function to foreshadow coming events, and loss of belief in their efficacy impoverishes the whole community. Their exclusion from *Soleils* would undoubtedly be a loss, since the temporal oscillation between memory and projection not only lends animation of surface, to which Kourouma's richness of language and graphic oral performance contribute, but also conveys a deeper sense.

Fama's anguished speculations in the past conditional, of what might have happened at crucial junctures, and equally somber awareness in the preterite of what in fact did occur, are offset by an implied or actual future form. This, symptomatically, is no more optimistic in tone: "Ces soleils sur les têtes, ces politiciens, tous voleurs et menteurs, tous ces déshontés, ne sont-ils pas le désert bâtard où doit mourir le fleuve Doumbouya?"[30] (99). Salimata's closing contribution to the first part points backwards and forwards simultaneously, reflecting the extensive temporal embrace of her conviction that she is destined to die sterile (80).

Throughout the novel, the theme of time is elastically handled. Koné's shade, a shade faster than sound, covers two thousand kilometers in a flash (7), while Fama's mortal injury occurs like lightning (201). At Togobala the forty days of mourning hang heavily on him, and Balla's hunting yarns help to "kill" time. In the internment camp, where time is neither observable nor relevant, weeks seem years, and Fama loses all sense of duration (165). He becomes totally disorientated by the sun's appearance at night, and the moon's by day.

The *caesar ex machina* of the president's pardon is couched in terms of temporal erasure: to forget the past and to think only of the future, "cet avenir que nous voulons tous radieux"[31] (181). Temporal indices are also provided by Fama's continual physical decline. With a diarrhetic's gait, already too old to work in the first part, markedly aging by the second, he contracts worms in prison, and becomes "ce vieux maigre et décharné, les yeux clos comme un aveugle"[32] (191), on his release in the third part.

Each of the three parts reveals a steady acceleration in time-ratios. Whereas the first part requires seventy-two pages to cover two days, the second part's seventy pages account for forty days, and the third part, extending over several months, is embraced in forty-eight pages. The first part shows temporal concentration by stressing the typicality of events, skillfully and evenly alternating present action with past memory, and representing a marriage by seeing it literally from its two constituent viewpoints. Salimata's sleepless night is paralleled by Fama's in the second part, the quickening tempo is now paralleled by the growing vagueness of time indices and by individual rather than typical events, now restricted to a single character.

Fama's increasing indifference to life might also be calibrated with the narrative's imprecision of time, so that his two dreams, with their essentially atemporal characteristics, are aptly placed in the temporal flux of the final part. Here, after an initial reference to the nine days of harmony between Salimata and Mariam, there is scarcely another specific reference to present time or, for that matter, to harmony. Fama's journey home becomes a journey toward voluntary death, a journey through time toward voluntary timelessness.

When *Soleils* is compared not with some abstract or hypothetical treatment of the topic of Independence, but with another, almost-contemporary French-African novel: *Le cercle des Tropiques* (1972) by the Guinean, Alioum Fantouré, the significance of the handling of sequential dynamics is patent. The two works show great differences in orders of representation and represented worlds. At least seven major events or dated anniversaries in *Soleils* are prenarrative.[33] In *Cercle*, virtually only one episode, from the protagonist Bohi Di's birth to his schooldays, a minute portion of the total narrative, belongs to this retrospective category.

Neither *Soleils* nor *Cercle* covers the entire period between the central character's birth and death; the months of *Soleils* are dwarfed by the years of *Cercle*, even given that the latter is nearly twice the length of Kourouma's novel. The intervals between the three parts of *Soleils* remain temporally indeterminate, allowing for relaxation of narrative tension. Between the two parts of *Cercle*, there is no such pause. The electoral victory at the end of part one is immediately followed by the Independence celebrations at the start of part two, so that the sequence reflects an irresistible forward drive. *Soleils* begins after Independence, with Fama already in decline, and closes with his death, whereas *Cercle* moves from Bohi Di's youth, not to his death but to an ambivalent close.

At the formal center of *Soleils* lies the prophecy made to Bakary in a remote past; its equivalent in *Cercle* is Independence itself.[34] Though the episodes of *Soleils* take place in the era of Independence, the event itself has been relegated to the prenarrative, while in *Cercle* it supplies the centerpiece of the narrative but not the title. A present and future, bland at best, confront a vivid prenarrative past in *Soleils*; in *Cercle*, a vivid narrative present, with no prenarrative past. Here, it is pertinent to distinguish between the characters of Fama and Bohi Di, and between two separate viewpoints.

Fantouré's novel is presented by a first-person narrator-participant; Kourouma's, by a near-omniscient narrator not identical with Fama. *Soleils* reveals the effects of Independence on a specific aristocratic individual, while *Cercle* reveals its advent and effects on a representative "son of the soil." Opening symptomatically in a past tense, with an allusion to a Malinké's death a week before, *Soleils* establishes an early tone of rumination. *Cercle* commences with elliptical hypotaxis, directly and graphically conveying a scene of action, before using an imperfect tense suited to evoke the repetitive labor of the fields.

Fantouré's novel progresses linearly from sequence to sequence, thematically propelled by Bohi Di's basic needs for food, job, security, so that his course can be charted in a picaresque manner, by degrees of advancement from an initial zero. By contrast, the sequential dynamics of *Soleils* mean that present oscillates tirelessly with past. At the beginning, Fama has already moved in the reverse direction from Bohi Di, arriving at, rather than departing from nothing. Kourouma sets himself greater difficulties than Fantouré, by his conscious choice of nonlinearity over linearity, as well as by a partially bifocal (Fama, Salimata) over a single perspective (Bohi Di).

The circular course of *Soleils*, from a representative death to the main character's own death, is marked by the refusal of change; the linear progress of *Cercle*, concerned with the development of the main character who is also representative, shows growing awareness of the possibility of change. In the broadest terms, the orientation of *Soleils* is backwards, that of *Cercle* forwards; the terms involve time in its technical and thematic aspects. One crucial element in Kourouma's novel, however, remains to be discussed.

Close to the start, the narrator, with an ironic feeling for incongruity, attempts to elicit the reader's admiration and sympathy for Fama by allusion to a central problem, related in its essence to that of temporality and the pressures it exerts: "Fama Doumbouya! Vrai Doumbouya, père Doumbouya, mère Doumbouya, dernier et légitime descendant des princes Doumbouya du Horodougou, totem panthère, était un *vautour*. Un prince Doumbouya! Totem panthère faisait bande avec les hyènes. Ah! les soleils des Indépendances!"[35] (9). Close to the end, a repetition of similar phrases during the exchange with a frontier guard produces an even more ludicrous effect. Such linguistic inflation of a name is seen to be totally incompatible with the actuality of its prosaic social context (197–99).

Throughout *Soleils*, liturgical reminders that Fama is the last scion of a princely line reinforce the fact that neither he nor his wife, jointly or individually, can produce an heir. It remains unclear, however, to whom responsibility should be apportioned. Salimata and Abdoulaye accuse Fama of being infertile, while it is pointed out that Salimata's own mother suffered from sterility (37). Fama's attempt to prove himself with the fecund Mariam in a bizarre ménage à trois is a disastrous fiasco. Later in the third part, even if the will to reproduce still exists, he learns on his release from prison that the opportunity is lacking: Salimata has joined Abdoulaye, and Mariam has found a taxi driver.

The formal and temporal balance of the first part, in which Fama and Salimata are accorded two chapters and one day each, might well lead, in an iconic reading of sequential dynamics, to the conclusion that they also share the balance of blame. As early as this first part, Fama has referred to his own life, as "un soleil éteint et assombri"[36] (29), an indicatively negative metaphor in view of the omnipresent sun of the novel's title. The imagery elsewhere, especially in the central prophecy to Bakary, alludes to a stream running dry in sand and desert, far from rivers and sea (101). No bad anticipation, perhaps, of Fama's final journey from coastal capital to arid Togobala.

Fama may be seen variously as a unique individual, as representative of traditional aristocracy, of a whole race: "et l'espèce malinké, les tribus, la terre, la civilisation se meurent, percluses, sourdes et aveugles . . . et stériles"[37] (21), or of a whole continent prior to Independence: "Vraiment les soleils des Indépendances sont impropres aux grandes choses; ils n'ont pas seulement dévirilisé mais aussi démystifié l'Afrique"[38] (149). Whatever the emphasis, the metaphor of sterility implies an absence of succession and the end of a particular human development.

Thematically, the notion of sterility plays a key role in terms of time, since it denies any future tense, and suggests an inability to reproduce the past and to project it into the future. Formally, the temporal oscillation in *Soleils* between past and future has a deeper sense, in dramatizing the insufficiency and instability of the present. Ultimately, thematic and formal aspects of time fuse in the concept of a past that forecasts a sterile future and thereby deprives the present of value. The novel's nonlinearity, its divergence between orders of representation and represented events, can be viewed as a projection of the relationship between its central character and his age, a narrative demonstration rather than simply a statement of his awareness that for him, as for Hamlet, the time is "out of joint."

In terms of sequential dynamics, the uncomplicated arrangement in Fantouré's *Le cercle des Tropiques* is challenged by the ordering in *The Interpreters* (1965), by the Nigerian Nobel Prize-winner, Wole Soyinka, or in the earlier *Nedjma* (1956), by the Algerian Kateb Yacine. Here, a circular course projects a political situation in which time is a closed circuit.[39] Where such procedures avoid mere virtuosity, they awaken the reader to the importance of content by means of suggestiveness of presentation.

Since sequential dynamics are a necessary if overlooked part of the total work of fiction, casual handling by an author can, as much as any other aspect, jeopardize the work's impact. The achievement of *Les soleils des Indépendances* is due not solely to its mastery of oral polyphony and evocative use of language, or its ability to sustain repeated readings. Neither as temporally transparent as Fantouré's, nor as radical as Soyinka's or Yacine's, Kourouma's novel occupies a position in-between. It is a measure of his integrative handling that sequential aspects remain formally unostentatious, yet promote Kourouma's thematic concerns.

NARRATIVE DIS/CONTINUITIES: GRAHAM SWIFT, *WATERLAND*

... let me tell you

3

About the Fens

Which are a low-lying region of eastern England ...
—Graham Swift, *Waterland*

Contemporary, especially Postmodernist authors challenge the notion of continuity in various ways, thereby instilling uncertainty in readers, and encouraging them to impose their own sense of cohesion on texts. Continuity itself has both a technical aspect (syntactic, grammatical), and a thematic aspect, the latter being subdivided into an internal linkage of motifs and figures, and into external practices of derivation (Genette 1982).

In British novels of the 1980s, increasing degrees of such dis/continuities are evident.[40] Peter Ackroyd's first novel, *The Great Fire of London* ([1982] 1987a), for example, explicitly continues, in the form of sequel, a familiar text, Dickens's *Little Dorrit* (1857). By his ordering, Ackroyd creates merging and diverging narrative lines, which echo *in parvo* the thematic range and density of Dickens's novel. Despite applying devices, such as cross-cutting, that promote discontinuity, Ackroyd's novel remains conventionally linear in its sequential dynamics.

Graham Swift's *Waterland* (1983), by contrast, explores continuity in both its thematic and technical aspects as part of its strategy of metafictional "process." For one critic, the novel "suggests artlessness while being meticulously ordered" (Hawtree 1983), and Swift himself refers to a "seemingly loose form ... not in fact ...

loose" within a novel of "seeming digressions" (Jach, 8). In this third, most accomplished and complex of Swift's novels, the reasons for complexity are less interpretative than presentational.

The material is distributed into five separate narrative lines, and the reader, as in much Postmodernist fiction, must connect the apparently disconnected. Given the surface disorder, it is all the more piquant to learn that Tom Crick, its schoolmaster-narrator, is at work on *A History of the Fens* (Swift 1984, 5). This absent *mise en abyme* is presumably both linear and academic: a reverse-image, in fact, of "these fantastic-but-true, these believe-it-or-not-but-it-happened Tales of the Fens" (35) that make up Swift's novel.

Waterland deals with twofold barrier-states: thematically, by exploring the boundaries between the factual and fictional that belong to Magic Realism; and technically, by challenging conventions of segmentation, to introduce across chapters fresh syntactic and semantic relationships. These involve transitional devices of titles and connectives, as well as larger categories of narrative sequence. By employing a range of taxonomies, which include levels of time, narrative lines, and specific types of transition, we can expose the vital function of dis/continuities in the overall economy of the text.

Narratorial Continuity

Much of Swift's narrative rationale stems from the dynamic relations of audience and narrator. Tom Crick, as London history master, is driven by the religious obsessions of his wife, Mary, and a challenge by his pupil Price into teaching-by-confession. This, combined with the scandal of his wife's baby snatching and committal to an asylum, forces his "retirement." The narrative-Now of Greenwich 1980 alternates with earlier crises which center around 1943, when a youthful Mary, pregnant by Tom, underwent a crude abortion by the local Fenland "witch" Martha Clay, an event condemning her to a childless marriage.

At the same time, her sexual initiation of Tom's mentally retarded brother Dick resulted in the latter's fatal attack upon the local boy responsible, he believed, for her condition. The double blow to Dick, of learning the truth about Mary's pregnancy and about his own origins (conceived by his mother and *her* father), leads the "potato-head" to dive into the Ouse and vanish. Intent on refuting Price's claims that history is a fairy-tale, Crick uses his own personal and family experiences as object lessons. His self-conscious address to his pupils, and foregrounded deployment of rhetorical devices, emphasize the status of *Waterland* as metafiction, as fiction of "process" that focuses, if in a different way than Kourouma, on the nature of oral storytelling.

Textual Space

To retain the interest of pupils with notoriously short attention-spans, Crick resorts to the kind of suspense and enigma familiar in detective-fiction: a nonlinear presentation, with restless shifts of topic and levels of time, variety of unit-scale and narratorial voice. In terms of textual space (see Fig. 2.1), the pre–1943 group contains the three longest chapters: chapter 9 an inordinate protrusion of history, that of Crick's maternal ancestors since the eighteenth century. The average chapter-length and sheer quantity of this group, as if statistically to underline the importance of forebears and past, is the highest of any period. It surpasses the 1943 material, which is evenly spread throughout the text, and also occupies the crucial first and final chapters.

Only two chapters are devoted to the 1943–80 period, the first of which (ch. 12) deals with the thirty years of Tom and Mary's marriage. Tom justifies such an enormously accelerated handling of time by the routine nature of their relationship. Apart from three purely essayistic chapters, focusing on the River Ouse (ch. 15), eels (ch. 26) and phlegm (ch. 51), with only slight temporal links to the other material, the remaining chapters, half the total, concern 1980. In this narrative-Now, Tom relates the most recent developments to his class, but the chapters, though frequent, are extremely brief, suggesting their role as framework markers.

Narratorial Ordering

Critical for continuity is the way Crick orders his material. Recent events alternate with episodes from two centuries back, and these in turn with geographical, biographical and philosophical reflections, so that this fiction of "process" dramatizes interconnected levels of time and experience. It is almost as if, by shifting rapidly from one narrative line to another, he can best illustrate this notion. In the pendulum movement between the five lines (see Fig. 2.2), and the commutation of each, there are obvious differences between the order of represented events, indicated by letters, and their representation, by chapter numbers.

The Dick and Mary line is by far the most "rearranged." Events A-C deal with 1940, and D with early 1943, E being set in July 1943 and O in August 1943. A mere month's "progression" between ini-

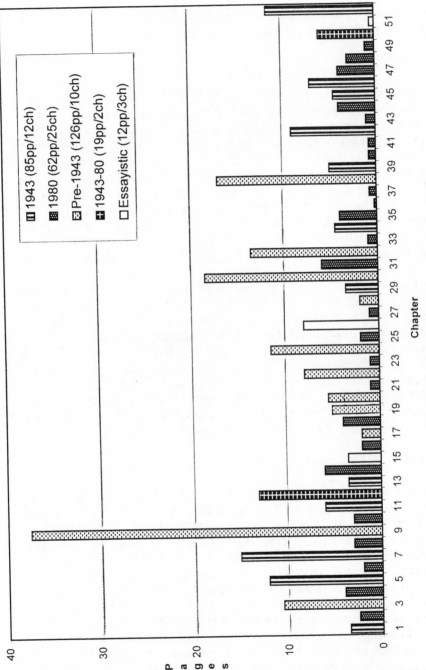

Figure 2.1 Graham Swift, *Waterland*: Chapter Length/Level of Time

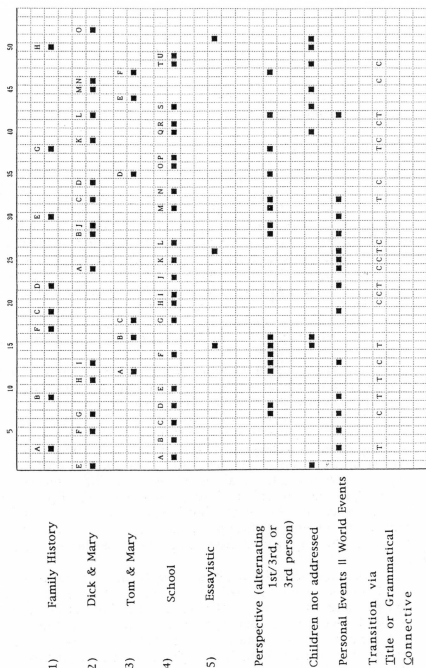

Figure 2.2 Graham Swift, *Waterland*: Narrative Lines/Features

tial and closing chapters not only broaches the notion of circularity, but also reinforces the key role of that year's events. Of the Tom and Mary line, only A, covering 1943–80, does not belong to the narrative-Now of 1980, site also of the School line. This is the busiest and threatens, through the regular rhythm of its appearance, to become monotonous and mechanical. Only after the halfway stage does the School line, in alternate chapters of roughly similar length, grow more irregular, yielding by way of variety to blocks of consecutive chapters.

Crick recognizes that storytelling must work backwards from what came after to what came before, from reaction to action. Since the process is never uncomplicated, its narrative continuity should match this. His audience is warned, that history is not a "well disciplined and unflagging column marching unswervingly into the future" (117). Rather, he insists, it "goes in two directions at once. It goes backwards as it goes forwards. It loops. It takes detours." History also "repeats itself . . . it twists, turns . . . goes in circles and brings us back to the same place" (123). Crick might almost be describing the movement of his own narrative, or that of the eel: the creature typifying Fen waterland, to which the whole of the essayistic chapter 26, symmetrical center of the novel, is devoted.

That chapter's shape, matching the topic of the eel's return to its origins, and with final words (177) echoing opening sentence (169), is appropriately cyclic. It represents a *mise en abyme* for the novel's entire movement. Tom Crick's choice of the French Revolution for his ideological excurses, is motivated not only by its role, which he defines as "*water*shed" and "*land*mark" (119; my italics), but also by the etymology of "Revolution": the notion of completing a cycle. The return of the fatal beer-bottle to the attic whence it was removed, is only a mundane illustration of the force of past upon present. Dick, for whom the bottle served as weapon, is last glimpsed in the final chapter plunging, like the eel, into a familiar element: "Obeying instinct. Returning. The Ouse flows to the sea" (310).

Even Crick's model for progress is no dynamic, forward-looking one, but closely bound up with his Fenland origins: land-reclamation, the never-ending retrieval of what is lost. What Crick has lost, besides his wife, is the chance, shared with protagonists in Sōseki and Kourouma, to produce descendants, a situation again grounded in the past. Suitably enough for one who is childless, last of the family line, his model for progress is not forward-looking. Unlike the mentally disturbed Dick and Mary, both amnesiacs, he can at least complete the circuit of past and present in his memory, and produce a (literary) offspring in *Waterland*.

Thematic Boundaries

Thematically, the notion of barrier-states implies a concern with the boundaries between the historical and the imaginative, "fact" and "fiction," and *Waterland* joins a series of works since 1960 qualifying as historiographic metafiction (Hutcheon 1988, 105–23). These works question the idea of an "innocent" history, view historical knowledge as problematic, are little engaged by traditions of detached objectivity and consistent record. Several go beyond Swift's novel, by inserting real historical events and personages into an overtly fictional context, presenting history as a "multiplicity of 'alternative worlds,' as fictional as, but other than, the world of novels" (Waugh 1985, 260).

Tom Crick's aim is more modest: to indicate how present is intimately connected with past by relationships of cause and effect. Thus, his wife's baby snatching stems from her infertility, in turn the outcome of a bungled abortion. Dick's mental handicap, his fatal attack on Freddie Parr and putative suicide, is traced to his grandfather/father Ernest Atkinson's incest and actual suicide. Crick's own crisis forces him to seek explanations in his Fenland forebears. The result testifies that the definition of *Historia* in the epigraph indeed embraces both history and story.

As with Salman Rushdie and Günter Grass, the formulaic "once upon a time" is used to blur thematic boundaries. Swift introduces his quasi-documentary account of the Fens as "both palpable and unreal" (6), like, he claims, the settings of all good fairy-tales. To counter, or complement the unreal aspects, Swift provides detailed passages on the East Wind, Greenwich Observatory and a Fenland cottage. Like Saleem Sinai in *Midnight's Children*, Tom Crick records world events that coincide with personal and local happenings. Unlike Saleem, he is not "handcuffed to history" (Rushdie [1981] 1982, 9) by an ingenious conceit, but free to allow dates, names and places to even up the balance between "fact" and "fiction." Such chapters, aligning personal with world events, and lending a broader perspective to the family history, decline after the halfway stage, when the historical underpinning is more secure (see Fig. 2.2).

Technical Boundaries:

TITLES

Technically, the notion of barrier-states involves transitional devices such as titles and grammatical connectives between narrative units, as well as relationships between categories of sequence. The traditional role of titles, to telegraph the gist of a chapter or section, to introduce a fresh stretch of narrative, to supply a strategic pause for reflection, or sleep, is, however, frequently usurped in *Waterland*. Over half its chapters, as if reinforcing their oral and pedagogical status, bear titles beginning, "About . . ." Though many summarize material, or anticipate a phrase in the coming chapter, other titles serve as topic-puns. "A Feeling in the Guts" (ch. 41), for example, intends more than gastroenteritis or conviction-politics.

Playfully, the unfinished last sentence of chapter 10 ("he's really only telling a-" [94]), is unexpectedly completed by the title of chapter 11 ("About Accidental Death"), while the closing reference to a beer bottle in chapter 5 appears to be taken up in the title of chapter 6 ("An Empty Vessel"). Only toward the end of that chapter does the motivic continuity prove spurious. In other cases, similarities and contrasts of content, not otherwise obvious, are emphasized by the pairing of titles in consecutive chapters: "About Natural History" (ch. 27), "About Artificial History" (ch. 28); "Goodnight" (ch. 47), "And Adieu" (ch. 48).[41]

With the most important group of titles, an identical formula effects the transition from a previous chapter. Crick addresses his children at chapter end with the words, "let me tell you," before immediately announcing the next chapter title ("About . . ."), and completing the grammatical sense across the chapter boundary. In nearly every case, the new chapter introduces factual material, by way of contrast to the foregoing chapter. The practical result of grammatically embedding the title in a continuing sentence is to deny division and difference, and to stress the idea of easy interchange. Like run-on lines in poetry, the absence of final punctuation sponsors a smooth flow between chapters. Titles become bridges, part of, rather than separate from text. Fluency of movement is further encouraged in those chapters beginning with relative pronouns, as the opening epigraph demonstrates.

GRAMMATICAL CONNECTIVES

Like titles, grammatical connectives can either aid or impede flow, promote a genuine, ambivalent, or false sense of continuity, and force the reader to make semantic links across chapter boundaries. Only rarely are such links realized here. "And," for example, operates simply to open a new chapter in a gradual unabrupt way, to remind us of the oral and informal mode of Crick's presentation. Despite its normal function, it does not conjoin narratively with what immediately precedes; rather, it resumes material from earlier stages. One chapter that ends, "Mary says: 'I know what I'm going to do,'" (ch. 34) and is then succeeded by a chapter beginning, "So one day . . ." (ch. 35), might seem to guarantee semantic continuity, but the conjunction glosses over an ellipsis of nearly forty years. The actual ordering runs from 34f to 39i, and chapter 35 takes up where chapter 18 left off.

Anaphora, as in the opening sentences of chapter 25 ("Hey this is good. This is juicy. Forget the Bastille" [167]) and chapter 27 ("What is this—a biology lesson?" [177]), offers semantic continuity with preceding chapters, but the level of events gives way in each case to the level of presentation. In a different case, when Price refers to the possibility of Crick's having children (ch. 33), the teacher's response has a bifurcated continuation ("But it's all right, Price" [224] and "Don't apologize, Price" [232]). The first opens chapter 34, the second chapter 36.

Whole-Chapter Transitions

Aided by *categories of sequence*, degrees of strictness can be measured between adjacent chapters and chapter-segments. Although it is Tom Crick's mind, like Shandy's, that generates the novel, transitions and all, the narratorial voice never sounds alike in all chapters. Stylistically, Crick is a man of many parts, raising doubts in the reader about the consistency and credibility of the frame-audience (present for over 80 percent of the total chapters). He ranges from contracted forms, verbless phrases, ellipsis, and breathless flow, to highly self-conscious diction, enumeration, and strings of rhetorical questions. In the final stages, indeed, as if his pupils are redundant, with the other narrative lines to sustain, six out of the last twelve chapters omit any address to them (see Fig. 2.2).

As in four of Swift's other novels,[42] the chapters of *Waterland* are not grouped into parts or sections, so that a sense of overall rhythms must derive from the reader's own perception of how material is distributed. Given Tom Crick's role, we are inevitably concerned with *narratorial* categories of sequence. In those chapters, however, where titles or connectives offer direct transitions from a preceding chapter, we may speak of *narratorial immediate ties.* Such cases comprise over 40 percent (22 chapters) of sequences. Fifteen chapters have spurious connectives, and the rest little continuity at all. Some 60 percent of *Waterland,* then, may be regarded as discontinuous from chapter to chapter.

A pattern of ebb and flow in transition via title or connective is therefore established (see Fig. 2.2). There is a noticeable grouping of immediate ties in alternating chapters (chs. 7–15), and around the halfway stage (chs. 20–27), when Crick moves rapidly between topics, to hold his class's attention, and illustrate historical theories in practice. These spans contrast with their infrequent occurrence later.

Though title transitions appear regularly, they cease after chapter 42, and with only two instances of grammatical connectives, the last ten chapters are increasingly disjointed. Different narrative lines are taken up and dropped, and their separate, contrasted topics grow increasingly more isolated. The average chapter length for this last quarter shrinks dramatically, to become the shortest in the novel (see Fig. 2.1). It suggests the rising tempo of Crick's anxiety to conclude each line.

Despite the outward guarantee of continuity lent by titles and connectives, such transitional devices prove no more than tenuous and temporary, in nearly half the chapters where they feature. A bridge accomplished, the bulk of the material reverts to *analeptic* sequence, which accounts for 60 percent of all chapters. The effect is to force upon the reader a fresh orientation, activate the memory of an earlier narrative line, promote expectation of developments in a episode just suspended. By alternating analeptic sequences with apostrophes to the class and Price, in the narrative-Now of 1980, the narrator creates a sense of complex temporal intermingling, in which the dependence of present on past, on history, is graphically reinforced by sequential dynamics.

Such is the case, for example, in chapter 41, barely a page long. It comprises Crick's inward reactions to Price's nightmare visions in chapter 40 (i.e. 41i→40f), shifting back for four lines to evoke Mary's decision in 1943 (ch. 39) to visit Martha Clay (41m→39f), before concluding with three lines addressed to the children. The sentence then flows across the chapter boundary to take in the title, and a further line of chapter 42. That chapter's nub, however, Mary's abortion, again reverts to 1943, though references to the pupils help recall Crick's oral presentation in 1980.

Internal analepsis is the most important phase-type in *Waterland,* since it applies to relationships between chapters, rather than any fixed starting point. The most striking example, and lengthiest ellipsis, joins the final segment of chapter 7 (7f), where Tom Crick relates how he conceals the beer bottle, with the initial segment of chapter 29 (29i). Here, he describes, 129 pages and twenty-two chapters later, how he then uses the bottle to test Dick's guilt in the death of Freddie Parr. That same bottle, moreover, was not discovered in chapter 7, but at the end of chapter 5. Continuity thus runs 5f→7f, producing an *alternate phase*, but not the normative final to initial segment (f→i). Given that identical words as in 5f are employed to resume the episode in 7f, the sequence may be qualified further as *narratorial immediate alternate*. This indicates that an earlier sequence is resumed, as if ignoring the presence of intervening chapters.

Segmental Transitions

Despite the variety of sequences in Fowles's *FLW* (Ireland 1986), there is small need there to subdivide chapter segments. In *Waterland*, however, we must identify first and second *initial, medial,* and *final segments*, in order to account for chapter continuity. Thus, the normative final to initial transition between chapters, appears in a variety of whole-chapter relationships (see Fig. 2.3). A range of permutations involves other segmental and subsegmental transitions, together with differing phase types. By noting the frequency and positioning of these examples and categorizing the varieties, new subtleties of articulation can be detected.

At 12f (Mary's announcement of "pregnancy"), her words are followed by a four-line exhortation from narrator to pupils, so that the final segment has to be designated as f1 and f2, respectively. That exhortation is then taken up without a break in the opening of chapter 13, making an *immediate tie*, though the bulk of the chapter constitutes an *alternate phase*, resuming material from 11f:

And then suddenly she announces: "I'm going to have a baby. Because God's said I will." (12f1; 113)

Children, don't stop asking why. Don't cease your Why Sir? Why Sir? Though it gets more difficult the more you ask it, though it gets more inexplicable, more painful, and the answer never seems to come any nearer, don't try to escape this question Why. (12f2; 113)

	Whole-Chapter Transitions		
Narratorial Immediate Tie		NICP	2f➡3i
/Span			24f➡25i;
			25f➡26i
Narratorial Internal Analeptic Phase		NiAN	40i➡36f
/Immediate		NIiAN	15i➡1f
Narratorial Alternate Phase		NALP	45i2➡42f
/Immediate		NIALP	17i➡15f

	Segmental Transitions		
f➡i	2f➡3i	[NICP]	
f➡i1	33f➡34i1	[NICP]	
f➡m	34f➡13m	[NIiAN]	
f➡f	7f➡5f	[NIALP]	
f2➡i	14f2➡15i	[NICP]	
m➡i	50m➡51i	[NICP]	
m➡m2	7m➡5m2	[NIALP]	
m➡f	41m➡39f	[NIALP]	
i➡i	4i➡2i	[NALP]	
i➡m1	11i➡5m1	[NIiAN]	
i➡f	5i➡1f	[NIiAN]	
	17i➡15f	[NIALP]	
	40i➡36f	[NiAN]	
i➡f1	16i➡12f1	[NIiAN]	
	22i➡19f1	[NIALP]	
i2➡f	45i2➡42f	[NALP]	
i2➡f2	31i2➡18f2	[NiAN]	

i = initial; m = medial; f = final segments of chapters

i1, i2, etc. as subdivisions of chapter-segments

All examples of transitions are narratorial and illustrated from text.

Figure 2.3   Graham Swift, *Waterland*: Whole-Chapter and Segmental Transitions

13

Histrionics

Because when I was your age and Jack Parr was asking Whywhywhy and my father was asking Whywhywhy . . . (13i; 114)

The Greenwich scene suspended at 12f1 is then continued at 16i, with a subtle shift of focalization: Crick and Mary are presented by an external narrator. Such shifts from a normative first person are internal features of at least a dozen chapters (see Fig. 2.2). These allow Crick to detach himself from his own history, furthering self-criticism and self-mockery, as well as reinforcing the barrier state implied by the "once upon a time" formula.

An example of *narratorial immediate alternate phase* takes the reader directly from 19f1 to 22i. The biography of his grandfather prompts Crick to draw parallels in a second final segment (19f2) for the benefit of his class, while reference to a "curly-haired lad named Price" affords an immediate syntactic and grammatical transition to the next chapter ("Whom I call to order"). Thus, the continuity runs as an *immediate tie* from 19f2→20i. The words, moreover, with which master calls pupil to order, follow directly upon Price's provocative outburst: "You can stuff your past!," yet this lies six chapters back, at 14f1, making the relationship *analeptic*. As so often with a second final segment in *Waterland*, 14f2 is another of Crick's apostrophes to his class.

In two closing examples, polyphonic density and linear intricacy result from a combination of sequential types and dramatic accentuation. In chapter 34, the first initial segment forms part of Crick's response at 33f about having children of his own, before the second initial segment takes up again the theme of Dick's "sentimental education" from 32f1. The final segment lexically repeats Mary's resolve, to seek an abortion, from 13m (i.e. 33f→34i1; 32f1→34i2; 13m→34f). In chapter 45, the last stage of Dick's "education" commences, but the continuation via *alternate phase* from the abortion scene at Martha Clay's (42f) is to the second of the initial segments.

The first (45f1) is represented by Dick's retrieval, from the mouth of a stuffed pike, of the hidden key to the black trunk. Dick's action takes place in the diegesis, after the medial segment made up of Crick's reflections on his father. So teasing a sequence (42f→45i2→45m→45i1→45f), which sharply opposes orders of events and representation, eventually allows Crick, in chapter 46, to solve the mystery of the trunk. The shattering revelation about Dick's parentage leads directly into the final chapter (45f→46i→46f→52i), when, ten lethal Coronation Ales later, he dives into the Ouse and disappears.

Both technically and thematically, then, *Waterland* deals with barrier states. The separate realms of past and present, story and history meet and mingle in a complex interplay of syntactic and semantic relationships across chapter boundaries, producing effects now of combination, now of divergence, always of surprise for frame audience and reader alike. Any cult of discontinuity per se is pointless, as the reviewer of a Postmodernist Spanish novel indicates: "no amount of surface complexity can hide the fact that what is going on underneath . . . is ordinary. No matter how jumbled the sequences, how baffling and numerous the flashbacks, asides, elisions and superimpositions, the writer is always the same and his voice unvarying" (Butt 1977, 121). Such accusations scarcely apply to Swift's novel, with its range of narratorial voices and its stylistic variety, its interweave of narrative lines and its sophisticated repertoire of narrative sequence. These features are summarized in the simultaneous continuities and discontinuities, flux and fixity of its title, *Waterland*.

3

HISTORY: SEQUENTIAL DYNAMICS
IN FICTION, 1550–1900

SURVEY OF TEXTS

When we isolate the story like this from the nobler aspects
through which it moves, and hold it out on the forceps—
wriggling and interminable, the naked worm of time—it presents an appearance that is both unlovely and dull. But we have
much to learn from it.

> —E. M. Forster, *Aspects of the Novel*

I like to mark the time, and connect the course of individual
lives with the historic stream. . . .

> —George Eliot, *Daniel Deronda*

THE FOLLOWING SURVEY HIGHLIGHTS FEATURES OF TEMPORAL AND
continuity relations in samples of prose fiction from Cervantes to
Conrad, and hopes, by so doing, to furnish the basis of a historical
poetics. Since relevance to sequential dynamics, rather than aesthetic or critical standing, has been paramount, there is no intent
to establish a Great Sequence, and no need for works omitted to
fear canonic disqualification. Less familiar examples have often
been given more detailed attention, while length of treatment generally does not reflect length of text or accepted reputations.

This account concentrates on the period pre–1900, since the
broad thematic and technical aspects of temporality have been
more extensively explored in Proust, Joyce and Woolf, Faulkner
and Mann, and their successors, among other twentieth-century
figures. Earlier developments, however, have not been studied to
the same depth, and for that reason supply the focus here.

Innovative, striking or unusual features represent the criteria for
selection. The kind of case study devoted to Austen's *Persuasion*
(§2.1), for instance, could scarcely be applied with identical rigor
and detail to all hundred or more of the texts considered. To exam-

167

ine each in terms of categories of transition alone, would inevitably become mechanical, tedious, and (even more) prolix. Thus, the aim has been to indicate tendencies, rather than pretend to completeness.

Attention will be directed, therefore, toward such features as chapter linkage and cohesion, scale and grouping, semantic projections, relationships of tempo and rhythm, prominence of specific continuity phases at specific periods, positioning of dialogue, types of order-transform. Most of the texts chosen are already typographically divided by their authors, since issues of transition, in unsegmented texts, can be especially problematic, leading to interpretative questions that detract from the central discussion.

Anonymous, *Lazarillo de Tormes* (1554)
Miguel de Cervantes, *Don Quixote* (1605–15)

Inaugurating Spanish picaresque, a first-person protagonist recounts his career to an aristocratic audience. From birth to the writing-Now of his marriage and post as town-crier, *Lazarillo's* linear ordering reflects the sequence of his masters. Each merits a new chapter [*tratado*], but his unmentionable or uneventful experiences with friar and artist, shrink chapters 4 and 6 to less than half a page each. The gap of four years in the latter episode (1969, 76) produces an obvious imbalance in the overall coverage of time.

Within the tight compass of a mere seven chapters, such unevenness of tempo, as well as scale, is obvious. The autobiographical context alone motivates allocation of separate chapters to what, objectively, appear unfruitful encounters. That the material is allotted to chapters that do not adjoin, testifies to a basic narratorial sense of contrast, vital in a work so dependent, as is the picaresque, on episodic addition, and unified solely by an omnipresent Lazarillo. In less skilled hands, the risks of rambling series of incidents, easily transposable, lacking in character growth or change, remain great. At the same time, picaresque fiction offers archetypal potential for simplicity, lucid arrangement, forward motion in the novel as a genre.

Barely fifty years later, Cervantes's masterpiece heads a more self-conscious tradition. Symptomatic of the split perspectives of its two main figures, is their radically differing attitude to time: in the cave of Montesinos (2.23), what Sancho Panza deems an hour is inflated by Don Quixote into three days. One of the striking contrasts between the first and second parts, is a virtually seamless continuity over thirty chapters, from 1.14 to the end, the great majority being immediate ties. Most time-lapses, like the periods of two and fifteen days during the Knight's Second Expedition, are intrachapter, so that misadventures smoothly yield to further tales and encounters.

The brief chapter-summaries, moreover, foreground events continued or concluded, allowing temporal to underline thematic links. By literally suspending the action at 1.8f, Don Quixote and the Basque are left with swords aloft, in a frozen tableau uncannily precinematic: "At this critical point our delightful history stopped short and remained mutilated, our author failing to inform us where to find the missing part" (1965, 75). A second author happily chances upon an Arabic translation of the history. Its continuance, at 1.9m, from the precise point of suspension, sharply dramatizes a delayed version of an immediate tie.

Nocturnal gaps between chapters, so familiar in later fiction, scarcely appear in Cervantes. Not that events are confined to daylight: the adventures with Asturian maid, and corpse, in the first part, the meeting with the Knight of the Wood and the disenchantment of Dulcinea in the second, are nocturnal. Don Quixote and Sancho, furthermore, wait until midnight for a glimpse of her house at El Toboso. To avoid interrupting narrative flow, however, the passage between nightfall and dawn is frequently positioned *within* chapters.

As for analepsis, the first part limits itself to 1.10, where Sancho, left beaten by the monks' servants (1.8m), rejoins his master, newly victorious over the Basque. In the second, by contrast, Sancho's governorship means that for nine chapters the focus switches between him and the knight, until each appears separately in 2.54, to be reunited in the next chapter. This alternate phase sequence (varied in 2.50 by analeptic overlap), contributes to a striking drop of immediate ties in the second part.

Its less regular rhythms and wider problematizing are echoed by an increase in proximate phases, marking larger gaps between incidents. A similar growth in delayed presentations results from the narrator's playful assumption of translator's and Cide Hamete's masks, to debate fictional truthfulness (2.24), ironize authorial meticulousness (2.40), argue claims for digressions and inserted tales (2.44). The longest chapters and narrative phases, however, belong to the first part.

As embedded narratives, the Tale of Foolish Curiosity (1.33–35) and the Captive's Tale (1.39–41) cover three chapters apiece, both include verses and are preannounced, so promoting easy transitions. The tales involve differing degrees of hypodiegesis, levels of temporality beyond the main narrative. While the second tale is relatively self-contained, the first suffers violent intervention by Don Quixote, mistaking wineskins for giant, reality for romance. Devices such as apostrophes to readers, internal reference to specific chapters, or questioning the "originality" of text, form only part of Cervantes's large narrative legacy.

Madame de Lafayette, *La Princesse de Clèves* (1678)
John Bunyan, *The Pilgrim's Progress* (1678–85)
Aphra Behn, *Love-Letters Between a Nobleman and His Sister* (1684–87)

Driven by timeless rather than temporal concerns, the first part of Bunyan's prose allegory coincides with Madame de Lafayette's secular and psychological novel, *La Princesse de Clèves* (1678). Divided by its printer into four volumes, which sponsor immediate ties between books one and two (M. de Clèves's story), and two and three (Vidame de Chartres's), to contrast with the more leisurely gap between three and four (political realignments after the King's death), the French work traces out linearly its heroine's "sentimental education." By strategic use of historical distancing and keen dramatic concentration, alternating narrative with dialogue, the novel explores the inner conflict between passion and duty in an ultimately unchanging heroine, within an aristocratic world of formal conventions.

In Bunyan, on the other hand, Christian's didactic centrality and teleology underline the forward dynamic implied in its title, and which from the start thematically minimizes analepsis. The outer framework of a narrator who recounts his dream, and reiterates the fact at regular intervals, is crucial. Christian's status, in particular, becomes that of a distanced dream-figure, with whom the reader finds it difficult to identify. Furthermore, the topic of dream is transferred to the hypodiegetic level, as a man describes to Christian and the Interpreter his vision of the Last Judgment (Bunyan 1960, 36–37), or when Mr. Sagacity, within the outer narrator's dream, tells of Christiana's own dream (178).

If the oneiric perspective determines the quality of events, so that Mercy's marriage to Matthew at the innkeeper Gaius's suggestion seems inconsequential, it also affects fluidity of presentation. The absence in either part of chapter division, means that sequences are delimited by other means. Topographical markers on the route from the City of Destruction to Mount Zion supply the most obvious punctuation, as do the numerous insertions of verse and marginal headings, while the pilgrim's encounters with a range of helpers and foes offer temperamental and ideological contrasts.

Such exchanges are rendered in direct speech and dramatic format, even when, as is the case with Christian's summary of his progress to Prudence, Piety, and Charity (48–52), the reader is already familiar with the events, and reported speech would suffice.

In the treatment of temporality, the dream framework also plays a key role. Lacking specifics of age and period, the text is content to allow half a day for Christian's combat with Apollyon, an hour for Great-heart's struggle with Giant Maul, and an indeterminate "season" for Christian and Hope to sojourn in Beulah. Ultimately, the passage of time is insignificant. The number of days spent by Christian (first part) or his wife Christiana (second part) at Palace Beautiful, his imprisonment by Giant Despair at Doubting-Castle, "from Wednesday morning till Saturday night" (114), are factors that scarcely register on Bunyan's scales of eternity.

Influenced at least partially by *La Princesse de Clèves*, Aphra Behn's *Love-Letters*, her first and longest prose fiction, appears in three separate parts (1684–87), each incrementally larger in scale. Each differs too in generic format: part one is entirely composed of letters, nearly all exchanged between the lovers Silvia and Philander; part two mingles, in a 6:4 ratio, narrative and epistolary modes; part three has scarcely any letters, though like part two, it includes much direct speech, reflecting Behn's stage practice. As a roman à clef, real-life English political and erotic scandals of the 1680s, despite ostensible transfer to France, model its plot and characters. Its hybrid form, moreover, serves to project shifts of feeling and attitudes by its chief protagonists, as well as to inspire later novels.

From innocent daughter, Silvia, unlike Mlle. de Chartres, changes into manipulative libertine, as the romance-form of expressive love-letters gives way to a synoptic editorial narrative. In sequential terms, the textual proximity and regular alternation of letters in part one, suggests the lovers' emotional and geographical closeness. Few letters are dated, but all follow the "found text" convention, whereby they are arranged in putative order of despatch by an editor. The use of temporal and spatial deictics enables the reader to occupy imaginatively the addressee's role.

One of Philander's letters to Silvia, for example, opens lyrically in blank-verse mode, then refers to "this Oak where now I ly Writing on its knotty root" (Behn 1996, 36); another alludes, in its postscript, to composition so hasty that the hand is not counterfeit, while the next, editorially noted to be on ivory or wooden sheets, records that " 'tis now seven a Clock, I have my Watch in my hand" (48); Silvia's reply is incomplete, being "found in pieces torn," but anaphorically and materially rejoined by her maid Melinda (51). This instance, like others in parts two and three, focuses on letters as both communicative medium and topic.[1]

When Philander is exiled, and Silvia is drawn towards Octavio, the part-narrative part-epistolary mode hints at their gradual estrangement. Ironically, the two longest letters of the whole "three-decker" appear in this second part: Philander's confessions to Octavio, of his meeting and pursuit of Calista. Appropriately, in a novel of intimate relations, where Silvia is Philander's sister-in-law, Calista turns out to be Octavio's sister. The reader becomes involved by direct address from the narrator, who resorts to historical present tenses and prefigurations, and claims personal contact with the characters.

At the start of part three, the editor-narrator detachedly lists Silvia's vices in advance of her amours, and the satire of institutions and individuals accelerates. Parallel events in close proximity, such as the accidental shootings of Uncle Sebastian (303) and old Clarinau (309), link diegesis and hypodiegesis, leading to a plot-meld as Silvia visits her rival Calista at the nunnery. Epistolary problematics culminate in the reference to Philander's incriminating letter sent to Octavio, which Silvia had given to Calista, and the latter in turn to the Lady Abbess (318). One of Aphra Behn's most important legacies to the eighteenth-century novel, must be the adventure of, as much as the adventure in letters.[2]

Alain-René Lesage, *Gil Blas* (1715–35)
Tobias Smollett, *Peregrine Pickle* (1751)
Abbé Prévost, *Manon Lescaut* (1731)
Pierre Carlet de Chamblain de Marivaux, *La Vie de Marianne* (1731–42)

Both Lesage and Smollett continue the journey motif of Bunyan but in picaresque guise, and raise in acute form the issue of balance in the arrangement of episodes. Heroes whose careers are retrospectively and chronologically detailed, also embed numerous stories recounted by characters they meet. Disregarding quibbles about prodigious feats of memory, we might question the narratorial control over their material. In Lesage, Don Raphaël's tale (1.5.1) amounts to eight times the average chapter length of volume 1, while Scipion's tale (2.10.10–12) straddles three chapters, ten times in total the average for volume 2. In Smollett, the disproportion is still greater.

"The Memoirs of a Lady of Quality," interpolated toward the end of the novel (ch. 78), bulk no less than fifteen times the chapter average of *Peregrine Pickle*. Set against Smollett's statement that a novel, as "large diffused picture [needs] . . . a principal personage to attract the attention, unite the incidents, unwind the clue of the labyrinth," ([1753] 1971, 2–3), Peregrine's ability to "unite" his experience appears tenuous at best. If the self-contained quality of picaresque fiction is shown at its most extreme by the "Lady of Quality," most chapters conform to the disjointed, episodic rule. Only the Belgian incidents (chs. 54–63), culminating in the farce of Pallet's ass at the inn of Alost (ch. 60), show immediate ties.

Neither Prévost nor Marivaux adopts a direct mode. The Chevalier des Grieux's story of Manon is narrated within the extradiegetic memoirs of Renoncourt, while Marianne's autobiography allegedly emerges from a manuscript discovered in a country-house. Breaks between parts are alike instructive. At the end of part 1, Prévost's tempo can be judged from the disclosure that des Grieux has taken more than an hour over a hundred pages ([1731] 1965, 116). At a similar point, Marivaux's narrator, resorting to proleptic *Hakenstil*, foreshadows a crucial event which ushers in the second part of her life. This justifies a second part in the text, allowing the same-sex reader, "madame," to catch her breath. In later parts, prefiguration encourages suspense, as with Victorian serialization, though the gap in calendar time between parts two and three amounts to nearly two years:

> . . . on frappa à la porte. Nous verrons qui c'était dans la suite; c'est ici que mes aventures vont devenir nombreuses et intéressantes . . .
> (2e partie; [1731–42] 1957, 100–101)

> Oui, madame, vous avez raison, il y a trop longtemps que vous attendez la suite de mon histoire.[3]
> (3e partie; 105)

Samuel Richardson, *Pamela* (1740)

In his first novel, Richardson uses epistle, rather than chapter as his basic narrative unit. Thus, length and content, tone and frequency depend, ostensibly, on individual correspondents. Their thoughts and feelings are expressed in the first person, at the moment they emerge, conveying a sense of immediacy to recipients and readers alike. Length is adjusted by writer alone, as much in response to other letters as to outside events, while the identity of recipients tends to color what is said, and how.

The arrangement of letters is typically chronological; the interplay of *fabula* and *syuzhet* is virtually absent, since the level of presentation rules. If the events of *Pamela* cover less than one and a half years, the internal tempo can be judged by the relative frequency of letters: the heroine pens five in a year, then nine in two months, to climax in six journal entries on her wedding day.[4] The avoidance of specific year-dates continues in the much longer *Clarissa* (1748), with only the vaguest of references to Queen Anne and the South Sea Bubble.[5]

By "twinning" letters, restricted focalization can be partially overcome: the same event is recorded from different angles by different correspondents. Later epistolary novels, such as Laclos's *Les Liaisons Dangereuses* (1782), exploit these possibilities, at the risk of an artificial presentation involving military-style campaigns by the "writer-composites," Valmont and Mme. de Merteuil.

Another example, Goethe's *Werther* (1774), features year-dating and biographical closeness, with a sequence of confessional monologues interrupted to allow an editor to complete its hero's fate. The purely epistolary novel, however, though betraying an author's hand in the disposal of letters, contains no obvious intrusions. Peopled literally by men and women of letters, so hermetic a realm is bounded primarily by the worldviews of its writers, who determine its yardsticks and values. In temporal and continuity relations, the very self-enclosure of the form means, ultimately, that it is less rewarding than other types of novel in the way it contributes to sequential dynamics.

Henry Fielding, *Tom Jones* (1749)
————, *Amelia* (1751)

Aside from the aesthetic balance conveyed by its tripartite rhythm, *Tom Jones* shows a hitherto unusual control of temporal relations. Each heading in its eighteen books indicates how much time is contained, and this overt foregrounding enables readers and narrative statisticians to plot a constant deceleration: from five years in book 3, and three weeks in book 6, to a bare twelve hours for the Battle of Upton in the symmetrically central book 9. Having the smallest number of chapters in the novel, this only contrasts with the previous book 8, with the largest, partly due to the history of the Man of the Hill. Unlike Lesage and Smollett, Fielding typically avoids delivery in bulk. The Man of the Hill's account occupies five average-sized chapters, and is interrupted by comments from Partridge and Jones. Like the history of Mrs. Fitzpatrick (bk. 11), and the dénouement (bk. 18), its chapters form an immediate continuity, projecting an extended and concentrated narrative flow.

Among more than a dozen cases of analeptic phase are the incident of Sophia's pet bird, five years past (4.3), and her experiences prior to Upton (10.8), which appear in chapters boldly entitled "the history goes backward." The latter actually specifies the point in the text ("the ninth chapter of the seventh book"), at which the heroine was last featured ([1749] 1963, 467). Her escape from home (10.9) is, however, recorded later than her arrival at Upton (10.3), which the escape antedates, while her adventures after Upton are only continued at 11.2.

This complex sequence begins at the juncture where Tom leaves the inn, as well as the narrative, for two whole books (10.7→12.3). Squire Western is absent for a similar period (10.8→12.2). Such resumptions may straddle book divisions, as, for example, when Tom bids farewell to the lieutenant (7.15→8.2). Since Tom and Sophia are separated from each another, one of the narrative lines must trail behind the other, until by the penultimate book the rapid deployment of alternate phase conveys a climactic tempo.

Control by a strong authorial narrator is apparent from delayed presentation, and the "ornamental parts" heading each book. Such essayistic inserts further suspend the continuity of events not resolved at the end of each book. In 2.1, especially, the "founder of a new province of writing" declares himself free to disregard periods which are mere "blanks in the grand lottery of time," and to vary text-lengths: "My reader, then, is not to be surprised if in the course of this work he shall find some chapters very short, and others altogether as long; some that contain only the time of a single day, and others that comprise years; in a word, if my history sometimes seems to stand still and sometimes to fly" (1963, 65). When he juxtaposes a "little chapter, in which is contained a little incident" (5.4), with a "very long chapter, containing a very great incident" (5.5), closes book 14 with a "short chapter" of two pages (14.10), and opens the next book with one "too short to need a preface" (15.1), Fielding testifies to mastery of sequential dynamics and playfulness alike.

In *Amelia*, presentational options are central: scenic mode, whereby a character rehearses his or her "history"; and narratorial, conveying necessary background. Early on, Miss Matthew in prison tells Booth her life-story, and the account includes his reactions to it. Booth then responds with his own autobiography interspersed with her questions and comments in books 2 and 3, while Amelia listens to another first-person "history," Mrs. Bennet's, in the ten chapters of book 7.

Together, the accounts by Miss Matthew and Booth form an unbroken span of immediate continuity across twenty-seven chapters.

These make up nearly one-quarter of the novel, between his arrival in her cell (1.6), and their being "locked up double" for the night (4.1). Thus, the length and continuity of scenic mode at so early a stage, lends it a tactical advantage. Narratorial mode is exemplified by the scene in which Mrs. Ellison persuades Amelia of her noble cousin's attraction to her (6.3), and by the account of the background to Dr. Harrison's actions (9.1). In both chapters, the exactitude of the titles, "In which the history looks [a little] backwards," draws attention to overt analepsis.

As in *Tom Jones*, linearity reflects Fielding's stage practice, but fiction sponsors parallel phases rarely essayed in the theatre. While Amelia converses with Mrs. Ellison, Booth visits Colonel Bath (6.2f), and while Amelia visits Mrs. Bennet (bk. 7), Booth is arrested (6.9). This event, physically separating the couple, results in separate narrative lines for Booth and Amelia, as with Tom and Sophia. Alternate phase is most striking in book 8. Having reverted to the circumstances of arrest (8.1–2), chapters 8.3, 4, 7 and 9 continue with Amelia, but interweave Booth's fate in chapters 5, 6, and 10, switching in 8.8 to the plot-complicating designs of Colonel James upon the heroine. By contrast with the ending of *Tom Jones*, where a present-tense, but distant narrator reports finally on his cast, the last sentence here, "Amelia declared to me the other day" (12.9f; [1751] 1987, 545), suggests by its writing-Now a greater closeness on the part of the narrator, even if *Amelia* lacks the author-reader intimacy of the earlier novel.

Voltaire, *Candide* (1759)

Brevity and compression govern the overall strategy of a text, which embodies a critique of ideas within a thematic and formal parody of the Baroque novel. Alongside such heroic-galant monsters as Herzog Anton Ulrich's *Römische Octavia* (1677–1711), and Caspar von Lohenstein's *Arminius* (1689), ranging from 4,000 to 6000 pages, Voltaire's 120 pages look paltry indeed. To divide that total into thirty chapters, then threatens to bring divisions into disrepute. Voltaire takes that risk, and exploits diminutive scale for a variety of effects.

The initial and final segments of any chapter, therefore, may be no more than single sentences, or sentence-paragraphs. Shifts of tempo range from mercurial to ironically labored, but are always unpredictable. In the account of the auto da fé at Lisbon (ch. 6), a clause covering a week's imprisonment is followed by another detailing cassocks. The next sentence evokes a sermon, a third summarizes death by fire and gallows ([1759] 1960, 149).[6] From that point, up to the encounter with the Oreillons in South America (ch. 16), a sequence of nine chapters forms a span of immediate continuity, as if to erase, by dynamics of narrative ordering, vast temporal and spatial distances.

That span includes lexical repetition, the histories of Cunégonde and of the old woman. The latter bridges a chapter boundary (chs. 11–12) and involves a further embedded tale, to echo *in parvo* the novel of adventure. Of two delayed presentations, that in chapter 9 features a double delay, at chapter end (8f), and chapter start (9i). The event of Don Issachar's surprise arrival, gives way to the narrator's explanation. A new chapter then offers narratorial characterization of Issachar, before the focalized object takes over, as the banker assaults Candide. In mock-homage to models of suspense, Voltaire ends the significantly numbered chapter 13 with a dramatic curtain: "Il n'y avait pas un moment à perdre; mais comment se séparer de Cunégonde, et où se réfugier?"[7] (166).

Daniel Defoe, *Moll Flanders* (1722)
Lawrence Sterne, *Tristram Shandy* (1759/67)
———, *A Sentimental Journey* (1768)

Setting *Moll Flanders* beside *Tristram Shandy*, is to contrast "real-life" with intellectual picaresque. Barely four decades after Defoe's novel, Sterne subverts conventions of chronology, plot, typography, and much else. The absence of divisions in Defoe, excepting the journal entries in *Robinson Crusoe* (1719), invites the reader's own delimiting of sequences, as with Bunyan.

It is the arrival of Moll's fresh spouses and lovers, new stages of travel and crime, which now govern the scale of episodes. Analeptic phases are brief, limited to summaries of intervening events, or to a telescoped history of Moll's Lancashire husband. Overall tempi alternate markedly, in a personal retrospective spanning seventy years, and without chapter-regulation. Defoe's basic linearity is also at variance with Sterne's critique, and discussion of "time-scheme" in Defoe, tends towards comparison of fictional chronology with putative use of almanac or calendar.[8]

With Sterne, divisions are introduced only to be ridiculed: chapters are missing (4.24), rewritten (4.33), blank (9.18–19), or so reduced (4.5), as to be absurd. A preface postponed until volume 3, matches the wilful humor of an author who synchronizes his own and his book's procreation. Continuity relations are typified by chapters which fracture after a single page, as with Dr. Slop's portrait:

Imagine to yourself; — but this had better begin a new chapter.
                                                    (2.8f; [1767] 1967, 123)
                            Chapter IX
Imagine to yourself a little, squat, uncourtly figure . . . (2.9i; 123)

Lexical repetition alternates with syntactical continuity across chapter boundaries. Walter Shandy's dissertation on trade is graphically interrupted:

. . . for as he opened his mouth to begin the next sentence,
                                                    (2.14f; 135)
                            Chapter XV
In popped Corporal Trim with Stevinus . . .   (2.15i; 136)

Typographical play radicalizes trends present in Fielding, but which in him stop short of assaulting the print surface.

Inserted material echoes the lists and genre mixes in Rabelais's *Gargantua et Pantagruel* (1532–34), but in an everyday rather than fantastic context, fulfilling Tristram's aim to show digressions as "the soul of reading" (1.22). Thereby, he focuses on the serious as well as humorous implications of "progression" and linearity, and that "vicious taste" of "reading straight forwards . . . in quest of the adventures" (1.20; 83). Such novelistic stock in trade goes the same way as divisions and insertions, since external "plot" has been replaced by the Lockean history "of what passes in a man's own mind" (2.2). Tristram's highly self-conscious inner workings compose the novel itself, and the equation affords Sterne unrivalled freedom.

A virtual anthology of temporal elasticity projects Tristram's mind, ranging backwards and forwards, ostensibly "to keep all tight together in the reader's fancy" (6.33). That reader is multiple, directed by internal prolepsis to a door opening in the next chapter but one (3.11), by external prolepsis to a map added to the end of (an unrealized) volume 20 (1.13). Among the many analeptic phases, are those which specify particular chapters (2.12), even pages (3.31), resume thoughts or wishes from many chapters back, transgress narrative levels ("I have left my father . . . and my uncle Toby . . . promised I would go back to them in half an hour, and five-and thirty minutes are lapsed already," [3.38; 240]). Throughout, Tristram's datings give a sense of time advancing on one front at least. Seven years' labour brings him, resplendent in purple jerkin and yellow slippers, to volume 9, on 12 August 1766.

Comfortable, at least, unlike Yorick's seesawing in a chaise, as, in

A Sentimental Journey (1768), he pens a preface, displaced this time to chapter 7. In its place is a chapter with as celebrated a verbal in medias res ("They order, said I, this matter better in France—" [1986, 27]), as its physical counterpart in *Shandy*. Its incomplete final sentence only anticipates that of the final chapter, providing a terminal fracture or explicit non-ending (Lotman 1977, 212).

At barely one-third the length of *Shandy*, Yorick's "travelogue" is nonetheless divided into seventy unnumbered chapters. Its miniature dimensions are then combined with wholly superfluous headings, to accentuate authorial irony. By noting that scarcely an hour has elapsed since his arrival (ch. 18; 51), Yorick allows the reader to contrast the tempo of these seventeen Calais chapters, with the three weeks in Paris dismissed in a single paragraph later (ch. 63; 136). It is symptomatic that a single span of immediate ties unites the Calais scenes, while those in Paris are dominated by proximate ties, signifying a less intense focus.

Tempo markings more ingenious enable Yorick to count "twenty pulsations" on the beautiful Grisset's wrist (34i; 75), as well as to indicate, with ironic precision, the chapter's sequential status. Elsewhere, a range of continuity relations is evident. Yorick's proleptic allusion to a concert at Milan (36m; 79), remains external to a text that does not even reach Italy. An inserted fragment about Cupid (ch. 23; 57) seems entirely discontinuous, neither prepared for, nor commented on. False continuity is demonstrated in the episode with the Parisian *fille de chambre*, where the grammatical bridge ("and then—" [52f; 118] // "Yes— and then—" [53i; 118]) appears, two chapters later, to conceal two whole hours quietly elided by Yorick.

His self-conscious play with ordering recurs in the episode of the passport, apparently left behind in London. Yorick now feels it is time to inform the reader, "for in the order of things in which it happened, it was omitted; not that it was out of my head; but that, had I told it then, it might have been forgot now" (40i; 92). Simple ellipsis, devious paralipsis, consideration for the reader, hastily retrospective motivation? Yorick keeps his own counsel.

Denis Diderot, *Jacques le Fataliste* (1773)

Further intellectualizing Sterne, Diderot takes as point of departure the episode in *Tristram Shandy* (8.19), where Corporal Trim tries to tell uncle Toby the history of his wound and romance. This slight, but intertextual frame is then enormously expanded, though unsegmented apart from alternating prose and dialogue sections.

The effect resembles the cinematic switch from closeup to zoom-back, as scenic presentness is replaced by distanced commentary, near-isochrony by variable tempi.

So unusually sustained a dialogue format, already found in Rabelais, is the chief mode for the development of Jacques's relationship with his master, as well as for the frequent discussions with inn-keeper and wife, surgeon and marquis. The textual foregrounding of dialogue thus stresses the level of presentation over events, while its affinity with drama extends to the use of stage directions. Even within this format, however, brief one-line exchanges between Jacques and his master suggest sudden shifts of tempo, contrasting with the authorial account.

Jacques's own story, like Trim's, is discontinuous, constantly interrupted by others' stories, by fresh tacks and incidents, by authorial interpolations. Inserted stories, unlike those in earlier novels, never grow disproportionate enough to threaten the main narrative. That is far more at risk from the author-reader relationship, which assumes an even greater role than with Fielding: "Vous avez donc deux balances pour les actions des hommes? Mais dites-vous, *la Pucelle* de Voltaire est un chef d'oeuvre!—Tant pis, puisqu'on ne l'en lira que davantage.—Et votre *Jacques* n'est qu'une insipide rapsodie de faits, les uns réels, les autres imaginés, écrits sans grâce et distribués sans ordre. —Tant mieux, mon *Jacques* en sera moins lu. De quelque côté que vous vous tourniez, vous avez tort. Si mon ouvrage est bon, il vous fera plaisir; s'il est mauvais, il ne fera point de mal"[9] ([1773] 1959, 714).

The reader's queries and complaints about Jacques's ever-postponed love affairs are given voice, curiosity and expectations are rudely mocked and reprimanded. An inscribed reader sets up another level of activity, to compete with or to fracture exchange of dialogue or authorial report on other characters. A self-conscious author flaunts the ability to interrupt any sequence at will, seems dubious about which character's fortunes to follow, how best to continue a plot, tardily offering to describe a room, wondering aloud whether to overturn a coach.

Alternative versions of what Jacques did after lights-out are presented for the reader's choice. At the close of the novel, likewise, three different resolutions, supplementing the reader's own continuation, to the romance of Jacques and Denise. Of these endings, the 'editor' has copied the second directly from Trim's account in *Tristram Shandy* of the fair Beguine (8.22), thereby completing the framework inspired by a chapter-sequence from a kindred spirit.

Christoph Martin Wieland, *Die Geschichte des Agathon* (1766)
Johann Wolfgang von Goethe, *Wilhelm Meisters Lehrjahre* (1795)

Heading the German bildungsroman, Wieland's novel achieves temporal and spatial distance by inhabiting Ancient Greece. In delineating spiritual growth, development over a period of time is paramount. Agathon's search for an ideal balance takes him through the testing-stations of philosophy, love and politics. His personal history, however, is held over from part 1, with its stock plots of piracy and slavery, until the middle books of part 2, where he relates it to his lover Danae. Her own story, in turn, has to wait for a further six books, when, in part 3, she emerges in a typical recognition scene.

By positioning centrally Agathon's history-to-date in the first model of an influential novel form, Wieland establishes the precedent of a *B-A-C* macrosequence.[10] Later practitioners may follow or disregard this, but at any rate must take it into account. This holds true, whether we attribute the novel's ordering to skilful delaying tactics, or gentle irony, by a writer in tune with the contemporary wit and elegance of the Rococo style.

If the hero of *Agathon* moves physically between Delphi, Athens, Smyrna, Syracuse, and Tarento, the hero's experiences in *Wilhelm Meister* tend to be both less strenuous and more contemporaneous. Goethe's revisions over two decades, since the *Urmeister* begun in 1777, mean that changes of emphasis and ordering occur. The later version no longer begins with childhood; its dramatic entry in medias res crystallizes the key topic of theatre (1.1i; [1795] 1964, 10), but this is now only one of many elements in its hero's *Bildung*.

During the first half of the novel, chapter-lengths average no more than three or four pages, promoting a lightness of mood and rhythm. A span of immediate ties, virtually restricted to the first five books, unifies Wilhelm's account of his life to Mariane (1.3→8). Another combines news of her loss, the meetings with Mignon and harpist (2.10→14), while the Aurelie encounter bridges two books (4.19→5.3). Mixed continuity spans are also used in the episode of the bandits (4.4→9), and the *Hamlet* discussions (4.13→16). By devoting the long, unsegmented book 6 to embedded confessions of pietistic isolation ("Bekenntnisse einer schönen Seele"), a new stage is reached.

The lyrical inserts pervading earlier books, typified by "Kennst du das Land" at the head of book 3, recede. Narratorial pronouncements are now delegated to characters, though the theoretical debate on novel and drama, between Wilhelm and Serlo, is still summarized by the narrator (5.7). Symptomatic for the final two books is a decrease in the number of chapters, and an increase in their length. Therese's first-person history (7.6), and the account of Mariane's fate (7.8), become the longest chapters in the novel. Further interpolations: the "Lehrbrief" announcing Wilhelm's paternity of Felix, and the drama format introduced for Mignon's funeral, suggest the variety of narrative textures and thematic shifts.

By stressing in *Wilhelm Meister,* a potential for slow tempo in the novel as a genre, and the receptive, rather than active character of its hero (5.7), Goethe argues from within a specific novel for progression according to laws of organic growth. Time, measured externally by Fielding, appears less relevant to Goethe than the gradual development of inner personality, reacting and changing in response to differing modes of life.

Horace Walpole, *The Castle of Otranto* (1765)
Ann Radcliffe, *The Mysteries of Udolpho* (1794)

While pedagogy underpins the bildungsroman, the engine behind early Gothic fiction is terror, allied to the miraculous. Containing no "flowers, digressions, or unnecessary descriptions" (Walpole [1765] 1978, 40), all in *Otranto* tends directly to the catastrophe. By page two, young Conrad has already been dashed to pieces by an enormous helmet, and the atmospheric keynote is set. Reappearing at the close of chapter 2, the same casque with its sable plumage triggers a further emotional climax in Manfred, and immediate continuity (2f→3i; 92–93) graphically serves to suggest how strong feeling surges across narrative divisions.[11]

Typifying the Gothic and its temporal relations, are heightened tempi, and an initial enigma: a mysterious prophecy resolved only in the final pages by Manfred's confession. Walpole's macrosequence is B-C-A,[12] the last term representing an external analepsis. Part of the Gothic's attraction stems from an essentially linear scheme, stressing forward succession, but complete only by narratorial revelation of a prehistory. At the start, the reader knows enough about Manfred to enter confidently into the narrative, but does not suspect that the opening scene belongs to the B, rather than A component. Subsequent tension is produced by uncertainty, as to if, and when, gaps in knowledge will be filled.

By alluding, on title-page and in preface, to its status as a translation from an original Italian manuscript of 1529, discovered in a private library in England, Walpole introduces a further temporal and thematic dimension. To set events at the period of the First Crusade, and employ editorial devices *[Herausgeberfiktion]* as a way to convey their authenticity to a mid-eighteenth-century readership, involves framework techniques. In later writers, these shift, significantly, from the paratext of preface, to become part of the text itself.

With nearly six times as many pages, and eleven times as many divisions, the economy of Ann Radcliffe's best-known work, *The Mysteries of Udolpho*, is quite different. In terms of sequential dynamics, one of its most striking features is the predominance of nocturnal gaps. The rhythm from chapter end to new chapter start, of Emily's retiring at night/waking next day, accounts for over half the total chapters. Nocturnal phase directly binds books 1 and 2, as Emily parts from Valancourt (1.13), and leaves her aunt's house next morning (2.1). Half of book 2 and more than half of book 3 use nocturnal gaps, which again bind the larger divisions (2.12→3.1).

By the last book, now linked, symptomatically, to book 3 by proximate phase, that proportion is lower, but the close of 4.1, which in the very same sentence sees Emily both retire and wake, stands out, precisely by its deviation from the strong nocturnal rhythm already established: "Thus passed the night in ineffectual struggles between affection and reason, and she rose, in the morning, with a mind, weakened and irresolute, and a frame, trembling with illness" (4.1f; [1794] 1970, 518).

This break in rhythm also enables the narrator to shift rapidly between characters, as the plot moves to its climax. Whereas books 2 and 3 have two (internal) analeptic phases apiece, resuming, after seven chapters, the Valancourt line (2.8→2.1), or tracking Montoni and Count Morano, the last book uses parallel, as well as analeptic phase, to register the sense of events running powerfully together. The inserted "Provençal Tale" read by Ludovico (4.6), his subsequent adventure with the bandits (4.7), and the history of Signora Laurentini (4.17), forming part of the dénouement, further fragment the continuity of the Emily line.

If reader expectations of Gothic horror on horror, articulated as immediate continuity across divisions, is realized only once in Walpole's five chapters, there is no single example in Radcliffe's fifty-seven. Events do occur at night, but the device of recording time-lapses *inside* chapters, and so theoretically freeing chapter gaps for overflows of feeling, is allied to the comfortable regularity of nocturnal phase, and a lyrical tonality diffused by epigraphs and interspersed poems.[13]

Jean Paul Richter, *Die Unsichtbare Loge* (1793)
———, *Hesperus oder 45 Hundsposttage* (1795)
———, *Flegeljahre* (1805)

Speculative and idealistic, like Hölderlin and Kleist at odds with Weimar Classicism, Jean Paul takes up and develops the fictional critiques of his mentor Sterne. Divided into chapter-length units, his works have curious nomenclature: "Sectors," "Filing-Cabinets," "Jubilee Years," "Official Reports," or lapidary titles. In the first major novel, *Die Unsichtbare Loge* (1793), "Jean Paul" even appears as a character, to rival Gustav for Beata's love, and he supplements divisions with extra sheets, lines, and thoughts. He reduces "Sectors" 39–46, because of his illness, to a few lines, so that his sister has to take over, while long digressions alternate with instances of writing-Now.

In *Hesperus*, division-titles are strongly motivated: "Dog-Post Days" allude to reports about the local duchy, which reach the author by canine despatch. Often surpassing Sterne in bizarre fantasy, as well as appellations, Jean Paul adopts his sequential practices, and his play with narrative levels. Thus, the first "day" blends with the next:

Und so führt mich das Schicksal selber in den
2. HUNDSPOSTTAG
Beim Tor des ersten Kapitels fragen die Leser die Einpassierenden: "Wie heissen Sie—Ihren Charakter?—Ihre Geschäfte?"—
Der Hund nimmt für alle das Wort.[14]

([1795] 1927b, 1. 512)

A self-consciously ironic narrator admits the improbability of many events (5. "Hundsposttag" [henceforth, H.]; 551), resolves to add a witty "Leap Day" after every four divisions, but is later forced into a preemptive strike against critics who might reproach him for omission.[15] Shandy-like, he includes details of his hero Viktor's arrival from Göttingen, excluded earlier from 3. H., then notes in a postscript, that he has only a month's gap to bridge (1175), between the end of the story and the writing-Now: a triumph denied to Tristram.

Viktor, at one point, reads *Die Unsichtbare Loge*, and its author too is introduced. "Jean Paul" himself discusses *Hesperus* with Dr. Fenk (45. H.), only to ask how the book will end (1228). This challenge to fictional conventions which demarcate author, narrator, and character, joins with satire against the Germans themselves, whose love of order underlies expectations of narrative linearity: "Chronologisch solls noch dazu gemacht werden . . . Dadurch wird die Ordnung grösser. Denn ich kenne die Deutschen: sie wollen wie die Metaphysiker alles von vorn an wissen, recht genau, in Grossoktav"[16] (22. H.; 817).

Flegeljahre (1805) focuses on twin brothers who cooperate on a novel-within-a-novel, which fictionally embodies their doubleness. In spite of digressions, in speeches, play of footnotes, and letters from "Jean Paul" as biographer, the plot line is typically linear. Paul's fusion of Sternean disorder and ideals of *Bildung* proves, despite its panache, unsatisfactory. Without the justification of Shandy's internal focalization, events often seem arbitrary, and characters are patently stage-managed.

William Godwin, *Caleb Williams* (1794)
Matthew Lewis, *The Monk* (1796)
Mary Shelley, *Frankenstein* (1818)
Charles Maturin, *Melmoth the Wanderer* (1820)

Godwin points out that *Caleb Williams,* in its exploration of individual psychology, was conceived end-first, in the series: pursuit, flight, murder.[17] In the finished novel, to accord with reader conventions, he reverses this sequence. The higher proportion of pages and chapters in volume 3, shows, nonetheless, the greater weight placed on the murder motif. Unlike Radcliffe, Godwin makes use of immediate ties, to project such dramatic action as Caleb's escape from prison, bridging volumes 2 and 3. This contrasts with the more distanced, self-contained quality of volume 1, where Caleb renders Collins's story of Falkland's life. By the final chapter of volume 3, action overtakes record, as the writing-Now is dated three days after Falkland's warning that escape is impossible.

The melodramatic tenor and tempo of Lewis's "romance," *The Monk*, is set by its opening: "Scarcely had the Abbey-Bell tolled for five minutes" ([1796] 1973, 7). Thereafter, the focus moves chiefly between Abbot Ambrosio, and Don Lorenzo, both attracted to Antonia. In the early scene of Matilda's seduction by the monk (1.2), the narrative is broken off, and Lorenzo gives a three-chapter account, using immediate ties, of the elopement and apparent death of his sister Agnes. Only then ("The burst of transport was past: Ambrosio's lust was satisfied" [2.3; 223]), is the scene resumed.

Its status is discontinuous with Lorenzo's account, but its action immediately succeeds 1.2f (" 'Thine, ever thine!' murmured the Friar, and sank upon her bosom" [91]). The reader's surprise at this direct resumption, rather than the expected proximate tie, or discreet silence, then yields to shock. Speculations about Agnes (3.1), are replaced, in the same chapter, by Ambrosio's suffocation of Antonia's mother, with immediate continuity carrying the narrative across into 3.2.

Two alternate phases prepare for the climax of 3.4, when the monk rapes and stabs Antonia in the vault. Appearing now within the same chapter as Ambrosio, Lorenzo arrives, but too late to revive her. Agnes is also rescued, her "History" adding external to the internal analepses. Emotional tension is heightened throughout by poetic epigraphs and interpolations. Simultaneous chapter- and volume-end suspense ("[Ambrosio] . . . waited with impatience for the approach of midnight" [2.4f; 279]), typifies the Gothic genre.

Fifty years after Walpole's *Otranto*, with framework confined to preface alone, Godwin's daughter, Mary Shelley, incorporates prefatory material into the actual text of *Frankenstein* (1818). Within the last of Walton's letters to his sister, comprising the frame narrative, is a journal detailing his encounter with Victor Frankenstein. This leads to embedded autobiographies, oral and chronological, by Frankenstein to Walton, by the Monster to Frankenstein. Although first-person forms ensure immediate continuity between chapters, breaks are justified on grounds that the contents of a letter need a fresh division (ch. 6), or that a brief pause encourages recall of horrific events (ch. 20). Despite these, immediate ties are used, not to convey emotional surges, but to ease continuity. Walton returns two hundred pages after Frankenstein begins his account, to complete the epistolary frame.

In *Melmoth*, though twice its length, the proportion of frame to enframed is almost identical to *Frankenstein*. The outer frame of John Melmoth's stay at his uncle's decaying mansion on the Irish coast, gives way to "Stanton's Tale." In this mutilated manuscript about seventeenth-century Spain, fragmentation is typographically reproduced:

—"That is false; you imagined you did, and that has been the
cause of all the wild   *   *   *   *   *
                              *   *   *   *
of the   *   *   *   *   *   *   *
*   *   *   of your finally being lodged in this
mansion of misery."

(1.3; [1820] 1968, 55)

By contrast, in the central narrative delivered orally to Melmoth, over several days and nearly five hundred pages, an outer narrator intends that the Spaniard Monçada's tale, discontinuous in actuality, will be given, "without the endless interruptions, and queries and anticipations of curiosity, and starts of terror" (1.5; 73), with which it was broken by its audience.

The tale includes a span of immediate continuity (2.7→3.13), bridging volumes 2 and 3, and dramatizing the escape from a convent (2.9→10). This rapid tempo (2.9f) contrasts sharply with a slow-motion sequence (2.10i), then four months of convalescence, telescoped into a paragraph:

> *"He is safe,"* cried Juan, following me. *"But are you?"* answered a voice of thunder. Juan staggered back from the step of the carriage,—he fell. I sprang out, I fell too—on his body. I was bathed in his blood,—he was no more.   (2.9f; 215)
>
> Chapter X
>
> One wild moment of yelling agony,—one flash of a fierce and fiery light, that seemed to envelope and wither me soul and body,—one sound, that swept through my ears and brain like the last trumpet, as it will thrill on the senses of those who slept in guilt, and awake in despair,— one such moment, that condenses and crowds all imaginable sufferings in one brief and intense pang, and appears exhausted itself by the blow it has struck,—one such moment I remember, and no more.
>
> (2.10i; 216)

Monçada's tale embeds further oral tales, as well as another manuscript ("Tale of the Indians"), containing illegible and obliterated pages, though these are not typographically reproduced as such. A different kind of embedding occurs before the climax. The Wanderer appears in person, and his mental state is expressed in the brief "Wanderer's Dream," prior to his plunge from the cliff.

Friedrich Schlegel, *Lucinde* (1799)
Clemens Brentano, *Godwi* (1801)
Anonymous, *Die Nachtwachen des Bonaventura* (1805)
E. T. A. Hoffmann, *Lebensansichten des Katers Murr* (1821)
Karl Immermann, *Münchhausen* (1839)

Where Gothic overstresses external events, much German Romantic fiction discounts plot per se. Viewing the novel as a genre of subjectivism and fantasy, symphonic in its all-inclusive variety,[18] the critic Friedrich Schlegel attempts to embody theory in his novel *Lucinde*. Its very incompleteness matches his claim that the Romantic ethos resides in a constant process of growth or *Werden*: a fundamental inability to be completed. One corollary is the high value attached to the fragmentary, together with an emphasis on the organizing imagination.

In a central section, "Lehrjahre der Männlichkeit",[19] consciously echoing *Wilhelm Meister,* Julius switches to a more objective third person. From a mature standpoint, he surveys his spiritual growth, and recognizes "eine Masse von Bruchstücken ohne Zusammenhang"[20] ([1799] 1962, 37). Disjointedness is clear, when Julius breaks off a letter to his mistress Lucinde, resolving to abandon conventional order for "das Recht einer reizenden Verwirrung"[21] (9), and then introduces his "Dithyrambische Fantasie." To convey complex experience, in the homogeneous framework of a letter, is impossible for him. Only by resorting to the scattered papers Lucinde has preserved, can "the fine chaos" of love be expressed (9).

Ipso facto, the sequential dynamics of the novel's thirteen sections, of varying size and topics, demonstrate Julius's positive application of imaginative "confusion," in the way he selects and presents his material. Proceding from, and dis/organized by a central consciousness, that presentation resembles Shandy's, rather than Schlegel's professed models in Jean Paul and Diderot. Juxtaposition, however, rather then transition, is the governing principle behind the sections, symmetrically grouped around the lengthy, central "Lehrjahre." Sensuality and idealism, idyll and piquant dialogue, abstract reflection and dramatic format compose Schlegel's "artistically ordered confusion." While it provokes the bourgeois morality of its time, it also foreshadows literary experiments a century later.

Beside Schlegel's confessional "arabesque," *Godwi* (1801) seems massive and overwhelmingly lyrical. In thematizing the play of authorship, Brentano gestures toward Jean Paul, and his inclusion of poetry adds a dimension not attempted in *Lucinde*. Subtitled "ein verwilderter Roman,"[22] its first part comprises letters, mainly between Godwi and his friend Römer, but including play-format, journal, and poems. With the preface to the second part, a self-enclosed epistolary world is subverted. Those letters, it now appears, had been handed over by Römer to the fictive author Maria, who has sought out Godwi in order to continue the narrative.

Maria later shows the first part of the novel to Godwi himself, who points out to her a pool in the park: "Dies ist der Teich, in den ich Seite 266 im ersten Bande falle."[23] (2.18; 1978, 379). Self-consciousness reaches self-parody, when they discuss the content of that first part, and Godwi supplies family papers for Maria to reorganize in the second part (ch. 20). Thereafter, the narrative becomes increasingly disconnected.

Whole chapters (chs. 17, 21, 26) are virtually given over to poetry, and Maria presents the fragmentary, aphoristic mémoires of Godwi's father, completed by his son (chs. 28–29). Her illness leads to a "fragmentary continuation," after which Godwi addresses the reader about her condition, then largely takes over the narrative. In a final section, another friend edits the material, and reinforces the elegiac mood following the couple's deaths with a coda of poetic parodies, the last being dedicated to Brentano himself.

Like Schlegel, the unidentified author of *Nachtwachen* offers brief sections, unified only by a central consciousness. With title inspired by Jean Paul, the sixteen sections lack the equivalent of Julius's pivotal "Lehrjahre," as Kreuzgang pieces together episodes from his own life. Far from picaresque linearity, the sequential dynamics of the night-watches correspond more closely to Shandean association. Seasonal progression proves illusory, as the autobiographer works backwards and forwards over his material.

Already, by focusing on the topic of night, the narrator displaces a fictional norm, whereby nocturnal phase marks a regular transition between daytime events. His aim, "ein gutes und vollständiges Chaos zu vollenden"[24] (ch. 6; [1805] 1960, 55), justifies the wayward ordering, and the movement toward negation. With resort to prose-poems, letters, and fictive woodcuts, a succession of scenes and visions, ranging from farce and horror, to satire and madness, culminates in a return to the opening watch. Reordered chronologically (16-4-7-9-14-15-6-1-2-3-[4]-5-8-10-11-12-13-[16]),[25] *Nachtwachen* reveals how temporal and continuity relations depend on a fragmented consciousness, and no longer on external plot.

Editorial play, as an aspect of Romantic irony, is radicalized in *Lebensansichten des Katers Murr* (1821). E. T. A. Hoffmann, in its preface, announces himself as a mere editor to the authorial tomcat, whose pompous foreword, which the printer was directed to suppress, has "unfortunately" been printed. Blame for the book's peculiar format is attributed to the compositor, who has published Murr's manuscript as received. This included pages from a biography of *Kapellmeister* Kreisler, which Murr tore up to use as pad and blotter while writing his autobiography. To this humor of textual origins, and the novelty of a feline narrator, must be added the irony, that Kreisler's "fragmentary" biography in fact exceeds Murr's own, by a factor of three to two. The narratives alternate symmetrically throughout. Murr's sections are semantically and syntactically continuous, as well as chronological, while Kreisler's are random and discontinuous.[26]

Playful suspense is created at section ends, as, for instance, when the tomcat is interrupted mid-sentence in the description of a fire. At the novel's halfway stage, precisely, Murr's courtship of Miesmies is rudely broken off: "Silbern glänzte ihr weisser Pelz im Mondschein, in sanftem schmachtendem Feuer funkelten die grünen Äuglein. 'Du—' "[27] (1.2; 1967, 289), only to be continued grammatically by an address to the reader from Kreisler's biographer: "—hättest, geliebter Leser, das freilich schon etwas früher erfahren können"[28] (289). That section, in its turn, is humorously interrupted by a further "Du—" which now allows Murr to resume his amatory address:

> Es ist nun an der Zeit, dass jene verhängnisvolle Frage des Biographen:
> "Du—"   (1.2; 301)
> (M.f.f.) liebst mich also, holde Miesmies?[29]   (301)

Editorial manipulation of material is evident later, in marginal interventions on Murr's plagiarisms of Shakespeare, Chamisso, and Kreisler himself. In a closing postscript, the editor remarks that Murr's death means that his autobiography must itself remain a fragment. Ironically, so much of Kreisler's book has been discovered, that the editor proposes to bring out a third volume. This will reverse the original hierarchy, interspersing what are now merely fragments by the philistinistic cat, between sections by the genuine artist.

Nearly two decades later, *Münchhausen*, Karl Immermann's own *Doppelroman*, alternates books of village idyll and courtly satire, targeting especially the real-life aristocrat, Fürst von Pückler-Muskau. The latter's travel journal, *Briefe eines Verstorbenen* (1831), arranged letters from 1826–28 after those from 1828–29, ostensibly to boost sales. Immermann, subtitling his last novel "a history in arabesque," thereby alluding to the Sterne-Schlegel-Paul tradition, parodies Pückler by starting, in medias res, with ch. 11.

In fictive correspondence between editor and bookbinder printed after chapter 15, and before chapters 1–10 appear, the latter defends his "reordering" by declaring linearity unfashionable. Any worthwhile author, he claims, "muss sich auf die unordentliche verlegen, dann entsteht die Spannung, die den Leser nicht zu Atem kommen lässt und ihn parforce bis zur letzten Seite jagt"[30] ([1839] 1906, 1.68–69). Nowadays, "confusion" must be the watchword. This, indeed, is the effect of Münchhausen's own famously mendacious stories, digressive and incomplete, leading the distraught schoolmaster Agesilaus to plead for "etwas geordneter und schlichter"[31] (1.1.13; 35).

The entry of the "well-known writer" Immermann (3.6.5) forcibly undercuts, as in *Hesperus* and *Godwi*, the fictional illusion, by resort to metaleptic transgression. While the author-as-character criticizes Münchhausen, he is himself accused of being shallow and mediocre by a creation who now declares his independence.

Immermann's ironic fractures enable him, by including a personal letter to the poet Ludwig Tieck, and inventing letters to bookbinder and real-life fiancée (4. Teil), to confuse narrative levels still further and to celebrate the virtues of improvisation.

Sir Walter Scott, *Guy Mannering* (1815)
———, *The Heart of Midlothian* (1818)
———, *Ivanhoe* (1819)

By directing attention to national tradition and historical consciousness, Scott influences cultural trends within and outside Britain. While raising issues of "progress," pointing up spiritual and physical changes between the period of the narration and of the narrated events, he sets important dynamics in train. To deal also with individuals in their multifarious contexts, necessarily involves, in terms of sequential dynamics, managing several narrative lines at once.

The problem is less complex in *Guy Mannering* than elsewhere, though Scott is at pains to keep the reader apprised. His narrator warns of the hero's initial disappearance (5f) for what proves to be seven chapters, since "it is to another and later period of his life that the present narrative relates" ([1815] 1987, 49). An epigraph from *The Winter's Tale* (4.1.5–6), referring to a "slide / O'er sixteen years," prepares the reader for a specific ellipsis of "nearly seventeen years" (10f→11i). This feat of outdoing the Bard, comes with the reassurance, that in the interim, "nothing occurred of any particular consequence" (11i; 83).

Contrasts of tempi are typical of Scott: leisurely expositions of places, events and characters, as in the sketch of family and estate in *Guy Mannering*, chapter 2, together with *presto* passages, such as Mrs Bertram's reactions at a later chapter end, to her son's abduction: "she was far advanced in her pregnancy; she fell into the pains of premature labour, and, ere Ellangowan had recovered his agitated faculties, so as to comprehend the full distress of his situation, he was the father of a female infant, and a widower" (9f; 75).

Speed, in the dramatic terms of Bertram's return and arrest, is conveyed by a span of immediate continuity (chs. 40→43). Resort to letter-extracts (chs. 16→18), even whole letter-chapters (chs. 29→31), with no authorial commentary, brings a sharp change in tempo and focalization, and announces analepsis. The choice of particular sequential phases foreshadows the climax. Developments in the Bertram line (chs. 44→45) are paralleled in Mannering (ch. 46), before alternate phase takes the reader from Woodbourne (ch. 47), to Portanferry (ch. 48), back to Woodbourne (ch. 49), and both lines merge in the culminating ch. 50.

For *The Heart of Midlothian*, Scott invents a frame narrator who edits a schoolmaster's manuscript, to combine the political events of the Porteous Riot, with the personal mission of Jeanie Deans. Invoking the "digressive" Ariosto as authority, the narrator comments aloud on the need, "of connecting the branches" of the story ([1818] 1954, 174), bringing other characters up to the point reached by his heroine (16i). Here, he leaves Jeanie with the stranger on the heights above Edinburgh, to switch to a legal debate in the city below, only to resume her line two chapters later with immediate internal analepsis, and specifying its point of interruption: "here our story unites itself with that part of the narrative which broke off at the end of the fifteenth chapter" (18i; 194).

Against the same backcloth, the history of Reuben Butler is given, in an external analepsis of three chapters (chs. 8–10), an indication of his importance in the novel. Scott takes advantage of the retrospective, to suggest parallels between narrating and narrated: "We have been a long while in conducting Butler to the door of the cottage at St. Leonard's; yet the space which we have occupied in the preceding narrative does not exceed in length that which he actually spent on Salisbury Crags" (11i; 122).

For young Staunton's history, Scott prefaces the invalid's disjointed oral account to Jeanie (ch. 33), with an admission that the overdetailed, impassioned manner of delivery has required editorial telescoping. Throughout the novel, key scenes are unified by spans of immediate continuity: Butler's visit to the Deans (chs. 11→13), Jeanie and her father preparing for Effie's trial (chs. 18→20), the trial itself (chs. 21→23), Jeanie's journey to London (chs. 29→34), her decisive meeting with the Queen (chs. 36→38).

In *Ivanhoe*, immediate continuity is prominent. Though minimally reduced by epigraphs, it effectively binds the two long opening spans of chapters set at Rotherwood (chs. 1→6), and at Ashby (chs. 7→11). It helps to fuse the chapters describing Rebecca's trial at Templestowe (chs. 35→38), and, in the novel overall, accounts for the high proportion of thirty-two out of forty-four chapters. Within those spans, however, short stretches of internal analepsis occur: to render the scene in the hall before the Templar's horn sounds (3i2→3m), to sketch previous courses of the tournament (9m). A medial scene-change, to Rebecca's father's house (10m), then allows immediate continuity at chapter end.

Enigmatic motifs, above all, require more extended use of analepsis. Ivanhoe's disappearance after the Ashby lists, means a ten-chapter gap until the opening of chapter 28. Here, "our history must needs retrograde" ([1819] 1987, 331), even if an intelligent reader is given credit for linking Ivanhoe's fate with Rebecca's. Similarly, the "Black Knight" vanishes for long periods, to be recalled four chapters (chs. 16→12f1), then seven chapters later (chs. 40→33), when he is identified as King Richard.

Characters physically separated from one another add complexity to the narrative. Scott's solution for recounting the sufferings of Isaac, Rowena, and Rebecca, imprisoned in different cells at Torquilstone Castle, is to allocate successive chapters (chs. 22→24) to each. Since the captives arrive together, the chapters run in parallel phase, and their limits are pre-set by their registration of the same horn-blast (21f), a device remarkably anticipating Modernist simultaneity.[32]

Finally, to convey the tension of the siege and destruction of Torquilstone, both parallel and analeptic overlaps appear. The former, during an interval in the attack, switches from Ivanhoe (29m) to the Templar and De Bracy (30i), advances the action to Ulrica's locking up Front-de-Boeuf, as the fire begins to take hold (30f). The latter phase tracks back (31i) to her promise of vengeance (27m), only to take the scene of the burning Castle to its conclusion, as Ulrica herself perishes in the flames (31f).

Honoré de Balzac, *Le Père Goriot* (1835)
Victor Hugo, *Notre-Dame de Paris* (1831)
───────, *Les Misérables* (1862)

Balzac's normal novelistic practice, exemplified in *Le Père Goriot* (1835) and *Ursule Mirouët* (1841), broadly involves an *A-B-C* rhythm, in which the initial component bears an unusually heavy freight of accumulative realistic detail. The entire first section of *Goriot,* covering nearly one-third of the length and memorably evoking the Pension Vauquer and its lodgers, is described by Balzac as expository, and forward action commences only halfway through it. Each of the remaining three sections declines progressively in size, matched by a reduction of intervening time-lapses, to leave only a nocturnal phase at the start of the fourth section. In *Ursule Mirouët*, moreover, the exposition occupies half the novel, with a historical review of developments up to 1829. Its second part then moves on eight years, close to the actual period of composition.

By such tactics of "front-loading," and deliberate imbalance of parts, another novel such as *La Recherche de l'Absolu* (1834) has its very raison d'être in the contrast of initial plenitude with final desolation. Balzac's general stress on self-sufficient sections, measured pace, and relatively few divisions, means, ultimately, that interest lies much more obviously within, rather than between sections, so that he offers less, in terms of sequential dynamics, than does Hugo.

Medieval settings transfer from England, in *Ivanhoe*, to France in *Notre-Dame de Paris*, the first of Hugo's great popular novels, where, like Scott, he contrasts past with present. From the start, the action is precisely dated (6 January 1482), in relation to the writing-Now (25 July 1831). Its sequential movement is clear throughout, but marked by an alternation of events and block exposition, and governed essentially by a large-scale rhythm of *B-A-C* identical with that used in Balzac's *La Peau de Chagrin*, also of 1831.

In *Notre-Dame*, the first book (of eleven) has immediate continuity for all six chapters, as the main figures enter the Palais de Justice. A discrete account of the Place de Grève, occupying its own chapter (2.2), interrupts a flow of events culminating in the "wedding night" of the poet Gringoire and gypsy Esmeralda. Here, two books and a single day completed, Hugo suspends forward action for three whole books, devoting separate chapters to the architecture of Notre-Dame (3.1), a virtuoso topography of Paris (3.2), thrice the average chapter length, and an analeptic account of the relationship since 1467 of foundling Quasimodo and archdeacon Frollo. The large-scale retrograde concludes with another detachable, essayistic chapter, treating the role of books in the fifteenth century (5.2), as the novel reaches the two-fifths stage. Henceforth, the third term of *B-A-C* reached, events are broadly linear.

Resuming and balancing the first two books, book 6 likewise covers a single day, the very next (7 January 1482), witness to Quasimodo's flogging. The tempo then slackens prior to Frollo's jealous stabbing of Phoebus (7.8), the outcome of which is suspended for a month, until another closing chapter (8.6), when analeptic overlap produces the melodramatic "curtain" of hunchback flourishing rescued gypsy from bell-tower. Further internal analepsis in the last books reflects Hugo's need to track the separate lines of Frollo, Gringoire, and Quasimodo.

The latter's heroic defence of Notre-Dame (10.4), for instance, is discontinued for two chapters, until the cliff-hanging close (10.7), when he discovers the cell sheltering Esmeralda to be empty. His reaction, stressed by lexical repetition, is discontinued until 11.2, while the analeptic 11.1 reverts to her rescue by Gringoire in the longest chapter of the novel. The shortest (11.3), typifying Hugo's love of contrasts, is almost adjacent, and summarizes developments after Esmeralda's hanging, and Frollo's plunge from cathedral tower.

Tripling the scale, and intensifying features of the earlier novel, *Les Misérables* displays similar transparency of sequence, and attention to the dynamics of segmentation. In so extensive a work, books, rather than chapters, represent key narrative units. At the same time, increased demands upon the reader's memory opt against the kind of nonlinear macrosequence found in *Notre-Dame*. While Valjean's recent history can be confined to single chapters (1.2.6, 1.2.8), a solid book of nineteen chapters is given over to an exposition of the Battle of Waterloo (2.1).

Other books, necessarily suspending forward events, deal exclusively with convent (2.6), and religious life (2.7), political events of the 1830s (4.1, 4.10), argot (4.7), and the Paris sewers (5.2). Analeptic phases are comparatively rare, restricted to continuing the fortunes of characters geographically separated. Thus, the Valjean (1.7.7→5), and Fantine (1.8.1→1.7.6) lines must alternate, while the secretive personality and activities of Javert demand temporal reversion (1.8.3, 2.5.10).

Immediate continuity is evident in the use of anaphora. In successive chapters (1.5.2, 3), the openings, "C'était un homme" and, "Du reste, il était demeuré"[33] both refer back to Madeleine, alias Valjean. Dramatic events, especially, invite immediate spans. Fantine's seduction (1.3.7→9), Valjean-Champmathieu's trial (1.7.9→11) and his pursuit by Javert (2.5.2→9), all occur climactically at the end of books, with the scenes at the Barricades (4.14.3→6) and the chase through the sewers (5.3.8→10), very close to the end. In treating such eventful material, Hugo resorts to a proleptic *Hakenstil*, as well as suspense techniques.

What follows at chapter start, is foreshadowed by previous chapter end: "voici ce qui se passait" (1.7.2); adjacent chapters announce "un incident singulier" (4.5.1), and "un nouvel incident"[34] (4.5.2). A pursuit, conveyed by immediate span, is preceded by a climactic chapter end: "Jean Valjean reconnut parfaitement Javert"[35] (2.5.1). A typical chapter end, "En ce moment on frappa à sa porte"[36] (5.9.3) is left unresolved for two chapters. Hugo's stylistic flexibility operates not only in terms of varying lengths of chapters and books, but also on the microlevel of sentence. Drama of theme is matched by drama of typography:

Ils prient.
Qui?
Dieu.[37]   (2.7.5; [1862] 1957, 1.617)

Stendhal, *Le Rouge et le Noir* (1831)

In his best-known, contemporaneous rather than historical novel, Stendhal transfers dividedness of title and temperament into bipartite arrangement of text. Julien Sorel's movement from provincial Verrières (book 1), to cosmopolitan Paris (book 2), is also registered in temporal and continuity relations. Immediate continuity marks adjacent chapters, in which his father orders Julien to tutor the children of Madame de Rênal (1.5), whose house he enters, with mutual interest aroused (1.6). Later, the same immediate tie logically binds chapters, by disposing two halves of an action across boundaries, which come to signify both separation and juncture. The thoughts and feelings of Madame de Rênal's night are recorded at chapter end; Julien's at chapter start:

> Les nuits de ces deux êtres furent bien différentes.
> Mme. de Rênal . . .   (1.13f; [1831] 1976, 76)
> Pour Julien . . .[38]   (1.14i; 77)

A chapter later, the need for divided record has disappeared.

By book 2, immediate ties increase fourfold, accompanied by more, and shorter chapters. Together, the features project the changed pace of Paris. The mutual reactions of Mathilde de La Mole and Julien (2.9, 10, 12, 15), clerical and political intrigues (2.21→23), scenes at home and opera (2.29→31), efforts to save Julien (2.39→40, 44→45) after the climactic shooting of Mme de Rênal: all involve immediate ties. It is also symptomatic that book 2 opens with unmediated dialogue, engaging the reader from the start, alerting to a shift of tempo, and introducing singulative frequency. The continuity of the ball scene at the Hôtel de Retz (2.9i) is likewise marked by unmediated dialogue, succeeding, at previous chapter end, unmediated thought (2.8f).

This last device, indeed, occurs in nearly half the chapters of book 2. It suggests the centrality of direct access to the inner workings of the hero, and encourages reaction and comment from the reader. At certain points, chapter-end thought and chapter-start event are directly continuous, with no narratorial intervention (2.22→23, 2.39→40). Mathilde's thoughts bridge the chapter-boundary (2.11→12), and Julien's mental reaction to her third letter is also immediate (2.14→15). Her first motivates a rare example of analeptic overlap (2.14), but a brief external analepsis elsewhere (1.5m) only indicates the novel's very limited anachrony. Mathilde's second letter, flung at Julien in the library, elicits his typically ironic, self-conscious response: "Il paraît que ceci va être le roman par lettres, dit-il en relevant celle-ci"[39] (2.14m; 315).

Later, echoing the tactics of Diderot and German Romantics, the narrator brackets an exchange between author and publisher. This debates the merits of allowing characters to talk politics, but fractures the flow of events (2.22m). Here, as in the account of Julien's seminary days (1.27f), attention is drawn to the fact that, to spare the reader's fatigue, material is being condensed. Stendhal's mercurial shifts of tempo, contributing to the animation of the narrative, mean that months shrink to brief summaries. A pregnancy is brusquely announced (2.32), a climax tersely recorded at chapter end: "[Julien] tira sur [Mme de Rênal] un coup de pistolet et manqua; il tira un second coup, elle tomba"[40] (2.35f; 432). It is ironic, as well as symmetric, that if the longest chapter of the novel (1.30), dealing with Julien's melodramatic departure from Verrières and Mme. de Rênal, closes book 1, the shortest (1.15), exactly halfway through the book, treats her initial seduction.

Clemens Brentano, *Die Geschichte vom braven Kasperl und dem schönen Annerl* (1817)
Jeremias Gotthelf, *Die schwarze Spinne* (1841)
Annette von Droste-Hülshoff, *Die Judenbuche* (1842)
A signal achievement of the German *novelle* lies in its development of framework techniques. Resuming a tradition stretching back from Goethe's cyclic *Unterhaltungen deutscher Ausgewanderten* (1795), to Chaucer, Boccaccio, and Homer, Clemens Brentano combines separate but related stories and narrators. Since frames, by definition, mark off boundaries between containers and contents, they tend to disturb continuity and linearity, often serving to highlight differential elements. Within the small compass of the *novelle*, application of such techniques, takes on proportionately greater importance than in the ampler reaches of the novel.

Brentano's frame-narrator introduces accounts by Kasperl's grandmother of Kasperl's career prior to suicide two days before, and Annerl's infanticide following her seduction. The inset-narrator proceeds in disjointed, episodic fashion, interrupting her tale to resume conversation with the frame-narrator, so that, overall, frame and tale are virtually equal in scale.

Only after the three-quarter stage of *Kasperl und Annerl* (1817), is it suddenly clear that Annerl faces execution within the hour. What seemed a second leisurely account of bygone events is now transformed from external analepsis into overlap. Actual erupt into narrated events, and the boundaries between frame and enframed dramatically dissolve. The reasons for the frame-narrator's precise time-notations during the old lady's account become apparent, with an impending deadline graphically intensifying narrative tempo. Too late, however, a rescue attempt by the Duke, and the subsequent revelation of Graf Grossinger as Annerl's seducer. This retrospective detail tragically colors the past, as, in view of the Duke's love for Grossinger's sister, and Grossinger's suicide, it also affects the extranarrative future.

While Brentano collapses narrative frames and temporal planes, Jeremias Gotthelf uses a near-contemporary baptismal celebration in *Die schwarze Spinne* (1841), as framework for another pair of narratives. Another Aged Grandparent, more didactically inclined than Kasperl's, traces the impact of a black spider in two historical epochs. His two accounts suffer no interruption, but establish an alternating rhythm between affirmative present-day frame, and admonitory past events, in the ratio 1:2.5. Implicit in this five-stage sequence, dominated by two external analepses, is the suggestion that any additional, sixth stage might fuse external and internal forms, intruding the demonic into a heedless present.

Die Judenbuche tackles a span of time more appropriate for a novel. In a highly compressed linear narrative, covering in as many pages the fifty-one years of Friedrich Mergel's life, key episodes are selected, and vital data withheld. Heinrich von Kleist's approach, in *Die Marquise von O-* (1808), was to announce an enigma boldly in the opening sentence, revert to the narrative prehistory in the longest section of the *novelle*, and record subsequent events in the third stage of an unbalanced *B-A-C* macrosequence. In retrospect, an informational or generative hiatus (being a case of unwitting pregnancy), can be seen, early in Kleist's second stage, as a vital paralipsis.

Droste's method is less narratorial omission, than incomplete disclosure. Near the halfway point, Mergel tells his mother of an encounter with forest-ranger Brandes, "mit Ausnahme einiger Kleinigkeiten, die er besser fand, für sich zu behalten"[41] ([1842] 1955, 40). Brandes's death gives way, near the three-quarter point, to the Jew Aaron's, accompanied by a mysterious Hebrew inscription. A rapid ellipsis of twenty-eight years leads to a dénouement, in which Mergel's body is found hanging from the eponymous beech. Nonreaders of Hebrew and detective fiction, by way of "completive" internal analepsis, are ultimately enlightened by translation.

Charles Dickens, *Oliver Twist* (1838)
———, *A Tale of Two Cities* (1859)
———, *Our Mutual Friend* (1865)
Even two installments of the twenty monthly parts of thirty-two pages, making up a typical mid-Victorian novel, would exceed the

length of most *novellen*. Dickens's fondness for serialization after *The Pickwick Papers* (1837) has wide ramifications. The need to supply, at fixed intervals over nearly two years, numbers of given length, effective breaks and evenly spread interest, means that novelists necessarily interrupt narrative flow, to create self-sufficient units. Readers expect repetition, fear complex plots, recognize that in a work-in-progress the memory of past installments and anticipation of future ones are alone relevant.

Focusing on the adventures of its rotund hero, his first novel proceeds by additive sequences typical of picaresque. Each of the opening six numbers of *Pickwick*, in a manner familiar since Cervantes, contains an embedded story, necessarily interrupting forward motion. Examples of analeptic or parallel phase in the main plot are virtually absent. Half of the relatively few immediate ties coincide with serial breaks, but lack, since most episodes are self-contained, the climactic effects that mark later novels.

In *Oliver Twist* (17i; [1838] 1978b, 168–69), Dickens defends the regular alternation of tragic and comic scenes, rapid changes of time and place, as equally common in real life and melodrama. His choice of theatrical model is no accident, in the light of such extravagant villains as Fagin and Bill Sikes, and the deliberate chapter contrasts that anticipate "parallel montage" in film (Eisenstein 1951, 223). The hundred-odd pages between Oliver's arrest at Clerkenwell (ch. 10), and his shooting at Chertsey (ch. 22), introduce unusual sequential complexity.

Immediate ties unite his arraignment and release (ch. 11), with convalescence at Mr Brownlow's (ch. 12). His fainting (12f) then contrasts with the analeptic chapter 13, which continues the Dodger's escape after Oliver's arrest, and advances to verification of Oliver's removal to Pentonville, so that 13f parallels 12i. By alternate phase, chapter 14 continues Oliver's line from chapter 12, with his fateful mission to deliver Brownlow's books. Switching to Fagin's countermeasures (ch. 15), by an alternate phase which conceals a lapse of many days, the two lines combine when Nancy recaptures Oliver.

Before they reach the den (ch. 16), a brief, typographically separated closing paragraph at 15f returns, cinematically, to glimpse those waiting for Oliver at Brownlow's. The tension of the moment is marked, appropriately, by a serial break, and the new installment continues Oliver's journey:

In another moment [Oliver] was dragged into a labyrinth of *dark narrow courts* . . . [my italics]

The gas-lamps were lighted; Mrs Bedwin was waiting anxiously at the
open door; the servant had run up the street twenty times to see if there
were any traces of Oliver; and still the two old gentlemen sat, persever-
ingly, in the dark parlour, with the watch between them.   (158)
                              Chapter 16
The *narrow streets and courts* . . . [my italics]   (158)

Dickens's excursus on transitions in life and art (17i), veils the
analeptic phase that conveys Bumble to Brownlow's. An identical,
but unseparated paragraph to that at 15f, then crystallizes Oliver's
despondency in the den (17f), a point coinciding with a further serial break. His apprenticeship climaxes in a sequence of three
chapters (chs. 20→22) joined by immediate ties, composing a single installment, which treats the robbery at Chertsey. Acting
counter to his own arguments for violent transitions, Dickens starts
the new installment (23i) by lexical repetition of "cold," which, at
22f overtakes Oliver's consciousness. Only gradually does it become clear, that the second reference, at 23i, is not to Chertsey,
but to the weather at Oliver's birthplace, so that the continuity, far
from being immediate, is false.[42] The magazine reader of the late
1830s must suffer through two more numbers, before a lively oath
from Sikes, six chapters and an immediate analepsis later, resumes
Oliver's fate (28i).

A relatively high proportion for Dickens, of one chapter in four of
Oliver Twist, uses immediate ties, half of which coincide with serial
breaks. Typical of the loaded placement of such breaks, is the
enigma of Oliver's parentage. This is finally revealed mid-chapter
(51m), necessarily as an external analepsis, sandwiched between
the deaths of Sikes and Fagin. *The Old Curiosity Shop* (1841) has a
similar proportion of immediate ties, but more serial coincidences,
perhaps predictable in view of its weekly, rather than monthly
deadlines. Interweaving the narratives of Little Nell, Kit, and Quilp
results in cases of lengthy narrative neglect, alleviated by analepsis.
The dwarf reappears after four chapters (chs. 62→67), Nell is left
in the church-porch for five (chs. 46→52), displaced by Dick Swiv-
eller and Kit for ten chapters (chs. 32→42), while Kit himself has
fifteen to settle in at Abel Cottage (chs. 22→38), as the narrator
explicitly notes (38i).

So rare, in *Dombey and Son* (1848), are immediate ties, that they
carry particular weight. Thus, they reinforce the impact of Doctor
Blimber's "hot-house" on little Paul (12i), Major Bagstock's parad-
ing with his friend Mr Dombey, Florence's flight from home (ch.
48), Carker's from Edith (ch. 55). Carker's death under a train

(55f), followed by a chapter celebrating Flo's engagement (ch. 56), typifies Dickens's attraction to abrupt transitions. In four successive chapters, attention switches from J. B. and Dombey at Leamington (ch. 21), to Carker (ch. 22), Florence (ch. 23), and the Skettles (ch. 24) in London.

Lincolnshire is the alternate pole to the capital in *Bleak House* (1853), and Esther Summerson the alternate first-person narrator to an external third-person. In *Little Dorrit* (1857), geographical expansion means that Marseilles and London (1.2, 3), Italy and London (2.7, 8) clash in adjacent chapters. Within the metropolis, the worlds of the Marshalsea and Bleeding Heart Yard contest the Merdles (1.19, 20; 2.12, 13), at similarly close, opposed quarters.

More than other novels, *A Tale of Two Cities* (1859), is entitled to alternate venues. Only after three paragraphs (1.5) of studied indirection, is it confirmed that Dover has been left behind (1.4), that the wine shop is in Paris. A chain of immediate ties (2.1→4) featuring Darnay's trial at the Old Bailey, is echoed by Manette's imprisonment in the Bastille (3.9→12). An average of one chapter in four ends with speech, leaving characters, rather than narrator, with the last word. In the climactic third book, set exclusively in France, simultaneous (3.9) and parallel phases (3.14) fuel suspense. The final chapter opens with pseudo-analepsis, a memorable image of temporal reversal, and prototype of the cinematic "dissolve" (Eisenstein 1951, 213): "Six tumbrils roll along the streets. Change these back again to what they were, thou powerful enchanter, Time, and they shall be seen to be the carriages of absolute monarchs, the equipages of feudal nobles, the toilettes of flaring Jezebels" (3.15; 1975, 399).

Discontinuous presentation reaches its head in Dickens's last completed novel, *Our Mutual Friend* (1865). In the chapters which make up the first monthly part, for example, focalization switches from the Hexams (1.1) to the Veneerings (1.2), from Mortimer Lightwood (1.3) to the Wilfers (1.4). Wegg and the Boffins appear with the second installment, the Podsnaps with the fourth, but the important figure of Bradley Headstone only emerges with the sixth, at the start of book 2. His rival, Rogue Riderhood, reflecting the novel's concern with identity, is unnamed on first sighting (1.1), the outward "tic" of a squinting leer alone recalling him for the installment-reader.

Indices of time, following a veto on exact year (1.1), tend to be buried within a chapter (2.1m), or related, like the Lammles' anniversary, to fictional events (2.16). Use of present-tense verbs in depicting Society (2.2, 3.17), hints satirically at its overriding of everyday temporality, and contrasts markedly with the historically conditioned world of *A Tale of Two Cities*. Repetition of the phrase, "up came the sun" (3.11f→3.12i), apparently harmonizing the realms of Headstone and the Lammles, proves the exception to Dickens's rule of abrupt transition.[43]

From chapter to chapter, it is characters rather than advancement in time that assume importance, but their fates are only resumed after imprecise intervals. With the same proportion of immediate ties as *Pickwick*, only one, rather than half the total, now coincides with serial break, an indication of the author's reduced reliance on mere temporal progression.

The final book of *Our Mutual Friend*, in its focalizing shifts from Riderhood and Headstone (4.1) to the Boffins and Lammles (4.2), from Wegg and Boffin (4.3) to the Rokesmiths and Wilfers (4.4), demands, like the first book, no less nimble a reader, alive to the challenges of discontinuity. That Dickens recognizes those difficulties, is evident from his postscript. Text becomes textile, as the "story-weaver at his loom" sympathizes with the installment-reader, attempting to perceive "the relations of [the story's] finer threads to the whole pattern" (1988, 893).

Eduard Mörike, *Maler Nolten* (1832)
Gottfried Keller, *Der grüne Heinrich* (1855; 1880)
Adalbert Stifter, *Der Nachsommer* (1857)

Published in the year of Goethe's death, Mörike's modest four-hundred-page *novelle* inevitably challenges *Wilhelm Meister*. The artistic *Bildung* of Theobald Nolten, however, is evoked retrospectively with a late-Romantic apparatus of magic and somnambulism. Progress is constantly hampered by interpolated material: the first part includes the (external analeptic) entries from his youthful journal, and fourteen scenes of a "phantasmagorical interlude" directed by his actor-friend Larkens, and occupying one-quarter of the part.

Aside from discussions and descriptions of art, the second part features a series of twenty poems, among which are the celebrated "Peregrina-Lieder" and the "Sonette an Luise Rau." As in Brentano's *Godwi*, lyricism yields to darker tones, when Agnes becomes insane and dies. The text is divided into unnumbered segments, nearly all of which open with a clear time index, though the absence of immediate ties suggests a view of sequential dynamics that is essentially episodic and self-contained.

Gottfried Keller's is the best-known Swiss bildungsroman. In its first version (1855), *Der grüne Heinrich* corresponds to the B-A-C macrosequence of Wieland's *Agathon*, even if relative proportions of the chronologically prior (A) component vary greatly. The critical issue of starting-point, is sharply illustrated by Keller's beginning with the eighteen-year-old Heinrich Lee's arrival in Munich, to become an artist. Barely unpacked, he opens a manuscript of his own "Jugendgeschichte," a first-person account covering his Zürich period, occupying well over half the novel.

The convention of autobiographer and novel reader moving simultaneously through the manuscript appears difficult to sustain when, at its termination, it is noted that Heinrich is almost at the end of the second year of his stay (3.4i). His narrative has served a secondary role of glossing over an extended stretch of time. By its sheer bulk, Heinrich's external analepsis also causes what precedes and follows to assume the role of framework, albeit couched in third-person form.

Reworking the novel later (1880), Keller introduces linear sequence, emphasizing causal and developmental aspects, harmonizes perspectives by using first person throughout, and makes changes in content and style. Titles, drawing attention to stages of growth, are now given to chapters, which virtually double in number. One effect of this reduction in their length, is that immediate ties appear, as longer stretches of narrative are broken up, and the creation of new gaps contributes to a livelier tempo.[44] The uneven scale of the retrospective in the 1855 version, overall and in excessive chapter length, is exchanged, by 1880, for a more balanced rhythm.

Although Adalbert Stifter's Austrian bildungsroman covers a similar quarter-century of time, in scarcely more pages than Keller, their approaches differ considerably. Heinrich Drendorf is already eighteen by the end of the first chapter in *Der Nachsommer* (1857), a feat that takes Keller's second Heinrich half his novel (Keller 3.5f; 1961, 299). Like Keller in his *Urform*, Stifter prefers extended chapters, but still allots only seventeen, where Keller uses seventy (1880). The figures are symptoms of a novel that lays small store by brisk tempi and lively contrasts, but has much sound advice on rose growing and insect prevention (1.5).

Having adopted as model the infinitely slow processes of nature, however, Stifter mirrors its qualities of microscopic detail and near-stasis in his text: lengthy stretches of undivided narrative, conveyed in measured prose. With so few outward events, and much attention to domestic routine, devices of enumeration and repetition predominate, furthering a sense that the hero's gradual accumulation of experience can be expressed most effectively by a *lentissimo* tempo marking.

Entirely typical is the presentation of passion, as a force affecting someone else, long ago. Stifter's equivalent of Keller's "Jugendge-schichte" is old Baron Risach's cautionary tale of his relationship with Mathilde. His account (3.3–4), produces the longest chapters of the novel, and its first half concludes with dense pages of un-paragraphed text. Toward the end, he alludes to events that might form the core of another novel: "Die Kriege brachen aus, ich wurde abwechselnd zu verschiedenen Stellen versetzt, grosse umfassende Arbeiten, Reisen, Berichte, Vorschläge wurden erfordert . . . der Kaiser wurde, ich kann es wohl sagen, beinahe mein Freund"[45] (1964, 560). Such compression, and so rapid a tempo belong, sig-nificantly, to an external analepsis well beyond the hero's unprob-lematic present.

Charlotte Brontë, *Jane Eyre* (1847)
Emily Brontë, *Wuthering Heights* (1847)
Anne Brontë, *The Tenant of Wildfell Hall* (1848)

In one of the most important first-person novels, a middle-class heroine is the focus of her own retrospective. By plunging abruptly into the opening chapter ("There was no possibility of taking a walk that day" [1847] 1978, 39), and using an immediate tie to relate self-defense (1f) to unjust confinement (2i), *Jane Eyre* establishes a dramatic tempo from the outset. Both Keller and Stifter, by con-trast, open with the conventional "Mein Vater war" ["My father was"], and feature few events at the start. Jane's account, in any case, records emotional rather than artistic or intellectual develop-ment. It proceeds chronologically, by clear stages, signalled by place-names, and engages the reader in direct address.

Of the rare analepses, the most outstanding also occupies the longest chapter: Rochester, after the sensational wedding service, explains his enigmatic history (ch. 27). Where Dickens withholds a secret, via external analepsis, until a late stage, Charlotte Brontë resolves her enigma at the three-quarter point, since Jane must un-dergo, in the second-longest chapter, an offer from the glacial St. John Rivers (ch. 34). Her heroine is refreshingly self-conscious about her choice of material. Unlike Lazarillo de Tormes, she omits what is unfruitful, and is alive to ratios of life and text: "to the first ten years of my life I have given almost as many chapters. But this is not to be a regular auto-biography: I am only bound to invoke memory where I know her responses will possess some degree of interest; therefore I now pass a space of eight years almost in si-lence: a few lines only are necessary to keep up the links of connex-ion" (115).

Wuthering Heights opens, like *Jane Eyre*, in medias res. Already, however, its format hints at a remove in time and perspective: "1801. —I have just returned from a visit to my landlord" ([1847] 1965, 45). The journal entry by Lockwood, outsider to the Heights, becomes part of an outer framework, the inner being delivered orally by the housekeeper Nelly Dean. Lockwood introduces further embedded levels, by quoting from Catherine's diary, and evoking his own nightmare at a juncture that barely precedes Heathcliff's end. Nelly's own narrative reaches back to the eighteenth century, and far from being an analeptic whole, is presented discontinuously.[46]

Though all the important events are dateable, allowing a detailed genealogy of the Earnshaws and Lintons (Sanger 1967), they are filtered twofold, through outer and inner frame narrators. The device creates distance, even as it sponsors authenticity. Since Lockwood does not witness the climactic scenes, he must rely on Nelly, a close observer, but not a central participant. Her fragmented narrative means that Lockwood comes to resemble an intradiegetic installment reader, positioned within the fiction. The irregular gaps between sittings and journal entries, are occupied by his own encounters with the family, which afford a contrast with Nelly's reports. They also heighten the reader's speculations about the most recent events, since Lockwood's journal inevitably lags behind.

The gradual reduction between his writing-Now, her narrating-Now, and the narrated events, seems to close with her conclusion (30f), only to increase again on Lockwood's temporary departure (31f). Even the elegiac coda completes a framework in which a year of *Erzählzeit* has exposed thirty years of *erzählte Zeit*. Its temporal status, therefore, differs from Brentano's *Kasperl*, where analeptic overlap dissolves narrative boundaries, and *Jane Eyre*, where the heroine dramatizes her final position: "Reader, I married him" (38i; 1978, 474).

In Anne Brontë's *The Tenant of Wildfell Hall* (1848), by contrast, a *B-A-C* macrosequence embeds, within an epistolary framework, Helen Huntingdon's journal. Chronological and dated, occupying over half the novel, it is consumed overnight by the frame-narrator in a single uninterrupted session. Critical objections to Helen's suppression of feelings in a diary format, and to her handing over a confessional manuscript to young Gilbert, tend also to raise questions about technique. Would the same material be more effective in Charlotte's first-person, linear retrospective, or in Emily's distanced, discontinuous dual framework?

W. M. Thackeray, *Vanity Fair* (1848)
Elizabeth Gaskell, *Mary Barton* (1848)
————, *North and South* (1855)

Dedicating to Thackeray the second edition of *Jane Eyre* (1848), Charlotte Brontë deems him a wit, humorist, and "the first social regenerator of the day" (Brontë 1978, 36). In *Vanity Fair* (1848), the author appears as puppeteer, his characters as figures, dolls, and puppets, while the subtitle of "a novel without a hero," suggests little risk of his being downstaged. This strong stance determines temporal and continuity relations, and much besides. Banter with the reader matches an unhurried tempo, naturalizing a digression on likely reactions of a clubman to the novel (1m), or an anecdotal reminiscence about old Miss Toady (15m).

Since the authorial narrator dominates his material, he takes full advantage of proleptic phase, to indicate early on that Amelia will feature prominently (1m), alert the reader to the historical role of Dobbin's fight vis-à-vis Waterloo (5m), encourage tired spirits, by puffing "terrific chapters coming presently" (6i; 1950, 48). Narrative prescience means that the reader is privy to a confidence, that "Becky has often spoken in subsequent years of this season [in high society]" (51m; 521).

Vanity Fair has few immediate ties, after those at the outset to introduce Misses Sharp, Sedley, and Jos (chs. 1→3), and that to mark their reunion in ducal Pumpernickel, at the end (ch. 66). A striking exception occurs after Becky's sensational reply to a declaration (14f): " 'Oh, Sir Pitt!' she said. 'Oh, sir—I—I'm *married already*' " (144). The baronet's violent reaction is delayed until the second paragraph of the new chapter (15i), and the identity of her husband until the chapter's last line (15f). For the hapless installment reader, prior to book publication, a whole month must drag by until the secret is out, since the serial break unfortunately coincides with Becky's shocking confession.

The combination of serialization and multiple plot lines brings considerable complexity, as the groupings of Amelia and George Osborne, Becky and Rawdon, Dobbin, Jos Sedley, Miss Crawley, Mr. Osborne, Pitt Crawley, must all be kept in the reader's purview. Thackeray himself shows awareness of the problems, and in the longest chapter, set at Brighton, declares that: "Our history is destined . . . to go backwards and forwards in a very irresolute manner seemingly, and having conducted our story to to-morrow presently, we shall immediately again have occasion to step back to yesterday, so that the whole of the tale may get a hearing" (25m; 244–47).

Such narrative interweaving involves parallel and analeptic

phases. Dobbin canvasses in London (ch. 23), at the same time as the Osbornes honeymoon at Brighton (22m), the widowed Amelia's Christmas (ch. 46) is set beside the Rawdons' (45m), both parallels accentuated by serial breaks. Rawdon's arrest by bailiffs (51f), is explained in chapter 52, which concludes at an identical point, so that his subsequent visit to the sponging-house (ch. 53) has the status of a double continuation.

Half of the analeptic phases also coincide with serial breaks, so that the fate of the Bute Crawleys is suspended for five chapters (34m→39i) and a whole installment, the active Becky for eight chapters (55m→64i), but a double installment. Here, chapter 64, resuming her career, must itself backtrack internally, when the author realizes that allusion to her arrival at Florence advances matters too far, and the following pages must retrograde to that point.

Another startling "curtain" to an installment has Amelia at Brussels, "praying for George, who was lying on his face, dead, with a bullet through his heart" (32f; 334). In the next monthly number, an ironical author perversely shifts to old Miss Crawley at Brighton (ch. 33). It is not until two chapters later that, in an analeptic overlap, the effects of George's death on his family, the contents of his last letter, and finally, the events leading to his death are revealed. Deliberate contrasts and discontinuities, reinforced by serial breaks, are elsewhere evident.

"Cuff's fight with Dobbin," the opening words of the second number (ch. 5; 38), appear abrupt and obscure, since neither name is familiar to the reader. The tenuous linkage with George's schooldays, in an external analeptic phase, comes only later. By introducing, without obvious linkage, such new material as the Crawley dynasty (ch. 7), and an auction-sale (ch. 17), or, at serial breaks, Madras (ch. 43), and Gaunt House (ch. 47), the author intends no smooth passage. For Dobbin, the reader must connect a letter sent to India (43f), and a visit to Amelia's son fourteen chapters and three monthly parts later (56f). The visit itself is a surprise, since an account of the major's history (57m→60f), has not yet been presented.

While Elizabeth Gaskell prefers provincial to panoramic, social to fashionable, she also features dramatic scenes which affect novelistic rhythm. In *Mary Barton* (1848), the murder of Harry Carson at the end of volume 1 (ch. 18), determines the tempo of volume 2. Events spread over several years now yield to intense activity over several days, as a Tuesday deadline is set for Jem Wilson's trial. Although the novel has a relatively high proportion of one chapter in three with immediate ties, the majority are concentrated in volume 2.

To follow the separate movements of Mary, the Wilsons, the Carsons, and Esther, means that the four chapters in the aftermath of the murder (chs. 18–21), adopt a range of sequential dynamics: parallel, immediate alternate overlap, and analeptic overlaps. Together they create a strong contrast with the succeeding span of immediate continuity, which advances the action to the Monday. Thus, with the exception of a nocturnal gap (chapter 26), a single continuous span joins ch. 22, when Mary realizes that her father and not Jem is guilty, to the climactic sea chase of chapter 28.

Mary's realization occurs in a chapter that contrasts the heroine's inner turmoil, with the serenity of the (outer) narrative instance: "very different to this lovely night in the country in which I am now writing" (22m; 1983, 303). The shortest chapter ends dramatically with dialogue, before an immediate tie highlights her reaction:

"Sailed, my dear! sailed in the *John Cropper* this very blessed morning."
"Sailed!"   (26f; 346)
                              Chapter 27
Mary staggered into the house. . . .   (27i; 347)

With both Mary and Will literally at sea (ch. 28), the patient Job Legh and the Wilsons must prepare, as best they can, for the trial. The heightened mood of the Monday is conveyed sequentially (chs. 29→32) by successive parallel, immediate, alternate, and parallel overlap phases.

As Job waits, a brief narratorial interpolation, in a flash of simultaneous phase, suggests a Modernist moment: "Mary (tossing about in the little boat on the broad river) did not come, nor did Will" (29m; 365). At the end of the trial, in the longest chapter (ch. 32), Jem's repeated "Where is she?" underlines the value of speech-closure as dramatic device, and also ensures that the heroine is not forgotten. It is the narrator who responds, by tracing the course of Mary's delirium: "She was where no words of peace, no soothing hopeful tidings could reach her" (33i; 401).

Despite the need, in *North and South* (1855), to fulfil tight weekly schedules for submission to Dickens's periodical *Household Words*, the number of immediate ties is lower than in *Mary Barton*. By contrast, nearly all occur in the first half of the novel. A span of immediate continuity diffuses an elegiac mood over the opening chapters (chs. 2→5), marking the last days of the Hale family at

Helstone. Another immediate span welds scenes which culminate in the dramatic attack by the mob on the factory-owner's house (chs. 19→23).

Since events are closely bound up with the perspective of Margaret Hale, there are few instances of analepsis. Both the shortest and longest chapters involve Margaret; Mr. Bell's proposal of a visit to her old home (ch. 45), is immediately succeeded by a sentimental return to Helstone (ch. 46). The contiguity reinforces a contrast of scale, and also focuses attention on the importance of the latter chapter in which confession and epiphany are joined.

By using speech in the very opening line of the novel, and extending the notion of in medias res to strengthen the oblique character of the opening chapters, Gaskell also prefigures the role of speech and thought as chapter-end marker. A dozen chapters end with untagged speech, half that total with untagged thought. The implications of reducing obvious narratorial presence at those points, can be judged in critical scenes, such as chapters 41→44, where the closing words are allocated to different speakers. In the final chapter, Margaret, significantly, anticipating marriage, has the last word (52f).

Nathaniel Hawthorne, *The Scarlet Letter* (1850)
Herman Melville, *Moby-Dick* (1851)

Two masterpieces of American fiction, remote either in temporal or spatial settings, arrive at midcentury. In Hawthorne's case, the introductory "Custom-House" offers editorial authentification, and maps out the "neutral territory" ([1850] 1982, 66) of the romance writer. Both passion and marriage antedate the starting point of *The Scarlet Letter*, leaving the narrative itself under an aspect of tension and secrecy. Whereas the dating within "The Custom-House" can be elicited from autobiographical references, that in *The Scarlet Letter* has to be inferred from the factual data of Puritan New England.

Thus, at the literal center of the text, in the twelfth of twenty-four chapters, the Rev. Dimmesdale's vigil at the scaffold coincides with the death (26 March 1649) of the historically attested Governor Winthrop, attended by an actual Rev. Wilson, and a fictional Roger Chillingworth and Hester Prynne. Winthrop's death has been fictively delayed by some six weeks, however, to raise the tempo of events preceding the Election Sermon in late May, as well as to make more bearable Dimmesdale's night-long vigil in a traditionally cold and blustery month (Ryskamp 1968, 22).

Despite an overall coverage of seven years (Hays 1972, 251–53), the period is symmetrically organized by recurring scenes at the Boston pillory, and by sequential rhythms. Five chapters account for nearly the whole seven years, leaving eighteen of the remaining nineteen chapters to concentrate on seven days. A broad alternation of singulative and iterative narrative, of intensive focus and extensive flux, marks the first half of the text, with a reference to Pearl's age (ch. 8) as the only direct time index. With only four out of the work's eleven immediate ties (dominant transition in *The Scarlet Letter*), this half also has the sole analeptic phase (ch. 9), tracing changes in Chillingworth and Dimmesdale since the opening scene.

By chapter 13, at the beginning of the second half, the ellipses between major episodes, each covering one day, are now reduced from several years, to mere days. Forward momentum is established by a second private "interview" between Hester and the physician (ch. 14), in a chapter that registers the highest proportion of dialogue. The importance of this exchange between former husband and spouse, is not only underlined in sequential terms by immediate ties with preceding and succeeding chapters, but also by the adjacent occurrence (11f, 13f) of *Hakenstil*, with episodes making preemptive appearances at chapter end.

Since external events in *The Scarlet Letter* play only a limited role, narrative tension shifts to an internal stage, where the careful disposition and linkage of material make a large contribution to the overall tautness of effect. The most crucial episode deals with Hester's meeting in the forest with Dimmesdale, and his subsequent return to the town as a new man. This single day accounts for one-fifth of the total text, its five chapters (chs. 16→20) compose an uninterrupted span of immediate ties, whose tight unity impresses upon the reader a sense of concentrated significance, of irreversible shifts in the couple's attitudes to each other.

Ever-increasing allusions to the seven years of "trial," culminate in the final chapter of the span and joint-longest chapter of all (ch. 20), with the introduction of "barrier-time" (Higdon 1977, 74–105), whereby the establishment of a terminal point (the departure of a Bristol-bound vessel within three days), further heightens tension. On the climactic day of Dimmesdale's Sermon, public events now counterpoint the private exchange. In the second-longest span of juxtaposed phases (chs. 21→23), the reader moves from Hester at the market-place to Dimmesdale's graphic revelation at the scaffold, with the actual text of the Election Sermon being omitted, lest the emotional level become reduced. By inviting any curious investigator to view the heraldic device on Hester's tombstone, the narrator imaginatively annuls, in the work's final paragraph (24f), the distance between narrative instance and narrated events.

Melville's Dedication of *Moby-Dick* to Hawthorne, is directly succeeded by the Shandyesque Etymology of a "late consumptive usher" and Extracts by a "sub-sub-librarian" (Melville [1851] 1988, xlii–liv). From playful paratexts, the novel itself remains largely shorebound for the opening twenty chapters: a juxtaposed span of twelve chapters, dominated by immediate ties, conveys, by its narrative fluency, the relatively secure conditions at New Bedford. The shorter section allotted to Nantucket (chs. 14–21), indicates by its majority of proximate phases, a gradual attenuation of chapter linkage prior to the *Pequod*'s departure (ch. 22). For the remainder of the work, the settings are oceanic, and Melville's chief concern is to engage the reader's interest by variety of material and presentation.

Alive to the possible *langueurs* of whaling yarns, Ishmael-as-narrator opts for contrast as guiding principle. Even the longest chapter (ch. 54: "The *Town-Ho*'s Story"), published separately in *Harper's* of October 1851, at five times the average chapter-span, is set directly after an average-length chapter. One of the first detailed essayistic chapters, "Cetology" (ch. 32) follows two of the shortest chapters, occupying less than a page (ch. 30) and two pages (ch. 31), respectively. The bare three lines of chapter 122 ("Midnight Aloft.—Thunder and Lightning"), however, takes the palm, terminating a brief sequence of chapters that employ dramatic format. This serves elsewhere as a highly effective means of switching from Ishmael's voice, and of introducing in rapid succession, through their own first-person monologues, Ahab, Starbuck, and Stubb (chs. 37–39), before an international sailors' chorus takes over (ch. 40).

Concluding the New Bedford leg of the shorebound section, an embedded biography of Queequeg (ch. 12) prefigures the status of the majority of chapters in *Moby-Dick*. Well over one-quarter are essayistic or descriptive in their content, so that continuity is thematic or narratorial, while nearly one-quarter are marked by temporally indeterminate gaps. The high incidence of immediate ties predeparture, including two instances of *Hakenstil* (5f, 20f), thus contrasts with largely atemporal linkages up to the novel's three-quarter point. In the final thirty chapters, essay gives way to action, and the increasing number of proximate gaps culminates in the assault on the Whale (chs. 133–35), with closing stages divided by nocturnal phase.

The climax has been anticipated too, by manipulation of chapter-titles. Mates and harpooneers are treated in identically styled chapters (chs. 26–27: "Knights and Squires"), a series of four chapters charts progress from sunset to midnight (chs. 37–40), a pairing offers contrasted views of sperm- and right-whale's heads (chs. 74–5). Over half a dozen chapters bear the formula "The *Pequod* meets . . .", and these maritime encounters at regular ten-chapter intervals, punctuate, in the absence of landfalls, the whaler's and reader's journey. When, toward the end of the novel, a meeting with the *Rachel* (ch. 128) is shortly followed by that with the sadly misnamed *Delight* (ch. 131), the next encounter is bound to be leviathanic.

In terms of continuity, the interplay of essay and action necessarily produces rupture or suspension of forward motion. At the end of chapter 61, for example, Stubb surveys the corpse of the whale he has killed, but that topic is not resumed until the start of chapter 64; intervening chapters deal in turn with the iron "dart" employed in chapter 61, then, in chapter 63, with the wooden "crotch" alluded to in the excursus of chapter 62. It is to an organic metaphor, of twigs growing from branches growing from a trunk, that the narrator resorts, in order to justify the digressive way that his chapters grow in "productive subjects" (297). In a later instance of dual continuity, no fewer than five chapters debate ship victuals and whale skeletons, before Ahab, alongside the *Pequod* (100f), is permitted to alight (106i). Though an immediate tie binds chapters 100 and 106, the bracketed chapters 101–5 are atemporal.

Elsewhere, digressions on Father Mapple's reputation and pulpit (ch. 8) or Stubb's indignation at Ahab (ch. 29) mean that (immediate) continuity is sub-segmental (8f1→19i; 29f1→30i), while the frequent presence of direct speech at chapter end and start, especially noticeable in the dramatized sequence (chs. 120–22), emphasizes the epic dimension. As if to demonstrate the principle of contrast, Melville inserts within adjacent chapters of one of the novel's longest sections of atemporal, essayistic chapters, two specific calendar references. At the end of chapter 84, Stubb celebrates the Fourth of July; in the opening paragraph of chapter 85, the narrator, with an ironic precision worthy of Shandy, notes that this "blessed minute" is in fact "fifteen and a quarter minutes past one o'clock P.M. of this sixteenth day of December, A.D. 1850" (379).

Gustave Flaubert, *Madame Bovary* (1857)
————, *L'Education sentimentale* (1869)

With a writer so meticulous in matters of style, it is no surprise to note a kindred attention to sequential dynamics. A tangential

opening scene, in which Charles Bovary's first day at school is recounted from a schoolmate's perspective, already hints at an ironical approach. The application of temporal and continuity relations
is varied and flexible throughout. Nearly one chapter in three contains an example of proleptic *Hakenstil*, a lower proportion than in
either part of *Don Quixote*, but, by virtue of scale and intent, more
subtle and telling in its effects.

Thus, Emma's wedding-party, hitherto the most important event
in her life, is prefigured in size and duration at the end of a previous
chapter (1.3f), thereby reducing its impact (1.4). Her inspection of
the new house (1.5), and her literary imagination (1.6), are likewise anticipated. The dinner at La Vaubyessard (1.8), the walk with
Léon (2.5), the Agricultural Show (2.8) are all foreshadowed at
chapter ends, as hopeful escapes from tedium.

A critical theme, such as Charles's money worries, is broached at
a similar position of high visibility (2.13f), as is advance notice of
Emma's trip to meet Léon at Rouen (3.2f). That their three-day
stay is despatched in the novel's shortest chapter, only testifies to
Flaubert's deflationary mode. The longest chapter, and as seven-
teenth of thirty-five, the virtual center of the novel, treats another
relationship, that of Emma and Rodolphe, as they listen in the
Council Chamber to the chairman's speech below. Temporally isolated from previous and following chapters, this contrapuntal scene
at the Comices (2.8) has inspired spatial form and film montage
alike (Eisenstein 1951, 12–13).

In its textual succession, and comic alternation of high feeling
undercut by earthy banality, it conveys simultaneity of events:

> Et il saisit sa main; elle ne la retira pas.
> "Ensemble de bonnes cultures!" cria le président.
> —Tantôt, par exemple, quand je suis venu chez vous . . .
> "A M. Bizet, de Quincampoix."
> —Savais-je que je vous accompagnerais?
> "Soixante et dix francs!"
> —Cent fois même, j'ai voulu partir, et je vous ai suivie, je suis resté.
> "Fumiers."[47]   ([1857] 1955, 139)

One chapter in four has immediate ties, though over half are delayed versions, neutralizing any potentially dramatic momentum.
Of the three in part 2, the second combines immediate and proleptic ties:

> . . . elle fût ainsi demeurée en sa sécurité, lorsqu'elle découvrit subite-
> ment une lézarde dans le mur.   (2.4f; 94)
> Ce fut un dimanche de février, une après-midi qu'il neigait.[48]
>
> (2.5i; 94)

In the first example in part 2, Flaubert offers an interesting variant, whereby the delay in presentation occurs at chapter end. Thus, with the Bovarys inside, the *Hirondelle* drives up to the Yonville inn (2.1f). One paragraph details the coach, a second the onlookers, and the final paragraph is analeptic, in recounting the recent escape of Emma's greyhound. Only then does the new chapter resume events following the coach's arrival (2.2i).

Apparently projecting a gathering tempo, part 3 has four immediate ties. Léon's student-days, analeptic matter of the part's opening paragraphs, give place to an immediate continuation of his movements after leaving the Bovarys the night before (2.15f), which creates an unobtrusive narrative bridge across the two parts. An immediate span unites the climactic chapters (3.7→10): Emma's vain journey to borrow money from Rodolphe (3.7→8), Charles's reaction to her death, delayed by narratorial comment (3.8→9), and old Rouault's reaction, delayed even more by analeptic background (3.9→10). At other points, narratorial discourse flows so unconcernedly across boundaries, as to deny their existence:

> Et Emma cherchait à savoir que l'on entendait au juste dans la vie par les mots de *félicité*, de *passion*, et d'*ivresse*, qui lui avaient paru si beaux dans les livres.   (1.5f; 32)
> Elle avait lu *Paul et Virginie* . . .[49]   (1.6i; 33)

By so smooth a transition, Flaubert brings the reader into Emma's imaginative world, at odds with the dull provincial round symbolized by a recurrent imperfect tense. At a later point, lexical repetition across chapters promises expansiveness and hope:

> Dès le lendemain, elle s'embarqua dans l'*Hirondelle* pour aller à Rouen consulter M. Léon; et elle y resta trois jours.   (3.2f; 237)
> Ce furent trois jours pleins, exquis, splendides, une vraie lune de miel.[50]   (3.3i; 238)

Not only the irony of allocating to this idyll the smallest chapter, but the boatman's allusion to the philandering Rodolphe, serves to puncture its tenuous pleasure.

Typical of a general ebb-and-flow from monotonous routine, to events that promise much but yield little, is Flaubert's fluctuating tempo. Emma's pregnancy is laconically and impersonally recorded in the last sentence-paragraph of part 1: "Quand on partit de Tostes, au mois de mars, Mme Bovary était enceinte"[51] (1.9f; 64).

The detailed focus of the Comices chapter is followed by a six-week ellipsis (2.9i); six months slip by in mid-sentence (2.10m).

Homais's longwindedness contrasts sharply, in another scene, with staccato notations of Emma's condition:

> On crut qu'elle avait le délire; elle l'eut à partir de minuit: une fièvre cérébrale s'était déclarée.
> Pendant quarante-trois jours Charles ne la quitta pas.[52]   (2.13; 195)

Even the writing-Now at the end (3.11f), in reporting the award of a Legion of Honor to Homais, functions as more than a temporal index, by leaving the reader with a sense of injustice and bitter irony.

The tendency toward discontinuities of tempo and sequence, is taken further in *L'Education sentimentale* (1869). In parts 1 and 2, whole years are quietly elided, months slip by unobtrusively (3.3), while a single external analepsis (1.2) near the start, sandwiched between two months in 1840, takes care of Frédéric's prehistory. Time-lapses occur between chapters, rather than between parts. Thus, an immediate tie binds parts 1 and 2, with Frédéric's reaction to news of his uncle's inheritance. The rattle of musket fire, during the 1848 insurrection, joins parts 2 and 3, using proximate phase. By its very size, the opening chapter of the last part, nearly five times the average length of a chapter in *Madame Bovary*, and well over twice that in *L'Education* itself, only throws into relief the tiny scale of the closing chapters, evoking a sense of progressive bathos.

With greater aplomb than Droste in *Die Judenbuche* and Scott in *Guy Mannering*, Flaubert effortlessly despatches time. After an astonished Frédéric, in December 1851, recognizes Sénécal as the gendarme who cuts down Dussardier (3.5f), no commentary or elaboration follows, only a new chapter, the novel's second-shortest and penultimate. Sixteen years flash by in a dozen lines, in sentence-paragraphs of terse economy and remarkable typography:

> Il voyagea.
> Il connut la mélancolie des paquebots . . .
> Il revint.
> Il fréquenta le monde . . .
> Vers la fin de mars 1867 . . .[53]   (3.6i; 1989, 455)

Theodor Storm, *Immensee* (1851)
———, *Der Schimmelreiter* (1888)
Otto Ludwig, *Zwischen Himmel und Erde* (1856)
Gottfried Keller, *Der Landvogt von Greifensee* (1877)
Conrad Ferdinand Meyer, *Die Hochzeit des Mönchs* (1884)

Further examples of the German *novelle* illustrate increasing complexity in continuity and framework techniques. Nearly forty years separate Storm's early from final works, but both emphasize mood and atmosphere, which techniques of sequential dynamics intensify. A realization that the start of a narrative has frame status generally comes with a transition, variously signalled, to another sequence. Only then can a temporally prior segment be confirmed.

Storm's provision of titles for the ten short sections of *Immensee*, affords easy overview of a basic *B-A-C* scheme, where the central retrospective of eight chronological sections dominates the frame by a factor of 16:1. Here, the transition is explicit, as an old man on a late-autumn evening gazes at a black-framed portrait: " 'Elisabeth!' sagte der Alte leise; und wie er das Wort gesprochen, war die Zeit verwandelt—er war in seiner Jugend"[54] ([1851] 1969, 4). His incantation triggers a sequence of lyrical episodes, with interpolated verses, culminating in his failure to reach the symbolic waterlily. With the onset of darkness, the images fade, and the housekeeper's arrival closes the frame.

In the triple framework of *Der Schimmelreiter*, by contrast, the first narrator, reader of the magazine story, does not return at the end to complete the outer frame. Transition to the magazine-narrator of the middle frame occurs after a typographical break, and a half-century regression to the bleak Friesland coast in the 1830s. A schoolmaster, as inner frame narrator, traces, in distinct stages, the rise to dike-reeve of the part-historical, part-legendary Hauke Haien in the previous century. He interrupts a linear account at several points, when the spectral rider is sighted. Close to the climactic storm tide of October 1756, the schoolmaster breaks off again, to warn that his narrative no longer has dependable sources. His account concluded, he stresses its necessary subjectivity, as the middle frame narrator takes his leave.

In a *C-B¹-A-B²* scheme, the outer 1880s frame is dwarfed, 1:23, by the 1830s frame of traveller and schoolmaster, while the inset 1750s events bulk a further tenfold. Tonally, seasonally and geographically, container matches contents. Unlike *Immensee*, the central figure of frame and enframed is not identical, and the issue is not personal but communal memory. Frame sightings of the enframed rider not only fragment narrative continuity, but, by interpenetrating past and present, myth and fact, dramatically set in question the delimiting activity of framework itself.

Another recessive, but completed scheme, is used in Otto Ludwig's *Zwischen Himmel und Erde* (1856). Divided into more than twenty sections, it summarizes at the start the key events: Fritz Nettenmair's fatal fall thirty years ago, and his brother's homecoming earlier. An external analepsis, composing nine-tenths of the narrative, focuses on that single year between Apollonius's return and Fritz's death.

Underlying this psychological study, is an event six years prior to Apollonius's return from Köln, his meeting with Christiane, Fritz's future wife, at a Whitsun dance. This scene, as well as Apollonius's stay in Köln, and Fritz's marriage, comprise the antecedent A to the B framework (Apollonius's homecoming) of section 2. Thereafter, up to the last two sections, which restore the C component of the writing-Now, all the events are linear.

Gathering tensions between the two slaters on the church roof, and frictions with old Nettenmair and Christiane, are suggested outwardly in a Poetic Realist detailing, and inwardly by resort to *erlebte Rede* or narrated monologue (Cohn 1978). In making the homecoming scene (sec. 3) the longest in the book, Ludwig hints at its impact in terms of subsequent events, but neither domestic nor rooftop drama sponsors immediate ties across section boundaries. No single section begins or ends with speech, while transitions are often from event to reflection.

Narratorial control is further asserted by abrupt movement between sections, underlining the autonomy of episodes:

> Leise weinend sank sie über ihr totes Kind.   (11f; 1971, 143)
> Die Reparatur des Kirchendaches hatte begonnen.[55]   (12i; 143)

After Fritz's plunge from the roof (sec. 18), and Apollonius's fire-fighting during the storm (sec. 21), the outer framework returns and, by telescoping decades into a single sentence (sec. 23), indicates that the significant events are now over.

In Keller's *Der Landvogt von Greifensee* (1877), the central, analeptic component of the *novelle*'s B-A-C scheme is represented by a series of five miniature biographies of the title-figure's "old flames." Sighting the first at a military parade near Zürich, inspires Salomon Landolt to invite others to a celebration, so that the B framework anticipates the gathering itself (C). Before linear presentation of the biographies (A), the narrator upholds the need for such orderliness, since this can only further the reader's appreciation (1944, 15).

Salome, the first-sighted, receives in fact less coverage than does Figura, while the last two have to share their titled section. With Governor Landolt uniting frame and enframed, though not himself narrating, nearly a year separates idea (B) from realization (C). The B-A-C ratio of 1:6.5:3, suggests that the festivity and its sequel are not, by contrast with the last component in *Immensee*, inconsequential, but exemplify the genial humor of Landolt as host, and Keller as creator.[56]

Die Hochzeit des Mönchs (1884), by a fellow-Swiss, employs quite different frameworks. Three decades after *Immensee*, Meyer's *novelle* is equally removed from the sequential lucidity of Storm's work. Historical, it fastens not on Keller's provincial Switzerland, but on the most celebrated poet of Medieval Italy. Dante, at Cangrande's court in Verona, is at once narrator and author of the eponymous story. The audience, however, has provided its theme (a change of profession), and Dante has chosen its ending (a tombstone-epitaph).

His narrative, apparently analeptic, is in fact quasi-analeptic. He is neither recounting from experience, nor memory, but improvising in a past tense as he goes along. Having evoked an initial image of the tyrant Ezzelin on the riverbank, unwittingly causing a bridal boat to overturn, the goal of the work-in-progress is to invent material culminating in the burial of the monk Astorre beside his wife, Antiope.

In a virtuoso display, Dante transfers traits of Cangrande's wife and mistress from the framework to figures in his story, and adopts the Alsatian butler for his fictional major-domo. Although the ratio of frame to story is 1:6, the narrative is broken no fewer than fifteen times within ninety pages. Dante interrupts to explain and elaborate, the audience to make connections and offer help, Cangrande to relate a puppet play.

Meyer's stress, ultimately, is on the creative force of the moment, the narrative contract between performer and audience, the sequential dynamics of discontinuity. With frame no longer subservient to story, but providing its own justification, and act of narration taking precedence over plot, it is not surprising that this complex *novelle* is the last by Meyer to employ frame techniques, nor that it foreshadows developments in the twentieth century.

Anthony Trollope, *Barchester Towers* (1857)
————, *Can You Forgive Her?* (1864)
————, *The Way We Live Now* (1875)

Trollope's social comedy has often been accused of dull presentation, predictable scenes of strict chronology, but the claims are not borne out by closer analysis. While chapter openings provide overviews, his commentaries on characters remind of authorial control. Passages within chapters, however, self-consciously reflect Trollope's views on sequential dynamics. At the three-quarter point of *Barchester Towers* (1857), after its leading figures assemble at the expansive Ullathorne party (chs. 35→42), an authorial narrator publicly airs the problems of dealing justly with them all: "But we must go back a little, and it shall be but a little, for a difficulty begins to make itself manifest in the necessity of disposing of all our friends in the small remainder of this one volume. Oh, that Mr. Longman would allow me a fourth!" (43m; 1981, 391).

Failing that unlikely event, he must pursue them severally as they depart. Thus, of the rare instances of internal analepsis, two resume the Eleanor Bold (chs. 44→42), and Stanhope (chs. 45→42) lines after Ullathorne. Proleptic phase serves to underline authorial prescience, to stress the need for mutual confidence, to reassure empathetic readers, at an early stage (15f), that fears are groundless ("It is not destined that Eleanor shall marry Mr. Slope or Bertie Stanhope" [15f; 121]), though interest still rides on the enigma of her intended.

By devoting whole chapters to depiction of the Stanhopes (ch. 9), Rev. Arabin (ch. 20), or the Thornes (ch. 22), a near-static tempo results. With fewer than one chapter in ten having immediate ties, moreover, the rare examples attract correspondingly greater attention. Archdeacon Grantly's reaction to the ambitious Slope (ch. 6), Eleanor's after boxing his ear at Ullathorne (ch. 41), therefore, markedly increase narrative tempo. Two delayed versions of immediate ties also indicate the value of subdividing chapter-segments.

When Mrs. Proudie bursts into the conference between her husband and Slope (25f→26i), her inner fury at Slope is evoked in the first paragraph (26i1), before receiving outward expression in the second (26i2). Similarly, Eleanor's meeting with the Archdeacon (28f→29i) is directly continued into the second paragraph (29i2), the first summarizing Dr. Grantly's feelings. Elsewhere, grammatical connectives ("But there was another visitor" [29f→30i]; "And now there were new arrivals" [36f→37i]), stress narratorial continuity, though only in the second case is there continuity of represented events.

In *Can You Forgive Her?* (1864), the proportion of immediate ties is no greater, though two bridge serial installments, without creating dramatic "curtains" (chs. 13, 60). The novel's multiple plot lines necessarily interweave, chiefly by internal analepsis. Thus, the reader meets the Pallisers again, eight chapters after Lady Monk's party (chs. 58→50), Burgo after twice as many (chs. 66→50). That party's end also represents the most advanced point of action. George, in the next chapter, leaves his cousin Alice, and resumes a line from several chapters back (50i→46f), when he flung his gift ring under the fire-grate. His fight with Grey (ch. 52), the old Squire's death and will (chs. 53–55) advance the time up to, then beyond the party.

In other examples of analepsis, Trollope makes specific reference to events recorded some pages earlier (36i→34m), as well as non-specific reference to co-occurring events (71i; 1986, 734). A more complex instance, belying accusations of artless Trollopian linearity, is found in chapter 32. Its final segment, postlude to an exchange of letters, invites three subdivisions. Although letters exchanged in fiction involve complications of temporal ordering, the situation here owes less to vagaries of the Royal Mail, or Trollope's own Post Office expertise, than to his narrative delivery.[57]

The tendency in Trollope for most chapter-openings to be explanatory or descriptive, is attested in *The Way We Live Now* (1875). Dialogue is rare at the start, since it would surrender control to characters, as well as delay temporal orientation. In the multiplot novel, analepsis serves almost exclusively to "catch up" with developments elsewhere. Other uses would unduly complicate the flow of action: "A few days before that period in our story which we have now reached, Miss Longestaffe" (60i; 1992, 1.87). The narrator suspends the Melmotte line, to take up another, necessarily neglected in the interim. This novel typically resumes actions from two and three chapters previously: Lady Monogram's doings after leaving Melmotte's reception (65i→62i), or Lord Nidderdale's after the Commons (85i→83m). Neither episode registers normative linkage between final and initial chapter-segments (f→i).

Barely a couple out of the novel's hundred chapters show immediate ties. The first, as in similar examples from chapters 4 and 5 of *Orley Farm* (1862), employs proleptic *Hakenstil* and virtually identical phrasing:

"And now," [Mr. Broune] said, "I also have something to say to you."
(30f; 1. 286)
"And now I have something to say to you." Mr. Broune as he thus spoke to Lady Carbury rose up to his feet . . .   (31i; 1. 286)

While paucity of immediate ties suggests relative self-containedness of chapters, as well as lack of interest in dramatic or accelerated transitions, this lexical repetition hints at the influence of serial breaks. Brief mnemonic formulae bridge monthly readings, but are retained when published in book form. Trollope rejects dramatic or melodramatic events at chapter start. Having concluded at a point of expectation, the result must be anticlimax:

> "There's mamma," said Henrietta;—for at that moment there was a double knock at the door.   (38f; 1. 362)
> So it was. Lady Carbury had returned home from the soirée . . .
>   (39i; 1. 362)

Ivan Turgenev, *A House of Gentlefolk [Dvoranskoe Gnezdo]* (1858)
———, *Fathers and Sons [Otzy i Deti]* (1862)
———, *Virgin Soil [Nov]* (1877)

Shrewd observation, in psychological and sociological terms, does not set Turgenev apart in Russian fiction, but his elegance and concision do mark him out. Modesty of scale, too, means that he dispenses with volume/part divisions, and articulates his texts, instead, by a rhythm of chapter-groupings. Thus, in *A House of Gentlefolk* (1858), the reader distinguishes seven stages, composed of a varying number of chapters. In most cases, the end of each stage is signalled by a specific temporal lapse recorded at the start of a subsequent chapter, or the "one day" formula (33i) denoting singulative frequency.

The first stage, for example, spanning chapters 1–17, occupies over one-third of the novel, and ends with Lavretsky's journey home four days later (18i). Within that stage, all the main characters are introduced with the aid of five immediate ties. External analepses provide a chapter-length background of the musician Lemm (ch. 5), and a nine-chapter treatment of the central figure, Lavretsky (chs. 8–16), which far exceeds the scale of its containing framework. Subsequent stages, inevitably, decline in number of chapters and immediate ties.

If the whole-chapter exposition of the heroine Lisa is held back until the three-quarter point (ch. 35), the grounds prove tactical. She and Lavretsky have confessed their mutual love in the previous chapter (ch. 34); the next brings the shock arrival of his wife (ch. 36). In terms of sequential dynamics, the ruptured idyll means that the sixth stage includes the only parallel and simultaneous phases: tracing Lisa's movements on the fateful day (ch. 38), and in tears upstairs, as her lover's wife sings in the drawing-room (ch. 40). Throughout, very brief chapters promote light rhythms.

Each of the first three chapters of *Fathers and Sons* (1862) has initial speech, while all but one of the novel's immediate ties occur in its first stage. With a starting-date very close to the novel's own composition, the reader gains an early sense of penetrating the fictional world of the main characters. The first stage (chs. 1–9), like its counterpart in *A House of Gentlefolk*, overshadows the five subsequent stages, in which Arkady and Bazarov visit the town of X and its hinterland.

After the longest chapter, treating the climactic duel between Bazarov and Pavel Petrovich (ch. 24), the end of the stage, exceptionally, is marked by a double shift, to Katya and Arkady at Nikol'skoye, and to a parallel overlap sequence, since Bazarov then appears with news of the duel (25m). Internal time shifts supplement overall rhythms, while Turgenev's delayed presentations typically focus on architectural setting in an opening paragraph, before figures enter, in proximate (ch. 16), or nocturnal sequence (ch. 26).

Virgin Soil (1877), longest of the three novels, has eight distinct stages, but its distribution of chapters, and immediate ties, amounting to a relatively high average of two chapters in five, is more equally balanced. All four chapters of the opening stage, set in St. Petersburg, and introducing Paklin, Nejdanov, and Sipiagin, have immediate ties. In its accelerated tempo, 4f thus contrasts sharply with the previous scenic norm, as one sentence encompasses an hour's conversation, ten days' gap, and a journey to Moscow.[58] Not only the background of Nejdanov, as hero, but that of Markelov, Mme Sipiagin, and the Old Believer Golushkin, is placed medially in chapters. An exception is that of Paklin's eccentric relatives, who, in the longest chapter, are detailed initially (19i).

While the fortnightly gaps, announced at 14i and 30i, typify the starts of new stages, the first internal analepsis, at 23i, broaches the fifth stage and suggests the future role of the engineer Solomin. In the same stage, two further analeptic overlaps, in successive chapters, present the thoughts of Mariana (ch. 25), and Sipiagin (ch. 26) about Solomin, who, after Nejdanov's suicide, eventually marries the heroine. The final stage, in which the suicide occurs, is broached, as at 23i, by shifts of focalization and temporal levels.

Following the visit by Sipiagin and Paklin to the imprisoned Markelov (ch. 35), Mariana is shown with Nejdanov (ch. 36). This last chapter, like others, has several functions. It resumes, after a night's gap, events of the previous evening which relate to the couple (33f); temporally, it coincides with the visit to Markelov (34m), but is also discontinuous with the immediately preceding segment (35f). Effected so smoothly, Turgenev's sequential handling goes virtually unnoticed.

George Meredith, *The Ordeal of Richard Feverel* (1859)
———, *The Egoist* (1879)

Like Turgenev, Meredith is a student of French culture, as well as English stage comedy, and German philosophy. His contribution to the bildungsroman in *The Ordeal of Richard Feverel* (1859), shows the consequences of Sir Austin's rigid application of a system to his son's upbringing. Tracing his "trials" from the age of seven onwards, the narrative is of necessity episodic, but united by its title-figure. The novel's theoretical bias is as evident in allusion to the aphoristic "Pilgrim's Scrip," as in the paucity of unmediated speech at chapter ends. The sole instance of direct character utterance at chapter start occurs in the coda-like chapter 45, in which Lady Blandish writes of Richard's duel in France, and the death of the forsaken Lucy. As pure epistle, free of narratorial commentary, it functions as dramatic curtain to a novel otherwise resonant with ironic address.

With so few analeptic or immediate phases, those that do appear are noteworthy. An initial dictum from the "Scrip," and abstract speculations on Love, eventually give way to a brisk exchange between Richard and Lucy (ch. 27). Exhibiting a delayed version of an immediate tie, this shortest chapter of the novel also indicates Meredith's range of tempo and style, shifting from solid paragraph to terse stichomythia:

> She blushed deeply.
> "Call me that name," he repeated. "You said it once today."
> "Dearest!"
> "Not that."
> "O darling!"
> "Not that."
> "Husband!"
> She was won.   (1984, 255)

The next two chapters both contain nocturnal gaps, again in delayed versions, to reinforce the narratorial hand. An opening discourse on beauty precedes Richard's breakfast (28i), an ingeniously oblique passage on Caesar and the Rubicon yields to another River of Ordeal on Richard's wedding-morn (29i). Completing the continuous span, the next chapter attaches itself by immediate tie and grammatical connective:

> . . . the coachmen drive off, and the scene closes, everybody happy.
> (29f; 290)
>
> And the next moment the Bride is weeping . . .   (30i; 291)

By way of ironic counterpoint, the novel's longest chapter treats the hero's last evening with the "Enchantress," Mrs. Mount (ch. 38). Meredith's deft transitions allow him to shift from a Spanish ballad, to images of night-flowers and stars, and thence, via Champagne, to Venice. His reverie fades, as a bewitching Bella inspires a metrical chapter end:

Not a word of Love between them!
Was ever Hero in this fashion won?   (38f; 445)
At a season when the pleasant South-Western Island has few
attractions . . .   (39i; 445)

The switch to Lord Mountfalcon at the Isle of Wight could scarcely be more deliberate, or abrupt.

In *Beauchamp's Career* (1876), and *Diana of the Crossways* (1885), there is little anachrony, while the relative scarcity of immediate ties means that their appearance, in continuity spans, again highlights specific encounters in specific chapters. Diana's first (chs. 7–10) and latest (chs. 41–43) interviews with Redworth, with Dacier (chs. 30–32), Beauchamp's visit from Renée (chs. 39–42), and rejection by Cecilia (chs. 46–48) all use immediate ties, accompanied in half those cases by proleptic *Hakenstil*.

In *The Egoist* (1879), a "comedy in narrative," by contrast, nearly one chapter in three has immediate ties. The majority occur in the second half of the novel, which, with its twenty-five chapters spread over a mere four days, has the intensity of drama. It is here that a long span of continuous phase (chs. $27 \rightarrow 39$), composed, with three exceptions, of immediate ties, moves from Clara's attempted flight, up to Sir Willoughby Patterne's climactic rendezvous with Laetitia Dale. His midnight declaration, however, is preceded by young Crossjay's unintended, but critical eavesdropping. This involves a (minor) parallel overlap ($39m \rightarrow 40i$), so as to conceal him on the ottoman before the hero pleads his cause.

In a further (major) parallel overlap ($41i \| 40i$), Clara's thoughts occupy the same night and next day; analepsis, in the following chapter ($42i \rightarrow 39$), then tracks back to Vernon's activities. An immediate span (chs. $42 \rightarrow 45$) binds events fuelled by disclosure of Crossjay's secret, up to a moment of stage farce (45f), when Sir Willoughby enters the drawing-room expecting to find Clara, only to be overwhelmed by the assembled females. That same juncture is then retraced by analepsis ($46m \rightarrow 46i$), to motivate his sudden entrance. Thereafter, his pursuit of Laetitia is relentless, linear, and eventually successful.

Since *The Egoist* largely dispenses with the complex action of most Victorian novels, Willoughby's surname suggests how psychological and comic, rather than narrative elements become important. Sequences of reflective and speculative soliloquies are followed by verbal encounters between different characters. It is the need to shift between them that chiefly accounts for the several analeptic, and rare parallel phases.

Chapter titles anticipate such groupings, with scene shifts, rapid single-line exchanges, and a high overall proportion of dialogue likewise recalling stage practice. A simple change to present tense would make an immediate tie eligible as stage direction:

> The door opened; Lady Busshe and Lady Culmer were announced. (44f; 1968, 541)
> Lady Busshe and Lady Culmer entered spying to right and left. (45i; 542)

Meredith's control of tempo matches abrupt switches of perspective. These are keyed to a rhythm of successive, single-line paragraphs with direct visual appeal:

> [Clara] took a breath before she moved.
> Vernon strode out of the house.
> Clara swept up to Laetitia.
> "You were deceived!"
> The hard sob of anger barred her voice.   (32f1; 394)

In other places, a shift of focalization across chapter boundaries evokes a precinematic transfer from a point-of-view shot, gradually distancing itself from the scene, to a zoom-in, complete with sound:

> A glance behind [Sir Willoughby], as he walked away with Dr. Middleton, showed Clara, cunning creature that she was, airily executing her malicious graces in the preliminary courtesies with Mrs. Mountstuart. (34f; 416)
> "Sit beside me, fair Middleton," said the great lady. (35i; 417)

Wilkie Collins, *The Woman in White* (1860)
———, *The Moonstone* (1868)

Unlike Trollope and Thackeray, Collins in his "sensation novels" operates with multiple narratives, rather than multiple plots: diversity of manner rather than matter, with issues of ordering and focalization paramount. The Gothic thriller aspects of the first, and the detective mystery of his second novel, are equally harnessed to a procedure in which participants collect and edit accounts by themselves and others, after the close of events.

As Hartright in the first, and Betteredge in the second novel make clear, the reader becomes judge, weighing the evidence of eyewitnesses. Their testimony, Betteredge points out, has impositions: "I am forbidden to tell more in this narrative than I knew myself at the time. . . . I am to keep strictly within the limits of my own experience, and am not to inform you of what other persons told me" ([1868] 1967, 175). An overzealous, proselytizing Druscilla Clack, is taken to task by the editor, when she attempts to infringe her narrative contract, by including later discoveries. Their exchange of notes (ch. 6), as in German Romantic examples, creates another, hypodiegetic level of text.

Each contributor transfers the baton to another in the narrative relay team, while covering similar ground. Individual tempi vary and, as quasi-editors, Hartright and Blake are responsible for overall fitness. They choose not to reveal events chronologically, from origins to outcome, but to investigate gradually, through distinct, often conflicting views, the source of a central enigma. In terms of sequential dynamics, the shifts from one narrator to the next involve disruption, as factors of reliability, omission, distortion, and ignorance take hold.

The Woman in White (1860) is begun and concluded by the drawing teacher Walter Hartright. He supplies over half the narrative, and intends, "to present the truth always in its most direct and intelligible aspect; and to trace the course of one complete series of events" (1978, 33). His second contribution near the end includes Anne Catherick's letter and Count Fosco's papers, which, as external analepses, offer keys to the mystery. Extracts from Marian Halcombe's diary make up more than one-quarter of the whole. Two entries, for 20 June, are separated by an hour, before dramatically tailing off, as her illness increases. A note in the text refers to the illegibility of the writing, and introduces a new entry on the next page: Postscript by a sincere friend (358). The new writer, creating a frisson in the reader, signs himself Fosco.

Six other witnesses, of lesser intensity and varying pace, make contributions. No phrase is left unturned, even Lady Glyde's epigraph composing The Narrative of the Tombstone (426). At this point, Hartright starts his final contribution, so that the Second Epoch closes with an effective "curtain." Though his narrative includes several immediate ties, he resumes the Third Epoch in London, a week later, in a similar way to that whereby Marian resumes her narrative in the Second Epoch, six months after Laura's marriage.

While Hartright needs to summarize and trim, Franklin Blake in

The Moonstone (1868) insists that he will not tamper with any of manuscripts he has collected. Both prologue and epilogue furnish an exotic, Indian framework for the seven main narrators, and precisely dated events of 1848–49. As in *The Woman in White*, the large-scale divisions ("Periods") seem to echo Dickens's "Staves" (*A Christmas Carol* [1843]), or "Quarters" (*The Chimes* [1844]), while the separate narratives, for the convenience of part publication, are subdivided into chapters. Though the double narrative of *Bleak House* (1853) provides inspiration, Collins refines the procedure to produce a multifocal, multitonal richness.

To judge *The Moonstone* by later detective fiction, ignoring reader expectations and publication requirements of the 1860s, inevitably results in a verdict of "too long and too slow." With two-fifths of the novel given over to Lady Verinder's steward, Betteredge, unable, Shandy-like, to pursue a straight course, it is not surprising that the opening tempo is leisurely and confused: "How hard I try to get on with my statement without stopping by the way, and how badly I succeed! But, there!—Persons and Things do turn up so vexaciously in this life, and will in a manner insist on being noticed. Let us take it easy, and let us take it short; we shall be in the thick of the mystery soon, I promise you!" (1967, 18–19).

Over thirty pages later (8f), he reaches the eve of Miss Rachel's crucial birthday, occasion of the theft. Each of the narratives in the Second Period then illuminates, from its self-restricted perspective, events bearing on the loss of the diamond. Temperamentally distinct narrators approach their task from diverse angles and starting-points, since their knowledge pertains to different portions of the whole.

Miss Clack, from her writing-Now in a small Breton town, goes back to June 1848; Mathew Bruff commences before Sir John's death, years earlier; Franklin Blake directs the reader's attention back to points in Betteredge's narrative; Sergeant Cuff, heading the final serial installment, succinctly establishes the facts. By external analeptic overlap, he exposes a hitherto unknown side of Godfrey Ablewhite, Blake's cousin. Discovery of Ablewhite's body, beneath its disguise, produces one of the many shock chapter ends in the novel (410). The forward impetus of the narrative means that at least half the main narratives (by Betteredge, Blake, and Miss Clack) use immediate ties, and these coincide in nearly every case with serial ends.

Frequent resort to proleptic *Hakenstil* underlines the virtual absence of anachrony at chapter starts, though it occurs internally, especially in the steward's narrative. The suspense aroused at each of the two volume ends, however, is dramatic enough. Thus, Betteredge, after Rosanna Spearman's death: "Through the driving rain we went back—to meet the trouble and the terror that were waiting for us at the house" (145). Still more intense, is Blake's realization, after recovering his nightgown from the Shivering Sand, of his own suppressed Doppelgänger nature: "I had penetrated the secret which the quicksand had kept from every other living creature. And, on the unanswerable evidence of the paint-stain, I had discovered Myself as the Thief" (283).

George Eliot, *Adam Bede* (1859)
——, *Romola* (1863)
——, *Middlemarch* (1872)
——, *Daniel Deronda* (1876)

Like Flaubert's, George Eliot's approach to the craft of fiction suggests the significance of all moves made or omitted. The specificity of dates, at the opening of Books First, Third and Fourth, for instance, is as relevant to *Adam Bede* (1859) as the indeterminacy of time-lapses between chapters in *The Mill on the Floss* (1860), where selective episodes over several years reflect its character as bildungsroman. Writing nearly sixty years after the depicted events, the narrator of *Adam Bede* enlists the reader's aid in evoking the age of Old Leisure (52f; 1981, 557–58). Lengthy paragraphs and weighty commentary contribute to a slow tempo, apparent too from the relations of *Erzählzeit* and *erzählte Zeit*.

Its first three books show a progressive reduction in the number of days covered, from 2.5 (bk. 1), to 2 (bk. 2), to 1 (bk. 3): the single day of Arthur Donnithorne's twenty-first birthday. Little outward action occurs at this celebration, though Adam begins to suspect that Hetty has a lover, and by its end, the halfway point of the novel has already passed. Natural and narrative processes demand that a good stretch of Hetty's pregnancy elapse uncommented. Coverage of seven months (bk. 4), therefore, contrasts sharply with the single day of book 3, with an identical page count as for the two days in book two, and for the restricted focus on her trial for infanticide (bk. 5).

While the few immediate ties reflect the tempo of a novel in which the narrator has leisure to reflect, like Fielding or Cervantes, on truthfulness and realism in art (ch. 17), analepsis functions chiefly to follow separate figures. Adam's early appearance (ch. 1) yields to two chapters of Seth and Dinah's Methodism, before he reaches home (1f→4i). Hetty and Donnithorne's tête-à-tête in the dairy (ch. 7), requiring an analeptic phase to report the co-occuring exchange between Dinah and Mr. Irwine (ch. 8), only hints at the way in which the courses of Hetty and Adam diverge, and must be separately tracked. Her vain journey to Windsor, for example, means that the activities of Adam (38i→35f), and Donnithorne (44i→29f) are presented in analeptic relation to Hetty's.

As if to underline the moral issues of the novel, its longest chapters (chs. 2, 18) deal, respectively, with Dinah's preaching and with Hayslope Church. Its shortest takes up a mere page, as if to demonstrate visually Hetty's dramatic release from execution (ch. 47).[59] The song by Adam (1f) typifies a novel in which more than one chapter in three has unmediated speech or thought at chapter end, with two examples coinciding with volume, as well as epilogue end. That proportion, as a measure of narratorial presence, declines progressively after *Adam Bede*. By the 1870s, the corresponding figure in *Middlemarch* and *Daniel Deronda* is no more than one chapter in seven.

Romola (1863), dealing with quattrocento Florence, is Eliot's only serialized novel. Grouped later into three volumes, its monthly instalments cover a historical period of six years, with dates exactly specified at the start of each volume. Its temporal and continuity relations echo its thematic concerns at many points. In the first volume, the novel's longest chapters, introducing Tito to Romola (chs. 5, 6), straddle the two opening serial parts. Tito's progress through society, echoed in a narrative flow of two close spans of immediate ties (chs. 1→4, 8→12), accounting for half the volume's chapters, culminates in the Carnival, and his betrothal to Romola.

The wedding itself is relegated to the ellipsis between volumes. The second volume is the most temporally concentrated, treating a five-week period at the end of 1494. Its proportion of continuous linkages declines, as the Romola and Tito lines draw apart, facing new pressures: Tito's relationship with Tessa, and the introduction of Baldassarre and Savonarola, bringing issues of ethics, politics, and religion into play.

Increased analepsis reflects a thickening of intrigue, as narrative lines move at different speeds and unite different figures. The resort, at the start of a new instalment, to simultaneous phase (27i), which shows the waiting Romola at home, as Tito crosses the bridge (26f), to return after more than two hours (27m), proves ominous. Not until seven chapters later, however, is his protracted journey revealed as a narratorial paralipsis (34m): Tito has visited his young mistress, Tessa. The omission is symptomatic rather than functional, as it is in *Silas Marner* (1861). Dunstan's fate, which affects Silas, is concealed for fourteen chapters and sixteen years, prior to his dramatic rediscovery in the Stone-pit.

By the last volume of *Romola*, the proportion of immediate ties has dropped to an average of one chapter in five, from the first volume's one in two, index to growing disintegration. Apart from analepses, to track Tito's separate course, variable chapter ellipses accentuate an air of uncertainty. A parallel phase brings Romola and Tessa together (chs. 49, 50), a simultaneous phase promotes the convergence, in death, of Tito and Baldassarre (ch. 67). This narrative crescendo marks the end of the thirteenth instalment, for Tito certainly an unlucky one, but also one during which Romola has been entirely absent.

The care with which Eliot organizes the serial parts is evident from the smoothness of transitions, and the consignment of longer ellipses to the volume gaps. Past memories are not placed at chapter starts, but framed within: Tito's by the San Giovanni festival (ch. 9), Baldassarre's by the crowd on the Piazza del Duomo (ch. 30). In the fourteenth, and final instalment, Romola takes control, all male contenders now eliminated. Last glimpsed by the reader at the end of the twelfth instalment, drifting alone at night in a fishing boat (ch. 61), she awakens next morning (ch. 68) to a lyrical landscape. This sharply contrasts with the violent events recorded in the intervening chapters, and prefigures reunion with Tessa, and renewal of hope.

With multiple plot lines contributing to its panoramic sweep, *Middlemarch* (1872) covers a period of nearly three years. Focusing on the year of the Great Reform Bill, its treatment may be contrasted with that of *Felix Holt* (1866), with far narrower limits of seven months, starting in 1832. Such temporal constraints mean that action in the earlier novel is more tightly compressed; the loss of Philip Debarry's pocket-book triggers a continuous span of ten chapters (chs. 13–22), mainly composed of proximate ties. In *Middlemarch*, equivalents extend no more than four chapters, and appear intermittently (chs. 1–3, 19–22). They convey a sense of developments marked off by several days or weeks, rather than being dramatically heightened by adjacency. The very rare instances of immediate ties thus attract attention.

Such is Casaubon's letter proposing marriage (ch. 5), earlier handed to Dorothea by Mr. Brooke (4f), thus involving proleptic *Hakenstil*. Another is the unusual start to chapter 21, part of the longest continuous span: "It was in that way Dorothea came to be sobbing as soon as she was securely alone" (1982, 198). A full account of the reasons for her distress during the Roman honeymoon has already been furnished in chapter 20, whose second paragraph makes identical allusion to her "sobbing bitterly" (187), so that a narrative circle is completed, then summarized at 21i. In another immediate tie, the vigor of Dorothea's defence of Lydgate to Mr. Farebrother (ch. 72) bridges both chapter and book boundaries, by continuing an important topic into the last book.

Analeptic phases are used in *Middlemarch* to follow the courses of different characters, as too are simultaneous or parallel phases (chs. 59, 61). At one critical juncture (ch. 77), Dorothea interrupts an embrace between Mrs. Lydgate and Ladislaw: "She laid down the letter on the small table which had checked her retreat, and then including Rosamond and Will in one distant glance and bow, she went quickly out of the room, meeting in the passage the surprised Martha, who said she was sorry the mistress was not at home" (77m; 737).

Bifurcation results, as Dorothea proceeds to her sister's house (77f), thence, two chapters later, to her own home (80i). The consequences for the couple, from the instant of Dorothea's exit (78i) are then traced out in those intervening chapters, among the shortest in the novel: "Rosamond and Will stood motionless—they did not know how long—he looking towards the spot where Dorothea had stood, and she looking towards him with doubt" (78i; 739).

As early as chapter 1, there appear other moments of temporal suspension. In successive paragraphs, internal prolepsis (Sir James's plan to dine with Casaubon), and past action (Dorothea's visit to the school) suggest a disorientation in the present (1m; 12–13). Narratorial control is evident in the low proportion of unmediated speech at chapter start and end, while the inclusion of epigraphs means that even the rare immediate ties are, at least momentarily, retarded. Deflecting suspicion of purely decorative intent, one chapter (ch. 85) has a lengthy epigraph (from Bunyan) succeeded by a commentary, then an application of that epigraph to a character (Mr. Bulstrode). Elsewhere, narratorial presence is strongly asserted, and activity on the level of events frozen, by an opening excursus on Fielding (ch. 15), or by the parable of the pier-glass (ch. 27).

In her last novel, *Daniel Deronda* (1876), Eliot introduces similar devices. One tangential opening moves from an epigraph by Shelley, to a lengthy reference to Dante's Madonna Pia, before Grandcourt's yachting expedition is broached (ch. 54). Another chapter opens with an epigraph in German from a work on Jewish medieval poetry, which is then translated, before being glossed (ch. 42). Immediate ties are as rare as in *Middlemarch*, and as noticeable. Two involve letters: that which recalls Gwendolen Harleth home from Leubronn (ch. 2); a second, in which Daniel's mother summons him to Genoa (ch. 50).

Both events are announced proleptically. The second is also typographically foregrounded, preceded by the novel's shortest chapter, barely two pages long, while the letter's immediate presentation bridges volumes 6 and 7. Another immediate tie occurs during the archery scene at Brackenshaw Park, when Gwendolen meets Grandcourt (ch. 11). So vital an introduction belongs, however, not to the most advanced stage of action, but forms part of a striking initial large-scale analepsis: an unusual *C-B-E-A-D* macrosequence occupying the first twenty-one chapters.[60]

The narrative then proceeds chronologically, if we allow for Grandcourt's lingering on the Continent (chs. 15–25), and the need to switch from his line to that of Deronda and Mirah, involving further analeptic sequences. As in *Romola,* the novel's longest chapters are adjacent. These signal the contrastive relationship of Gwendolen and Grandcourt (ch. 35), Gwendolen and Deronda (ch. 36). As with Esther in *Felix Holt,* Deronda's enigmatic background remains unresolved until the three-quarter point of the novel.

Leo Tolstoy, *War and Peace* (1869)
———, *Anna Karenina* (1877)

So large and panoramic a work as *War and Peace* (1869) is almost bound to contain models to suit every need. Since only a limited number of characters can be featured in a single chapter, however, other narrative lines must be resumed later. At social gatherings, for instance, Tolstoy's narrator switches focus from one figure to another. The deployment throughout of relatively brief chapters creates a flexible rhythm of short segments, which are then assembled into parts constituting the major units. Early on, at the Rostov name-day, young Natasha runs out of the drawing-room followed by Boris (1.1.8f). What ensues is related in the chapter next-but-one. Their parents and Countess Vera occupy the intervening chapter (1.1.9), and their discussion resumes in another chapter, next-but-one again.

This type of interwoven sequence occurs more broadly, as multiple plot lines resume from geographically distinct groups, on country estates, in townhouses, at scenes of battle. If analepsis continues the fortunes of the injured Prince Andrei (1.3.19→16), or Princess Maria (3.2.8→2), Pierre Bezuhov's career, on nearly twenty occasions, is determined by this aspect of sequential dynamics. Parting from his wife, he is absent from the novel for ten chapters (2.1.6–2.2.1); after Andrei's engagement to Natasha, he slips away for a whole part (2.3.24–2.5.1). His imprisonment by the French removes him for a further sixteen chapters (4.2.14–4.3.12).

It is during this period that one of the lengthiest immediate spans occurs. Petya and Denisov attack the French near Shamshevo (4.3.4→11), lending book 4, part 3 its dramatic core. This is framed by Tolstoy's reflections in the opening and closing chapters, on Napoleon's campaign in particular, and on military science in general. Slightly less than one chapter in five, overall, has immediate ties, with the majority appearing after the halfway mark: in the longest part (book 3, part 2), treating the Battle of Borodino, and in discussions of military tactics (book 3, part 3).

War and Peace offers a compendium of immediate ties: dialogue transitions (2.1.5), delayed presentation (2.1.9), narratorial repetition of character utterance (2.1.15). More than one chapter in four of part 1 has immediate ties, in a series of social settings from Anna Pavlovna's soirée and Countess Rostov's name-day, to scenes at Count Bezuhov's and Prince Bolkonsky's. Transitions between venues involve simultaneous (1.1.18i) and parallel phase (1.1.19), inter- and intrachapter (1.1.18m). Continuity spans blend different types. In book 2, part 5, the Rostovs visit Moscow, and Natasha is torn between Prince Andrei and Anatole Kuragin, who attempts to abduct her. The sequence (2.5.6→18) employs a different phase in each chapter: nocturnal, proximate, immediate, with their associated delayed versions.

Essayistic chapters, often at the beginning of parts, as with Fielding, or powerfully sustaining the novel's double epilogue, add variety. By contrast, the unmediated speech which opens the novel, foreshadows the important role, at chapter start and end, of character utterance. Although the longest part (book 3, part 2), centering on Borodino, is twice the average for the novel, and the shortest (book 2, part 4), dealing with the Rostovs and culminating in the wolf hunt, is one-third its size, there is no great imbalance overall of chapters and parts. The brevity of chapters, moreover, proves a key component in the work's economy.

Of the relationships in *Anna Karenina* (1877), the least crucial and perhaps most normal, in its ups and downs, that of Stiva and Dolly Oblonsky, is presented first. That of Levin and Kitty Shtcherbatsky follows, with whole chapters given over to the background of each (1.6, 1.12). Kitty's other suitor, Count Vronsky, has another complete chapter (1.16), but his lack of interest at the ball (1.22), proleptically marked, reflects the impact of his recent meeting with Stiva's sister, Anna. After she and Vronsky meet again on the Petersburg train (1.30), the series of parallel chapters which closes part 1 tracks their separate movements on arrival in the city. This sequential arrangement foregrounds the importance of their relationship.

As with *War and Peace*, the need to switch between character groupings, here centred around Anna and Levin, involves analeptic phase. One particular episode, Vronsky's fatal ride on Frou-Frou, has a centripetal function. First viewed from his perspective (2.25), it is then amplified from that of Anna and Karenin (2.26→29), and serves to betray publicly her interest in Vronsky. By way of contrast, Tolstoy then devotes the last six chapters of part 2 to Kitty and her family at the German spa. Levin dominates the opening chapters of part 3, capped by the epiphanic night on the haycock, and his glimpse of Kitty in the carriage (3.12). Only then does the narrative return to the consequences of Anna's day at the races, as they separately affect Karenin (3.13→14), Anna (3.15→18), and Vronsky (3.19→21), before Levin's line is once again resumed (3.12→24). Similar interwoven sequences obtain throughout.

Immediate ties, averaging nearly one chapter in three, are distributed evenly in the novel, though most prevalent in book 7. Here, two of the longest continuity spans occur. Earlier examples have included the scenes of Levin's courtship of Kitty (4.13→16), and Dolly and Anna in the country (6.18→20). In this last episode, the extensive use of unmediated speech at chapter end, coincides with that at chapter start (6.19f→20i), emphasizing Anna's prominence. Her seductive manner, in a later immediate span (7.7→11) impresses Levin, as a speech/thought combination underlines:

"I will tell her by all means . . ." said Levin, blushing. (7.10f; 1973a, 733)
"What a wonderful, sweet, pathetic woman!" he was thinking, as he stepped out into the frosty air with Oblonsky. (7.11i; 733)

Her suicide contributes to the novel's longest immediate span (7.26→31), which brings the penultimate part to a dramatic climax. Between parts 7 and 8, a two-month lapse typifies an overall trend for longer passages of time to be assigned to the large-unit gaps. *Within* parts, events triggered by Anna's encounter with Vronsky assume an inevitability. They are projected, as in *War and Peace*, by a succession of relatively brief chapters, with a measured coverage of time. In addition to contrastive sets of characters, which produce contrasts of sequential dynamics, individual chapters incorporate their own polarities. The only titled chapter (5.20: "Death"), combines the demise of Levin's brother with the pregnancy of Levin's wife. The birth of her child (7.16) is followed directly by an account of Oblonsky's money problems (7.17), thereby crystallizing again, in sequential terms, Tolstoy's sense of the heterogeneity of life.

Thomas Hardy, *Far from the Madding Crowd* (1874)
———, *The Return of the Native* (1878)
———, *Tess of the D'Urbervilles* (1891)
———, *Jude the Obscure* (1896)

With his command of detail and atmosphere, Hardy's exploration of impassioned feelings in restricted settings relies a good deal on plots of cause and effect. The triggers, often trivial and accidental, join with strong inward forces to produce dramatic episodes of tragic tinge. His thematics of rivalry in love, exhibited in rhythms of attraction and rejection, are sequentially articulated by a variety of phase types. In *Far from the Madding Crowd* (1874), the number of immediate ties, nearly one chapter in five, represents Hardy's average. They occur, however, at key junctures, often combined with other features.

Unmediated speech, as in Gabriel Oak's chapter-end question to Bathsheba about her need for a shepherd (6f), carries his rick-fire heroics directly into the next chapter (7i), with her recognition of reliance on him. Her inner response to Farmer Boldwood's proposal (ch. 19), comes in the opening sentence of the new chapter (20i), to differentiate it from her more guarded spoken reactions earlier. A renewed offer (ch. 23) is immediately followed by a contrasting encounter, among the firs, between her and Sergeant Troy (ch. 24). Troy's spoken address in the hayfield justifies another immediate tie (25f→26i). Bathsheba is again indebted to Gabriel during the overnight storm, its vividness being conveyed in chapters of immediate ties (chs. 36→38). Identical transitions appear in sequels to Troy's denunciation of his wife at Fanny Robin's coffin (ch. 44), and Boldwood's shooting of Troy (ch. 54).

The sergeant's triangular affair involves parallel and analeptic overlaps, the former to track Fanny's desperate journey to the refuge (40i→39f1), the latter, Bathsheba's increasing suspicions (41i→39f2), and Troy's planting at Fanny's grave (45i→43f). In the aptly titled "Converging Courses" (ch. 52), Hardy pre-Modernistically splinters perspective by dividing the chapter into seven sections, two apiece to Boldwood, Bathsheba, and Troy, as each prepares separately for the farmer's Christmas-Eve party. The parallel phases are underscored, by placing direct speech in the mouths of each main character at the start of their respective second sections.

As if to recall Gabriel's accusation against Bathsheba of vanity, foregrounded at the end of chapter 1, a scene at Weatherbury Church prefiguring their union, also adopts Flaubertian counterpoint for the hymn "Lead, Kindly Light":

> "Are you going in?" said Bathsheba; and there came from within the church as from a prompter—
> > *I loved the garish day, and spite of fears,*
> > *Pride ruled my will: remember not past years.*
> "I was," said Gabriel. "I am one of the bass singers, you know. I have sung bass for several months."
> "Indeed: I wasn't aware of that. I'll leave you, then."
> > *Which I have loved long since, and lost awhile,* sang the children.
>   (56m; 1975a, 389–90)

Despite the rural backcloth of Egdon Heath, *The Return of the Native* (1878) has a slow Balzacian epic exposition. By contrast with the years covered in *Far from the Madding Crowd*, and the striking nineteen-year ellipsis in *The Mayor of Casterbridge* (1886), Hardy devotes all book 1 of *The Return of the Native* to a mere two days, but exactly a year to the next four books. The narrative moves between two specific November days, a year apart (1.1→11; 5.5→9), with intensive treatment of other key days, such as the "closed door" episode on 31 August (4.5→8). Using an immediate continuity span for the first five chapters, the novel shifts gradually from Egdon's timeless to its timebound aspects, to people the heath, then lend it names and voices. Hardy symptomatically makes one of those chapters (1.3), featuring local gossip, the longest of the novel.

Its counterpart in *Far from the Madding Crowd*, the chat around another fire, at the Malthouse (ch. 8), likewise exudes vernacular atmosphere. A complete chapter portraying Eustacia Vye (1.7), another, reddleman Venn (1.9), further retard any forward action as the first day of *The Return of the Native* ends (1.1→9). The second, and book 1 with it, ends by matching Oak's verdict on Bathsheba (1f), with another unmediated proleptic allusion, to Clym Yeobright's return from Paris, that "rookery of pomp and vanity" (1.11f).

As partners permutate, Hardy's preference, reinforced in *The*

Woodlanders (1887), is for parallel over analeptic sequences. In detailing Venn's antics to thwart Eustacia's old lover Wildeve (4.4), the focus within this single chapter switches from Clym and Eustacia reacting to moth and door-knock, to Venn's discharging shots near Wildeve, to his call on Mrs. Yeobright, and to resumption of Clym and Eustacia's talk. Each brief internal section runs parallel with and overlaps its predecessor.

In the four chapters that conclude book 4, moreover, the events of the fateful last day of August are all recorded by parallel overlaps: Mrs. Yeobright's journey of reconciliation to Eustacia's (4.5); Wildeve's visit and departure, coinciding with the apparent rebuff to and return of Clym's mother (4.6); Clym's awakening, and his discovery of her on the heath (4.7); a final "in the meantime," which unites Eustacia and Wildeve, Clym, and his mother, the latter dying from snakebite (4.8).

A similar sense of converging courses, articulated by parallel phases, informs the end of book 5. The phases suggest destinies interlocked in actuality, but ironically unaware of and isolated from one another. On Guy Fawkes Night, the separate activities of Eustacia and Wildeve (5.5), Clym and his cousin Thomasin, Thomasin and her husband, Wildeve (5.6) are recorded. At 8 P.M. next night, Eustacia signals to her lover Wildeve, and her grandfather discovers her escape near midnight. The narrative returns to detail its circumstances, before tracking her to Rainbarrow; the last section evokes the concurrent modeling of her in wax by the witchlike Susan Nunsuch (5.7).

In the initial sentence of the following chapter, the last two plot lines are conflated, and a third, that of Yeobright, added.[61] In this striking example of progressive simultaneous phase, Clym is first shown in search of Eustacia, later joined by Thomasin in search of Wildeve. The latter's activities, from the same 8 P.M. onwards, are then traced out by parallel overlap in the book's last chapter (5.9), up to the catastrophe of Shadwater Weir.

With attention, in *Tess of the D'Urbervilles* (1891), more tightly concentrated on a single heroine and two rival suitors, both of whom go unreported for long stretches, the narrative has less occasion for parallel and analeptic phases. While Alec d'Urberville's background is briefly sketched during Tess's first visit (ch. 5), Angel Clare's history involves a fuller external analeptic overlap. This reaches back to his career prior to the novel's starting point at the Marlott dance, then traces it beyond his second encounter with Tess, at Talbothays Dairy (ch. 18). Of the few parallel phases, one allows Hardy to comment on fatal mismatching of character, and reveal Alec's reaction (5f2) to his cousin, before we accompany Tess back home (6i→5f1). Another parallel phase records her parents' feelings, after she goes off a second time (7f2). The next chapter immediately resumes Tess's perspective, as Alec drives her away in the cart (8i→7f1).

Nearly all the novel's immediate ties concern travel, and stimulate comparison and contrast at chapter start, as the heroine is progressively reduced from horse (11i) to foot transportation (50i). Two further examples report Tess's feelings: about Angel after the Marlott dance (ch. 3), about Alec preaching in the barn (ch. 45). The latter is more striking, since it also bridges a Phase division, dramatizing Alec's reappearance after thirty-two chapters. His separation from his "four months' cousin" (ch. 12), likewise takes place after a Phase break, eliding the weeks that follow the night ride in The Chase, and justifying Phase the Second as "Maiden No More."

The baptism and death of Tess's baby, in the novel's longest chapter (ch. 14), and her decision, in the shortest, to move elsewhere (ch. 15), prepares for Clare's courtship in the next two Phases. Hardy's sense of narrative rhythm is again apparent, in his decision to omit details of Tess's wedding-night confession to Clare. The narrative evokes only the antecedent image of the couple beside the dying fire, at Phase end (ch. 34), and recommences in the novel's longest Phase, "The Woman Pays," with the sequel to her honesty, Clare's ominously unforgiving response (ch. 35).

In *Jude the Obscure* (1896), as in *The Return of the Native*, an immediate continuity span unites the opening chapters: no heathland, however, but the idealism of youth, when Jude Fawley, at eleven, sights distant Christminster. The bildungsroman format entails a selection of episodes from two decades. Among them, Jude's relationships with Arabella Donn, his cousin Sue Bridehead, and schoolmaster Phillotson are crucial. Though Arabella emigrates to Australia at the end of part 1, returning as barmaid two parts later, it is the news of joint divorces (5.1) that creates the flux and reflux of emotions in the last two parts. Both parallel and analeptic phases articulate this movement.

Typical is a sequence after Sue's promised marriage to Phillotson, when she and Jude visit Wardour Castle and are forced to overnight at a shepherd's cottage, returning to Melchester next day (3.2). In a parallel overlap, the reactions of fellow-students at curfew, and of the principal at breakfast, result in her escape to Jude's lodgings (3.3). Two immediate ties advance the action, to her departure thence next day, and her expulsion (3.4→5). A further parallel overlap then traces Phillotson's activities up to his encounter with Jude in the cathedral (3.6). Jude's speculations about Sue's tearful state after her sudden wedding to Phillotson are aptly conveyed by immediate tie (3.7→8), ironically in the very chapter of Arabella's reappearance.

In the chapter recording Sue's separation from Phillotson (4.5), a double parallel phase first tracks back to a note sent twenty-four hours previously to Jude (4.5i1→4m). It then resumes almost immediately her omnibus journey (4.5i2→4m), the final segment of 4.4 focalizing their farewell through Phillotson. In the chapter next-but-one (4.6), an analeptic overlap returns to the period of the schoolmaster's appointment at Shaston (3.6), marriage (3.7), and separation (4.4), before advancing by a month to his dismissal from the school.

Hardy's last novel also sees the highest proportion, one in three, of chapters ending with unmediated dialogue. Appearing in five successive chapters of part 5, and in six of the last eight chapters of the novel itself, this deployment allows voices, personalities and issues to resonate across boundaries, for chopped and proleptic discourse to register, for questions, pathos and irony to linger with the reader.

The hopeful arrival of Sue and Jude in Christminster one Remembrance Day, is signified by an immediate tie bridging parts 5 and 6. All the more poignant, therefore, three childrens' deaths and two remarriages later, is Jude's own death on another Remembrance Day. It occurs to a triple counterpoint of his pained incantations from the Book of Job in his room, of public festivity and his wife's philandering outside:

> The hurrahs were repeated, drowning the faint organ notes. Jude's face changed more: he whispered slowly, his parched lips scarcely moving:
> *"Let the day perish wherein I was born, and the night*
> *in which it was said, There is a man child conceived."*
> ("Hurrah!") . . .
> Meanwhile Arabella, in her journey to discover what was going on, took a short cut down a narrow street and through an obscure nook into the quad of Cardinal.   (6.11m; 1975b, 408–9)

Fyodor Dostoyevsky, *Crime and Punishment* (1866)
——, *The Brothers Karamazov* (1880)
    With Dostoyevsky, the combination of violent physical actions in the external world, and extreme feelings and reactions in the inner

world, produces unbearable tension in the reader. Since narrative perspectives identify so closely with central figures, there is little relief from intense mental life, and much of the power of Dostoyevsky's novels derives from this claustrophobic enmeshment in anguished and unpredictable minds.

Any protracted historical and topographical descriptions, therefore, would only divert attention from issues more vital to an understanding of Raskolnikov, Myshkin, Stavrogin, or the Karamazovs. In his presentation, Dostoyevsky shows the advantages of drawing events closely together temporally, to concentrate their impact. It is the effects of Raskolnikov's murders, in *Crime and Punishment* (1866), rather than any laborious premeditation, which are central, so that the axe falls early, at the end of part 1 out of six parts.

The majority of the novel covers several days, with immediate ties linking more than half the chapters. In *The Idiot* (1869), the proportion is identical, but its opening part occupies a mere day, with an immediate continuity span of fourteen chapters. These convey the prince between different social settings, before a specified absence of six months away from Petersburg (2.1) marks the end of the opening stage. Given the high percentage of dialogue and monologue in Dostoyevsky's novels, it is not surprising that they color chapter transitions. In *The Idiot*, one chapter in three begins, in *Crime and Punishment* one in five begins or ends with unmediated speech or thought. The latter group is particularly significant in a novel of inward obsessions.

Raskolnikov's reply, at one particular chapter opening—" 'It's true, I did think of asking Razumikhin to help me find some work recently' . . . The recollection suddenly dawned upon Raskolnikov" (1.5i; 1991, 87) is to his own question, as to why he visits an old university friend. That question was addressed to himself, not at chapter end, but more than a page of background memories earlier. In another example, which bridges part divisions, and uses proleptic *Hakenstil*, Raskolnikov's nightmare about the murders is succeeded by the arrival of Svidrigailov, pursuer of his sister (3.6f). The new chapter (4.1i) directly records Raskolnikov's first thoughts about the stranger ("Can this really still be my dream?" [337]), before he speaks out aloud. Questioned next day at the police station, Raskolnikov comes near to frenzy, broken by a proleptically marked "strange incident" (4.5f).

Symptomatically, this scene of Nikolai's confession to the double murders of the Ivanovnas, is registered through the hero's own thoughts, but with minimal delay, and aposteriori: "Later on, whenever he remembered that moment, it presented itself to Raskolnikov in the following manner:

The commotion that had made itself heard on the other side of the door grew louder, and the door opened a little way" (4.6i; 412). Similarly, after the mêlée from which Sonya escapes, Raskolnikov goes after her, his inner apprehension about her response to his confession being directly expressed (5.3f). The opening of the next chapter briefly details his grounds for anxiety, before exactly repeating his earlier thoughts: "And thus it was that when, as he left Katerina Ivanovna's he exclaimed: 'Very well, Sonya Semyonovna, let's see what you'll say to this?' (5.4i; 473). In part 6, culminating in Raskolnikov's deposition, a span of immediate continuity unites the first five chapters. Porfiry's explanation for his unexpected arrival (6.2i), broached by unmediated speech, follows upon his victim's urgent desire for him to proceed. Typically, the final words ("Go on, why don't you tell me what it is you've got to say?" [6.1f; 519]) remain unspoken. Likewise, after Porfiry leaves (6.2f), Raskolnikov rushes off to see Svidrigailov (6.3i), with immediate continuity across chapter gap again marked by unmediated speech at chapter end (6.3f), and chapter start (6.4i).

In *The Idiot*, Ippolit's "Essential Explanation" bridges three chapters (3.5→7), to provide similar immediate transitions. An average of one chapter in three has chapter-end speech, to underline again the many-voiced quality of Dostoyevsky's fiction. Two lengthy spans in *The Devils,* or *The Possessed* (1872), contribute to the high average of over one chapter in three with immediate ties. The first example features the events of a crucial Sunday. These commence not at the start of a new section, but rather in the last chapter of a previous one (1.4.7), continue without break across the divide (1.5.1), and, seven chapters later, at part end, culminate in the drama of Shatov striking Stavrogin (1.5.8). A second span, two chapters and eight days later, prefigured as "the new troubles" (2.1.2f), comprises a sequence of nine chapters, bridging the next book, to climax in Stavrogin's visit to his secret wife, Mary Lebyatkin (2.2.3).

Although book 1 of *The Brothers Karamazov* (1880) covers thirty years, the remaining eleven books focus on three days out of a period of months, so that a sense of strict concentration and unrelenting momentum is again evident. The longest chapter is Ivan's quasi-independent "poem," "The Grand Inquisitor," (2.5.5). At the end of another chapter, singly devoted to the origins of the foundling Smerdyakov, key to Dmitri's later trial, the narrator ironically and symptomatically apologizes for digressing from the central plot line: "I ought to say a little more about him in particular, but I am ashamed to distract my reader's attention for such a long time to such ordinary lackeys, and therefore I shall go back to my narrative, hoping that with regard to Smerdyakov things will somehow work themselves out in the further course of the story" (1.3.2; 1990, 100).

The whole of book 2.6 is an external analepsis, dealing with the life of the Elder Zosima, and Dmitri's own "Confessions" to Alyosha occupy three linked chapters (1.3.3→5). With a high proportion of content made up of dialogue and thought, nearly one chapter in five ends with unmediated speech. It is in the last book that the feature is most prevalent. Here, at Dmitri Karamazov's trial, an immediate continuity span extends over twelve chapters to the end of the book. The span carries the reader through the judicial proceedings in a single sustained sweep.

Theodor Fontane, *Irrungen Wirrungen* (1887)
———, *Unwiederbringlich* (1891)
———, *Frau Jenny Treibel* (1892)
———, *Effi Briest* (1894)

One of the first novelists in German to focus on urban life, Fontane employs factual accuracy and realistic detail in handling social themes. He embraces specific settings and contemporary references, while clear time indices and linear chronology articulate formally the notion of order, which his characters likewise uphold. In the absence of part or book divisions, his novels unfold, like Turgenev's, in clear stages marked off by temporal gaps.

Five such chapter-groupings can be distinguished in *Irrungen Wirrungen* (1887), the second stage separated from the first by one week (6i), the third from the second by several weeks (11i). By the end of this third stage, Botho von Rienäcker has been recalled to the duty of marriage within his own aristocratic class, so that the country excursion with lower-middle-class Lene (chs. 11–13), anticipates a doomed relationship. As if to underscore by sequential dynamics this thematic break, the symmetry of three five-chapter groupings of mixed continuity gives way to separate chapters. These treat over three years of Botho and cousin Käthe's married life (chs. 16–17), capped by two final chapter–groupings (chs. 18–23; 24–26) of unequal length.

By introducing a simultaneous phase (8i), to convey officer's club gossip about Botho's parlous finances, Fontane reinforces the familial pressures being exerted on him at the very same moment (ch. 7) by his uncle. A parallel phase within the same opening sentence (19i), contrastively shifts subject and society levels, from Botho's wife en route for a spa cure, to Lene's tending her asthmatic foster mother. As common factor, the bright sun on 24 June 1878: "Käthe zog zwischen Berlin und Potsdam schon die gelben Vorhänge vor ihr Kupeefenster, um Schutz gegen die beständig stärker werdende Blendung zu haben, am Luisenufer aber waren an demselben Tage keine Vorhänge herabgelassen, und die Vormittagssonne schien hell in die Fenster der Frau Nimptsch und füllte die ganze Stube mit Licht"[62] (1963c, 431–32). A visit, during Käthe's absence, by Lene's intended, sponsors the novel's only span of immediate ties (chs. 20→23), as Botho burns Lene's old letters, reluctantly making final severance.[63]

Aristocracy mingles with royalty in *Unwiederbringlich* (1891), with Count Holk's infatuation by a lady-in-waiting at the Danish court. His own marriage, followed by construction of a new Baltic castle is recorded, in retrospect, from the starting-date of September 1859 (ch. 2). In that chapter, the narrative moves in parallel phase between the conversations of Holk and his brother-in-law Arne, Countess Christine and the Principal Schwarzkoppen, before a span of immediate continuity (chs. 3→5) brings visitors together on terrace, in dining-room, and vicarage.

Fontane's interest in suggesting co-occurring talk and activity, results in a simultaneous phase, which then bifurcates: "Holk und Asta schritten, während Christine dies Gespräch mit der Dobschütz führte, die Säulenhalle hinunter, und erst . . . hundert Schritte weiter . . . trennten sie sich"[64] (1963d, 609). Thereafter, Asta visits Elizabeth Petersen in Holkeby village (ch. 7). A parallel overlap then traces Holk's steps to gardener and servant (8i), until Christine, then Asta return.

Though temporal continuity is maintained by mixed nocturnal and proximate phases until chapter 17, where a gap of several days intervenes, spatial continuity is broken. Holk leaves for Copenhagen, his family remaining behind (9i). His stay culminates in an outbreak of fire, and a swift sequence of immediate ties marks the departure of himself and Ebba von Rosenberg from Fredericksborg Castle (28i). The closing chapters are separated by gaps of up to eighteen months (31i), and the novel's shortest chapter (ch. 32), celebrating the renewal of Holk and Christine's marriage vows, quantitatively foreshadows her all-too-brief future.

Covering a mere two months, by comparison with the three years of *Irrungen Wirrungen* and the two years of *Unwiederbringlich*, *Frau Jenny Treibel* (1892) is one of Fontane's most temporally concentrated novels. It shares with them a high proportion of direct speech, over two-thirds of the text, and likewise contains unmediated speech at nearly half its chapter ends. The device not only projects, by its lack of narratorial closure, a character's presence beyond the textual division, but also accentuates the fact that none of the four novels has speech at chapter start, where narratorial control again resumes.

In tracing the relations between the son of a wealthy industrialist, his materialistic mother, and a schoolmaster's daughter, Fontane uses parallel phase to emphasize class differences. Social events, anticipated and recalled, become central, with reactions to the Treibels' dinner (ch. 8), and the Halensee excursion (ch. 10), producing the longest chapters.

The gathering at the Treibels' villa (chs. 2–5), textually linked by immediate and proximate phases, is then counterpointed, at a socially inferior level and at shorter length, by Professor Schmidt's collegiate assembly on the same evening (chs. 6–7). By dividing the two parallel accounts at similar junctures (7i‖3i), with entries by the two parties into respective dining-rooms marked by immediate ties, Fontane offers richly ironic contrasts:

> Und die Ziegenhals am rechten, die Bomst am linken Arm, ging er auf die Flügeltür zu, die sich, während dieser seiner letzten Worte, mit einer gewissen langsamen Feierlichkeit geöffnet hatte. (2f; 1963b, 324)
> Und Distelkamp an der Hand nehmend, schritt er, unter Passierung des Entrees, auf das Gesellschaftszimmer zu, drin die Abendtafel gedeckt war. Ein eigentliches Esszimmer hatte die Wohnung nicht. Friedeberg und Etienne folgten.[65] (6f; 356)

Rounding off the novel's first stage at exactly the halfway point, chapter 8 uses sequential parallelism to record, firstly, discussions over breakfast by Treibel and his wife, secondly, by their son Otto and his wife at the same moment. The third parallel phase evokes an early morning ride by Leopold, topic of both debates, who has left before his father appears, and returns before his brother has finished eating. During the Halensee chapter (ch. 10), when Leopold and Corinna become engaged, typographically marked subdivisions suggest the centrality of talk as the fuel of society, in separate but parallel conversations between the various couples, as they promenade around the lake. In the following chapters, the separate, contrasting responses by old Frau Schmolke to Corinna's, by Jenny to Leopold's announcement, are viewed in parallel phase from chapter start onwards (12i‖11i). The title-figure's shock, and near-fainting, triggers the final stage, during which her forceful personality prevails over unwanted attachments.

In Fontane's best-known novel, *Effi Briest* (1894), the passage of time is pivotal rather than incidental. Baron von Instetten's discovery, at the three-quarter stage, of letters from Major Crampas to his wife Effi dating back more than six years, prompts Instetten to a duel. The event is recorded succinctly and unemotionally (ch. 28), typifying Fontane's studied detachment: "Es lief darauf hinaus, dass man *a tempo* avancieren und auf zehn Schritt Distance feuern solle. Dann kehrte Buddenbrook an seinen Platz zurück; alles erledigte sich rasch: und die Schüsse fielen. Crampas stürzte"[66] (1963a, 242).

Aside from the moral issue of time limits on retribution, and Effi's own sense of guilt, forcefully expressed in the novel's longest chapter (ch. 24), the technical problems involve unusual accelerations of tempo. Thus, the narrative moves continuously forward from the starting point of Instetten's visit to Hohen-Cremmen and, in the shortest chapter (ch. 2), his offer for Effi's hand. Two-thirds of the novel, up to chapter 24, cover a period of two years, including two chapters devoted to Effi's first day as Baroness Instetten, at Kessin (chs. 7–8).

The novelistic need to advance more rapidly, so as to dramatize the dilemma of time limits, then means that a single chapter (ch. 25) must show some four years to have elapsed, with Instetten now in the seventh year of his ministerial appointment. Similarly, following the banishment by her parents, a further three years go by (32i), foreshadowing Effi's downward path.

Like Fontane's other novels, *Effi Briest* has a high proportion of direct speech, within and at the end of chapters. Especially poignant are the heroine's misgivings early on about her marriage, in tones that reverberate after chapter end: "Sieh, Mama, da liegt etwas, was mich quält und ängstigt. Er ist so lieb und gut gegen mich und so nachsichtig, aber . . . ich fürchte mich vor ihm"[67] (4f; 35). At the new chapter start (5i), a brief ellipsis then alludes to the close of the wedding festivities (*B*), before an account of wedding eve and ceremony (*A*), and parents' reactions next day (*C*). The brief order-transform stresses that the consequences rather than the ceremony itself deserve attention.

Immediate ties, in a novel spanning a whole decade, are rare, but occur at key junctures: Innstetten's sharp glance at his wife, as she and Crampas return from a sleighride (20i); his silent meal with his daughter, just prior to discovery of Crampas's letters (27i); Effi's fainting, after abandonment by her parents (31i). It is the epistolary evidence of her affair that affords the only significant analepsis, or paralipsis, in the novel. It is pastness, as in Austen's *Persuasion*, that crucially affects the remaining action. In an order-governed society, where even Effi's child, as if to parody Prussian efficiency, is born precisely nine months after her wedding, observance of social codes proves strict and unyielding.

Mark Twain, *The Adventures of Huckleberry Finn* (1885)
Edith Wharton, *Ethan Frome* (1911)

In the radically different world of Twain's Mississippi, a self-conscious hero opens his first-person narrative by allusion to the status of the text as a sequel to *The Adventures of Tom Sawyer* (1876), the conclusion of which he then summarizes ([1885] 1995, 11). This case of *transtextual sequence* (Watts 1993, 118) involves the earlier hero, but the sequential profile of *Huckleberry Finn* is a good deal more distinctive. Though *Tom Sawyer* adopts a picaresque mode, it deviates at two key junctures from that linearity: three chapters at midpoint (chs. 17–19), recording the boys' "funerals" and Alfred's revenge, are analeptic overlaps, while Tom and Becky's adventure in the cave (chs. 31–32) employs alternate phase. The context of this second disappearance, moreover, is sequentially represented by paired transitions of proximate (chs. 27–28), nocturnal (chs. 29–30), and immediate phases (chs. 33–34). In this last pairing, the book's climax: Injun Joe's death and the boys' display of the robbers' treasure, is aptly projected by immediate ties, contrasting with the irregular pattern of transitions up to the midpoint.

By replacing Tom's third-person perspective with Huck's first person, the later and longer work gains in directness of effects, as the apostrophized reader must concede, as well as approaching more closely to traditional picaresque models, albeit of river rather than road fiction. With the exception of chapter 18, an iterative account of the Grangerford family, virtually all chapters in *Huckleberry Finn* have determinate transitions. The opening chapters, especially chapters 8–14, alternate regularly between immediate and proximate ties, as the early adventures in the woods or on the river inspire switches between closeup and middle-distance relationships.

Typical of the sequence is chapter 8: its proximate, rather than nocturnal, gap reflects Huck's return from a night excursion, completed at dawn by a nap before breakfast (7f). Thus, a relatively brief, but greater-than-immediate transition is marked by his waking up after eight o'clock (8i). An iterative medial segment then covers three days and nights of his solitary camping on Jackson's Island, until he encounters Miss Watson's Jim, and the second half of the chapter records a correspondingly large increase in the proportion of direct speech. The transition to chapter 9, following Jim's closing words, is immediate, a feature common in *Huckleberry Finn* after chapter-end speech.

Overall in the novel, two-fifths of chapter ties are immediate, while the rare instances of nocturnal, as opposed to proximate phases, have chiefly to do with Huck's unconventional inversion of day and night hours. The fluidity and linearity of *Huckleberry Finn*, by contrast with *Tom Sawyer,* is most evident, however, in the series of twenty-four chapters from chapter 18 to the end. By creating a single elision at 31i, as the raft floats downstream "for days and days" (1995, 237), and by allowing the passage of several days (ch. 27) or weeks (ch. 39) to elapse within rather than between chapters, two balanced sequences, each of twelve chapters, emerge.

Broached by the singulative "one morning" at 19m (141), the first continuous span begins with the arrival of the King and Duke, and their subsequent thespian activities up to their graveyard escape and drunken embarkation at 30f. The central episodes of Wilks's funeral, fraudulent uncles and embezzled funds are unified by a succession of six immediate ties. In the second, mixed continuous span (chs. 31→42), triggered by the singulative "early one morning" at 31m (238), proximate ties, indicating less intense cohesion, dominate, though the episodes of tar and feathers, and plans to rescue Jim (chs. 32→35) are related by a span of three immediate ties.

Of the next generation, Edith Wharton is artistically closer to her friend Henry James, but in *Ethan Frome* (1911), published just after Twain's death, she produces another classic of American fiction, and a landmark of early Modernism. Technically, in its use of framework, and atmospherically, in exploiting personal and environmental isolation, it recalls *Wuthering Heights*. Its novelistic density, however, means that within its mere ten chapters, it creates a range of varied emotions and responses.

The author's introductory note, representing the work's outer frame, insists on the gradual assembly of narrative fragments, before an enforced lodging with the title-figure supplies the "gaps" lending the story its "deeper meaning" ([1911] 1995, 13). Between first-person frame and third-person enframed, is a twenty-four-year remove. The main narrative, in the compressed manner of the German *novelle,* covers four days, until the frame is resumed in chapter 10, the story is pieced together, and village voices comment next morning.

That narratorial resumption after ten chapters is immediate, and lexically underlined by the opening reference to a "querulous drone" (98), which takes up the voice "droning querulously" from the close of the author's introductory note (22). Since Ethan himself terms his wife Zeena a "bitter querulous woman" (76), it is all the more ironic and tragic that the narratorial allusions in the outer frame prove to be to the hapless Mattie, irreparably transformed by the accident. As in Conrad's *The Secret Agent* (1907), another contemporary work demonstrating time shift, no successive chapters have identical continuity relations, indicative of fluctuations and uneven rhythms of feeling. Several chapters in particular exhibit complexities of sequential dynamics.

Following Ethan's return with Mattie from the Starkfield dance (2f; *[B]*), chapter 3 begins with an evocation of the fine weather on the next day (3i1; *[D]*), only to shift back (3i2) to an account of Zeena's frosty reception the evening before (*C*), and Ethan's thoughts of Mattie's warm embrace (2m; *[A]*). The fourth paragraph again takes up the bright winter scene (*D*), but superimposes on it Ethan's image of Mattie's face, which then gives way to his memories of her first arrival at the station. While the latter episode represents an external analepsis, the other incidents establish a microsequence from 2m onward, of *A-B-D-C-A-D*.

This recessive texture, amplified by details of Mattie's family background (3m), is counterpointed in the next chapter by reference to Zeena's own arrival years before. The chapter (ch. 4) is dominated by proleptic, or quasi-proleptic hints, set off by prenarrative memories of studies at Worcester and marital disillusionment, about how Ethan and Mattie might benefit that evening from Zeena's absence. Zeena's unexpected return from the doctor's is aptly rendered in the novel's shortest chapter (ch. 6), with an immediate tie converting Ethan's dysphoria into hatred, as he confronts Zeena (ch. 7).

At chapter end, the effects of her fury at discovery of the broken pickle dish, are stylistically prefigured by the use of ellipsis points indicating incompleteness. In the next chapter (ch. 8), no fewer than seven instances of this device occur, most visibly at the end of three successive paragraphs, recording Ethan's outburst at Zeena's decision to replace Mattie (77). The chapter itself (ch. 8) opens analeptically with a reference to the illness of Ethan's father years ago, and Ethan's occupation of a small "study" room, to which he now descends after the showdown with his wife.

Within the second paragraph, however, allusion is made to the speechless reactions of Mattie and Ethan immediately after Zeena's departure (7f), before Ethan in his "study" reads Mattie's note, triggering his rebellion. Here, sequential complexity and stylistic foregrounding of incompleteness combine to create a powerful narrative impact which extends into the climactic accident of chapter 9. Ellipsis points appear nine times here at paragraph end, as well as internally, to reinforce the tension, in this longest chapter of the novel, between a doomed present and the potential promise of an irrecoverable past.

Emile Zola, *Germinal* (1885)
Thomas Mann, *Buddenbrooks* (1902)
Arnold Bennett, *The Old Wives' Tale* (1908)
    Like Balzac, Emile Zola tends to place greatest weight within chapters, rather than exploit sequential gaps and transitions, so that his chapters have a self-contained quality, separated by specified ellipses from those that precede and follow. There are relatively few immediate ties or analeptic phases, while comparatively long chapters allow ample expansion of episodes, before chapter breaks announce shifts in time or setting. Zola's Naturalism, with its impersonal analysis of social forces in an anti-idealistic, material world, accentuates content rather than structure or style, documentary cross-section rather than dramatic sequence.
    By utilizing a cyclic framework, that of the Rougon-Macquart dynasty, Zola is also able to reduce anachrony, for provision of his characters' past careers. Thus, the half-sister of Étienne Lantier, protagonist in *Germinal* (1885), is title subject of *Nana* (1880). Her childhood, with an alcoholic father, and a mother fated by hereditary weakness, has already been evoked separately, in *L'assommoir* (1877), thereby obviating any requirement in *Nana,* to go back before going forward.
    Étienne appears in *Germinal* as unemployed newcomer to an industrial crisis. Nearly one-quarter of the novel, two out of seven parts, records the initial impact made on him by the suffering of the mining community of Le Voreux. That impact is all the sharper, by condensing the events of the first two parts into a single day, and stretching the remaining parts over a further year. It is the Maheu family that links Étienne and the mine-owning Grégoires. By 1.3, the courses of Étienne and the Maheus have converged at the pit, and the first part concludes with a rare immediate tie, as Étienne resolves to leave for good (1.6i), but allows Maheu to find him lodging for the night.
    In total contrast, part 2 opens analeptically, at 8 A.M. the same day, but in the luxuriant setting of the Grégoire's mansion, and 2.1 ends with the entry there of Maheude and her children. By way of

explanation, 2.2 retrogrades to 6 A.M.: after the departure of Maheu and his daughter for the day shift (1.2f), but before Maheude vainly seeks to obtain credit, and tramps to the mansion. Here, the narrative loop is completed:

> Alors, la Maheude et ses petits entrèrent, glacés, affamés, saisis d'un effarement peureux, en se voyant dans cette salle où il faisait si chaud, et qui sentait si bon la brioche. (2.1f; 1968, 104)
> Dans la salle à manger, la mère et les enfants se tinrent immobiles, étourdis par la brusque chaleur, très gênés des regards de ce vieux monsieur et de cette vieille dame, qui s'allongeaient dans leurs fauteuils.[68] (2.2m; 111)

Maheu's return home after settling Étienne (2.4i) analeptically resumes from the medial segment of 1.6. Étienne's walk through the village after parting from Maheu (2.5i→1.6f) advances the hour beyond that reached by 2.4f, to establish an analeptic overlap. In a later example, following Catherine's escape from the disaster underground (5.2f), the narrative returns to the predawn political activity. It then continues from her emergence out of the shaft (5.3m), with new moves against other pits. The next part sees another rare immediate tie, as Étienne, having disarmed Chaval, his rival for Catherine (6.3f), leaves Rasseneur's house with her (6.4i). Catherine's death in the flooded mine, after Étienne's hereditary blood lust has conquered Chaval, brings to a close what is, significantly, the novel's longest chapter (7.5).

Thomas Mann's early *Buddenbrooks* (1902) also traces the decline of a family, but solidly bourgeois, and, within a single work it covers four decades and generations. By adopting linear chronology, a sense of long-established tradition as revered Lübeck merchants, is only reinforced. Little Antonie's opening words: " 'Was ist das.—Was—ist das' "[69] (1974b, 7) draw the reader in medias res, into the opening scene of the regular fortnightly soirée in the Mengstrasse.

At the same time, the words, representing Tony's attempt to remember the next line of her catechism, sound, by allusion to future and succession, the novel's thematic concerns. With a single exception, all chapters of book 1 carry forward, by immediate ties, the stages of the Thursday gathering in October 1835. Thereafter, the clan's unity, articulated by such ties, begins gradually to disintegrate, and few ties appear after the sixth, of eleven books.

The arrivals of the banker Kesselmeyer (4.6), then Consul Johann Buddenbrook (4.7→9), to retrieve Tony from her bankrupt husband Grünlich, and the problems with her second husband, Permaneder (6.7→9), furnish scenes which exploit immediate ties as dramatic markers. In the latter instance, one tie is primarily narratorial (6.7→8); the second includes *Hakenstil*:

> Als das Jahr 1859 sich zu Ende neigte, geschah etwas Fürchterliches . . . (6.8f; 252)
> Es war ein Tag gegen Ende des November . . .[70] (6.9i; 252)

That "frightful" event, the sight of Permaneder's nocturnal wrestling with Babette the cook, triggering Tony's second return home, is presented after its effects. The analepsis appears, typically, in a medial rather than initial position (6.9m), so as to minimize any linear digression.

In another rare analepsis, Senator Thomas Buddenbrook is allowed the chapter space occupied by Tony's contemplation of the sleeping Hanno (8.3), to mull over her proposal to invest in the Pöppenrade harvest, before taking the fateful plunge (8.4i→8.2f). A chapter later, the Jubilee celebrations are interrupted by news of the disastrous hailstorm, and Thomas sinks down, with a festive serenade in the background:

> . . . die Musik setzte wieder ein, mit . . . einem aufdringlichen und in seiner naiven Unbefangenheit unerträglich aufreizenden Tohuwabohu von Knarren, Schmettern und Quinquilieren, zerrissen von den aberwitzigen Pfiffen der Pikkoloflöte.—(8.5f; 336)
> "Oh Bach! Sebastian Bach, verehrteste Frau!" rief Herr Edmund Pfühl, Organist von Sankt Marien, der in grosser Bewegung den Salon durchschritt, während Gerda lächelnd, den Kopf in die Hand gestützt, am Flügel sass, und Hanno, lauschend in einem Sessel, eins seiner Knie mit beiden Händen umspannte . . .[71] (8.6i; 336)

Here, the bridge is doubly musical, if contrastive, and the temporal continuity promised by the opening words of 8.6 rapidly proves illusory. It is Thomas's inability to appreciate his son's musical sensitivity, but his violinist-wife's appreciation of the musical Leutnant von Throta, which the chapter division symbolically foreshadows. Likewise, the double line ruled by Hanno across the family-tree, in the next chapter (8.7). His explanation to his father (" 'Ich glaubte . . . ich glaubte . . . es käme nichts mehr' "[72] [8.7f; 356]), by virtue of its status as unmediated speech, at chapter end, resonates long in the reader's, not to mention Thomas's memory.

At another point, a chapter-end speech allusion by Thomas, to his sister Clara's tuberculosis (7.6f), prepares the reader for her impending death. The opening of the next chapter, with over a dozen angry conversational "turns" and delayed indices of speakers and time, has disorientating effects (7.7i). Gradually, it becomes clear that the exchange is no longer between Thomas and Tony, but Thomas and his mother, though not the interview promised for the following morning (7.6f). The false continuity, in fact, elides a period of over two weeks, during which Clara's funeral has taken place, and the Frau Consul has made over Clara's inheritance to her pastor son-in-law in Riga. This disputed gift is symptomatic of the downward course of events.

After whole chapters that reproduce letters exchanged between characters, without any narratorial comment (3.10, 4.1, 5.7), the longest chapter of the novel by far, over six times the average, evokes a single day in the life of the last Buddenbrook, Hanno (11.2). It climaxes a constant increase from part to part in the ratio of pages to chapters. In the next chapter, one of the shortest, seemingly unconnected to its neighbors, a dispassionate, clinical, and atemporal account of typhoid is presented (11.3). Not, ironically, until the fourth paragraph of the novel's final chapter (11.4), is there any reference to Hanno's burial, six months previously. Throughout, Mann handles his narrative flexibly, making particular use of the short chapters associated with Tolstoy, and accurately dating the passage of time.

For Arnold Bennett too, detailed chronology is relevant in *The Old Wives' Tale* (1908), a novel treating the effects of time, and concerned to register its movement within individuals. Like Mann, he covers over four decades of the nineteenth century, from 1862 onwards, focusing on the varied fortunes of two sisters born in the Five Towns. The petit-bourgeois setting of the Baines' drapery shop, on St. Luke's Square at Bursley, has the same centrality as with Mann and Zola, and furnishes an obligatory point of reference for all later measurements of change.

Having introduced Constance and Sophia at the ages of sixteen and fifteen, respectively, the narrative traces the routine of Potteries' life, until the arrival of the commercial traveler, Gerald Scales. Of the very few immediate ties in the novel, the majority relate to him: engaging a blushing Sophia in small-talk over the counter (1.4.2), delaying fatally her watch at her father's bedside (1.4.3); visiting on New Year's Day (1.5.3); storming out of their Paris hotel, after she has refused him money (3.4.2). This scene is critical, marking, after four years together, a parting of ways.

Sophia's parting from her family, by elopement with Scales, has occurred at the end of book 1. Her separate life from 1866 to 1878 occupies the separate book 3, culminating in her success at the Pension Frensham in Paris. Constance's career is presented, in book 2, as a large-scale parallel phase, running from her honeymoon return in 1867, to her son Cyril's scholarship in 1893. Her marriage to the shop-assistant Samuel Povey, a year after Sophia's departure, is characteristically occluded, by juxtaposing antecedent and sequel. Thus, the narrative shifts, within a few lines at book end, from allusion to Sophia's marriage-telegram in 1866, to their mother's removal to her sister's in 1867: "And ever since, in the solemn physiognomy of the triple house of John Baines . . . have remained the traces of the sight it saw on the morning of the afternoon when Mr. and Mrs. Povey returned from their honeymoon— the sight of Mrs. Baines getting into the waggonette for Axe" (1.7.3; 1966, 141).

By similar use of ellipsis, presenting a microsequence of *A-C-B*, Sophia's own honeymoon advances from London (*A*) at chapter end (3.1.2), to France. The past perfect tense at chapter start ("They had been to Versailles and had dined there" [3.2.1; 260]), swiftly indicates omission of an earlier event, their arrival in Paris (*B*), subsequently recorded in the second paragraph. Thus, the ellipsis is overt, the reversed order of events short-lived, serving to open the honeymoon episode with a verbal flourish.[73]

On a larger scale, Bennett is able to gloss over nearly two decades of Sophia's life in France, by adopting another *A-C-B* sequence. Thus, book 4 opens without dates, describing a stay by Cyril's friend in Sophia's Pension Frensham, about which he reports to Cyril. The year, it appears, is 1896 (*C*), book 3 having closed with Sophia's success in 1878 (*A*). In a rare parallel phase (4.1.4i‖4.1.1f), of a novel lacking analepsis, her reflections (*B*) on "a quarter of a century of ceaseless labour and anxiety" (400) trigger self-questioning and fever, until Constance's invitation arrives from England, and the sisters are reunited in the spring of 1897 (4.2.2). The relationship between them informs the longest chapter (4.3), in the longest book, before a specified nine-year gap brings first Sophia's, then, one year later, Constance's death. That narrative suspense is not paramount, becomes clear from the proleptic doubling of chapter title and textual foreshadowings of her end.

Earlier, so trivial a detail as Gerald's cheaply laundered collar suffices, in conjunction with the chapter-title "A Crisis for Gerald," to reflect "the shadow of impending disaster" (3.4.1; 292). His final outburst, before separation from Sophia in the same chapter, serves only to confirm the proleptic allusion made during his "fortuitous" New Year's visit:

And years afterwards, in the light of further knowledge of Mr. Scales, Sophia came to regard his being on the doorstep as the most natural and characteristic thing in the world.   (1.5.2; 82–83)
I remember beginning the New Year well with a thumping lie just to have a sight of you, my vixen.   (3.4.3; 301)

In addition to stressing signs of mortality, and recording victims of time, Bennett notes throughout, with dry irony, the distance between the period of the represented events and that of the narrative representation: "For Constance and Sophia had the disadvantage of living in the middle ages. The crinoline had not quite reached its full circumference, and the dress-improver had not even been thought of. . . . One went to Longshaw as one now goes to Pekin. It was an era so dark and backward that one might wonder how people could sleep in their beds at night for thinking about their sad state" (1.1.2; 11).

Henry James, *The Portrait of a Lady* (1881)
————, *The Wings of the Dove* (1902)
————, *The Ambassadors* (1903)

As with writers such as Flaubert and George Eliot, elements featured or omitted in the work of Henry James carry greater import than in practitioners less fastidious. With temporal and continuity relations, the hand of the highly self-aware artist of the Critical Prefaces is no less obvious in the novels themselves. So few, for example, are cases of immediate ties in *The Portrait of a Lady* (1881), that their appearance signals scenes of particular moment for the heroine, Isabel Archer: looking up from perusal of Caspar Goodwood's letter, to see before her another suitor, Lord Warburton (12i); trembling, after her proposal from Caspar (17i); bemused, after Gilbert Osmond's accusation about her influence over his Lordship (42i). The heroine's background, like that of Caspar and Ralph Touchett, is first presented in medial position (4m), so avoiding any Balzacian overweight at chapter start. In Ralph's case, the context involves analepsis.

After a chapter of Isabel's memories of Caspar at Albany (ch. 4), Ralph knocks before dinner on his mother's door at Gardencourt (5i1). He thus resumes, by proximate tie, his earlier discussion on the lawn with Warburton (2f). A narratorial account of Ralph's childhood (5i2) leads to resumption of his conversation with his mother (5m), until Ralph conducts his cousin through the gallery after dinner (5f). As with Austen, events internal to the narrative are frequently more pertinent than extratextual allusions. Thus, the death of Ralph's father (19f) becomes a reference point for later scenes.

During Isabel's visit to the hilltop villa, James resorts to simultaneous phase. Acknowledging that her discussion with Osmond, treated in chapter 24, continues in the background, the narrator switches to a dialogue between Madame Merle and the Countess Gemini, adopting the latter's perspective: "While this sufficiently intimate colloquy (prolonged for some time after we cease to follow it) went forward Madame Merle and her companion, breaking a silence of some duration, had begun to exchange remarks. . . . Her brother wandered with Isobel to the end of the garden, to which point her eyes followed them" (25i; 1991, 288).

A later chapter opens with Isabel at a window of the Palazzo Crescentini, expecting a visitor (31i). The bulk of the chapter then reviews her sister's travels in Europe, and her own in the Middle East, before the narrative circle is completed, with Ralph being mentioned, by *Hakenstil*, as prospective visitor (31f). Despite an immediate tie (32i), intimations of topic-continuity are unfounded: "It was not of him, nevertheless, that she was thinking while she stood at the window near which we found her a while ago, and it was not of any of the matters I have rapidly sketched. She was not turned to the past, but to the immediate, impending hour" (352).

James chooses, therefore, to introduce Caspar Goodwood at the beginning of the second paragraph, to prepare the reader during the first for a name other than Ralph's, rather than to spring any melodramatic surprise in the chapter's opening sentence. Like Fontane, one chapter in two has unmediated, or minimally tagged speech at chapter end. The great majority of cases are situated in the first half of the novel, while the absence of chapter-start speech also recalls the German novelist.

Though *The Wings of the Dove* (1902) has fewer instances overall of chapter-end speech, its final book alone has four. Merton Densher's question to Kate Croy, as to how Lord Mark learned of their engagement, prompts, via immediate tie, a climactic exchange between the couple (10.5i). In length, the final book is surpassed only by the central book 5, which focuses on two crucial encounters of the fatally ill heiress Milly Theale, at Lord Mark's house, with the portrait by Bronzino (5.2), and at the National Gallery, with Densher and his accomplice Kate (5.7).

This last encounter prompts a second instance of speech at chapter start. Combined with an immediate tie that links books 5 and 6, it highlights the couple's relief at escape: " 'I say, you know, Kate—you *did* stay!' had been Merton Densher's punctual remark on their adventure after they had, as it were, got out of it . . . they had looked at each other, on gaining the street, as people look who have just rounded a dangerous corner" (6.1i;1984, 217). The stylistic use of past perfect forms, which, in an early chapter detailing Kate's background, serves to delay confirmation of sequential status for some eight pages (1.2), also features in the few cases of immediate ties.

Impatient with Densher's reluctance to visit Aunt Maud, Kate walks away (2.1f), so that, "His eyes had followed her at this time quite long enough, before he overtook her" (2.2i; 53). In the central book, Milly reviews the advice of the distinguished consultant, Sir Luke Strett, from a similarly distanced perspective, with its suggestion of ellipsis. Anaphoric reference and immediate tie at chapter start seem, again, at odds with past perfect verb form: "She had gone out with these last words so in her ears that when once she was well away—back this time in the great square alone—it was as if some instant application of them had opened out there before her" (5.4i; 176).

In *The Ambassadors* (1903), clear time indices at the opening of chapters and books, betoken a less internalized series of events. Its use of immediate ties, however, as well as anachrony, is again restrained, and James's care in positioning such ties is manifest. The critical sequence in *The Golden Bowl* (1904) is articulated by an immediate span culminating in chapter 33, longest of the novel. Fanny Assingham, having learned that Charlotte and Prince Amerigo were former lovers, shatters the eponymous vessel, just as the prince enters.

At a somewhat later stage in *The Ambassadors*, the counterpart to this scene takes place outdoors. Lambert Strether, during his rural excursion away from Paris, rests in the garden of the riverside inn:

> . . . while he leaned against a post and continued to look out he saw something that gave him a sharper arrest. (11.3f; 1986a, 460)
> What he saw was exactly the right thing—a boat advancing round the bend and containing a man who held the paddles and a lady, at the stern, with a pink parasol. (11.4i; 461)

The couple are identified at the beginning of the second paragraph as Chad and Madame de Vionnet, and the shattering effect of their intimacy becomes critical in the novel as a whole.

James foregrounds this scene by various means. Apart from its idyllic framework, it is placed in the final chapter of the penultimate book, longest of a novel where successive books contain an increasing number of chapters, to climax in books 11 and 12. Unlike the other rare instances of immediate ties, moreover, which follow chapter-end speech (5.2, 6.3), or even embody chapter-start speech (12.2), the riverside scene renounces dialogue. Remarkably, in a novel with unmediated speech at more than one in two of its chapter ends, as well as a high proportion of dialogue within chapters, the scene confines itself almost entirely to a report of Strether's consciousness, as he attempts to grapple with the implications of what he has seen. Lexical repetition of the notion of sight, in combination with proleptic *Hakenstil* at the textual division (11.3f→11.4i), only serves to sharpen, for characters and readers alike, the novel's focus on issues of perception.

Joseph Conrad, *Almayer's Folly* (1895)
————, *An Outcast of the Islands* (1896)
————, *Lord Jim* (1900)
————, *Nostromo* (1904)
————, *The Secret Agent* (1907)

As early as *Almayer's Folly* (1895), Conrad eschews the linearity of mainstream Victorian fiction. Four of its opening five chapters are external analepses: before Dain's arrival in the middle of chapter 1, Almayer's memory returns him to Macassar twenty years back, and chapters 2–5 unfold these experiences, while Dain's plot line is not resumed until chapter 6. From the start, then, Conrad's exposition is retrospective, and by focussing on a late stage of Almayer's career, he reduces further the prospects of forward progression. Anticipating the complexity of Conrad's later fiction, are rapid alternations of time-level and perspective in chapter 5.

Babalatchi's thoughts regress from warm afternoon to gray dawn, when he observed Dain in Nina Almayer's canoe; an account of Almayer's activities on the same afternoon gives way to his preparations of the previous fortnight, yielding in turn to Dain's first encounter with Nina, and their liaison up to the evening prior to Babalatchi's sighting. The narrative loop is completed at the end of chapter 5 (1994, 57), with reference to the same thunderstorm that concludes chapter 1, so that events appear in an initial reverse transform, B-A-C.

The entry of new characters dominates the second half of *Almayer's Folly*, conveying a sense of restlessness. This is reinforced by a span of three minor parallel overlaps, and by the fact that nearly every chapter increases in length, making the climactic final chapter the longest in the novel. Separated as it is from the penultimate chapter by a nocturnal gap, one of only two in the novel, its opening also echoes the direct speech from the end of chapter 11. It thus emphasizes, by its scenic presentation, the participants' relative independence of the narrator.

At double the length of *Almayer's Folly*, Conrad's second novel, *An Outcast of the Islands* (1896), is also sequentially more complex. Exemplifying the notion of *hysteron proteron* [last put first], it uses *transtextual sequences*, but in reversed order (Watts 1984, 133; 1993, 118). *An Outcast of the Islands* thus deals with a younger Tom Lingard, while *Almayer's Folly*, the earlier novel, treats him at a later stage. The arrangement recalls one of Conrad's American models: in *The Prairie* (1827), Fenimore Cooper deals with the latest stage of Leatherstocking's career, in *The Deerslayer* (1841), with the earliest.

Like *Almayer's Folly*, *An Outcast of the Islands* shows end-loading, with each of its five parts expanding incrementally. The chapters in its final part are twice the length of its first, while the concluding chapter is again the longest of the novel, incorporating a coda not textually separated by a new chapter from the culminating events. Presaging the dramatic ellipsis between chapters 5 and 6 of *Typhoon* (1903), with its contrast of tempo between iconic match $(ST = DT)$ and weather summary,[74] the account of Willems's fate is broken off as he loses consciousness after being shot by Aïssa ([1896] 1986, 289). The overt gap is only completed many years later, ironically vouchsafed by Almayer to a visiting Roumanian naturalist.

By contrast with *Almayer's Folly*, the sequential profile of *An Outcast of the Islands* is quite different. An opening narrative loop, touching analeptically on Lingard's early career, is confined to a single chapter (1.2), which begins symptomatically with delayed presentation. Each of the first three parts has two instances apiece. They combine with frequent topic shifts and covert time gaps, to project indirectness. Thus, the reader's expectation of a nocturnal gap between parts 1 and 2 is shattered by the (delayed) revelation (2.1; 79), that Willems's liaison with Aïssa has already lasted five weeks: an example of false continuity.

With three chapters in part 3 of *An Outcast of the Islands* linked by immediate (3.2→3) and (delayed) proximate (3.4) ties, the jerkiness of the first two parts gives way to a more forward impetus, though the immediate ties mark Almayer's oral account to Lingard, foregrounded by the juxtaposition of chapter-end and chapter-start direct speech (3.2→3). Part 4 comprises a continuous span of immediate ties, recording the urgency and expansive flow of present-moment events centered on the confrontation between Lingard and Willems, directly reported over a considerable stretch of text and reading-time. By the final part, part 5, topic shifts and a single immediate tie return the narrative to its oblique mode again, typified by Almayer's distanced, and not personally witnessed retrospective of Willems's death (5.4).

In his approach to narrative, Conrad has affinities with Lawrence Sterne not related to whimsy and eccentricity. Both writers handle temporal relations with an elasticity which tracks the associative consciousness, rather than the dictates of an external plot line. Thus, Tristram Shandy and Charley Marlow, perversely and diversely, by their narratorial ordering, direct attention to material not chronologically successive, but subjectively significant.[75]

Marlow features first in the short story, *Youth* (1898), introduced abruptly by an outer-frame narrator unsure even as to how the name is spelled, with regular and rudimentary interruptions thereafter to fuel his recital. As inner-frame narrator again, in *Heart of Darkness* (1899), Marlow presents his African experience in a broadly linear sequence to a shipboard audience on the Thames. Within a narrative arch constructed by the colonial capitals of London, Rome, and Brussels, Marlow's voice recounts already completed events, but in a discontinuous presentation involving sequences such as proleptic analepses, whereby his retrospective narration betrays knowledge of future consequences.

In *Lord Jim* (1900), an outer-frame narrator oscillates between different periods of Jim's career, using ellipsis to avoid any suspicion of omniscient, and therefore conclusive treatment of the *Patna* affair (4i), until Marlow himself takes over (5i). Apart from occasional pauses, recalling the frame situation of an oral account several years later, Marlow continues in a virtually seamless span of thirty chapters of immediate transition, up to his last glimpse of Jim (35f). Within this span, however, the account wanders back and forth across the events surrounding the *Patna*. The subsequent Court of Inquiry becomes the only sure reference point in a temporally indeterminate world of narrative flux, and the linear norm of the topos of the sea voyage is further subverted.

As surrogate judge and jury, moreover, the reader has to filter out and weigh up a spectrum of eyewitness accounts. Marlow reports, for instance, Jim's report of his skipper's, or of Jewel's speech, and such recursive planes are complicated by a typical Marlow admission, that "at this distance in time I couldn't recall his very words" (9m; 1971a, 82). Within two pages, Marlow, with an oral narrator's license, shifts from the day before the inquiry, to "a long time after" and "very many years ago" (5m; 42–43), from "after more than three years" to "very lately," "not very long ago" to "years before" (13m; 116–17).

His oral account is incomplete, and only one privileged listener learns its sequel, in written form, more than two years later. In his covering letter, Marlow admits that even this information is fragmentary, much of it dependent on the dubious testimony of Gentleman Brown. The written narrative as presented, however, is now chronological (chs. 38→45), has immediate continuity, and in terms of end-loading, produces not the novel's longest chapter (reserved for Marlow's first impressions of Jim at the inquiry), but rather the novel's fastest tempi, in the climactic sequences of events in Patusan.

Nostromo (1904), like *Tristram Shandy*, tends to sort out lay readers from critics. The density of its opening chapters, in particular, denies instant orientation. Untroubled by calendar dates, though chronological tables, as with Sterne, have been reconstructed (Pettersson 1982, 115–22; Watts 1993, 171–73), readers are likewise ignorant of the proleptic force of the early allusions, so that the novel, more than most, insists on rereading as narrative strategy.[76] After Mitchell's reminiscences of the dictator Ribiera's arrival in Sulaco and Nostromo's defeat of the rioters (1.2), later chapters head backwards in earnest.

Having moved from the dinner party eighteen months before at which Ribiera inaugurated the railway (1.5), to the histories of the San Tomé silver mine and the Gould family since the early nineteenth century (1.6), the narrative loops back again at the close of part 1, in a large-scale variant of the opening of *Almayer's Folly*, to the same dinner party on board the *Juno*. Not scale, however, but complexity of anachrony is the key factor. More than a quarter of *Daniel Deronda*, for instance, forms a large-scale retrospective exposition, a progressive reverse order transform (*C-B-E-A-D*). Unlike *Nostromo*, however, it remains relatively transparent, focused upon one individual history at a time, and avoiding Conradian effects of simultaneity.

Halfway through part 2, and close to the halfway point, Martin Decoud writes to his sister in Paris. In the longest chapter (2.7) of *Nostromo*, typically embodying not action but reflection, he alludes to a riot in Sulaco the previous day, and Ribiera's arrival. To readers of a vaguely progressive bent, the forward quality of the twelve intervening chapters since Mitchell's own mention of those same events (1.2), must seem minimal. Conrad's justification differs from Shandy's account of how an apparently digressive movement is actually progressive (Sterne 1.22; [1767] 1962, 62–63). In Conrad's case, it would be more accurate to speak of quasidigression, a mode of narrative indirection rather than playful improvisation.

By part 3, the physical distance between Decoud and Nostromo on the Isabel Islands, and the Europeans at Sulaco, entails the use of internal analepsis (3.1i→2.7m, 3.9m→3.8f, 3.12i→3.10f). Simultaneous phases (3.2, 3.7) and immediate ties (3.3, 3.4) now register the gathering tension, as General Sotillo enters the town. Conrad's exploitation of ambiguous temporal adverbials, keeps readers in further suspense about gaps between events and their recall. The fate of Decoud, for example, is only confirmed by his medallion in the cathedral (3.10m), which Mitchell points out to a visitor, no less than seven years after his suicide. Compared with news of the fates of Willems and Lord Jim, this instance of delayed presentation looks scandalously belated.

The Secret Agent (1907), half the length of *Nostromo*, seems to promise easier access, if greater austerity. From opening participle onwards ("Mr. Verloc, going out in the morning" [1980, 13]), with its ambivalence of singulative and iterative markers, Conrad's sequential dynamics establish an ominously uneasy rhythm. Verloc's journey only commences in fact at 2i, to confirm chapter 1, with its survey of house and family, as an actionally static loop. Vladimir's deadline of a month (2m; 39) for the bomb outrage, then galvanizes a situation of threat and instability. Abrupt changes of focalization between chapters, from the Verlocs, to embassy officials, anarchists, high police and government representatives, recall the second half of *Almayer's Folly*, but also Dickens's tactics in the first serial parts of *Our Mutual Friend* (1865).

No successive chapters of *The Secret Agent,* in fact, have identical continuity relations. Between chapters 7 and 13, the transitions comprise an immediate tie, internal analepsis, a ten-day gap, parallel overlap, alternate phase, another immediate tie and an ellipsis, belatedly reported, of ten days. The Assistant Commissioner's ruminations about Michaelis bridge divisions, and delay for over eight pages any confirmation of the sequential status of chapter 6. Where normative transition is final segment to initial segment, the continuity here, in speech terms, runs from first final subsegment to medial segment (5f1→6m; 90→98):

"Two foreign anarchists coming from that place," he said, apparently to the window-pane. "It's rather unaccountable."

"Yes, sir. But it would be still more unaccountable if that Michaelis weren't staying in a cottage in the neighbourhood." (5f1; 90)

"You connect Michaelis with this affair?"   (6m; 98)

An earlier, intrachapter analepsis, linked to Chief Inspector Heat's encounter with the professor, again suspends forward movement, to give a police view of the Greenwich explosion (5m; 75–81). This central event, as if to illustrate the "unexpected solutions of continuity, sudden holes in space and time" (ch. 5; 76), which mark relations between conspirators and police, goes unrecorded in its order of occurrence.

By contrast with the overt gap of more than a month between chapters 3 and 4 of *Lord Jim*, spanning the *Patna* affair, the corresponding gap in *The Secret Agent* is covert. Not until the second half of chapter 4, does Ossipon refer to a bomb at Greenwich. Another four pages elapse, before he pronounces it to be a month since last he saw Verloc (69). The latter's own, laconic account, filtered obliquely through the keyhole to his wife Winnie, is reserved for the end of chapter 9. For the first time we learn the doings of the couple on the fatal day, though the text is coy about Adolf's role in the central event: "She was alone longer than usual on the day of the attempted bomb outrage in Greenwich Park, because Mr Verloc went out very early that morning and did not come back until nearly dusk" (156).

Lacking the mediation of a Marlow, the deliberate dislocation of events is all the more startling for the reader. In the month after Vladimir's ultimatum, incidents are shifted from chapter 4, where linearly they belong, to be post-positioned in chapters 8 and 9, creating a medial reverse transform, a macrosequence of A-C-B-D. Thus, a sympathetic account of the feeble-minded Stevie (ch. 8) is juxtaposed to the high-level political discussions of Sir Ethelred and the Assistant Commissioner (ch. 7), and to the grim aftermath of the explosion (ch. 9). In a much shorter text than Dickens's *Bleak House* (1853), with that novel's gradual convergence of societal extremes, and ironic juxtapositions of Jo the crossing-sweeper and the Dedlocks, *The Secret Agent* offers a sequential profile at once more abrupt and disconcerting, by virtue of its telescoped effects.

Verloc's murder, in the longest and most graphic chapter (ch. 11), is also the only major event presented scenically, rather than reported retrospectively. To discontinuity of topic, variability of transition and dislocation of sequence, Conrad now adds unevenness of tempo. In its closeup details, shifts of focalization, and, especially, its slow-motion realization of Winnie's revenge (during which three minutes subjectively expand across four pages [213–17]), the scene has cinematic affinities. It recalls similar decelerations of pace elsewhere: Fanny Robin's desperate five-hour crawl along the Casterbridge highway in Hardy's *Far from the Madding Crowd* ([1874] ch. 40), for instance. The *lento* of the murder scene testifies to an extreme irregularity of pace; it contrasts with *presto* markings later, as Ossipon leaps out of the boat-train.

While immediate continuity binds these adjacent chapters of action (ch. 11) and reaction (ch. 12), the dreamlike clarity in the account of Verloc's death renders Stevie's all the more obscure and contingent. Winnie's own death, however, is also reported indirectly and retrospectively, in a chapter (ch. 13) that, like chapter 4, delays for several pages confirmation of its sequential status. No month, this time, but ten days separate the chapters (12f→13i). Though reduced in scale, this second ellipsis shifts the accent again from event to reconstruction. When E. M. Forster, in *Howards End* (1910), has Mrs. Wilcox surprisingly expire between chapters 10 and 11, marked by apparent topic change and temporal indeterminacy, he may well, in his stress on consequences over circumstances, owe a debt to Conrad, who in *An Outcast of the Islands, Lord Jim, Nostromo,* and *The Secret Agent,* shows himself a master of the delayed obituary.

Conrad's wide international reading gives him access to a range of technical and formal devices, as well as thematic inspiration, but it is his particular handling of those devices in alliance with his choice of subject matter that accounts for his key role. Writing to Richard Curle in 1923, he insists that an attention to effects, often at the cost of directness of narrative, "can be detected in my unconventional grouping and perspective, which are purely temperamental and wherein almost all my 'art' consists. That, I suspect, has been the difficulty the critics felt in classifying it as romantic or realistic. Whereas, as a matter of fact, it is fluid, depending on grouping (sequence) [*sic*] which shifts, and on the changing lights giving varied effects of perspective" (Curle 1928, 191).

If Conrad himself regards his approach to sequence and perspective as "purely temperamental," many critics have linked expression with personality. His break with linearity, "ultimately reflects Conrad's sense of the fragmentary and elusive quality of individual experience" (Watt 1980, 357), his love of ironically contrasting viewpoints is natural for a *homo duplex* (Watts 1993, 118), his own insecurity is embedded in the tone of his narrative voice (Moore 1996, 238), while the sense of instability in *Lord Jim* can be partly traced to the cultural and linguistic dislocations of Conrad's youth (Stape 1996, 67).

Larger philosophical issues, moreover, underpin and sustain these biographical motivations. The reader's sense of cyclic repetition in *The Secret Agent,* for example, the need to grapple for orientation in *Nostromo,* to sift for evidence in *Lord Jim* project, at a textual level, essential concerns about general human progress, trust and truth. Multiple ironies, furthermore, attend actions occurring simultaneously, effects introduced before causes, appearances before motivations.

Dispersed across a number of different and independent works, rather than concentrated in a single *roman fleuve* like Proust's, Conrad's arsenal of sequential dynamics makes an arguably more dramatic impact, though an early work of the mid-1890s such as *Jean Santeuil* coincides with Conrad's own first publications. For the latter, "narrative experimentation is not an aim in itself" (Lothe 1996, 176). His achievement, therefore, is to adapt and combine, to intensify and radicalize technical resources for his own expressive and perceptual needs. By stressing reaction over action, reconstruction over construction, he eschews direct broaching of the main event, together with any authoritative account which might imply certainty or omniscience. To this end, his exploitation of framework narrative is crucial.

A landscape, according to Conrad, should be looked at in many ways, even to the extent of standing on our heads to avoid staleness. In literature, he goes on, "I am the only one in our generation who seems to be seeking a new form. Not that I deliberately sought it—stories came to me so. I had to have a number of different people seeing others from different angles. I had already adopted the form before I had fully realised it. And then I knew it was essentially mine, so I continue in it" (Randall 1968, 63). His statement dates from 1913. In that year, the first volume of Proust's novel appears; nearly all of Conrad's key works have already been published. Tardy obituarist of his fictional creations, Conrad remains an early master of ellipsis, a lacunaphile extraordinaire, rendering those "sudden holes in space and time" (Conrad [1907] 1980, 76) with a panache that reinforces his claim as the first great influential literary Modernist, as well as a distinguished contributor to the practice of sequential dynamics.

4

Conclusion

Sequential techniques do not thus merely offer an *available* approach; they are in many cases an *indispensable* means of analysis.

— P. M. Wetherill

The reader who neglects the order, frequencies and speeds of a text runs the risk of confusing story with truth, and could find himself to be the dupe of the disingenuous narrator.

— Jean Duffy

As INTERMEDIARY BETWEEN VICTORIAN AND MODERNIST ERAS, CONRAD serves as well as anyone to sum up and point ahead in terms of sequential dynamics. In a twentieth century of "time-novels," engendering critical self-consciousness about temporality, and inspiring in their turn oppositional works that celebrate achrony and nonlinearity, it is salutary to examine the contributions of texts prior to 1900, within contexts less patently fixated on time. The approach above to a historical poetics will, it is hoped, have helped to raise such issues as to which practices are conventional to and which transcend a given time and place. It is suggested too, that developments "within a single structural element of literature can provide important signs of literary process, laying a foundation for the study of relations between aesthetic form and social history."[1] This survey will also have served its purpose, if it demonstrates the need to analyze texts of every period from sequential perspectives.

Having taken Proust's *A la Recherche du Temps Perdu* as exegetical model, Genette later conceded that he was inevitably led to overstress the element of time (1980, 160), but his approach is justified by its exposure of what was only indistinctly observed by earlier critics. When his categories are applied, for example, to recent French fiction (Brooke-Rose 1983, 311–38), modifications of the kind he envisages and invites, find their place. Over the course of two decades, Genette's reconsiderations of his seminal "Discours

265

du récit" (1972) culminate in his own view, that there is little difference in the practice of anachrony between fictional and nonfictional narrative (1991, 73). The point reinforces the importance of testing techniques across a wide range of material. In terms of fictional texts, the present study has attempted to achieve this internationally, with broad surveys and detailed samples, antedating and succeeding Proust.

Many of the key literary developments noted above, emerge or come to fruition in that century that witnesses the births of both Conrad and Proust, when temporal awareness is polarized between discoveries in distant aeons of geology and biology, and the accelerating tempo created by contemporary industrialization and mass-production. The Romantic novel, ironic and confessional, poetic and supernatural, deliberately fragments and disorders its materials, plays with narrative and narratorial levels, and mixes literary genres. In the related historical novel, eras and cultures, factual and imaginative are contrasted, and a constant switch of focus between individuals and groups renders the form necessarily discontinuous. From the counter-Enlightenment Gothic tale, enshrining enigma and emotion, spring the detective fiction of the 1830s and the sensation novel of the 1860s. The latter relies on multiple, often conflicting perspectives, dislocations of chronology, and dramatic breaks that convert reader into judge.

With the Victorian multiplot novel, similar disruptive effects are seen, as techniques of cross-cutting and repeated transitions serve to regulate speeds, and advance action on all fronts. Frame narrative again involves complex transgressions of plot continuity, transitions between representing and represented worlds, and distancing and decelerating procedures. It differs from the unifying and organic bildungsroman, with its subjective record of stages toward individual maturation. The archetypal linear picaresque with which it is associated, also regains popularity with serial publication, whereby lengthy narratives first appear to readers in short monthly units.

Qualities of incompleteness and disjunction, suspense and contrast are here given a rational basis, while analogies with stage presentation are clear from the role of episodic development, spoken discourse, and climactic "curtains." Discontinuous presentation in the poetry of Tennyson's mid-century *Maud*, with its abrupt and fragmentary rhythms, prefigures more radically disjunctive work by late-century French Symbolists such as Laforgue, who champion juxtaposition over transition.

The invention of photography, the growth of journalism and the popularity of autobiography bring new impetus to classic realism in fiction, and partly reinforce its emphasis on causality, on precision of detail and linearity. Later developments, such as the quasiscientific impersonality and quotidian topics of Naturalism, the end of the triple-decker novel and the beginnings of cinema in the 1890s bring long-lasting effects on the novel form. The advent of Impressionism throughout the arts, however, is also pivotal. By dissolving mass, flow and continuity, it concentrates on means rather than ends, foregrounding the aesthetic perceptions of a subjective observer.

In terms of sequential dynamics, Impressionism instigates broken rhythms, which fracture the unidirectional motion and descriptive objectivity of classic realism and Naturalism. The "inward turn" of fiction means that material is arranged according to the way in which phenomena present themselves to the perceiving self. Outside stimuli and forward narrative are alike irrelevant for Huysmans's Des Esseintes, and the chapters of *A Rebours* (1884) cataloguing his esoteric tastes, are virtually interchangeable in their ordering within a basically circular form.

In other spheres, Whistler's attack on High Victorian values reinforces an increasing antinarrative tendency, which finds expression in a musicalization of topics and a blurring of artistic boundaries, elsewhere promoted by composers from Wagner to Scriabin. Exploitation of a specific medium, of manner over matter in the sense of *l'art pour l'art*, creates the decorative stasis and passive mood typified by Art Nouveau. Literary Impressionism, like painterly *taches*, accentuates the separateness of point-present sensations, treating them as isolated monads. Syntactically, their ephemeral quality is conveyed in brief phrases and verbless sentences, to project the self-communing consciousness, rather than phenomena in the outer world.

Parataxis and ellipsis underscore the looseness of relationships, while coordinating patterns emphasize additive rather than hierarchical properties. Suprasententially, smooth chapter transitions, assuring temporal and thematic continuity, give place to abrupt juxtapositions, whereby readers must supply their own sequential and semantic linkage. Such training will not go amiss in the twentieth century, with challenges posed by atemporality and aleatory, unsegmented fluidity and typographical abandon.

Recent critics of fiction and film alike have noted the difficulty of rendering any satisfactory account of temporality and causality in contemporary texts.[2] Works that seem merely quirky, marginal or perversely inscrutable today, however, cannot easily be dismissed as irrelevant to enquiry, since they may, like the "experiments" of

Joyce and Faulkner, assume a quasinormative status tomorrow. By applying sequential dynamics, it is not pretended that all contingencies can be covered, but analyses which utilize this approach can enrich their critical armory of technical resources, highlighting elements everywhere present, yet little regarded.

Outside the mainstream canon of fiction, moreover, other genres can benefit by examination from a sequential perspective. The espionage thriller represented by Ian Fleming's *Goldfinger* (1959), having already drawn the semiotic attentions of Umberto Eco and Roland Barthes,[3] invites disclosure, too, of its own organizational agenda. Contributing to its pace, tension and readability, are the facts that over half its chapters have immediate ties, its climactic third part features a continuity span of five such chapters, and immediate ties also bind together each part. The momentum of events is further stressed by the absence of analeptic phase, by the concentrated page/time ratios of individual chapters and overall time-cover.

In the genre of historiography, an example such as Thomas Pakenham's *The Boer War* (1979) displays a high level of sequential awareness. All its chapter headings announce their dates and venues, with constant shifts between character groupings echoing the kaleidoscopic movement of the multiplot novel. In temporal transparency, however, it exceeds its fictional exemplar, telegraphing parallel phases and analeptic overlaps with a clarity rarely encountered by the novel reader, and graphically demonstrating the dynamic possibilities of narrative sequence.

Less visible and often overlooked in fiction, the operation of sequential dynamics has been seen to vary according to different types of narrative and author, period, and culture. By supplying, for narrative transitions and order transforms especially, a more exact terminology and set of taxonomies than hitherto available, it is hoped that a new receptiveness to relations between, and dynamics across narrative units has been established. In association with other features, sequential analyses can illustrate the projection of semantic levels, convey pacing and proportions, bare skills or shortcomings of assembly, and sharpen the reader's sense of narrative as process, as experience of shifting and transforming elements.

Since issues of order, linkage, and continuity affect all texts, the role of sequential dynamics as a classifying and explanatory tool is equally relevant and applicable. At the beginning of a new millennium, moreover, when political and ideological concerns dominate theoretical approaches to the old form/content divide, it may be timely and tonic to redress the balance a little, and to direct critical energies once again toward potentialities of form.

Notes

INTRODUCTION

1. "Sequence" itself fundamentally alludes to the "fact of following after or succeeding" (*OED*, 2nd ed., 1989). This basic definition is then supplemented by further senses, involving "order of succession," "a continuous or connected series," "a logical consequence." "Sequential dynamics" as a term has been preferred to "sequencing," since it characterizes more accurately the nature of the syntagmatic operation.

2. For discussion of narrative and sequential ordering in relation to temporality in fiction, see especially Forster [1927] 1993, 17–29; Lämmert 1955, 73–94; Genette 1972, 71–121; Wetherill 1974, 230–47; Barthes 1977, 91–104; Chatman 1978, 62–84; Sternberg 1978, 8–34; Prince 1982, 48–60; Rimmon-Kenan 1983, 43–58; Bal 1985, 51–68; Toolan 1988, 48–62; Cohan and Shires 1988, 52–64; Miner 1990, 146–65; and Duffy 1992, 44–59.

3. Standard editions of texts have been used wherever possible, but chapter and part/volume indications have also been given, to allow convenient identification in other editions. Dates following titles indicate original year of publication; when two dates are given, the date in brackets represents the original publication. The symbol "§" alludes to a chapter section in the text, "‖" to a parallel phase, "→" to continuity linkage between narrative units or segments. Shorthand references to initial (i), medial (m), and final (f) segments of chapters are designed for economy; *Tom Jones* 12.10f, for instance, denotes the final segment of chapter 10 in book 12 of Fielding's novel. For the sake of uniformity, Arabic numerals appear throughout.

1. THEORY

1. In a vast literature devoted to the concept of time, the bibliographies included in Patrides (1976), Higdon (1977), Ritter (1978), Martin (1987), Ermarth (1992), serving interdisciplinary and literary interests, are particularly rich.

2. "Time is the principle of narrative, just as it is the principle of life" [my trans.].

3. For discussion of fictional narrativity, especially events, focalization and time, in relation to concepts of possible worlds, see Ronen 1994.

4. A. A. Mendilow refers to time as both absolute, since it is a primary aspect of experience, and relative, having a cognitive value "only as it is related to sensible phenomena" (1952, 145). For Paul Ricoeur, narrative is only meaningful "to the extent that it portrays the features of temporal existence" (1984, 3). To neglect a work's functioning in time, reduces it to "an assemblage of pieces" (Segre 1979,

269

viii). Time provides the "generative energy of fictional form" (Miller 1968, 16), while novelistic excellence can be gauged by the degree to which a work is convincingly "chronomorphic," the success with which materials of fiction are molded by time (Hutchens 1972).

5. For Robert Scholes, events are the only kind of thing that can be narrated (1980, 209), and sequences entail events being related in time. Seymour Chatman refers to "an event chain, operating through time" (1981, 808). Both formulations of events imply the idea of transformation or modification from one state of affairs to another.

6. Cohen (1979, 124) identifies a lack of progression and a static cluster of present moments; Hayman (1987, 151) notes the tendency to freeze verbal time and spatialize discourse.

7. For case studies of these internal aspects, see Lid 1961, Tanner 1967, Crawford 1981.

8. For external aspects, see Edwards 1969, Hornback 1963, Andrews 1968.

9. "Time went by, trickled away, time flowed" [my trans.].

10. For the effects of these different discourse types, see §1.4.

11. Contrasting the earlier with the later form, Georg Lukács recognizes that in the epic, the "life-immanence of meaning is so strong it abolishes time," whereas in the novel, "meaning is separated from life, and hence the essential from the temporal" (Lukács 1971, 122). In his view, the novel as the epic of a literally god-forsaken world is a form constantly seeking for the organic totality of the classical epic, with the novelistic hero alienated from his community, unable to achieve a unified personality by mastery of memory, or of time, which represents the fullness of life. Thus, "the entire inner action of the novel is nothing but a struggle against the power of time" (122). Though he foists ambitions on the novel to which it often did not aspire, in stressing a nostalgic yearning for epic totality, and underplaying the novel's flexibility and power of adaptation to new circumstances, Lukács valuably establishes a larger framework against which the newer form can be measured.

12. The Greek archetype of the romance represents "an alien world in adventure-time" (Bakhtin 1982, 89), its limits marked off by the lovers' first meeting and final union. Despite an improbable number of adventures between these two adjacent biographical moments, heroes and heroines appear as fresh and handsome at the end as at the beginning. Thus, for Bakhtin, Greek romance-time has no elementary biographical or maturational duration. Time ticked off in the separate and theoretically infinite series of events is not united into the real-life series of a human life. With initiatives belonging to divine or nonhuman forces, and humans at the mercy of chance, the realm of romance, not unsurprisingly, bears no indications of historical time or period.

13. In *Time and the Conways* (Priestley 1937), act 2 is a subjective prolepsis of twenty years; in *Death of a Salesman* (Miller 1947), act 1 employs an analepsis-within-analepsis. A large-scale analepsis between acts 1 and 4 represents the King's friendship and betrayal of the prelate in *Becket* (Anouilh 1959); act 3 of *Top Girls* (Churchill 1982) takes place a year earlier than the opening acts.

14. Lessing, in his *Laokoon*, contrasted the plastic arts as visible bodies in space and governed by the principle of juxtaposition, with the poetic arts as events following one another in time and governed by succession ([1766] 1990, 219–20). Later aestheticians have argued that any process of perception is temporal. If the elements of a picture, as a spatial object, have a certain order and inner consistency, that order makes it aesthetically compulsory that the elements appear to

the contemplator in a definite time sequence (Ivanov 1973, 32). As little prescient as Aristotle, in his *Poetics,* of the impact of prose fiction on aesthetic theory, so Lessing in his *Laokoon,* of the twentieth-century art of film, where narrativity involves the exploration of tensions between spatial mapping and temporal movement.

15. Emile Benveniste (1966) opposes "discours," as the grammatically indicated presence of a locutor, with "récit," the pure causal-chronological sequence.

16. Stevick (1970, 42–55) presents seven different types of chapter cadence: declarative; anticipatory; scenic; symbolic summary; broadening; reductive; repetitive, though he indicates that any given ending is likely to contain different types operating simultaneously.

17. Austen's completed chapters average six pages each, and range between 3.5 and 12; those in the sequel average eleven, the shortest being 6 and the longest 17.5.

18. Sternberg (1978, 50, 311 n), in discussing expositional gaps, is at pains to distance his own view of the literary text as a dynamic system of gaps, from the quite different conceptions of Ingarden and Iser. He himself distinguishes (236) between preliminary and delayed expositions (according to position in the *syuzhet*), concentrated and distributed (according to degree of formal continuity), while David Bordwell (1985, 78), referring to film, adds flaunted and suppressed gaps to the narrational types.

19. "The structure of an event from beginning to end as it is moulded in narrative" [my trans.].

20. See §1.5.

21. Reid 1992, 23–24, has questioned the view of narrative as representing a succession of events, and redefines it as "the discursive mode that imparts an illusion of eventful serial movement to its constituent figures." Thus, from a rhetorical perspective, action sequences appear as transformations, and narrative exchanges are dominated by tropes of substitution and dispossession.

22. His "story-type sujet" (picaresque fiction) denotes a temporal-additive presentation; "story-type fabula" a reader's reconstitution of stream-of-consciousness fiction; "plot-type sujet" identifies the deformed causal arrangement in *Oedipus Rex*; "plot-type fabula," the same material linearized (Sternberg 1978, 12).

23. Half of them adopt a two-part, the remainder a three-part system, in grouping components: events in chronological order; causally related; ordered artistically; text on the page; narration as enunciation. While Chatman, for example, associates "story" with the first component and subsumes all the rest under "discourse," Prince and Stanzel, his two-part colleagues, extend their "narrated" and "story" categories, respectively, to the various types of events, reserving "narrating" and "mediation" for the last two components. Genette and Rimmon-Kenan, on the other hand, identify "histoire," with its ambiguous connotations (Martin 1987, 108; Sternberg 1990, 919 n), and "story," respectively, with the first two types of event, "discours/récit" and "text" with the next two components, and, alone, employ "narration" for the enunciatory act. Bal, on her (three-) part, confusingly labels the first component "fabula," and uses "story" (and focalization) for the second and third, then widens the scope of "narration" from enunciation into the text itself.

24. Among the pairs, with their various shadings and emphases, the following are some of the more notable: temporal and syntagmatic orders (Genette); "ordre des événements" and "ordre des paroles," "temps raconté [de la fiction]" and "temps racontant [du discours]" (Todorov); presented world and presentational

process (Ruthrof); dispositional and expositional sequences (O'Toole); time order and textual order (Pavel); "erzählte Zeit" and "Erzählzeit" (Müller); chronological and communicative sequences, orders of occurrence and presentation (Sternberg); temporal sequence of events and textual order of presentation (Perry); "temps raconté" and "temps du raconter" (Ricoeur); narrated and narrating order (Prince); story-time and -order, text-time and -order (Rimmon-Kenan).

25. These comprise:

Fabula	Syuzhet
A. simultaneous events	simultaneous presentation
B. successive events	simultaneous presentation
C. simultaneous events	successive presentation
D. successive events	successive presentation

Only C and D are relevant to fiction.

26. "Nothing in this world comprises one single piece, but everything is a mosaic. Past history alone can be related chronologically, a system inapplicable to an ongoing present" [my trans.].

27. Chatman (1981, 802–9) argues against Smith's theory as being totally language-oriented, her speech-act model not being relevant to literary narrative. In a later statement, Chatman draws attention to the failings of contextualist narratology, among whose supporters he lists Smith, Mary Louise Pratt, Vincent Leitch and Susan Lanser. Denying that the story/discourse distinction is any more than a construct and "convenient heuristic" (1990, 312), he also strongly insists that narratology, "presupposes no ur-text in which 'story' exists autonomously, nor one whose discourse order perfectly parallels its story order . . . only that a narrative may present last events first and first events last and that an implied reader can recognize that ordering" (311).

28. Its dislocations of expositional order, its later instances of analepsis, including the temporal complexity of an exchange of letters between George Vavasor and Alice (chs. 30–32), and its multiplot interweavings mean, *contra* Smitten, that the violations in *Can You Forgive Her?* (1864) exceed those in Trollope's first significant novel *The Warden* (1855). Here, following initial returns to Mr. Harding's early life and to the foundation of the almshouse in chapter 1, the action moves forward with virtually no dislocations.

29. Paul Ricoeur (1980, 178) views narrative activity as a confrontation between, and combination of chronological and nonchronological dimensions, the former concerned with the formation of story out of events in terms of episodic sequence; the latter with the configuration of plot, construing significant wholes out of scattered events.

30. In his introduction to the later version, the editor Malcolm Cowley attempts to justify the revision project, left incomplete by Fitzgerald himself. He quotes a statement by the author, who traces back the problems of the novel's reception to the public's difficulties in distinguishing its central theme: "its great fault is that the *true* beginning—the young psychiatrist in Switzerland—is tucked away in the middle of the book" (Fitzgerald 1973, v).

31. Chatman 1978, 32.

32. Though conceding the relativistic character of speed labels, Bonheim tabulates subclasses for these varied modes (1982, 42). He proposes diagrams to represent the relationship between narrative time and narrated time (*Erzählzeit* and *erzählte Zeit*), in terms of parallel lines. When a panoramic report or flashback occurs, for instance, the narrated line is interrupted and a "time cave" results;

with a description or comment, the narrative line shows a "time pouch" (see figure below). In a different graphic scheme, Eckard Cwik adopts a single line for narrated time, which is broken by dots or horizontal dashes when it seems to be slowed down or stopped, and is given arrows when it seems to be speeded up (Bonheim, 44–46).

33. "As Instetten helped her out of the sleigh, he had looked closely at Effi but avoided any reference to the strange journey that she had made with her companion; and next morning, having risen early, he tried as far as possible to restrain himself, even though his ill-humour still persisted" (Fontane 20i; [1894] 1967, 151).

34. See Gide 1943, 44–45; Morrissette 1971; Ricardou 1967, 171–90; 1973, 47–75; Dällenbach 1977; also §2.2.

35. Genette's categories (1972) embrace singulative, anaphoric, repetitive, and iterative.

36. Müller's legacy is diverse. It allows readers to appreciate, for instance, how each book of *Tom Jones* draws on a progressively greater length of clock time to cover a progressively shorter period of fictional time (Mendilow 1952, 127); how an inserted flashback creates an illusion of length and slowness of time, in Castorp's first week at the sanatorium in *The Magic Mountain* (Harvey 1965, 107); how an uneven coverage of the period before and after Waterloo, in *Vanity Fair*, matches blurred dating and relaxed narrative (Sutherland 1971); how, with Balzac, the static structure of *Eugénie Grandet* contrasts with the forward drive of *Père Goriot* (Wetherill 1974, 239). Other commentators on the tempo of specific works cite thematic, conceptual and technical grounds. Conrad's fellow-novelist, Ford Madox Ford, speaks of a *progression d'effet* that governs the gradual increase of pace in *Lord Jim,* from Marlow's discursive account of Jim's trial to the dramatic action at Patusan (Ford 1924, 210).

37. "alike . . . as a flowing, as a succession in time, as one thing after another; and both differ from the plastic arts, which are complete in the present, and unrelated to time save as all bodies are, whereas narration—like music—even if it should try to be completely present at any given moment, would need time to do it in" (Mann 1927, 683)

38. At least at the level of the *represented world*, since, as Sturgess (1992, 135) reminds us, a sequence of *representation*, defying discontinuity and any sense of non sequitur, is always present in the narrative syntagm.

39. The treatment of temporal and continuity relations within the broader rubric of literary history, is explored in detail in §3.

40. In the case study of Austen's *Persuasion* (§2.1), the role of determinacy of data is illustrated at some length.

41. See, especially, Halliday and Hasan (1976, 295), and Van Dijk and Kintsch (1983, 204). Logical, expository, thematic, and associative, as well as narrative grounds can determine sequence (Leitch 1986, 14). Proust uses the topographical pattern of a train journey, to trigger episodes attached to towns on the route (Houston 1962, 42), thus creating an "achronic structure" (Genette 1980, 84). In his *Mobile,* Butor (1962) sweeps across America in a large-scale interweave of names and ideas.

42. Friedman (1955) offers a typology of eight categories of point of view; Stanzel (1955) sets up a continuum of authorial/figural/first-person situations. Subsequent refinements and modifications appear in Lanser (1981, 11–63), and Prince (1989, 73–76) offers a succinct survey of developments.

43. Both examples by Rimmon-Kenan of simultaneous focalization are taken

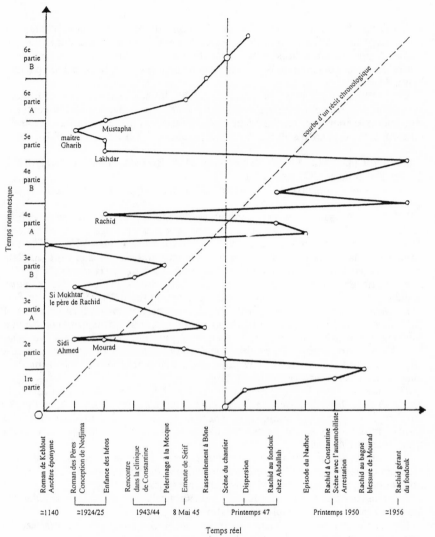

• Gontard 1985, 38 [*fabula* & *syuzhet*/Yacine, *Nedjma*]

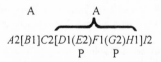

• Genette 1980, 41 [order/Proust: *Jean Santeuil*]

Graphic Representations

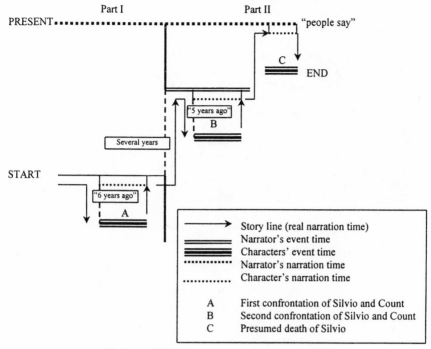

Part I   Part II

PRESENT ●●● "people say"

C   ↓
═══ END

"5 years ago"
B

Several years

START

"6 years ago"

A

──────▶	Story line (real narration time)
═══════	Narrator's event time
≡≡≡≡≡≡≡	Characters' event time
●●●●●●●	Narrator's narration time
·············	Character's narration time
A	First confrontation of Silvio and Count
B	Second confrontation of Silvio and Count
C	Presumed death of Silvio

• Shukman 1977, 51 [time structure/Pushkin: *The Shot*]

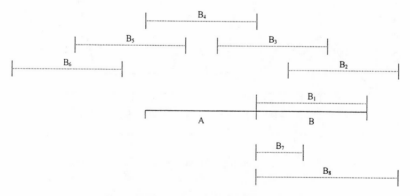

• Branigan 1992, 41 [story time/on-screen time]

A. Base time (beginning, into second paragraph) 5
B. Childhood (mid second par.) 1
C. Base time (end second par. and beginning of third) 5
D. (A complex section to be scrutinized more closely later on)
E. Recent past (Miss Gavan and the Stores) 4
F. Future ("her new home," p. 106) 6
G. Recent past (Saturday night, etc.) 4
H. Future ("She was about," p. 107) 6
I. Recent past (Eveline's relationship with Frank) 4
J. Earlier past (Frank's history) 2
K. Base time (p. 107—the "evening deepened" 5
L. Earlier time (Eveline's mother's illness and death) 3
M. Base time mixed with future (end of first section) 5/6
N. Ellipsis in base time 5
O. Base time (whole second scene, with only a hint of future) 5

• Scholes 1982, 93–94 [temporal movement/Joyce, "Eveline"]

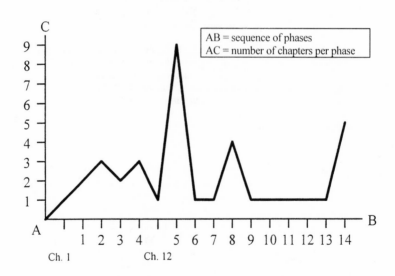

• Jungel 1953, 54 [phase & chapter relations/Forster: *A Passage to India*]

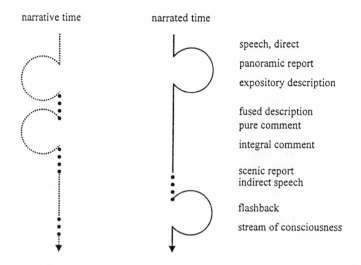

narrative time   narrated time

speech, direct
panoramic report
expository description

fused description
pure comment
integral comment

scenic report
indirect speech

flashback
stream of consciousness

• Bonheim 1982, 44 [time pouches and caves]

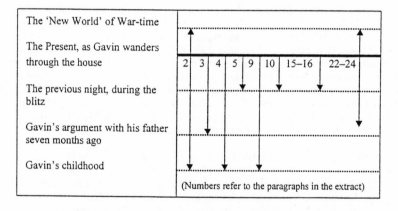

The 'New World' of War-time								
The Present, as Gavin wanders through the house	2	3	4	5	9	10	15–16	22–24
The previous night, during the blitz								
Gavin's argument with his father seven months ago								
Gavin's childhood								
(Numbers refer to the paragraphs in the extract)								

• Raban 1976, 66 [time shifts/Moore: *The Emperor of Ice Cream*]

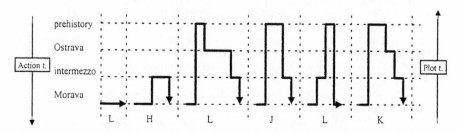

	prehistory
Action t.	Ostrava
	intermezzo
	Morava

L   H   L   J   L   K   Plot t.

• Dolezel 1973, 97 [plot time structure/Kundera: *The Joke*]

from Patrick White's *Voss*, and relate to contiguous sections within, rather than between chapters.

44. Thus, Fielding: "Jones departed *instantly* in quest of Sophia" (*Tom Jones*, 6.8i; [1749] 1963, 251); Tolstoy: "*At that moment* Count Rostopchin . . . strode into the room" (*War and Peace*, 3.1.23i; [1869] 1973b, 807); Dostoyevsky: "*As soon as* [Nastasya] had gone" (*Crime and Punishment*, 2.6i; [1866] 1991, 199) [my italics].

45. "He carefully withheld this from his mother"; "When he viewed these things in such a way" [my trans.].

46. "Everything in ashes. But *still* bound together"; "Botho gazed into the ashes. How little, yet how much" [my trans.].

47. "and Herr Kesselmeyer walked in"; "Herr Kesselmeyer entered unannounced, as a friend of the house . . . paused, however, near the door" (Mann 1971, 155).

48. "Ruined, robbed, forsaken! He had remained on the seat, as though shell-shocked" [my trans.].

49. "When he had taken his seat in the carriage . . . a feeling of intoxication seemed to overwhelm him" [my trans.].

50. In texts chosen virtually at random, the total number of occurrences for proximate/nocturnal/immediate phases yields, in *Pride and Prejudice*: 10/18/8; in *The Pioneers*: 2/7/22; in *The Warden*: 7/4/3; in *Middlemarch*: 15/10/3; in *Fathers and Sons*: 10/5/6; in *Irrungen Wirrungen*: 7/5/5; in *The Ambassadors*: 12/3/4. To generalize about differences between proximate and nocturnal phases, is less easy than to observe that Austen shows strong nocturnal rhythms, that Cooper's adventure fiction, as opposed to the societal concerns of Trollope and Eliot, stresses immediate phases. In James, these are similarly demoted in favour of the less sudden, more graduated proximate intervals, while Turgenev and Fontane nicely poise nocturnal and immediate gaps. A comprehensive profile would require data about where such instances occur within texts, the role of continuity spans, as well as the proportions of proleptic, parallel, and analeptic phases also present.

51. For Butor (1970, 20), the phase represents "an essential rhythm of our existence."

52. Brevity marks Scott's *The Fair Maid of Perth* (34i; [1828] 1969, 421): "Palm Sunday now dawned"; terse colloquialism, Fontane's *Frau Jenny Treibel* (8i; [1892] 1966, 74): "Treibel war ein Frühauf" ["Treibel was an early bird" (my trans.)]; Eliot underlines a peaceful night by entitling ch. 29 of *Adam Bede* ([1859] 1981, 356) as "The Next Morning." Elsewhere, Goethe focuses on social aspects in *Die Wahlverwandschaften* 1.12 ([1809] 1963, 94): "Als die Gesellschaft zum Frühstück wieder zusammen kam" ["When the company assembled again for breakfast" (my trans.)]. Dickens turns to pathetic fallacy, in *Bleak House* (26i; [1853] 1996, 416): "Wintry morning, looking with dull eyes and sallow face upon the neighbourhood of Leicester Square." Raabe uses facetious circumlocution in *Abu Telfan* (2i; [1868] 1980, 16): "Und die Erde drehte wieder einmal ihre Ostseite der Sonne zu" ["And the earth rotated its easterly portion once more towards the sun" (my trans.)].

53. "And Marcell really did write, so that on the following morning two letters addressed to Corinna lay on the breakfast-table" [my trans.].

54. With Forster, the absence of proleptic reference in the preceding chapter (*A*) to her death (*B*), and the postfacto assumption (*C*) of its occurrence, may be conveyed by the *microsequence A-C-B* on the level of the *syuzhet*. This ellipsis, or *medial reverse transform* (§1.3) is striking by virtue of its being completely unfore-

shadowed. In other cases, the constituent B may be merely downplayed or suppressed in the *syuzhet*, its effect softened by advance notice. Charles's interview with Ernestina's father (A), in Fowles's *FLW* 37, is followed by another with her mother (B) ([1969] 1970, 229). A new chapter then features the hero already outside the mansion (38i; (C)), the narrator having left unexpressed in chapter gap, because unimportant, the actual conversation with Mrs. Freeman (B). Here, the ellipsis amounts to no more than a proximate gap, untypical of a novel animated by paralipsis.

55. "How long ago it now is that I wrote the above. I am scarcely the same person, and my handwriting has long since altered" [my trans.].

56. "We sit and listen likewise for a moment to those footsteps which recede and those which approach, for henceforth there are two paths available, by which we can now attain the goal of our travels" [my trans.].

57. "something frightful" [my trans.].

58. Bal (1985, 66–67) defines three main kinds of deviations resembling achrony: anticipation-within-retroversion (referring forward within a back-reference); retroversion-within-anticipation (being told beforehand how circumstances in the 'present' will be presented); anticipation in *fabula* as retroversion in *story* (event yet to take place chronologically, already presented, e.g., in embedded speech, in story). Branigan (1992, 42; 235n), analysing film sequence, separates retrospective (nonsubjective) flashforward from (subjective) flashback.

59. "At the precise hour that the guests rose from dinner at the Treibels', Professor Schmidt's 'evening' commenced" [my trans.].

60. "Meanwhile, at that very moment, Fantine was in raptures" [my trans.].

61. Various lexica define it in a value-free way, as, for instance, an "interruption of the chronological sequence of events by interjection of events of earlier occurrence" (*Webster* 1976). An emphasis on the verbal component "flash" (*Longman* 1978, *OED* 1989) tends to accentuate the *speed* of transition. A separate connotation stresses the temporal *extent* of the reversion (Cook 1981, 64), but such quoted examples as "prolonged flashback" (*OED* 1989) only seem self-contradictory. Its filmic history and etymology is thoroughly explored by Turim (1989), while Chatman (1983, 64) argues that the use of both "flashback" and "flashforward" should be limited to film. For him, "flashback" should not refer to traditional summary passages, but rather to those that go back specifically visually, "as a scene, in its own autonomy, that is, introduced by some overt mark of transition like a cut or a dissolve."

62. "Let us retell those stories, at the same time dividing them up neatly, rounding them off and arranging them for our better appreciation" [my trans.].

63. "a kind of advance summary" [my trans.].

64. Even a basically nonepistolary novelist such as Scott, makes verbatim use of letters throughout the first of the three volumes of *Redgauntlet* (1824), and passim use of extracts in *Guy Mannering* (chs. 16–18; [1815] 1987, 115–32). In a predominantly linear novel, Stendhal must also regress, in *Le Rouge et le Noir* 2.14 ([1831] 1973, 312), so as to motivate Mathilde's letter to Julien.

65. "When he entered the cell, he found it empty" [my trans.].

66. "When Quasimodo saw that the cell was empty" [my trans.].

2. PRACTICE: FOUR CASE STUDIES OF SEQUENTIAL DYNAMICS

1. In the first quarter, imprecise or analeptic markers, as in 1.4, prepare the end of the exposition, with Sir Walter's and Anne's removals announced in ad-

vance, but detailed only in retrospect from the key date of Michaelmas. In the second quarter, with events increasingly viewed through Anne's eyes, and the return of Wentworth accompanied by renewed temporal imprecision, it is only in 1.11, before the fateful trip to Lyme, that the temporal extent of Anne's six-chapter stay at Uppercross is (retrospectively) made known. Of the third quarter, part is calculated from the (indeterminate) day of the accident at Lyme, the remainder, again retrospectively, as if to suggest Anne's lack of response to Bath in Frederick's absence, is measured from the key date of Mary's letter in February. Of the final quarter, only the final chapter cannot be assigned a specific day and number based concomitantly on this letter.

2. Lloyd Brown (1973, 105) describes time in *Persuasion* as "an experience that is integral to the emotional and moral development of character."

3. Nash (1967, 194–98) contends that *Pride and Prejudice* uses the calendar of 1802, whereas Chapman (1926, 2.400–407) opts for 1811–12. Chapman also points out (5.282) that there is no indication of a calendar being employed in *Persuasion*: 1 February 1815 was not a Monday, as the text suggests, but a Wednesday.

4. Chapman examines chronological consistency (5.280–82), and charitably allows that the initial date of Lady Elliot's death as 1800 must be a slip or printer's error. He points out that the time spans allotted Wentworth between Lyme and Bath do not fill the interval, though he omits the week spent at Plymouth and confirmed by Admiral Croft (344, 380). External evidence, that of entertainment nights at Bath, fixes the (otherwise indeterminate) concert evening (2.8) as a Wednesday, since the key link of "a day or two passed" (388) remains imprecise. Next morning, however, Anne visited Mrs. Smith, who learned of Mr. Elliot's "intentions" from Nurse Rooke on Monday evening, "two days ago" (404), so that it would now seem to be only Wednesday and not Thursday, as Chapman proposes. When it is recalled that the chapter in question (2.10) was added during rewriting of the two manuscript chapters of *Persuasion*, the temporal inconsistencies can be better explained. Since the novel was published after her death, it is a moot point whether further revisions would have been made: "we can assume that the text does not represent her intention in every detail" (Southam 1964, 86 n).

5. Pennala (1985, 230) alludes to the category of "process-time" (Higdon 1977) to characterize Austen's typical approach.

6. Her response to him, temporally simultaneous and emotionally plural, is contained in the time-noun "confusion"; his to her, of similar immediacy but recorded only externally, in the temporal adverbial "instantly." The increasing precision, amplification, eventual exchange and fusion of these temporal-linguistic counters, projects the course of their relationship.

7. *Persuasion* has nine continuous phases (vs. thirty-six in *Pride and Prejudice*), constituting 37 percent of its chapters (vs. 65 percent in *Northanger Abbey*), its largest continuity span of six chapters (vs. eleven in *Pride and Prejudice* and *Northanger Abbey*), its most extensive single day coverage of twenty-two pages (vs. twenty-eight in *Emma*).

8. Though continuous phases represent only 44 percent of chapters in *Mansfield Park*, they are disposed with similar care, so as to span all three volumes. In this lengthy novel, they establish subtle rhythms, through their unusual tendency to begin or end in the same rather than in adjacent chapters.

9. The first span (1.5–6; 9 pp.) literally enlarges on the change which Uppercross affords Anne; the second (1.11–2.1; 26 pp.) encompasses the momentous Lyme episode, and its echoes into volume two; the third (2.2–4; 10 pp.) steeps

Anne in the events of Bath; the fourth (2.6–11; 73 pp.) unites in a sustained sweep the final eleven days between Admiral Croft's conversation with Anne, to the Camden Place party of the Saturday evening.

10. At almost one-half the length of *Emma* (437 pp.), the longest and immediately preceding work, and of *Mansfield Park* (432 pp.), *Persuasion* is only slightly longer than the early *Northanger Abbey* (213pp.). It has by far the fewest chapters, half those of *Mansfield Park* (48), *Emma* (55), and of the prolific *Pride and Prejudice* (61).

11. In *Northanger Abbey*, the direction of this temporal concentration is reversed: from an average of twenty-five pages/week (vol. 1), to Austen's average of thirteen pages/week (vol. 2). *Persuasion* moves from five pages/week (vol. 1), to over nine pages/week (vol. 2).

12. Eclipsed only by Willoughby's repentance in *Sense and Sensibility*, if it occupies actually "only half an hour" (3.8; [1811] 1970c, 292) for its fifteen pages.

13. In terms of the distribution of dialogue, the first quarter of *Persuasion* reaches only 27 percent, with sharp contrasts between Sir Walter's self-portrait in direct speech (1.3) and the next chapter, which totally shuns dialogue in its return to 1806. There is a similar absence in 1.11 of the second quarter, where the celebrated evocation of Lyme Regis gives place to a narrative sketch of the Harvilles and Benwick: comparative stasis in preparation for the comparative activity of the accident to come (1.12). It is the relatively high proportion of direct speech in 1.8, where Wentworth delivers himself at greater length than on any occasion before the climactic 2.11, that boosts this quarter to 31 percent. In the third quarter, dialogue is more evenly apportioned, being present in every chapter, holding the overall percentage at 32 percent.

14. Literally a circular movement, if the allusion to Sir Walter's insertion of Anne's marriage in the Baronetage (452) is taken into account, and linked with similar allusions in 1.1.

15. For Brown, the metaphor joins other major symbols in dramatizing coincidental cycles of time and experience, linked with all three Elliot sisters (1973, 104).

16. See Gide (1893) 1943; Dällenbach 1972; 1977; 1989; Jefferson 1980.

17. See also Magny (1950, 269–78); Goebel (1972, 34–52); Geerts (1979, 9–37).

18. It is Hamlet who chooses the play and inserts lines of his own into the given text, while the avowed intention, to "catch the conscience of the king," proves successful. In its narrative relation to the main play, "The Mouse-trap" is retrospective, an *external analepsis*, and in its performance it is only half-completed, King Claudius leaving when the Player King is poisoned. The *mise en abyme* here has the status of a stage-work acted out in public, using a model familiar to initiator and performers, and carrying personal meaning for its chief spectator.

19. It is the unnamed narrator who, within the prose narrative, vainly chooses a prose romance, the *Mad Trist* of Sir Launcelot Canning, to divert the doomed recluse. Usher's own recognition of the kinship between events offstage during the reading, and those in the romance, stresses the narrowness of the *internal prolepsis*. Here, the *mise en abyme*, generating suspense but represented by a partial and uncompleted performance, barely foreshadows the catastrophe. As Roderick's friend, the first-person narrator is observer and participant in a private performance, the literary model for which is familiar to speaker and listener alike, and the outcome of which destroys both master and mansion.

20. When Sōseki censures Defoe, for being "detailed, exhaustive and detective-

like" ("Daniel Defoe and the Structure of the Novel," [Sakuko 1975, 270]), he clearly intends the last epithet in a different, and pejorative sense, that of trivialization.

21. Both artist and reader in *Kusa Makura*, according to Rimer (1978, 60), are educated to understand that any escape into the past, "is at best a tour, a spree; the present must command our attention, and our compassion."

22. Kourouma's other novels are *Monnè: outrages et défis* (1990); *En attendant le vote des bêtes sauvages* (1998).

23. See, for instance, Echenim (1978, 140); Schikora (1980, 811); Okafor (1988, 53); Mortimer (1990, 108).

24. Cortazzi (1993, 105–107) illustrates a global range of variations in the internal structure of narratives, affected by different linguistic and cultural features.

25. "a weary worn-out thing like an old chipped calabash" (Kourouma 1981, 35).

26. "in Africa [these days] . . . were of less account than one grain in a sack of millet" (1981, 78).

27. "Everything belonged to him here, even the river flowing at his feet, the river and the sacred crocodiles" (1981, 129).

28. By a lesser irony, Salimata is compared to a carp, and Fama himself to a crocodile (Kourouma 1970, 94).

29. "the cursed sun of Independence filled half the sky, scorching the universe" (Kourouma 1981, 5).

30. "These suns overhead, these politicians, all these shameless people, these liars and thieves, are they not the bastard desert where the great Dumbuya river must disappear?" (1981, 66).

31. " 'the glorious future we all hope for' " (1981, 120).

32. "the gaunt, emaciated old man, his eyes shout tight like a blind man's" (1981, 127).

33. These comprise the founding of the dynasty, Bakary's prophecy, Fama's birth in 1905, Togobala's escape in 1919, Salimata's excision and rape, her successive marriages, and Independence. The statement by Anita Kern (1973, 211), that "with the exception of two or three flashbacks in Salimata's thoughts, there are no scenes in the past," needs considerable amplification, and fails to take sufficient account of the novel's pendular motion.

34. The comparison would serve to support Ohaegbu's view (1974), that the title and theme of Kourouma's novel diverge, that Independence is merely the final tool of destiny.

35. "Fama Dumbuya! A true Dumbuya, of Dumbuya father and Dumbuya mother, the last legitimate descendant of the Dumbuya princes of Horodugu, whose totem was the panther—Fama was a 'vulture.' A Dumbuya prince! A panther totem in a hyena pack. Ah! the suns of Independence!" (1981, 4).

36. "a dead and darkened sun" (1981, 18).

37. "So the Malinke species, tribes, land and civilization, was dying: crippled, deaf, blind . . . and sterile" (1981, 13).

38. "Truly the suns of Independence are unsuited to great things; they have not only unmanned, but also unmagicked Africa" (1981, 100).

39. Mortimer (1990, 97) refers to *Nedjma* being organized around the leitmotif of a six-pointed star, with six parts each of twelve chapters. See page 274.

40. See, for example, Thomas (1981), Gee (1981), Gray (1984, 1985), Barnes (1984).

41. This whimsical pairing is highly reminiscent of titles in Dickens's *Little Dorrit* ([1857] 1987; I, 16–17; II, 5–6, 30–34).

42. *Shuttlecock* (1981), *Out of This World* (1988), *Ever After* (1992), *Last Orders* (1996).

3. HISTORY: SEQUENTIAL DYNAMICS IN FICTION, 1550–1900

1. Cf. the mislaid letter at the tennis court in *La Princesse de Clèves*, and its crucial role in the subsequent intrigue.

2. Day's relatively early claim (1966, 161–62), that in the "skillful and complex management of epistolary material, Mrs. Behn was second to none before Richardson," has since been supplemented by numerous studies, largely by feminist critics. Sylvia has been seen to prefigure Clarissa, Julie, and Cécile, Philander to foreshadow Lovelace and Valmont, and Calista, Mme. de Tourvel (Duyfhuizen 1992, 138). A strong case has been made out for Behn's role as "the first practitioner of the novel" (Fludernik 1996, 131), in terms of technical innovations: the report-cum-scene pattern, preliminary orientation, and the representation of consciousness (131–59).

3. "somebody knocked on the door. We will see who it was subsequently; here my adventures start to grow numerous and interesting . . ."

"Yes, you are right, Madame, you have been waiting too long for the continuation of my history" [my trans.].

4. See Parker 1969, 695–704.

5. See Sherbo 1957, 139–46.

6. See discussion in §1.4.

7. "There was no time to lose . . . but how was he to leave Cunégonde, and where was he to find shelter?" (Voltaire 1964, 60)

8. See Ganzel 1961; Macey 1969.

9. " 'You believe there are two scales for men's actions? But Voltaire's *Pucelle* is a masterpiece, you say!—So much the worse for him, since people will only read him more.—And your *Jacques* is simply a dull medley of events, some real and some imaginary, lacking any grace or sense of organization.—So much the better, since my *Jacques* will be read that much less. You're wrong whichever way you turn. If my work is good, you will be pleased with it, and if it is bad, then it won't do you any harm' " [my trans.].

10. Initial reverse transform, as in §1.3.

11. See passage in §1.4.

12. Final reverse transform, as in §1.3.

13. In Radcliffe's *The Italian* (1797), romance again prevails over terror; a single instance of immediate continuity binds books 1 and 2, though in no way conveying an emotional surge. Analepsis is typified by alternate phases, motivated by the separation of Ellena (1.6, 1.8), from her lover Vivaldi (1.7, 1.9), while the sparsity of nocturnal phases or other dominant rhythms contrasts sharply with its predecessor.

14. "And fate itself directs me to the
Second Dog-Post Day
At the gateway of the first chapter, readers ask those passing through: 'What is your name? your character? your business?'

The dog takes over as general spokesman" [my trans.].

15. See "Vierte Vorrede," 1. 1095–96.

"It should be done moreover in a chronological fashion. . . . That will make everything more orderly. I know the Germans: like metaphysicians, they want to know everything precisely and in large format right from the start" [my trans.].

17. Godwin 1832, vii–ix.

18. See his "Brief über den Roman" (Schlegel [1800] 1988, 2).

19. "Apprenticeship to Manhood" [my trans.].

20. "a heap of disconnected fragments" [my trans.].

21. "the privilege of delightful confusion" [my trans.].

22. "an unruly novel" [my trans.].

23. "This is the same pool I fall into on page 266 of the first part" [my trans.].

24. "to achieve a fine and total chaos" [my trans.]

25. Sammons 1965, 34.

26. See §1.3, for justification by Kreisler's biographer of this arrangement.

27. "Her white fur glistened like silver in the moonlight, her small green eyes sparkled in a soft glow of yearning. 'You—' " [my trans.]

28. "—could indeed, my dear reader, have been told about it somewhat earlier . . ." [my trans.]

29. "The time has now come for the biographer's fateful question: 'You—'
(Murr continues) 'love me then, sweet Miesmies?' " [my trans.].

30. ". . . must devote himself to the irregular, for that creates the tension which allows the reader no breathing space and drives him on forcibly to the final page" [my trans.].

31. "something a little more organized and straightforward" [my trans.].

32. See §1.5.

33. "It was a man"; "Besides, he had stayed" [my trans.].

34. "What happened was this"; "a remarkable occurrence"; "a new occurrence" [my trans.].

35. "Jean Valjean recognized Javert perfectly" [my trans.].

36. "At that moment there was a knock at the door" [my trans.].

37. " 'They are praying.' 'To whom?' 'To God.' " [my trans.]

38. "Each of them spent the rest of the night in a very different way. Madame de Rênal . . .
As for Julien . . ." (Stendhal 1959, 90–91)

39. " 'This is apparently going to be a novel in letter form,' he said as he picked this one up." (1959, 337)

40. "[Julien] fired one of his pistols at her and missed. He fired a second shot; she fell." (1959, 451)

41. "save for some details which he preferred to keep to himself" [my trans.].

42. See §1.5.

43. See §1.5.

44. See §1.4.

45. "Wars broke out, and I was transferred by turns to different posts. Important and far-reaching tasks and journeys, reports and proposals were demanded of me . . . the Emperor himself, I may say, became almost a friend" [my trans.].

46. Her first sequence, until she interrupts herself to note the hour, takes four chapters (4–7), and advances to 1777, while references to audience and present year remind the reader of the frame status. Two more chapters bring the hour to half past one, and she breaks off. Lockwood's month-long illness means a further interruption, until Nelly is persuaded to visit and narrate (chs. 10–14). In the fourth, and longest sequence (chs. 15–30), Lockwood condenses her story, derived from several sittings, and continues it in her own words. In a final entry for September 1802, he records Nelly's account of the dénouement, which occurred during his absence in London.

47. "He took her hand, and she did not withdraw it.

'General Prize!' cried the Chairman.

'Just now, for instance, when I came to call on you . . .'

'Monsieur Bizet of Quincampois.'

'. . . how could I know that I should escort you here?'

'Seventy francs!'

'And I've stayed with you, because I couldn't tear myself away, though I've tried a hundred times.'

'Manure!' " (Flaubert 1965, 161)

48. ". . . she would have continued to feel quite safe had she not suddenly discovered a crack in the wall.

It was a snowy Sunday afternoon in February."

(113)

49. "And Emma wondered exactly what was meant in life by the words 'bliss,' 'passion,' 'ecstasy,' which had looked so beautiful in books.

She had read *Paul et Virginie* . . ."

(47–48)

50. "The very next morning she took her seat in the *Hirondelle,* to go and consult Monsieur Léon at Rouen. She stayed there three days.

Three full, exquisite, splendid days they were: a real honeymoon."

(266–67)

51. "When they left Tostes in March, Madame Bovary was pregnant." (81)

52. "They thought she must be delirious. By midnight she was. Brain-fever had set in.

For forty-three days Charles never left her side." (221)

53. "He travelled.

He came to know the gloom of steamships . . .

He returned.

He moved in society . . .

Towards the end of March 1867" [my trans.].

54. " 'Elisabeth!" the old man softly breathed; and just as the word was uttered, time was transformed—he was in his adolescence again" [my trans.].

55. "She sank down, weeping softly, over her dead child.

The repair work on the church roof had started" [my trans.].

56. See §1.5.

57. By order of presentation, George's verbatim proposal to Alice is recorded and despatched (30m), and her reply arrives (30f). She then receives his letter (31i), reacts to it (31m), before replying (32i). When George's second letter arrives, Alice tells her family of the engagement (32m). In the final segment, the circumstances of his receiving her reply (32f1), its verbatim contents (32f2), his "careless" reaction and despatch of a second letter (32f3) are detailed. Rearrangement, by order of occurrence, yields a sequential looping back and forth (30m–31i–32i–30f/32f1–32f3–32m), not instinctively associated with Trollope. Other examples of analepsis dislocate the order of exposition, so that George's later history precedes an account of his boyhood wound (ch. 4), while a minor return is signalled by an initial past perfect: "On the occasion of [Lady Macleod's] preceding visit she . . . had sworn to herself that she would come to London no more; and here she was again in London." (ch. 2; 48)

58. See §1.4.

59. Ibid.

60. Gwendolen's return to England (C; 2f) triggers a lengthy external analepsis

(chs. 3–14), which recounts her background, up to Grandcourt's decision to seek her in Germany (*B;* 14f), and his subsequent arrival there, five days after her departure (*E;* ch. 15). A further analeptic sequence (chs. 16–20) then traces the history of Deronda (*A*), up to his glimpse of Gwendolen at Leubronn, already related in ch. 1. She reaches Offendene (*D;* ch. 21) after a lengthy eighteen-chapter journey from Germany.

61. See §1.5.

62. "Between Berlin and Potsdam, Käthe had already drawn the yellow window curtains in her compartment for protection from the increasingly strong glare, but there were no curtains lowered that same day on the Luisenufer, and the morning sun shone clearly through Frau Nimptsch's windows, illuminating the whole room" [my trans.].

63. See §1.5.

64. "While Christine was conducting this conversation with Julie Dobschütz, Holk and Asta walked down the hall and only separated a hundred yards further on" [my trans.].

65. "And with [Frau von] Ziegenhals on his right arm, and [Fräulein von] Bomst on his left, he approached the folding-doors, which, as he had been speaking, had been opening slowly and with a certain solemnity."

"And taking Distelkamp by the hand, he led the way past the entrance-hall to the drawing-room, where supper had been laid. There was no dining-room as such. Friedeberg and Etienne followed them" [my trans.].

66. "It was agreed that the two should advance simultaneously and fire at a distance of ten paces. Then Buddenbrook went back to his place. No time was lost; the shots rang out. Crampas fell to the ground." (Fontane 1967, 220)

67. " 'So you see, Mama, that's something that worries and frightens me. He's so kind and good to me and so considerate but . . . I'm scared of him.' " (39)

68. "And in came Maheude and her children, frozen, hungry, and panic-stricken at finding themselves in this warm room where there was such a lovely smell of brioche." (Zola 1961, 89)

"Mother and children stood motionless in the dining-room, dazed by the sudden warmth and overawed by this elderly gentleman and lady staring at them from the depths of their armchairs." (96)

69. " 'And—and—what comes next?' " (Mann 1971, 7)

70. "As the year 1859 drew to a close, something frightful indeed happened. It was a day towards the end of November . . ." (28)

71. "The music—it was beginning again . . . a naïve, insistent, intolerable hulla-baloo of snarling, crashing, and feebly piping noises, punctuated by the silly tootling of the piccolo."

" 'Oh, Bach, Sebastian Bach, dear lady!' cried Edmund Pfühl, Herr Edmund Pfühl, the organist of St. Mary's, as he strode up and down the salon with great activity, while Gerda, smiling, her head on her hand, sat at the piano; and Hanno listened from a big chair, his hands clasped round his knees." (383)

72. " 'I thought—I thought—there was nothing else coming.' " (404)

73. See §1.3.

74. See §1.5.

75. As early as 1925, Donald Davidson refers to Conrad's "inversive method," whereby import rather than chronology, significance rather than sequence is paramount (1992, 1.543). A decade later, Edward Crankshaw criticizes chronology for its "waste of space" and "thinness of texture" ([1936] 1976, 170–72), praising Conrad's "broken method."

76. Crankshaw claims (1976, 170–72), that to write *Nostromo* according to strict chronology would have been easy, but the outcome unreadable.

4. CONCLUSION

1. Lanser 1981, 280.

2. On this issue, see, for example, Bull 1970, 64–65; Chatman 1978, 263; Heath 1981, 115; Prince 1982, 65; Docherty 1983, 174; Bal 1985, 51; Bordwell 1985, 54; Gazzetti 1985, 186; Branigan 1992, 42; Gibson 1996, 198–99.

3. Fleming's hero features strongly in contributions to *Communications* 8 (1966): Eco, 77–93, Barthes, 1–27. Eco's essay is based on "Le struttore narrative in Fleming" (1965), which appears in a revised version in Eco 1981, 144–72.

Glossary

References in brackets after entries are to critics originating or closely identified with use of particular terms.

achrony: chronological deviation that cannot be measured since data is indeterminate or insufficient [Genette 1972; 1980].

alternate phase: subcategory of analeptic phase, resumes events from the last-but-one or occasionally from the third previous chapter.

alternate proleptic phase: subcategory of proleptic phase, anticipated events feature in next-but-one chapter.

alternation: one of three broad types of sequential combination, moving back and forth between sequences (see also embedding, and linking) [Todorov 1981].

anachrony: discordance between order in which represented events are supposed to have occurred, and the order of representation in the text.

analepsis/analeptic phase: antedates start of a previous sequence, evokes events retrospectively; in relation to work's starting point, may be either external/internal, alternate, overlap, double, analeptic prolepsis, together with delayed, narratorial, and immediate versions; may be measured according to reach ("portée") from most advanced stage of narrative, and extent ("amplitude") of period covered [Genette 1972; 1980].

analeptic overlap: subcategory of analeptic phase; internal version returns to juncture after work's starting point but prior to previous sequence, then exceeds temporal limit of most advanced stage of narrative; external version, comparable to Genette's "mixed analepsis," begins prior to and continues after starting point, then exceeds most forward stage.

analeptic prolepsis: reference backward within narrative sequence foreshadowing future events, retroversion-within-anticipation. [Bal 1985]

anaphoric relations/anaphora: coreferential feature, repeating or substituting earlier words or phrase, especially important at start of new narrative sequence (see also cataphoric).

anisochrony: variation of speed in narrative representation from deceleration to acceleration, via stages of descriptive pause, stretch/slow-motion, scene, summary, ellipsis [Genette 1972; 1980; Chatman 1978].

atemporal: sequence without specific temporal reference points or linkages to previous or succeeding sequences, often essayistic, furnishing context, speculation or reflection on topics related to main narrative (e.g., *Moby-Dick*).

autodiegetic: narrator present as hero of own narrative. [Genette 1972; 1980]

bildungsroman: novel of spiritual growth and inner development, preferred German novel form after Wieland's *Agathon* (1766) and Goethe's *Wilhelm Meister* (1795).

cataphoric relations/cataphora: coreferential feature, pointing forward or standing for later words or phrase, especially important at end of narrative sequence (see also anaphoric).

chronomorphic: temporal molding of fictional materials, degree of success as gauge of novelistic excellence [Hutchens 1972].

chronotope: fusion of temporal and spatial indices into single concrete whole [Bakhtin 1982 (1937–38)].

coherence: semantic and pragmatic relations in text [Reinhart 1980].

cohesion/cohesive relations: overt linguistic devices and lexicogrammatical ties binding sentences together [Halliday & Hasan 1976; Reinhart 1980].

commutation: diachronic tracking along horizontal/syntagmatic axis of elements belonging to same code or class.

continuity or continuous span: juxtaposition of same or different types of forward narrative sequences, minimum span of three directly contiguous chapters; its beginning as earliest point, its end as latest point at which gap of no longer than day (i.e., nocturnal phase) can be marked.

delayed presentation: late appearance of temporal data in narrative unit holding back reader's determination of unit's sequential status.

diegesis/diegetic segment: represented events in primary or first-degree narrative; narratorial telling of events vs. showing of events in imitated speech of characters in mimetic "scene."

discourse-time/DT: temporal duration of narrative representation, significant for account of narrative tempo (see also story-time/ST of represented events).

Doppelroman: double-decker novel, often of contrastive material and ironic juxtaposition (e.g., Hoffmann's *Kater Murr*).

double analepsis: second retrospective phase within phase already retrospective as measured from most recent stage of narrative, analepsis-within-analepsis.

ellipsis: gap in record of narrative events, either within or between units, may be explicit/implicit, completed/uncompleted, determinate/indeterminate; discourse-time (DT) infinitely less than story-time (ST) [Genette 1972; 1980].

embedding: one of three broad types of sequential combination, one sequence enclosed within another (see also alternation and linking) [Todorov 1981].

end-loading: pronounced emphasis on and concentration of specific elements, often in terms of length, at closing stage of narrative unit (e.g., assembly of explanatory detail in dénouement of detective fiction).

erzählte Zeit/Erzählzeit: story-time (period covered by narrated events)/ discourse-time (time taken by representation expressed in lines and pages of text), relationship between two elements crucial to account of narrative tempo [Müller 1950].

extradiegetic: level of act of narration producing diegesis or first-degree narrative [Genette 1972; 1980].

fabula: Russian Formalist term for raw materials of narrative, in chronological time sequence in which it is supposed they "originally" occurred (see also syuzhet).

false continuity: intentional mismatch, either temporal, characterological or locational, between expected resumption of events at new chapter or unit start, and actual frustration of continuity.

focalization: triadic relation between narrator, focalizer, and focalized object determining the technical representation of narrative events [Cohan and Shires 1988].

front-loading: pronounced emphasis on and concentration of specific elements, often in terms of length, at opening stage of narrative unit (e.g., descriptive intensity of exposition in Balzac's *Père Goriot*).

fugal narrative: type of nonlinear sequence, analogous with vertical chord of simultaneous notes in music, aiming to show past and present at once in spatial network of relations (see also linear succession of states and events) [Boa and Reid 1972].

Hakenstil: interlocking of chapter-end anticipation and chapter-start retrospective, preemptive appearance of episode at chapter end creating seamless onward continuity by proleptic tie [Lämmert 1955].

hermeneutic code: works against narrative flow by occlusive and stalling tactics of withholding information or misleading readers (see also proaieretic code of forward actions) [Barthes 1970].

heterodiegetic: relating to different, newly introduced, secondary figures, events or plot lines; absent narrator telling of other characters [Genette 1972; 1980].

homodiegetic: relating to the same figures, events or plot lines; narrator present as participating character [Genette 1972; 1980].

hypodiegetic: level of story or second-degree narrative, told by (intra)diegetic narrator or character within diegesis or first-degree narrative [Bal 1977] ; term preferred to Genette's "metadiegetic" [1972; 1980].

hypotactic/hypotaxis: arrangement of phrases or clauses in subordinate relationship to each other, often involving series of relative clauses.

iconicity/iconic match: imitation at formal level of meanings represented, chronological sequencing as example of syntactic iconicity, tempo of equal story-time (ST) and discourse-time (DT) as iconic match in "scene," where textual time enacts fictional reality [Leech and Short 1981].

immediate continuity/tie: reduction close to zero in degree of temporal ellipsis between narrative units, lengthier gap becomes proximate tie; most significant type of continuous phase in terms of transitional gap, reinforces sense of linear flow and impetus.

isochrony: ideal, unrealizable match between represented events and representation in terms of temporal consistency, "scene" as near-isochrony closest to metronomic norm [Genette 1972; 1980].

isotopy/isotopic relations: continuity of subject matter via kindred elements on either side of unit divide or segmentation, impact fluctuates according to transition type selected [Greimas 1966].

iterative: single telling of event that occurs more than once; pseudo-iterative, where events are said to occur many times but are narrated with specificity of single occurrence [Genette 1972; 1980].

kernel event: consecutive and consequential juncture of narrative, crucially advancing or outlining new developments, cardinal function [Chatman 1978 trans. Barthes's "noyau" 1966].

lexeme: virtually self-contained sequence or topic named by critic, forming linear series to compose text [Greimas 1976].

lexia: lexical unit of several words, microdivision of text designated by critic, organized by Barthes into five narrative codes [Barthes 1970].

linear ordering/linearity: arrangement of narrative elements in chronological sequence from cause to effect, as movement along straight line in single direction.

linking: one of three broad types of sequence in which different actions are juxtaposed in linear succession, also termed "enchaining" (see also alternation and embedding) [Todorov 1981].

macrosequence/-sequential: whole-text, or broad movement across different narrative units.

metalepsis/metaleptic: transgression of narrative levels, whereby an extra-diegetic narrator or narratee intrudes into diegetic universe, or diegetic into extradiegetic, or diegetic into hypodiegetic etc. [Genette 1972; 1980].

microsequence/-sequential: part-text, ranging upward from sentence and paragraph usually in same narrative unit.

mimesis/mimetic segment: showing of events in "scene" through imitated speech of characters vs. narratorial/diegetic telling of events.

minimum retard: device, usually paratextual, such as chapter title or epigraph, that briefly prevents uninterrupted flow from one narrative unit to next.

minus device: unused but meaningful element, such as spatial gap in text [Lotman 1977].

mise en abyme: internal mirror or condensed duplication at hypodiegetic level, micronarrative of diegetic events of larger narrative, capable of high-speed analeptic review or proleptic vision, literary model of play-within-play of *Hamlet* [Gide 1943].

narrative instance/-Now: narrator's writing-time, in present tense of discourse [Brooke-Rose 1983; Chatman 1978].

nocturnal phase/gap: temporal interval of up to twenty-four hours, may extend to evening or night of next day before notion of continuity begins to lose hold, area demarcated on one hand by proximate, on other by distant continuity.

nonlinear ordering/nonlinearity: arrangement of events out of chronological or causal sequence, e.g. by time shift, deviation [Bal 1985], transposition [Shklovsky 1990], "broken method" [Crankshaw 1976], "dynamic order" [Meyerhoff 1955], fugal narrative [Boa and Reid 1972].

order transform: types of nonlinear sequences in which narrative elements are presented in text in order different from that of their supposed occurrence; may operate at either micro- or macrosequential level, classified in Fig. 1.1.

page/time ratio: relationship between amount of text and period of narrative time for which it accounts, specific means for indicating contrasts of tempo, essentially identical with erzählte Zeit/Erzählzeit [Müller 1950].

paradigmatic: "vertical" relations along axis of selection, linked with operation of metaphor (see also syntagmatic) [Jakobson 1971].

paralipsis/paraliptic: lateral ellipsis whereby narrative information is deliberately omitted and retrospectively acknowledged by narrator [Genette 1972; 1980].

parallel overlap: subcategory of parallel phase; major overlap where phase temporally exceeds limit of last forward phase or most recent action, to establish new and more advanced date; minor overlap as more common and flexible, occurring at point within but not at start of previous sequence, then exceeding terminal point of that sequence.

parallel phase: involves reversion from point reached at previous sequence or chapter end, but reader is meant to assume that it co-occurs with that sequence despite post-position in text; major version where heterodiegetic action or set of events recorded at chapter start coincides with that at start of preceding chapter or sequence; minor version where action coincides with that within but not at start of preceding chapter or sequence.

paratactic/parataxis: clauses or phrases placed one after another without connectives, in coordinate rather than subordinate relationship (see also hypotactic).

paratextual: material elements of physical text such as titles, prefaces, dedications, notes, epigraphs, illustrations, tables [Genette 1982].

presentational sequence: type of nonlinear ordering (see also psychological sequence), grounded in relationship between focalization and order in which information is conveyed, narrator's role important by use of omission, playfulness, artistic dis-ordering [Leech & Short 1981].

proaieretic: code of actions, especially important for analysis of temporal sequence, counters stalling tactics of hermeneutic code [Barthes 1970].

proleptic analepsis: reference to future events from juncture prior to previous sequence, anticipation-within-retroversion [Bal 1985].

proleptic phase/tie: alludes to future events either within or beyond text, especially important at chapter end, ranges in function from explicit advance mention ("annonce"), hint ("amorce"), which reveals significance only later, false clue or snare ("leurre") [Genette 1972; 1980]; in combination with chapter-start retrospective designated *Hakenstil* [Lämmert 1955].

proximate tie/gap: most common temporal gap between narrative units, embraces periods from several minutes to several hours, area demarcated on one hand by immediate tie, on other by nocturnal gap.

psychological sequence: type of nonlinear ordering (see also presentational sequence), grounded in relationship between focalization and order in which information is conveyed, typified by detective-fiction whereby reader adopts investigator's perspective and order of pursuing case [Leech and Short 1981].

Rahmenerzählung: framework narrative, especially important in German short-story form of *novelle,* involves complexities of focalization and fractures of forward progression.

representation/represented world: textual arrangement of diegetic events, discourse/story relationship.

satellite event: consecutive or chronological juncture of narrative, optional action filling in or amplifying outline of sequence, secondary and replaceable element, functional catalyzer (see also kernel) [Chatman 1978 trans. Barthes's "catalyse" 1966].

segment types: broad divisions of chapter into initial (i), medial (m), and final (f) segments, necessarily approximate and flexible, normative transition as contiguous relationship of final to initial chapter segments.

semic code: one of five codes (including proaieretic, hermeneutic, symbolic, referential), distributes semantic features relating to character, less central than proaieretic and hermeneutic to temporal sequence [Barthes 1970].

simultaneous phase: beginning coincides with end of previous sequence but features heterodiegetic characters or events; nonprogressive version usually at medial junctures, new line of action not developed; progressive version usually at initial junctures, more comprehensive, new line of action continues to end of sequence or chapter.

singulative: single telling of single event, often "one day" or "one morning" marker initiating episode (see also iterative) [Genette 1972; 1980].

story-Now: moment when action begins to transpire, usually expressed in preterite tense [Chatman 1978].

story-time/ST: duration of events in represented story, significant for account of narrative tempo (see also discourse-time/DT of representation).

subsegmental types: subdivisions of chapter segments into first and second instances of initial (i1, i2) and final (f1, f2) segments, so as to track continuity with greater precision.

suprasentential: above or beyond limits of sentence-length, involving larger contexts that allow fuller analysis of narrative elements.

synopsis-sentence: reflects in its ordering of clauses and phrases the temporal and causal sequence of complete text [Fowler 1977].

syntagmatic: "horizontal" relations along axis of combination, linked with operation of metonymy and notion of continuity (see also paradigmatic) [Jakobson 1971].

syuzhet: Russian Formalist term for concrete textual rearrangement of raw materials of narrative, deviations sponsor discussion of ordering, tempo, continuity relations etc. (see also fabula).

temporal determinacy: identification of temporal data on scale modulating from specific to indeterminate; relative precision in designating degrees of temporal accumulation (e.g. character's age), lapse (interval preceding or succeeding another sequence), locus (juncture at which sequence begins); also direct/indirect, external/internal, recurrent/nonrecurrent aspects.

tense deviance: shift from norms of verb form, as in use of historical present where past tenses have been predominant.

transition categories: range of chapter and unit gaps, from forward continuous, parallel and simultaneous, to analeptic phases, classified in Fig. 1.2.

transtextual sequence: existing in, across and between two or more texts, may be in linear or reversed order [Watts 1984].

ulterior narrative: traditional fictional mode of narrating events after they have occurred, using past verb form [Genette 1972; 1980].

writing-Now: temporal position of narrator during act of narration in relation to narrated events, analagous with narrative instance.

Works Cited

Dates given in brackets represent the first publication of each work.

PRIMARY SOURCES

Achebe, Chinua. 1976. *A Man of the People*. [1966]. London: Heinemann.

Ackroyd, Peter. 1987a. *The Great Fire of London*. [1982]. London: Abacus.

———. 1987b. *Hawksmoor*. [1985]. London: Abacus.

Amis, Martin. 1991. *Time's Arrow*. London: Jonathan Cape.

Anouilh, Jean. 1959. *Beckett ou l'Honneur de Dieu*. Paris: La Table Ronde.

Austen, Jane. 1971a. *Emma*. [1816]. Edited by David Lodge. London: Oxford University Press.

———. 1952. *Jane Austen's Letters*. Edited by R. W. Chapman. London: Oxford University Press.

———. 1970a. *Mansfield Park*. [1814]. Edited by J. Lucas. London: Oxford University Press.

———. 1971b. *Northanger Abbey* and *Persuasion*. [1818]. Edited by John Davie. London: Oxford University Press.

———. 1926. *The Novels of Jane Austen*. 5 vols. Edited by R. W. Chapman. London: Oxford University Press.

———. 1970b. *Pride and Prejudice*. [1813]. Edited by F. W. Bradbrook. London: Oxford University Press.

———. 1970c. *Sense and Sensibility*. [1811]. Edited by Claire Lamont. London: Oxford University Press.

———, and Another Lady. 1976. *Sanditon*. London: Corgi Books.

Balzac, Honoré de. 1961. *Illusions perdues*. [1843]. Paris: Garnier.

———. 1982. *La Peau de Chagrin*. [1831]. Paris: Imprimerie Nationale.

———. 1960. *Le Père Goriot*. [1835]. Paris: Garnier.

———. 1950. *La Recherche de l'Absolu*. [1835]. Vol. 9 of *La Comédie Humaine*. Paris: Gallimard.

———. 1965. *Ursule Mirouët*. [1841]. Vol. 2 of *La Comédie Humaine*. Paris: Seuil.

Banville, John. 1993. *Kepler*. [1981]. London: Minerva.

Barnes, Djuna. 1961. *Nightwood*. [1937]. New York: New Directions.

Barnes, Julian. 1985. *Flaubert's Parrot*. [1984]. London: Picador.

Barth, John. 1961. *The Sot-Weed Factor*. [1960]. London: Secker and Warburg.

Behn, Aphra. 1996. *Love-Letters Between a Nobleman and His Sister*. [1684–87]. Harmondsworth: Penguin Books.

Bennett, Arnold. 1966. *The Old Wives' Tale*. [1908]. London: Dent.

Boswell, James. 1994. *The Life of Samuel Johnson*. [1791]. Edinburgh: Edinburgh University Press.

Brentano, Clemens. 1970. *Die Geschichte vom braven Kasperl und dem schönen Annerl*. [1817]. Vol. 1 of *Brentanos Werke*. Edited by Max Preitz. Bern: Herbert Lang.

———. 1978. *Godwi*. [1801]. Vol. 16 [*Prosa I*] of *Sämtliche Werke und Briefe*. Edited by Werner Bellmann. Stuttgart: Kohlhammer Verlag.

Brontë, Anne. 1985. *The Tenant of Wildfell Hall*. [1848]. Harmondsworth: Penguin Books.

Brontë, Charlotte. 1978. *Jane Eyre*. [1847]. Harmondsworth: Penguin Books.

———. 1962. *Villette*. [1853]. New York: Dell Publishing.

Brontë, Emily. 1965. *Wuthering Heights*. [1847]. Harmondsworth: Penguin Books.

Bunyan, John. 1960. *The Pilgrim's Progress*. [1678–85]. Oxford: Clarendon Press.

Butor, Michel. 1962. *Mobile*. Paris: Gallimard.

Carroll, Lewis. 1947. *Alice's Adventures in Wonderland* and *Through the Looking-Glass*. [1865; 1871]. London: Pan Books.

Carter, Angela. 1992. *Wise Children*. [1991]. London: Vintage.

Cervantes, Miguel de. 1965. *Don Quixote*. [1605–15]. Translated by J. M. Cohen. Baltimore, Md.: Penguin Books.

Churchill, Caryl. 1982. *Top Girls*. London: French.

Clarke, Lindsay. 1990. *The Chymical Wedding*. [1989]. London: Pan Books.

Collins, Wilkie. 1967. *The Moonstone*. [1868]. London: Dent.

———. 1978. *The Woman in White*. [1860]. Harmondsworth: Penguin Books.

Conrad, Joseph. 1994. *Almayer's Folly*. [1895]. Cambridge: Cambridge University Press.

———. 1971a. *Lord Jim*. [1900]. Harmondsworth: Penguin Books.

———. 1971b. *Nostromo*. [1904]. Harmondsworth: Penguin Books.

———. 1986. *An Outcast of the Islands*. [1896]. Harmondsworth: Penguin Books.

———. 1980. *The Secret Agent*. [1907]. Harmondsworth: Penguin Books.

———. 1991. *Typhoon and Other Stories*. [1903]. London: Dent.

Cooper, James Fenimore. 1993. *The Deerslayer*. [1841]. Oxford: Oxford University Press.

———. 1991. *The Pioneers*. [1823]. Oxford: Oxford University Press.

———. 1980. *The Prairie*. [1827]. New York: New American Library.

Defoe, Daniel. 1981. *Moll Flanders*. [1722] . Oxford: Oxford University Press.

———. 1972. *Robinson Crusoe*. [1719]. London: Oxford University Press.

Desai, Anita. 1982. *Clear Light of Day*. [1980]. Harmondsworth: Penguin Books.

Dickens, Charles. 1996. *Bleak House*. [1853]. Harmondsworth: Penguin Books.

———. 1978a. *The Christmas Books I*. [1843–44]. Harmondsworth: Penguin Books.

———. 1982. *Dombey and Son*. [1848]. Harmondsworth: Penguin Books.

———. 1973. *Great Expectations*. [1861]. Harmondsworth: Penguin Books.

———. 1987. *Little Dorrit*. [1857]. Harmondsworth: Penguin Books.

———. 1986. *Martin Chuzzlewit.* [1844]. Harmondsworth: Penguin Books.

———. 1985a. *Nicholas Nickleby.* [1839]. Harmondsworth: Penguin Books.

———. 1985b. *The Old Curiosity Shop.* [1841]. Harmondsworth: Penguin Books.

———. 1978b. *Oliver Twist.* [1838]. Harmondsworth: Penguin Books.

———. 1988. *Our Mutual Friend.* [1865]. Harmondsworth: Penguin Books.

———. 1983. *The Pickwick Papers.* [1837]. Harmondsworth: Penguin Books.

———. 1975. *A Tale of Two Cities.* [1859]. Harmondsworth: Penguin Books.

Diderot, Denis. 1959. *Jacques le Fataliste.* [1773]. *Oeuvres romanesques.* Edited by Henri Bénac. Paris: Garnier.

Dostoyevsky, Fyodor. 1990. *The Brothers Karamazov.* [1880]. London: Quartet Books.

———. 1991. *Crime and Punishment.* [1866]. London: Viking/Penguin.

———. 1977. *The Devils,* or *The Possessed.* [1872]. Harmondsworth: Penguin Books.

———. 1968. *The Idiot.* [1869]. Harmondsworth: Penguin Books.

Droste-Hülshoff, Annette von. 1955. *Die Judenbuche.* [1842]. London: Harrap.

Eliot, George. 1981. *Adam Bede.* [1859]. Harmondsworth: Penguin Books.

———. 1978. *Daniel Deronda.* [1876]. Harmondsworth: Penguin Books.

———. 1972. *Felix Holt.* [1866]. Harmondsworth: Penguin Books.

———. 1982. *Middlemarch.* [1872]. London: Chatto & Windus.

———. 1985. *The Mill on the Floss.* [1860]. Harmondsworth: Penguin Books.

———. 1980. *Romola.* [1863]. Harmondsworth: Penguin Books.

———. 1984. *Silas Marner.* [1861]. Harmondsworth: Penguin Books.

Elton, Ben. 1992. *Gridlock.* [1991]. London: Sphere Books.

Fantouré, Alioum. 1972. *Le cercle des Tropiques.* Paris: Présence Africaine. Adapted into English by Dorothy S. Blair. *Tropical Circle.* Harlow: Longman, 1981.

Faulkner, William. 1982. *The Sound and the Fury.* [1929]. Harmondsworth: Penguin Books.

Fielding, Henry. 1987. *Amelia.* [1751]. Harmondsworth: Penguin Books.

———. 1983. *Joseph Andrews* and *Shamela.* [1742]. London: Dent.

———. 1963. *Tom Jones.* [1749]. New York: New American Library.

Fielding, Sarah. 1979. *History of Charlotte Summers.* [1749]. Quoted in George Watson, *The Story of the Novel.* London: Macmillan.

Fitzgerald, F. Scott. 1973. *Tender Is the Night.* [1934]. Revised Version [1951]. Edited by Malcolm Cowley. *Three Novels of F. Scott Fitzgerald.* New York: Charles Scribner's Sons.

Flaubert, Gustave. 1965. *L'Éducation sentimentale.* [1869]. Paris: Gallimard. Translated by Douglas Parmée. *Sentimental Education.* Oxford: Oxford University Press, 1989.

———. 1955. *Madame Bovary.* [1857]. Paris: Garnier. Translated by Alan Russell. Harmondsworth: Penguin Books, 1965.

———. 1960. *Salammbô.* [1862]. Paris: Colin.

Fleming, Ian. 1964. *Goldfinger.* [1959]. London: Pan Books.

Fontane, Theodor. 1963a. *Effi Briest.* [1894]. Vol. 4 of *Sämtliche Werke. Romane*

Erzählungen Gedichte. Edited by Walter Keitel. München: Carl Hauser. Translated by Douglas Parmée. Harmondsworth: Penguin Books, 1967.

————. 1963b. *Frau Jenny Treibel.* [1892]. Vol. 4 of *Sämtliche Werke.*

————. 1963c. *Irrungen Wirrungen.* [1887]. Vol. 2 of *Sämtliche Werke.*

————. 1963d. *Unwiederbringlich.* [1891]. Vol. 2 of *Sämtliche Werke.*

Ford, Ford Madox. 1972. *The Good Soldier.* [1915]. Harmondsworth: Penguin Books.

Forster, E. M. 1967. *Howards End.* [1910]. Harmondsworth: Penguin Books.

————. 1981. *A Passage to India.* [1924]. Harmondsworth: Penguin Books.

Fowles, John. 1970. *The French Lieutenant's Woman.* [1969]. New York: New American Library.

Galsworthy, John. 1995. *The Forsyte Saga.* [1922]. Oxford: Oxford University Press.

Gaskell, Elizabeth. 1983. *Mary Barton.* [1848]. Harmondsworth: Penguin Books.

————. 1982. *North and South.* [1855]. Harmondsworth: Penguin Books.

Gee, Maggie. 1983. *Dying, in Other Words.* [1981]. London: Granada Publishing.

Gissing, George. 1973. *The Nether World.* [1889]. London: Dent.

Godwin, William. 1970. *Caleb Williams.* [1794]. London: Oxford University Press.

————. 1832. *Fleetwood; or the New Man of Feeling.* London: Richard Bentley.

Goethe, Johann Wolfgang von. 1965. *Die Leiden des jungen Werthers.* [1774]. Stuttgart: Philipp Reclam Jun.

————. 1947. *Unterhaltungen deutscher Ausgewanderten.* [1795]. Krefeld: Scherpe-Verlag.

————. 1963. *Die Wahlverwandschaften.* [1809]. *Werke Goethes.* Edited by Helmut Praschek. Berlin: Akademie-Verlag.

————. 1964.*Wilhelm Meisters Lehrjahre.* [1795]. München: Wilhelm Goldmann Verlag.

Gogol, Nikolai. 1972. *Diary of a Madman.* [1835]. Translated by R. Wilks. Harmondsworth: Penguin Books.

Golding, William. 1988. *Free Fall.* [1959]. London: Faber.

Gotthelf, Jeremias [Albert Bitzius]. 1956. *Die schwarze Spinne.* [1841]. Oxford: Blackwell.

Grass, Günter. 1963. *Die Blechtrommel.* [1959]. Frankfurt am Main: Fischer.

Gray, Alastair. 1985a. *Lanark.* [1981]. London: Panther Books.

————. 1985b. *1982 Janine.* [1984]. Harmondsworth: Penguin Books.

Green, Henry. 1979. *Loving, Living* and *Party Going.* [1945; 1929; 1939]. London: Picador.

Hardy, Thomas. 1975a. *Far from the Madding Crowd.* [1874]. The New Wessex Edition. London: Macmillan.

————. 1975b. *Jude the Obscure.* [1896]. London: Macmillan.

————. 1975c. *The Mayor of Casterbridge.* [1886]. London: Macmillan.

————. 1975d. *The Return of the Native.* [1878]. London: Macmillan.

————. 1975e. *Tess of the D'Urbervilles.* [1891]. London: Macmillan.

————. 1975f. *The Woodlanders.* [1887]. London: Macmillan.

Hawthorne, Nathaniel. 1982. *The Scarlet Letter.* [1850]. Harmondsworth: Penguin Books.

Hill, Susan. 1992. *Air and Angels.* [1991]. London: Mandarin.

———. 1981. *In the Springtime of the Year.* [1974]. Harmondsworth: Penguin Books

Hoffmann, E. T. A. 1967. *Lebensansichten des Katers Murr.* [1821]. Vol. 3 of *Werke.* Edited by Herbert Kraft and Manfred Wacker. Frankfurt am Main: Insel Verlag.

Homer. 1963. *The Odyssey.* Translated by Robert Fitzgerald. Garden City, N.Y.: Doubleday.

Howard, Elizabeth Jane. 1957. *The Long View.* [1956]. London: The Reprint Society.

Hugo, Victor. 1957. *Les Misérables.* [1862]. 2 vols. Paris: Garnier.

———. 1959. *Notre-Dame de Paris.* [1831]. Paris: Garnier.

Huxley, Aldous. 1972. *Eyeless in Gaza.* [1936]. Harmondsworth: Penguin Books.

Huysmans, Joris-Karl. 1981. *A Rebours [Against Nature].* [1884]. Paris: Imprimerie Nationale.

Immermann, Karl. 1906. *Münchhausen.* [1839]. Vols. 1–2 of *Immermanns Werke.* Edited by Harry Maync. Leipzig: Bibliographisches Institut.

Isherwood, Christopher. 1988. *The Memorial.* [1932]. London: Methuen.

James, Henry. 1986a. *The Ambassadors.* [1903]. Harmondsworth: Penguin Books.

———. 1983. *The Golden Bowl.* [1904]. Oxford: Oxford University Press.

———. 1991. *The Portrait of a Lady.* [1881]. Oxford: Oxford University Press.

———. 1986b. *Roderick Hudson.* [1875]. Harmondsworth: Penguin Books.

———. 1984. *The Wings of the Dove.* [1902]. Oxford: Oxford University Press.

Jean Paul [Johann Paul Friedrich Richter]. 1927a. *Flegeljahre.* [1805]. Vol. 10, Erste Abteilung, of *Sämtliche Werke.* Edited by Eduard Berendt. Weimar: Hermann Böhlau.

———. 1927b. *Hesperus oder 45 Hundsposttage.* [1795]. Vols. 3–4 of *SW.*

———. 1927c. *Die Unsichtbare Loge.* [1793]. Vol. 2 of *SW.*

Joyce, James. 1975. *Finnegans Wake.* [1939]. London: Faber and Faber.

———. 1961. *Ulysses.* [1922]. New York: Random House.

Kafka, Franz. 1965. *Der Prozess [The Trial].* [1925]. Frankfurt am Main: Fischer Bücherei.

Keller, Gottfried. 1926. *Der grüne Heinrich.* [1855]. Erste Fassung [Original Version]. Vols. 16–19 of *Sämtliche Werke.* Edited by Jonas Fränkel. Zürich: Eugen Kentsch Verlag.

———. 1961. *Der grüne Heinrich.* [1880]. 2nd Version. München: Goldmann Verlag.

———. 1944. *Der Landvogt von Greifensee.* [1877]. Vol. 9 [*Züricher Novellen I*] of *Sämtliche Werke.* Bern: Verlag Benteli.

Kleist, Heinrich von. 1965. *Die Marquise von O.* [1808]. In *Sämtliche Novellen.* München: Goldmann Verlag.

Korolenko, Viktor. 1954. *Makar's Dream.* [1885]. In *Korelenko's Siberia.* Translated by R. F. Christian. Liverpool: Liverpool University Press.

Kourouma, Ahmadou. 1998. *En attendant le vote des bêtes savvages*. Paris: Seuil.

———. 1990. *Monnè: outrages et défis*. Paris: Seuil.

———. 1970. *Les soleils des Indépendances*. Paris: Seuil. Translated by Adrian Adams. *The Suns of Independence*. London: Heinemann, 1981.

Kundera, Milan. 1973. *Zivot je jinde*. Translated by Peter Kussi. *Life Is Elsewhere*. London: Faber, 1986.

Laclos, Choderlos de. 1958. *Les liaisons dangereuses*. [1782]. Paris: Gallimard.

Lafayette, Madame de. 1980. *La Princesse de Clèves*. [1678]. Paris: Imprimerie nationale.

Lawrence, D. H. 1967. *Women in Love*. [1920]. Harmondsworth: Penguin Books.

Lazarillo de Tormes. 1969. *Two Spanish Picaresque Novels*. [1554]. Translated by Michael Alpert. Harmondsworth: Penguin Books.

Lesage, Alain-René. 1965. *Gil Blas*. [1735]. Paris: Garnier.

Lewis, Matthew. 1973. *The Monk*. [1796]. London: Oxford University Press.

Lively, Penelope. 1987. *Moon Tiger*. London: Andre Deutsch.

Loti, Pierre. 1989. *Pêcheur d'Islande*. [1886]. Paris: Éditions Jean-Claude Lattès.

Ludwig, Otto. 1971. *Zwischen Himmel und Erde*. [1856]. Stuttgart: Philipp Reclam Jun.

Manchester, William. 1967. *The Death of a President*. London: Michael Joseph.

Mann, Thomas. 1974a. *Buddenbrooks*. [1902]. Frankfurt am Main: Fischer Verlag. Translated by H. T. Lowe-Porter. Harmondsworth: Penguin Books, 1971.

———. 1974b. *Der Zauberberg*. [1924]. Vol. 3 of *Gesammelte Werke*. Frankfurt am Main: Fischer Verlag. Translated by H. T. Lowe-Porter. *The Magic Mountain*. London: Martin Secker, 1927.

Manzoni, Alessandro. 1972. *The Betrothed [I promessi sposi]*. [1827]. Translated by B. Penman. Harmondsworth: Penguin Books.

Marivaux, Pierre Carlet de Chamblain de. 1957. *La vie de Marianne*. [1731–42]. Paris: Garnier.

Maturin, Charles Robert. 1968. *Melmoth the Wanderer*. [1820]. London: Oxford University Press.

Melville, Herman. 1988. *Moby-Dick*. [1851]. Oxford: Oxford University Press.

Melville, James. 1990. *A Haiku for Hanae*. [1989]. London: Headline Book Publishing.

Meredith, George. 1896. *The Amazing Marriage*. [1895]. Edinburgh: Constable & Co.

———. 1913. *Beauchamp's Career*. [1876]. London: Constable & Co.

———. 1922. *Diana of the Crossways*. [1885]. London: Constable & Co.

———. 1968. *The Egoist*. [1879]. Harmondsworth: Penguin Books.

———. 1984. *The Ordeal of Richard Feverel*. [1859]. London: Oxford University Press.

Meyer, Conrad Ferdinand. 1961. *Die Hochzeit des Mönchs*. [1884].Vol. 12 [*Novellen II*] of *Sämtliche Werke*. Edited by Hans Zeller and Alfred Zäch. Bern: Benteli-Verlag.

———. 1958. *Jürg Jenatsch*. [1876]. Vol. 10 of *Sämtliche Werke*.

Miller, Arthur. 1993. *Death of a Salesman*. [1947]. In *Plays*. London: Methuen.

Moore, George. 1964. *Esther Waters*. [1894]. London: Oxford University Press.

———. 1898. *Evelyn Innes*. London: Fisher Unwin.

Mörike, Eduard. 1967. *Maler Nolten*. [1832]. Vol. 3 of *Eduard Mörike: Werke und Briefe*. Edited by H.-H. Krummacher, H. Meyer, and B. Zeller. Stuttgart: Klett Verlag.

Murdoch, Iris. 1972. *The Sandcastle*. [1957]. Harmondsworth: Penguin Books.

Nachtwachen des Bonaventura., Die. 1960. [1805]. München: Goldmann Verlag.

Naipaul, V. S. 1983. *The Mimic Men*. [1967]. Harmondsworth: Penguin.

Ouologuem, Yambo. 1968. *Le devoir de violence*. Paris: Seuil.

Pakenham, Thomas. 1979. *The Boer War*. London: Weidenfeld and Nicolson.

Poe, Edgar Allan. 1980. *The Fall of The House of Usher*. [1839]. In *Selected Tales*. Oxford: Oxford University Press.

Prévost d'Exiles, Antoine-François, Abbé. 1965. *Manon Lescaut*. [1731]. Paris: Garnier.

Priestley, J. B. 1979. *Time and the Conways*. [1937]. In *Six Plays*. London: Heinemann.

Proust, Marcel. 1954. *A la recherche du temps perdu*. [1913–27]. Paris: Gallimard.

Pückler-Muskau, Hermann Ludwig Heinrich, Fürst von. 1831. *Briefe eines Verstorbenen*. Stuttgart: Halberger.

Raabe, Wilhelm. 1980. *Abu Telfan*. [1868]. Vol. 2 of *Werke*. Edited by Karl Hoppe. München: Winkler Verlag.

Rabelais, François. 1991. *Gargantua et Pantagruel*. [1532–34]. Vol. 1 of *Oeuvres complètes*. Paris: Garnier.

Radcliffe, Ann. 1971. *The Italian*. [1797]. London: Oxford University Press.

———. 1970. *The Mysteries of Udolpho*. [1794]. London: Oxford University Press.

Ricardou, Jean. 1965. *La Prise de Constantinople*. Paris: Minuit.

Richardson, Samuel. 1985. *Clarissa*. [1748]. Harmondsworth: Penguin Books.

———. 1962. *Pamela*. [1740]. London: Dent.

Robbe-Grillet, Alain. 1955. *Le Voyeur*. Paris: Minuit.

Rushdie, Salman. 1982. *Midnight's Children*. [1981]. London: Picador.

Schlegel, Friedrich. 1962. *Lucinde*. [1799]. Vol. 5 of *Dichtungen*. Edited by Hans Eichner. München: Verlag Ferdinand Schöningh.

Schmidt, Arno. 1956. *Das steinerne Herz*. Karlsruhe: Stahlberg.

Scott, Sir Walter. 1969. *The Fair Maid of Perth*. [1828]. London: Dent.

———. 1987. *Guy Mannering*. [1815]. London: Soho Book Co.

———. 1954. *The Heart of Midlothian*. [1818]. London: Dent.

———. 1987. *Ivanhoe*. [1819]. London: Hamlyn Publishing.

———. 1993. *Kenilworth*. [1821]. Edinburgh: Edinburgh University Press.

———. 1997. *Redgauntlet*. [1824]. Edinburgh: Edinburgh University Press.

———. 1991. *Rob Roy*. [1818]. London: Dent.

———. 1920. *The Talisman*. [1825]. London: Dent.

Shakespeare, William. 1982. *Hamlet*. Edited by Harold Jenkins. The Arden Shakespeare. London: Methuen.

———. 1963. *The Winter's Tale*. Edited by Frank Kermode. New York: The New American Library.

Eagleton, Terry. 1983. *Literary Theory: An Introduction.* Oxford: Blackwell.

Echenim, Kester. 1978. "La structure narrative de *Soleils des Indépendances.*" *Présence Africaine* 107:139–61.

Eco, Umberto. 1966. "James Bond: Une combinatoire narrative." *Communications* 8:77–93. Translated by R. A. Downie. "Narrative Structures in Fleming." *The Role of the Reader,* 144–72. London: Hutchinson, 1981

Edwards, P. D. 1969. "The Chronology of *The Way We Live Now.*" *Notes and Queries* 16:214–16.

Eisenstein, Sergei. 1951. *Film Form.* Edited and translated by Jay Leyda. London: Dennis Dobson.

Erlich, Victor. 1955. *Russian Formalism: History-Doctrine.* The Hague: Mouton.

Ermarth, Elizabeth Deeds. 1992. *Sequel to History: Postmodernism and the Crisis of Representational Time.* Princeton: Princeton University Press.

Flint, Kate. 1990. "Reading *The Awakening Conscience* Rightly." In *Pre-Raphaelites Re-Viewed,* edited by Marcia Pointon, 45–65. Manchester: Manchester University Press.

Fludernik, Monika. 1993. *The Fictions of Language and the Languages of Fiction.* London: Routledge.

———. 1996. *Towards a "Natural" Narratology.* London: Routledge.

Ford, Ford Madox. 1924. *Joseph Conrad: A Personal Remembrance.* London: Duckworth.

Forster, E. M. 1993. *Aspects of the Novel.* [1927]. London: Hodder and Stoughton.

Fowler, Roger. 1977. *Linguistics and the Novel.* London: Rowan and Littlefield.

Frank, Joseph. 1945. "Spatial Form in Modern Literature." *Sewanee Review* 53:221–40; 433–56; 643–53. Reprinted in *The Widening Gyre,* 3–62. New Brunswick, N.J.: Rutgers University Press, 1963.

———. 1981. "Spatial Form: Thirty Years After." In *Spatial Form in Narrative.* Edited by Jeffrey R. Smitten and Ann Daghistany, 202–43. Ithaca: Cornell University Press.

Friedman, Norman. 1955. "Point of View in Fiction: The Development of a Critical Concept." *PMLA* 70:1160–84. Reprinted in *The Theory of the Novel.* Edited by Philip Stevick, 108–37. London: Free Press, 1967.

Ganzel, Dewey. 1961. "Chronology in *Robinson Crusoe.*" *Philological Quarterly* 40:495–512.

Garrett, Peter K. 1969. *Scene and Symbol from George Eliot to James Joyce.* New Haven: Yale University Press.

Geerts, W. 1979. "Réflexion dans *Cahiers d'André Walter.*" *Revue des Lettres Modernes* 547–553:9–37.

Genette, Gérard. 1991. *Fiction et diction.* Paris: Seuil. Translated by Catherine Porter. *Fiction and diction.* Ithaca: Cornell University Press, 1993.

———. 1972. *Figures III.* Paris: Seuil. Translated by Jane E. Lewin. *Narrative Discourse: An Essay in Method.* Oxford: Blackwell, 1980.

———. 1983. *Nouveau discours du récit.* Paris: Seuil. Translated by Jane E. Lewin. *Narrative Discourse Revisited.* Ithaca: Cornell University Press, 1988.

———. 1982. *Palimpsestes: La littérature au second degré.* Paris: Seuil. Translated by Channa Newman & Claude Doubinsky. *Palimpsests: Literature in the second degree.* Lincoln: University of Nebraska Press, 1997.

———. 1987. *Seuils*. Paris: Seuil. Translated by Jane E. Lewin. *Paratexts: Thresholds of interpretation*. Cambridge: Cambridge University Press, 1997.

Gibson, Andrew. 1996. *Towards a Postmodern Theory of Narrative*. Edinburgh: Edinburgh University Press.

Gide, André. 1943. *Journal I (1889–1912)*. Rio de Janeiro: Americ-Edit.

Goebel, Gerhard. 1972. "Funktionen des 'Buches im Buche' in Werken zweier Repräsentanten des 'Nouveau Roman.' " In *Interpretation und Vergleich: Festschrift für Walter Pabst*, edited by Eberhard Leube and Ludwig Schrader, 34–52. Berlin: Schmidt.

Gontard, Marc. 1985. *"Nedjma" de Kateb Yacine: Essai de la structure formelle du roman*. [1975]. Paris: Editions L'Harmattan.

Grabo, Carl H. 1928. *The Technique of the Novel*. New York: Charles Scribner's Sons.

Graham, John. 1949. "Time in the Novels of Virginia Woolf." *University of Toronto Quarterly* 18:186–201.

Gregor, Ian. 1980. "Reading a Story: Sequence, Pace, and Recollection." In *Reading the Victorian Novel: Detail into Form*. London: Vision Press.

Greimas, Algirdas Julien. 1976. *Maupassant: La sémiotique du texte: exercises pratiques*. Paris: Seuil.

———. 1966. *Sémantique structurale*. Paris: Larousse.

Guzzetti, Alfred. 1985. "Christian Metz and the Semiology of the Centre." In *Film Theory and Criticism: Introductory Readings*. Edited by Gerald Mast and Marshall Cohen. New York: Oxford University Press.

Halliday, M. A. K., and R. Hasan. 1976. *Cohesion in English*. London: Longman.

Halperin, John. 1974. *The Theory of the Novel: New Essays*. New York: Oxford University Press.

Harvey, W. J. 1965. *Character and the Novel*. Ithaca: Cornell University Press.

Hawtree, C. 1983. "Good Beer. Review of *Waterland*, by Graham Swift." *Spectator* 8 (October): 26.

Hayman, David. 1987. *Re-Forming the Narrative: Toward a Mechanics of Modernist Fiction*. Ithaca: Cornell University Press.

Hays, Peter L. 1972. "Why Seven Years in *The Scarlet Letter*." *Nathaniel Hawthorne Journal*: 251–53.

Heath, Stephen. 1981. *Questions of Cinema*. Bloomington: Indiana University Press.

Heise, Ursula K. 1997. *Chronoschisms: Time, Narrative, and Postmodernism*. Cambridge: Cambridge University Press.

Henderson, Brian. 1983. "Tense, Mood, and Voice in Film (Notes after Genette)." *Film Quarterly* (Summer): 4–17.

Higdon, David Leon. 1977. *Time and English Fiction*. London: Macmillan.

Hornback, Bert G. 1963. "Anthony Trollope and the Calendar of 1972: The Chronology of *The Way We Live Now*." *Notes and Queries* 10:454–58.

Houston, J. P. 1962. "Temporal Patterns in *A la recherche du temps perdu*." *French Studies* 16:33–45.

Hughes, Linda K., and Michael Lund. 1991. *The Victorian Serial*. Charlottesville: Virginia University Press.

Hutchens, Eleanor N. 1972. "Towards a Poetics of Fiction: The Novel as Chronomorph." *Novel* 5:215–24.

Hutcheon, Linda. 1988. *A Poetics of Postmodernism*. London: Routledge.

Ingarden, Roman. 1960. *Das Literarische Kunstwerk*. [1931]. Tübingen: Max Niemeyer Verlag.

Ireland, K. R. 1990. "Doing Very Dangerous Things: *Die Blechtrommel* and *Midnight's Children*." *Comparative Literature* 42 (fall): 335–61.

———. 1986. "Towards a Grammar of Narrative Sequence: The Model of *The French Lieutenant's Woman*." *Poetics Today* 7:397–420.

Iser, Wolfgang. 1978. *The Act of Reading: A Theory of Aesthetic Response*. Baltimore: Johns Hopkins University Press.

———. 1971. "The Reading Process: A Phenomenological Approach." *New Literary History* 3:279–99.

Ishiguro, Kazuo. 1989. "An Interview with Kazuo Ishiguro. Conducted by Gregory Mason." *Contemporary Literature* 30 (fall): 335–47.

Ivanov, Vjaceslav V. 1973. "The Category of Time in Twentieth-Century Art and Culture." *Semiotica* 8:1–45.

Jach, A. n.d. "An Interview with Graham Swift." Supplement to *Mattoid* 25:3–17.

Jakobson, Roman. 1975. "Two Aspects of Language and Two Types of Aphasic Disturbances." [1956]. In *Fundamentals of Language*. Edited by Roman Jakobson and Morris Halle, 69–96. The Hague: Mouton.

———, and Claude Lévi-Strauss. 1962. " 'Les chats' de Charles Baudelaire." *L'homme* 2:5–21.

Janeiro, Armando Martins. 1970. *Japanese and Western Literature*. Tokyo: Tuttle.

Jauss, Hans Robert. 1955. *Zeit und Erinnnerung in Marcel Prousts "A la recherche du temps perdu."* Heidelberg: Winter.

Jefferson, Ann. 1980. *The Nouveau Roman and the Poetics of Fiction*. Cambridge: Cambridge University Press.

Jonnes, Dennis. 1990. *The Matrix of Narrative: Family Systems and the Semiotics of Story*. Berlin: Mouton de Gruyter.

Josipovici, Gabriel. 1977. *The Lessons of Modernism*. London: Macmillan.

Jungel, Renate. 1953. *Die Zeitstruktur in den Romanen E. M. Forsters*. Ph.D. diss., University of Graz.

Kayser, Wolfgang. 1948. *Das sprachliche Kunstwerk*. Bern: Francke Verlag.

Kermode, Frank. 1980. "Secrets and Narrative Sequence." *Critical Inquiry* 7 (Autumn): 83–101.

———. 1967. *The Sense of an Ending: Studies in the Theory of Fiction*. New York: Oxford University Press.

Kern, Anita. 1973. "On *Les soleils des Indépendances* and *Le devoir de violence*." *Présence Africaine* 85:209–30.

Kestner, Joseph A. 1978. *The Spatiality of the Novel*. Detroit, Mich.: Wayne State University Press.

Knoepflmacher, U. C. 1971. *Laughter and Despair: Reading in Ten Novels of the Victorian Era*. Berkeley: University of California Press.

Kroeber, Karl. 1992. *Retelling/Rereading: The Fate of Storytelling in Modern Times*. New Brunswick, N.J.: Rutgers University Press.

————. 1971. *Styles in Fictional Structure: The Art of Jane Austen, Charlotte Brontë, George Eliot*. Princeton: Princeton University Press.

Kundera, Milan. 1988. *The Art of the Novel*. London: Faber.

Labov, William. 1972. *Language in the Inner City*. Philadelphia: University of Pennsylvania Press.

Lämmert, Eberhard. 1955. *Bauformen des Erzählens*. Stuttgart: J. B. Metzlersche Verlag.

Lanser, Susan Sniader. 1981. *The Narrative Act: Point of View in Prose Fiction*. Princeton: Princeton University Press.

Lawrence, D. H. 1924. *Studies in Classic American Literature*. London: Martin Secker.

Leech, Clifford. 1968. "The Shaping of Time: *Nostromo* and *Under the Volcano*." In *Imagined Worlds: Essays on some English Novels and Novelists in Honour of John Butt*. Edited by Maynard Mack and Ian Gregor, 323–41. London: Methuen.

Leech, Geoffrey, and Michael Short. 1981. *Style in Fiction*. London: Longman.

Leitch, Thomas M. 1986. *What Stories Are: Narrative Theory and Interpretation*. University Park, Pa.: Penn State University Press.

Lemon, Lee T., and Marion J. Reis. 1965. *Russian Formalist Criticism: Four Essays*. Lincoln: University of Nebraska Press.

Lessing, Gotthold Ephraim. 1990. *Laokoon*. [1766]. Vol. 5/2 of *Werke 1766–1769*. Edited by Wilfried Barner. Frankfurt am Main: Deutscher Klassiker Verlag.

Lévi-Strauss, Claude. 1958. *Anthropologie structurale*. Paris: Plon.

Lid, R. W. 1961. "On the Time Scheme of *The Good Soldier*." *English Fiction in Transition* 4:9–10.

Litz, A. Walton. 1976. "*Persuasion*: Forms of Estrangement." In *Northanger Abbey and Persuasion: A Casebook*. Edited by B. C. Southam, 228–41. London: Macmillan.

Lodge, David. 1990. "Composition, Distribution, Arrangement: Form and Structure in Jane Austen's Novels." In *After Bakhtin: Essays in Fiction and Criticism*, 116–28. London: Routledge.

————. 1979. *The Modes of Modern Writing*. London: Routledge.

Longman's Dictionary of Contemporary English. 1978. Harlow: Longman.

Lothe, Jakob. 1996. "Conradian Narrative." In *The Cambridge Companion to Joseph Conrad*. Edited by J. H. Stape, 160–78. Cambridge: Cambridge University Press.

————. 1989. *Conrad's Narrative Method*. Oxford: Clarendon Press.

Lotman, Yuri. 1977. *The Structure of the Artistic Text*. [1970]. Translated by R. Vroom. Ann Arbor: Michigan Slavic Contributions No. 7.

Lubbock, Percy. 1921. *The Craft of Fiction*. London: Cape.

Lukács, Georg. 1971. *The Theory of the Novel*. [1920]. Translated by Anna Bostock. Cambridge: MIT University Press.

Lynen, John F. 1969. *The Design of the Present: Essays on Time and Form in American Literature*. New Haven: Yale University Press.

Macey, S. L. 1969. "Time Scheme in *Moll Flanders*." *Notes and Queries* 16:336–37.

Magny, Claude-Edmonde. 1950. *Histoire du roman français depuis 1918*. Paris: Seuil.

Martin, Wallace. 1987. *Recent Theories of Narrative*. Ithaca: Cornell University Press.

McHale, Brian. 1987. *Postmodernist Fiction*. London: Methuen.

Mendilow, A. A. 1952. *Time and the Novel*. London: Peter Neville.

Metz, Christian. 1968. *Essais sur la signification au cinéma*. Paris: Klincksieck.

Meyerhoff, Hans. 1955. *Time in Literature*. Berkeley: University of California Press.

Mickelsen, David. 1981. "Types of Spatial Structure in Narrative." In *Spatial Form in Narrative*. Edited by Jeffrey R. Smitten and Ann Daghistany, 63–78. Ithaca: Cornell University Press.

Miel, Jan. 1969. "Temporal Form in the Novel." *MLN* 84:916–30.

Miller, J. Hillis. 1982. *Fiction and Repetition: Seven English Novels*. Oxford: Blackwell.

———. 1968. *The Form of Victorian Fiction*. Notre Dame, Indiana: Notre Dame University Press.

———. 1978. "Narrative Middles: A Preliminary Outline." *Genre* 11 (fall): 375–87.

Miner, Earl. 1990. *Comparative Poetics: An Intercultural Essay on Theories of Literature*. Princeton: Princeton University Press.

Moore, Gene M. 1996. "Conrad's Influence." In *The Cambridge Companion to Joseph Conrad*. Edited by J. H. Stape, 223–41. Cambridge: Cambridge University Press.

Morrissette, Bruce. 1971. "Un héritage d'André Gide: La duplication intérieure." *Comparative Literature Studies* 8 (June): 125–42.

Morson, Gary Saul, and Caryl Emerson. 1990. *Mikhail Bakhtin: Creation of a Prosaics*. Stanford, Calif.: Stanford University Press.

Mortimer, Mildred. 1990. *Journeys Through the French African Novel*. Portsmouth, N.H.: Heinemann.

Muir, Edwin. 1928. *The Structure of the Novel*. London: Hogarth Press.

Müller, Günther. 1947. *Die Bedeutung der Zeit in der Erzählkunst*. Bonn: Universitätsverlag.

———. 1944. *Die Gestaltfrage in der Literaturwissenschaft und Goethes Morphologie*. Halle: Niemeyer.

———. 1953. "*Le Père Goriot* und *Silas Marner*: Eine vergleichende Aufbaustudie." *Archiv für das Studium der neueren Sprachen* 189:97–118.

———. 1950. "Über das Zeitgerüst des Erzählens." *Deutsche Vierteljahrschrift für Literaturwissenschaft und Geistesgeschichte* 24:1–32. Reprinted in *Morphologische Poetik, Gesammelte Aufsätze*, 299–311. Darmstadt: Wissenschaftliche Buchgesellschaft, 1968.

Mumford, Howard. 1963. *Technics and Civilization*. [1947]. New York: Harcourt Brace Jovanovich.

Nash, Ralph. 1967. "The Time Scheme for *Pride and Prejudice*." *English Language Notes* 4:194–98.

Nash, Walter. 1980. *Designs in Prose*. London: Longman.

The New Shorter Oxford English Dictionary. 1993. Oxford: Clarendon Press.

Ohaegbu, Aloysius U. 1974. *"Les soleils des Indépendances,* ou le drame de l'homme écrasé par le destin." *Présence Africaine* 90:253–60.

Okafor, Raymond. 1988. "La recherche esthétique chez Kourouma: *Les soleils des Indépendances." Zagadnienia Rodzajów Literackich* 30:51–61.

Orange, Michael. 1989–90. "Aspects of Narration in *Persuasion." Sydney Studies in English* 15:63–71.

O'Toole, L. Michael. 1982. *The Russian Short Story: Structure, Style and Interpretation.* New Haven: Yale University Press.

The Oxford English Dictionary. 1989. 2nd. ed. Oxford: Clarendon Press.

Parker, Dorothy. 1969. "The Time Scheme of *Pamela* and the Character of B." *Texas Studies in Literature and Language* 11:695–704.

Patrides, C. A., ed. 1976. *Aspects of Time.* Manchester, Eng.: Manchester University Press.

Pavel, Thomas. 1985. *The Poetics of Plot: The Case of English Renaissance Drama.* Manchester, Eng.: Manchester University Press.

Peckham, Morse. 1967. *Man's Rage for Chaos: Biology, Behavior, and the Arts.* New York: Schocken Books.

Pennala, Judy L. 1985. "The Thematic and Structural Use of Time in the Novels of Jane Austen." Ph. D. diss., Georgia State University.

Perry, Menachem. 1979. "Literary Dynamics: How the Order of a Text Creates Its Meanings." *Poetics Today* 1:35–64; 311–61.

Pettersson, Torsten. 1982. *Consciousness and Time: a Study in the Philosophy and Narrative Technique of Joseph Conrad.* Acta Academiae Aboensis, Ser. A, Humaniora; v. 61, nr. 1. Åbo: Åbo akademi.

Pouillon, Jean. 1946. *Temps et roman.* Paris: Gallimard.

Poulet, Georges. 1949. *Etudes sur le temps humain.* Paris: Plon.

Prince, Gerald. 1989. *Dictionary of Narratology.* Lincoln: University of Nebraska Press.

———. 1973. *A Grammar of Stories.* The Hague: Mouton.

———. 1982. *Narratology: The Form and Functioning of Narrative.* Berlin: Mouton.

Propp, Vladimir. 1968. *Morphology of the Folk Tale.* [1928]. Translated by Lawrence Scott. Austin: University of Texas Press.

Quirk, Randolph, Sidney Greenbaum, Geoffrey Leech, and Jan Svartnik. 1985. *A Comprehensive Grammar of the English Language.* London: Longman.

Raban, Jonathan. 1976. *The Techniques of Modern Fiction.* London: Edward Arnold.

Rabkin, Eric S. 1981. "Spatial Form and Plot." In *Spatial Form in Narrative.* Edited by Jeffrey R. Smitten and Ann Daghistany, 79–99. Ithaca: Cornell University Press.

Randall, Dale B. J. 1968. *Joseph Conrad and Warrington Dawson: The Record of a Friendship.* Durham, N.C.: Duke University Press.

Reid, Ian. 1992. *Narrative Exchanges.* London: Routledge.

Reinhart, Tanya. 1980. "Conditions for Text Coherence." *Poetics Today* 1:161–80.

Ricardou, Jean. 1973. *Le nouveau roman.* Paris: Seuil.

———. 1967. *Problèmes du nouveau roman.* Paris: Seuil.

Ricoeur, Paul. 1980. "Narrative Time." *Critical Inquiry* 7:169–90.

———. 1983–85. *Temps et récit.* 3 vols. Paris: Seuil. Translated by Kathleen McLaughlin and David Pellauer. *Time and Narrative.* Chicago: University of Chicago Press, 1984–88.

Riessman, Catherine Kohler. 1993. *Narrative Analysis.* Newbury Park, Calif.: Sage Publications.

Rigney, Ann. 1991. "Narrativity and Historical Representation." *Poetics Today* 12:591–605.

Rimer, J. Thomas. 1978. *Modern Japanese Fiction and Its Traditions.* Princeton: Princeton University Press.

Rimmon-Kenan, Shlomith. 1983. *Narrative Fiction: Contemporary Poetics.* London: Methuen.

Ritter, Alexander, ed. 1978. *Zeitgestaltung in der Erzählkunst.* Wege der Forschung 447. Darmstadt: Wissenschaftliche Buchgesellschaft.

Robbe-Grillet, Alain. 1963. "Temps et description dans le récit d'aujourd'hui." In *Pour un nouveau roman.* Paris: Minuit.

Rodway, Alan. 1979. "Review of *Time and English Fiction,* by David Leon Higdon." *Notes and Queries* 224 (June): 284–85.

Ronen, Ruth. 1994. *Possible Worlds in Literary Theory.* Cambridge: Cambridge University Press.

Ross, Harris. 1987. *Film as Literature, Literature as Film.* Westport, Conn.: Greenwood Press.

Ruthrof, Horst G. 1981. *The Reader's Construction of Narrative.* London: Routledge.

Ryding, William W. 1971. *Structure in Medieval Narrative.* The Hague: Mouton.

Ryskamp, Charles. 1968. "The New England Sources of *The Scarlet Letter.*" In *Twentieth-Century Interpretations of "The Scarlet Letter."* Edited by John C. Gerber, 19–34. Englewood Cliffs, N.J.: Prentice-Hall.

Said, Edward. 1975. *Beginnings: Intention and Method.* New York: Basic Books.

Sakuko, Matsuo. 1975. *Natsume Sōseki as a Critic of English Literature.* Tokyo: Centre for East Asian Cultural Studies.

Sammons, Jeffrey L. 1965. *"Die Nachtwachen des Bonaventura": A Structural Interpretation.* The Hague: Mouton.

Sanger, C. P. 1967. "The Structure of *Wuthering Heights.*" [1926]. In *"Wuthering Heights:" An Anthology of Criticism.* Edited by Alastair Everitt, 193–208. London: Frank Cass & Co.

Schikora, Rosemary G. 1980. "Narrative Voice in Kourouma's *Les soleils des Indépendances.*" *French Review* 55 (May): 811–17.

Schlegel, Friedrich. 1988. "Brief über den Roman." [1800]. Vol. 2 of *Kritische Schriften und Fragmente.* Edited by Ernst Behler and Hans Eichner, 208–15. Paderborn: Ferdinand Schöningh.

Scholes, Robert. 1980. "Afterthoughts on Narrative II: Language, Narrative and Anti-Narrative." *Critical Inquiry* 7:204–12.

———, and Robert Kellogg. 1975. *The Nature of Narrative.* [1966]. New York: Oxford University Press.

Schow, H. Wayne. 1975. "Ironic Structure in *The Good Soldier.*" *English Literature in Transition* 18:203–12.

Segre, Cesare. 1988. *Introduction to the Study of the Literary Text.* Translated by John Meddemmen. Bloomington: Indiana University Press.

——. 1979. *Structures and Time.* Translated by John Meddemmen. Chicago: Chicago University Press.

Selden, Raman. 1989. *Practising Theory and Reading Literature.* Hemel Hempstead: Harvester Wheatsheaf.

Shattuck, Roger. 1959. *The Banquet Years: The Origins of the Avant Garde in France, 1885 to World War One.* London: Faber.

Sherbo, Arthur. 1957. "Time and Place in Richardson's *Clarissa.*" *Boston University Studies in English* 3:139–46.

Shklovsky, Viktor. 1990. *Theory of Prose.* [1925]. Translated by Benjamin Sher. Elmwood Park, Ill.: Dalkey Archive Press.

Shukman, Ann. 1977. "Ten Russian Short Stories: Theory, Analysis, Interpretation." *Essays in Poetics* 2.2 (September): 27–95.

Simpkins, S. 1988. "Magical Strategies: The Supplement of Realism." *Twentieth-Century Literature* 34:140–54.

Smith, Barbara Herrnstein. 1980. "Afterthoughts on Narrative: III: Narrative Versions, Narrative Theories." *Critical Inquiry* 7 (autumn): 213–36.

——. 1968. *Poetic Closure: A Study of How Poems End.* Chicago: University of Chicago Press.

Smitten, Jeffrey R. and Ann Daghistany, ed. 1981. *Spatial Form in Narrative.* Ithaca: Cornell University Press.

Southam, B. C. 1964. *Jane Austen's Literary Manuscripts.* Oxford: Oxford University Press.

Spiegel, Alan. 1976. *Fiction and the Camera Eye: Visual Consciousness in Film and the Modern Novel.* Charlottesville: Virginia University Press.

Staiger, Emil. 1939. *Die Zeit als Einbildungskraft des Dichters.* Zürich: Niehaus.

Stallman, R. W. 1977. *The Houses That James Built.* Athens: Ohio University Press.

Stanzel, Franz K. 1979. *Theorie des Erzählens.* Göttingen: Vandenhoeck & Ruprecht.

——. 1955. *Die typischen Erzählsituationen im Roman.* Wien: Braumüller. Translated by James P. Pusack. *Narrative Situations in the Novel.* Bloomington: Indiana University Press, 1971.

Stape, J. H. 1996. "*Lord Jim.*" In *The Cambridge Companion to Joseph Conrad.* Edited by J. H. Stape, 63–80. Cambridge: Cambridge University Press.

Sternberg, Meir. 1978. *Expositional Modes and Temporal Ordering in Fiction.* Baltimore: Johns Hopkins University.

——. 1990. "Telling in Time (1): Chronology and Narrative Theory." *Poetics Today* 11 (winter): 901–48.

——. 1992. "Telling in Time (2): Chronology, Teleology, Narrativity." *Poetics Today* 13 (fall): 463–541.

——. 1974. "What Is Exposition? An Essay in Temporal Delimitation." In *The Theory of the Novel.* Edited by John Halperin. 25–70. New York: Oxford University Press.

Stevick, Philip. 1970. *The Chapter in Fiction: Theories of Narrative Division.* Syracuse, N.Y.: Syracuse University Press.

Storey, Graham. 1987. *Charles Dickens: "Bleak House."* Cambridge: Cambridge University Press.

Sturgess, Philip J. M. 1992. *Narrativity: Theory and Practice.* Oxford: Clarendon Press.

Sultana, N. 1987. "The Principle of Chapter- and Volume-Division in *Tristram Shandy." Language and Style* 20:185–202.

Sutherland, John A. 1971. "The Handling of Time in *Vanity Fair." Anglia* 89:349–56.

Tambling, Jeremy. 1991. *Narrative and Ideology.* Milton Keynes, Eng.: Open University Press.

Tanner, J. E. 1967. "The Chronology and the Enigmatic End of *Lord Jim." Nineteenth-Century Fiction* 21:369–80.

Todorov, Tzvetan. 1969. *Grammaire du Décaméron.* Paris: Mouton.

———. 1981. *Introduction to Poetics.* Translated by Richard Howard. Brighton, Eng.: Harvester Press.

———. 1968. *Qu'est-ce que le structuralisme? 2. Poétique.* Paris: Seuil.

———., ed. 1965. *Théorie de la littérature. Textes des formalistes russes.* Paris: Seuil.

Toolan, Michael J. 1988. *Narrative: A Critical Linguistic Introduction.* London: Routledge.

Tovey, Donald Francis. 1981. *Essays in Musical Analysis: Concertos and Choral Works.* London: Oxford University Press.

Turim, Maureen. 1989. *Flashbacks in Film: Memory and History.* New York: Routledge.

Uspensky, Boris. 1973. *A Poetics of Composition: The Structure of the Artistic Text and Typology of a Compositional Form.* Translated by Valentina Zavarin and Susan Wittig. Berkeley: University of California Press.

Van Ghent, Dorothy. 1953. *The English Novel: Form and Function.* New York: Rinehart.

Vidan, Ivo. 1981. "Time Sequence in Spatial Fiction." In *Spatial Form in Narrative.* Edited by Jeffrey R. Smitten and Ann Daghistany, 131–57. Ithaca: Cornell University Press.

Viglielmo, Valdo H. 1964. "An Introduction to the Later Novels of Natsume Sōseki." *Monumenta Nipponica* 19:1–36.

Wales, Katie. 1989. *A Dictionary of Stylistics.* London: Longman.

Walker, Ronald G. 1984. "World without End: An Approach to Narrative Structure in Greene's *The End of the Affair." Texas Studies in Literature and Language* 26 (summer): 218–41.

Watson, George. 1979. *The Story of the Novel.* London: Macmillan.

Watt, Ian. 1980. *Conrad in the Nineteenth Century.* London: Chatto & Windus.

Watts, Cedric. 1984. *The Deceptive Text: An Introduction to Covert Plots.* Brighton, Eng.: Harvester.

———. 1993. *A Preface to Conrad.* London: Longman.

Waugh, Patricia. 1985. *Metafiction: The Theory and Practice of Self-Conscious Fiction.* London: Methuen.

Webster's Third New International Dictionary of the English Language. 1976. Springfield, Mass.: G. & C. Merriam.

Welsh, Alexander. 1978. "Opening and Closing *Les Misérables*." *Nineteenth-Century Fiction* 33 (June): 8–23.

Wetherill, P. M. 1974. *The Literary Text: An Examination of Critical Methods.* Oxford: Blackwell.

Wilhelm, Cherry. 1979. "*Persuasion:* Time Redeemed." *English Studies in Africa* 22 (September): 91–98.

Wolfe, Thomas P. 1971. "The Achievement of *Persuasion.*" *Studies in English Literature (1500–1900)* 11:687–700.

Yamanouchi, Hisaaki. 1978. *The Search for Authenticity in Modern Japanese Literature.* Cambridge: Cambridge University Press.

Yu, Beongcheon. 1969. *Natsume Sōseki.* New York: Twayne Publishers.

Index

Page references in italics indicate substantial discussions of topics. Works are indexed under their authors, and technical terms are defined in the Glossary above.

317